MYTHICISM

A Seven-Fold Revelation of the Buddhist 'Branch' Grafted onto Jesse's 'Lineage Tree'

Articles Compiled, Edited, and Commented on by
Michael Lockwood

Tambaram Research Associates
Tambaram, Chennai 600 059

ISBN 978-93-5137-607-1

Printed at Sudarsan Graphics, Chennai 600 017

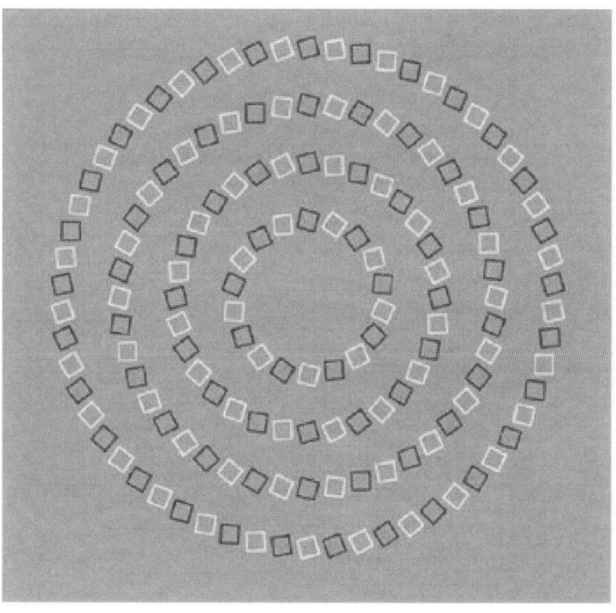

4 Perfectly Round Circles*

PREFACE

Multi-level Illusions

SOME OF THE AUTHORS whose works are included or reviewed in this book are atheists. Some are not atheists. But the articles and books reviewed have not been selected for their authors' views on that subject. Rather, the articles and reviews are presented under Section headings in the hope of progressively peering through seven veils of illusion concerning what was going on historically around the rise of Christianity (third century BCE to third century CE). Surprisingly, the sources of these illusions are chiefly *literary*! Seeing through each of the seven illusions involves a paradigm shift in one's thinking.

In Section I, Robert M. Price's article[1] **(1)** masterfully summarizes the writing of other scholars and his own instructive insights, and presents a mountain of evidence that the New Testament documents (the gospels, *Acts*, the epistles, and *Revelation*) are works of literary fiction, created, *in large part*, by a decidedly non-historical narrative method called 'midrash' that was based on the "Old Testament" (mainly, on its ancient Greek translation: the *Septuagint*). The narrative of the New Testament – the 'hypertext' – has been imaginatively written by borrowing themes, characterizations, and plots from the Old Testament – the 'hypotext'. Becoming aware of this artificial hypertext/hypotext relationship provides a glimpse of the ***first* of five major meta-narrative layers** to which the New Testament refers or alludes, and with that glimpse, one, hopefully, will experience the ***first* of five paradigm shifts** and be able to dispel the enthralling illusion that the New Testament narratives are based on historical, first century events, a number of which were "foretold" by Old Testament prophets. The third article **(3)**, a review by René Salm of Thomas L. Brodie's book, *Beyond the Quest for the Historical Jesus* (2012),[2] examines this same imaginative dependence by the New Testament on the Old, noting, as a particular example, a detailed analysis, in Brodie's seventh chapter, of the obviously fictional parallel structural dependence of Luke's gospel on the Elijah story in *1 Kings*.

---

*Neuroscience Research Techniques' optical illusion.

Both Price and Brodie would close down the "Quest for the Historical Jesus", realizing that it ends in "Mythicism". For Price, it also closes, for him, the belief in God. Not so, for Brodie, who invites us, instead, to seek God, and a Jesus who is beyond history!

In Section II, a second review article **(4)**, this by Richard Carrier, of Dennis R. MacDonald's book, *The Homeric Epics and the Gospel of Mark* (2000),[3] examines MacDonald's massive evidence that the gospel of Mark is a fictional, non-historical *literary* creation structurally dependent, in most significant ways, on Homer's epics, *The Odyssey* and *The Iliad*! In the order of our discussion here in the Preface, MacDonald's revelation of the mimetic relationship of *Mark* to Homer's epics will facilitate the experiencing of a ***second*** **paradigm shift** revealing a ***second*** (Homeric) **meta-narrative layer**, which underlies even the Old Testament layer. Since Mark's gospel is the earliest of the four canonical gospels, its fictional Homeric skeleton (its overall plot) has been adopted and adapted by the other three gospels. This means that *Matthew*, *Luke*, and *John* are also massively indebted to the underlying fictional literary model of Homer's epics.

It should be noted, however, that MacDonald does stop short of Mythicism. Nevertheless, his revelations are of the greatest importance for achieving liberation from a second layer of tradition's blinding illusions. And because he is a highly respected professor of more than one respected biblically related institution, members of the academic bodies of that discipline will, at least, tend to listen respectfully to him.

In Sections I and II, we thus have outstanding anti-illusory analyses of ***two distinct*** **meta-narrative layers** of influence in the New Testament: **first**, from the ***Septuagint***, and **second**, from the **epics of Homer**.

In Section III, in article **5**, I discuss John Pippy's book, *Egyptian Origin of the Book of Revelation*.[4] This book's first edition, in 2009, was followed by revisions in 2010 and, then, a second edition in 2011. Pippy's overall thesis is that the New Testament's final book, *Revelation*, has a distinctive parallel structural dependence on ancient Egyptian written sources. Now, if Pippy is right that the Bible's *Book of Revelation* is based point by point – by hundreds of points! – on very ancient Egyptian literary sources, then its historical and prophetic claims are brought into question. Yes, the seven churches may be historical, the challenging conditions those churches were suffering from may be historical, and the "Beast" may refer to a historical Roman emperor, but. . . ? Pippy thus presents us with grounds for a ***third*** **paradigm shift**: his analysis of the ***third*** **meta-narrative layer** of influence in the last book of the New Testament – this influence coming from ancient Egypt! Of the many, many parallels which Pippy finds between ancient Egyptian written records and *Revelation*, I quote here, as a foretaste, just the following three groups of parallels:

1. The opening scene in Egypt's *Book of the Dead* (Chp. 30B) is extremely similar to the opening scene of *Rev. 1-2*. Practically all the main elements (knowledge of people's deeds, rebellious activities, etc.) in the letters to the seven churches (*Rev. 3-4*) are present in a group of six consecutive chapters in the Egyptian *Book of the Dead* plus one in the *Book of Caverns*. The structure of two of the letters has the same form as Egyptian sources. [ref. Pippy, p. 568]
2. The entire middle section of the 6th Division of ancient Egypt's *Amduat* is similar to the one describing the opening of the scroll in *Rev. 5:1-9*. Almost all characters and events follow the same order in both sources. [ref. p. 197]
3. The unusual scene describing the cries of the souls of those slain in *Rev. 6:9-11* is remarkably similar to that depicting the cries of the souls slain in the 8th Division of the *Amduat*.[5] [ref. p. 223]

To my knowledge, in the four years since Pippy's research was first published, there has not been a single academic response to his book. One may argue that though he has a Ph.D., Pippy's degree is neither in Egyptology nor in New Testament studies. My opinion on the absence of academic reaction to his work is simply this: any Egyptologist who would engage in a serious review of Pippy's research, unless the review were totally dismissive of his research, would immediately be open to attack by critical Christian apologists. Pippy's theories, from the beginning, are explosive. Why would any Egyptologist care to enter such a contentious field? For other scholars, who are not conversant with the rather intimidating realm of Egyptology, how can they even comment? There is still hope that some Egyptologist who is also knowledgeable of New Testament studies will have the courage to evaluate Pippy's research, whether positively, negatively, or mixed. I, who am neither an Egyptologist nor a New Testament scholar, have hazarded some observations of my own in the Third Section.

In article **6**, I discuss D.M. Murdock's informative book, *Christ in Egypt: The Horus-Jesus Connection*[6] (2009). The influence of the Egyptian religion on the entire New Testament has been profound, and Murdock has dealt with that influence, comprehensively researching this ***third*** **meta-narrative layer**.

Among the many aspects of Egyptian influence on the New Testament which Murdock deals with are the Virgin Birth, the Nativity story, the Star and 'Three Kings', the Baptizers (Anubis and John), the 'Twelve followers', the Bread and Wine Eucharist, the 'Good Shepherd', Crucifixion, Burial, and Resurrection.

In Section IV are ten short reports (articles **7** to **16**)[7] from Christian Lindtner which add to his mind-boggling, paradigm-shifting series of eleven "News Bulletins" printed in my earlier book, *Buddhism's Relation to Christianity*.[8] The radical theory underlying all of his articles, the so-called 'Christian Lindtner Theory' (CLT), claims that the four canonical gospels, "perhaps even the NT as a whole" are copies of Buddhist gospels.[9] This theory of his was first heralded in an address he presented to an international gathering in Sarnath, India, in November, 1998, which address was subsequently expanded and then published as a pamphlet by the Ananda Buddha Vihara Trust, under the title "Buddhism in Relation to Science and World Religions" (1999). Lindtner thus, along with his startling **paradigm shift** (our ***fourth***), adds a ***fourth*** **meta-narrative layer**, the Buddhist, to the other three (the Septuagintal [Judaic], Homeric [Greek], and Egyptian layers).

Lindtner's Buddhist theory very quickly provoked strong reactions back in the West: the organizers of the 12th Conference of the International Association of Buddhist Studies, to be held in Switzerland, notified him in February, 1999, that his "presence would be unwelcome at the Conference". This would seem to be an extreme and unseemly academic distortion of the traditional Buddhist/Christian practice of 'Shunning'!

In Section V, in article **17**, Robert M. Price reviews Robert Eisenman's book, *The New Testament Code: The Cup of the Lord, the Damascus Covenant, and the Blood of Christ* (2006).[10] Eisenman's book could alternately be entitled *The Quest for Determining the Illusive and Fragmentary Historical Meta-Narrative Layer of the New Testament*! (In our tally, this would constitute a ***fifth*** **meta-narrative layer**, along with a multi-fold ***fifth*** **paradigm shifting revelation** of coded meanings of a great number of "historical" persons, places, and things (including titles of documents). The written Greek works of the historian Flavius Josephus (c. 37-100 CE) and Philo of Alexandria (c. BCE 20 to 50 CE) seem to have provided the gospel writers with many of the "historical" elements that they make imaginative use of. Eisenman holds that many of the names of places and names or titles of characters in the New Testament narratives must be viewed as coded references to different historical places or persons. The matter is extremely involved. For instance, there are, in the Dead Sea Scrolls, coded titles such as the 'Teacher of Righteousness' and the 'Spouter of Lies'. Eisenman's network of conjectures about which historical persons the New Testament may be referring to has opened promising avenues of research.

The remaining two paradigm shifts are: a ***sixth*** **paradigm shift**, which leads to comprehending interrelations *among* all five major meta-narrative layers (and even involving other more minor layers), and a ***seventh*** **paradigm shift**, which brings one to the realization that the New Testament gospels were highly complex works created by four Buddhist literary scholars who were interacting with other scholars of different ethnic and religious backgrounds in the environs of the great Library/Sarapæum of Alexandria.

Endnotes

[1]Robert M. Price, "New Testament Narrative as Old Testament Midrash", on his website, in 2004: (< http://www.robertmprice.mindvendor.com/art_midrash1.htm >); it also appears as the 53rd article in Vol. 1 of *The Encyclopaedia of Midrash: Biblical Interpretation in Formative Judaism*, 2 Vols., eds. Jacob Neusner and Alan J. Avery Peck (Leiden: E.J. Brill, 2005), pp. 534-74; and it is included in Price's book, *The Christ-Myth Theory and Its Problems* (Cranford, NJ: American Atheist Press, 2011), pp. 59-263.

[2]Thomas L. Brodie, *Beyond the Quest for the Historical Jesus* (Sheffield: Sheffield Phoenix Press, 2012); for another important work which examines the mimetic dependence of a NT work on OT stories, see Adam Winn's *Mark and the Elijah-Elisha Narrative: Considering the Practice of Greco-Roman Imitation in the Search for Markan Source Material* (Eugene, OR: Pickwick Publications, 2010).

[3]Dennis R. MacDonald, *The Homeric Epics and the Gospel of Mark* (New Haven, CT: Yale University Press, 2000).

[4]John H.C. Pippy, *Egyptian Origin of the Book of Revelation*, second edition (Raleigh, NC: J.H.C.P., Lulu Enterprises Inc., 2011).

[5]Quoted from: < http://www.revorigin.com/highlights.php > "Highlights" (2013), on the website promoting Pippy's book. These are website paraphrases – not verbatim quotes – of passages from the indicated pages of Pippy's book.

[6]D.M. Murdock, *Christ in Egypt: The Horus-Jesus Connection* (Seattle, WA: Stellar House Publishers LLC, 2009).

[7]These ten short articles have been selected from the brief bulletins from the "News" column of Lindtner's internet site: < http://www.jesusisbuddha.com/ >.

[8]Lockwood, *Buddhism's Relation to Christianity: A Miscellaneous Anthology with Occasional Comment* (Chennai: Tambaram Research Associates, 2010).

[9]Lockwood, *Buddhism's Relation to Christianity*, p. 147.

[10]Robert Eisenman, *The New Testament Code: The Cup of the Lord, the Damascus Covenant, and the Blood of Christ* (London: Watkins Publishing, 2006).

* * * * * * * * *

ACKNOWLEDGMENTS

Thanks to all of the scholars who have contributed to this book and to one who should be especially mentioned: Michael Anthony Barry, who critiqued drafts of the manuscript and proposed the Parables = Kōans equation.

I wish to acknowledge my late colleague, Prof. A. Vishnu Bhat, with whom I collaborated in translating Sanskrit, as the facilitator of whatever insights I may have attained in that field.

Thanks again go to those two eyes of the digital research world: Google and Wikipedia. (For one who has reached his eightieth year, they have also aided the waning powers of memory.)

'God is a comedian playing to an audience whose members just don't get the humor!'

– ML's version of H.L. Mencken's aphorism, misattributed to Voltaire!

'Your old men shall dream dreams'

– Acts 2:17 // Joel 2:28

"When asked by his assistant what his reaction would have been if general relativity had not been confirmed by Eddington and Dyson in 1919, Einstein famously made the quip:

'Then I would feel sorry for the dear Lord. The theory is correct anyway.'"

– Ilse Rosenthal-Schneider: *Reality and Scientific Truth* (Detroit: Wayne State University Press, 1980), p. 74

Photograph on title page
"Jesse's 'Lineage Tree'"
Courtesy of Wikipedia

CONTENTS

Arthur Schopenhauer (1788-1860)

His portrait by Ludwig Ruhl, in 1815, 2nd of the critical 5 years of the initial composition of *Die Welt als Wille*

Courtesy of Wikipedia

INTRODUCTION

Arthur Schopenhauer

MY ELDEST DAUGHTER, having had a look at a draft of this Introduction, was intrigued by the inclusion of a portrait of the great German philosopher, Schopenhauer, in a book dealing with, among other matters, a Buddhist "Branch" being grafted onto Jesse's "Lineage Tree". Let me explain.

In the many centuries after the rise of Christianity, Schopenhauer was the first person (beginning c. 1818) to articulate the significant *organic* relation between Buddhism and Christianity – and he was the first to characterize that relation metaphorically as an 'engraftment of the doctrine of Buddha upon the mythological dogmas of Judaism':

> *"The essence of the Christian religion is the centre dogma of Buddhism, – the doctrine of the worthlessness of terrestrial life. With this difference only, that Christianity dates that worthlessness from the transgression of our apple-eating forefathers. This modification implied the fiction of a *liberi arbitrii indifferentiæ*: but it was required by the necessity of **grafting the doctrine of Buddha upon the mythological dogmas of Judaism**. The myth of the Fall offered here the only basis for the insertion of the scion from the East Indian parent-tree." – Schopenhauer, *Die Welt als Wille* [1844], Vol. II., p. 694 [bolding added].

I came across this passage of Schopenhauer's quoted by Felix L. Oswald in his book, *The Secret of the East; or, The Origin of the Christian Religion, and the Significance of Its Rise and Decline* (Boston: Index Association, 1883), pp. 30-31, where Oswald states:

> Together with the unmistakeable* doctrine of Buddha Sakyamuni, the prophet of Galilee [i.e., Jesus] probably disseminated the current tradition about the miracles and adventures of his master [i.e., Buddha]; and, when in the oral traditions of the next century the records of Buddha and Christ had coalesced, the East Indian legend was transferred to the soil of Palestine, while the myth-making faculty of the monastic historians supplied the details of the local coloring. . . .
>
> . . . The records of the earlier Gospels are too fragmentary and contradictory to reconstruct a trustworthy biography of the Galilean Buddhist [Jesus], but his system of ethics proves that it was the main object of his mission to **graft** the doctrine of Buddha upon the optimistic theism of the Hebrew law-giver. Hence, the dogmatical contradictions of the Old and New Testaments. . . . [The asterisk in the paragraph above indicates the Schopenhauer quotation as its footnote; and the bolding in this paragraph has been added. – ML]

These two scholars are the earliest to understand the organic connection of Christianity to Buddhism. But, as Mythicists would assert, both Schopenhauer and Oswald have missed realizing the fact of the mythical nature of Jesus. If Jesus was not a flesh and blood follower of the Buddha, he must be a literary creation – a meta-Buddha – which has become so convincingly historicized, that nearly all scholars, today, still think he is historical.

In this book, I have chosen to play the part of *Advocatus Diaboli* and to argue in support of Mythicism.

Before I came across the Schopenhauer passage, I had already completed writing the two short essays presented in this Introduction in order to support the framework of my own theory that Christianity was the result of the engraftment of Buddhism on Judaism. Imagine my surprise to learn that Schopenhauer, almost two hundred years before me, had anticipated my own efforts!

The first introductory essay, entitled "Jesse's 'Lineage Tree' and Its Buddhist 'Branch'", presents the general framework of my theory. After having written the first essay, I chanced to read the thought-provoking article, "A Simile in Christine de Pisan for Christ's Conception", by William Wells, in the *Journal of the Warburg Institute*, Vol. II, No. 1 (July 1938), pp. 68-69. Wells's article revealed to me that the grafting metaphor had been made explicit, in 1399 CE, in Christian art's vivid portrayal of Buddhism's Isaiac Messiah-"Scion" being bound together with the "Stock"-of-Judaism by the goddess Isis/Mary!

My second, short essay, "Two Divine 'Engrafters': Isis and Mary", is meant to convey the significance of Wells's article, in support of Schopenhauer's incredible insight.

Reclining Jesse, a "Lineage Tree" arising from his navel, the Basilica of St. Quentin, France – *Courtesy of Wikipedia*

First Essay: Jesse's 'Lineage Tree' and Its Buddhist 'Branch'

Michael Lockwood

'Then a shoot shall grow from the stock of Jesse,
and a branch spring from his roots.'
– Isaiah 11:1

When King Aśōka, in the mid-third century BCE, sent out Buddhist monks from India as missionaries (the world's first Salvation Army, propagating the Buddha's Gospel: The Dharma) to the kingdoms beyond his borders, the king's 13th Rock Edict inscription specifically names rulers of the Seleucid Empire, Egypt, Macedonia, and the lands which are approximately today's Libya, Greece, and Albania:

> (XVI) So, what is [peaceful] conquest through Dharma is now considered to be the best conquest by 'The Beloved of the Gods' [i.e., by Aśōka].[1]
>
> (XVII) And such a conquest has been achieved by 'The Beloved of the Gods' not only here [in his own dominions] but also in the territories bordering [on his dominions], and as far away as six hundred Yojanas, [where] the Yavana [Greek] king named *Antiyoka*[2] [is ruling and], beyond [the kingdom of] the said *Antiyoka*, [where] four other kings named *Tulamāya*,[3] *Antikeni*,[4] *Maka*[5] and *Alikasundara*[6] [are also ruling]. . . .

And, in another Rock Edict, the 2nd, Aśōka assigned certain medical and botanical duties to be carried out:

> (I) Everywhere in the dominions of king 'Priyadarśin' [i.e., of Aśōka], 'Beloved of the Gods', and likewise [in] the bordering territories such as [those of] the Çoḍas [and] Pāṇḍiyas [as well as of] the Satīyā-putras [and in] Tāmraparṇī [i.e., Śrī-Laṅkā] and [in the territories of] the Yavana king named *Antiyoka* and also [of] the kings who are the neighbours of the said *Antiyoka* – everywhere King 'Priyadarśin', 'Beloved of the Gods', has arranged for two kinds of medical treatment, [viz.,] medical treatment for men and medical treatment for animals.
>
> (II) And, wherever there were no medicinal plants beneficial to men and beneficial to animals, everywhere they have been caused to be imported and planted.[7]

As Aśōka's main object was, of course, for the monks to spread the Buddhist Gospel (The Dharma) throughout these lands, these words about medicinal plants carry an additional, suggestive meaning. Aśōka is known to have sent to the island of Śrī Laṅkā a physical 'shoot' of the Bōdhi tree, under which the Buddha was said to have gained Enlightenment. One can view this venerated tree in Śrī Laṅkā, today, some 2250 years after its shoot was transplanted there. In Indian art during Aśōka's time, the Bōdhi tree was the very symbol of the Buddha's Enlightenment (his realization of The Dharma). Therefore, consider the following:

Proposition 1: Besides the physical medical plants which had been imported into these countries, Aśōka's inscription can be taken to signify that a metaphorical "medical shoot" (the Buddha's Gospel: The Dharma) had also been introduced in these lands.

Proposition 2: However, this "introduction" would not always have been a simple case of "transplanting" the Buddhist Gospel directly into foreign "soil". In the case of the western kingdoms beyond Afghanistan, the Buddhist monks accomplished it by slight of hand, a very clever and discreet (*upāya-kauśalya*) case of "engraftment"!

Proposition 3: Though it may never be known when exactly this "engraftment" was first initiated, it had already established, by the second century BCE, both the Essenes of Qumran with their followers throughout Palestine and the early Essenes of Mareotis (presumed forerunners of Philo's first century CE Therapeutæ, whose followers, he claims, were spread throughout *every district* of Egypt).

> **ESSENES** – The name of the sect is variously given as ***Essaioi*** (Philo) or ***Essēnoi*** (Josephus, Dio, Hippolytus) in Greek, ***Esseni*** in Latin (Pliny). Epiphanius mentions . . . ***Essēnoi***, which he identifies as a Samaritan sect. . . .[8]

Following Eusebius's confused claim that Philo's Therapeutæ were Christians, Epiphanius, who lived c. 315-403 CE, made the following interesting statement about these Therapeutæ in his *Panarion* (1.29.5.1-3):

> If you are a lover of learning and read the writings of Philo, you would find an account of these people in the book entitled ***On the Iessaioi***. He describes their way of life and their praiseworthy customs and recounts their monasteries in the vicinity of the Marean marsh, speaking about none other than the Christians. For he himself was present in the area (the place is called Mareotis) and spent some time with them, receiving hospitality in the monasteries in this locality. Since he was there during the time of Pascha [Passover/Easter], he observed their practices, how some of them prolonged their fast for the entire holy week of the Pascha, others ate every second day, while yet others broke their fast every evening. All these matters are dealt with by the man in his account of the faith and practices of the Christians.[9]

Further, in the prior section (1.29.4.9-10), Epiphanius, significantly, says:

> [S]ince I have come to the reason why those who came to faith in Christ were called Jessaeans [***Iessaioi***] before they were called Christians, I have said that Jesse was the father of [King] David. And they had been named Jessaeans [***Iessaioi***], either because of this Jesse; or from the name of our Lord Jesus. . . . In any case, they had acquired this additional name [***Iessaioi***] before they were called Christians.[10]

What Epiphanius is either obscuring or failing to understand, himself, is the fact that the Qumranites and Therapeutæ were ***Iessaioi***/Jessæans who, long before the beginning of the Common Era, had assumed the form and some of the practices of Jewish sects, and in this manner had engrafted themselves onto Jesse's 'Lineage Tree' of Judaism. It is in this fundamental sense that they originally came to be called 'Jessæans'/ Essenes.

Both Eusebius and Epiphanius were mistaken in saying that Philo's Therapeutæ were Christians. However, Philo's Therapeutæ and the Qumranites should, indeed, be counted among the *proto*-Christians.

Was Epiphanius mistaken in identifying the Therapeutæ with the Essenes (***Iessaioi***)? David Winston, in his book *Philo of Alexandria* (1981), had this to say:

> As for the relationship of the Therapeutae to the Essenes, the consensus is that, although originating from the same root, they nevertheless represent separate developments. Vermes, however believes that there is a close bond between them, and he interprets the opening sentence of the treatise [*On the Contemplative Life*] as implying that the Therapeutae were contemplative Essenes.[11]

Winston's translation of this opening sentence of Philo's work gives support to G. Vermes' view, when the word 'those' is understood as 'Essenes':

> After discussing the Essenes who zealously cultivated the active life, and excelled in all or, to put it more acceptably, in most of its spheres, I [Philo] shall now proceed at once, following the sequence demanded by the treatment of this subject, to say what is fitting concerning those [Essenes] who have espoused the life of contemplation.[12]

The Greek term ***Iessaioi*** is interchangeable with Greek ***Essaioi***, ***Essēnoi***, and Latin ***Esseni***, and these terms apply equally to both the Mareotis and Qumran monastics. Keep in mind that the name of King David's father, in Greek, is ***Iessai***, and therefore we can reasonably follow Epiphanius in saying that the ***Iessaioi*** (the Qumranites as well as the Therapeutæ) were Jessæans – 'of Jesse's lineage '. And both groups can equally be thought of as "Therapeutai" ('Devotees of God' [Greek] or 'Elders, sons (of Buddha)' [Pāli]) – but, by the first century CE, the Qumranites had little use for Greek terms, and even less, for Pāli or Sanskrit!

Isaiah, 11:1:

"There shall come forth a shoot from the stump of Jesse, and a branch shall grow out of his roots."

It was only toward the end of the disastrous Jewish revolts against the Romans, between 66 and 135 CE, that the *Alexandrian* Essenes (one 'limb' of that great western 'branch' of Buddhism which had been engrafted onto Judaism in the third century BCE by King Aśōka's Buddhist missionary monks) appear to have begun to interpret their Jessæan 'Lineage Tree', onto which they had been metaphorically engrafted, as now having become a mere 'Stump' – that is, what little was left of the Jewish nation. And, around the beginning of the second century of the Common Era, when, *in Alexandria*, the allegorical gospel accounts of 'Jesus' had begun to be written in Greek, this allegorical 'Jesus' – a disguised meta-Buddha – began now to be proclaimed by the Essene clergy as a *historical* person, the prophesied metaphoric 'Shoot' of Isaiah which had, supposedly, 'sprouted up' from the 'Stump of Jesse' some one hundred or so years before their own time.

The Isaiah passage would later be translated into Latin by Jerome, in the Vulgate Bible, as:

"*et egredietur virga de radice Iesse et flos de radice eius ascendet*"

". . . a rod out of the root of Jesse, and a flower shall rise up . . .".

('*Flos*, pl. *floris*, is Latin for flower. *Virga* is a "green twig", "rod" . . . , as well as a convenient near-pun with *Virgo* or Virgin, which undoubtedly influenced the development of the image. Thus Jesus is the *Virga Jesse* or "shoot of Jesse".' – Wikipedia)

Nazareth

The foregoing discussion offers a solution to the long-standing theological puzzle of the evangelist's statement in *Matthew 2:23*:

> And being warned by a dream, he [Joseph, with Mary and Jesus] withdrew to the region of Galilee; there he settled in a town called Nazareth. This was to fulfil the words spoken through the prophets, 'He [Jesus] shall be called a Nazarene.'
>
> – *The New English Bible*

The problem with this passage, of course, is that nowhere in the Hebrew Bible do the prophets mention a town called Nazareth. The fact is that the evangelists were rather careful about openly declaring that 'Jesus' was the Messiah/Christ (the messianic "Shoot" – N-Z-R, in Hebrew – from Jesse's "Stump"). They were under Roman rule, when even such an allegorical claim might appear treasonous. So Matthew's passage is camouflage: Jesus is called a Nazarene because of his having lived in Nazareth. Thus, Matthew, by means of this passage, is obfuscating the fact that the followers of 'Jesus', the Nazarenes (including 'Paul', of course), were, indeed, followers of Isaiah's messianic "Sprout" from the "Stump" of Jesse. But keep in mind, these Nazarenes were not the ordinary Jewish, militaristic variety of messianists: they were pacifistic crypto-Buddhist-"Jewish" messianists!

Employing Christian Lindtner's analytic method and following his use of gematria techniques, one can throw light on how 'Nazareth', the putative residence of 'Jesus', is actually derived from Jesus, the 'Shoot', which had been *grafted* onto the 'Stump' of Jesse. Take the word *netzer* in:

Isaiah 14:19

Hebrew (Strong 5342): *netzer* = N*e*TZ*e*R = N-T-Z-R

a sprout, shoot, branch, descendants

N*e*TZ*e*R / N-T-Z-R = N-Z-R-T / N*a*Z*a*R*e*T (*Nazareth*, in English transliteration)

It follows that the name of the town of 'Nazareth' is but a Greek metaphorical transmogrification of the Hebrew word for 'sprout' or 'shoot'; so 'Nazareth' can be rendered in English as 'Sprout-town'. In this way the theological puzzle is solved in one stroke. Arthur Drews, a century ago, presented an extensive scholarly analysis covering much of this same ground. (See First Appendix.) Only, Drews did not grasp the presence of Buddhism: the evangelists' conception and literary 'engraftment' of the Buddhist 'Jesus' onto the Judaic 'Stump' of Jesse's 'Lineage Tree'.

In the year 93 or 94 CE, Josephus used the Greek word '*Naziraios*' twice in his *Antiquities*: in iv, 4, 4, and in xix, 6, 1 (see Drews's remarks on p. 32 of this book [meta-page 204 of his work], where he gives '*Nazaraios*' for Josephus's first entry and '*Naziraios*', for the second). Note that the context of each appearance of the term in the *Antiquities* is crystal clear and unambiguous: it involves the 'Nazirite' tradition of the Hebrew Bible (think of Samson and Samuel). As Josephus was mainly addressing educated Roman Gentiles in his writings, the term '*Naziraios*', meaning 'Nazirite', would have thus appeared to them totally innocuous.

Thus, protected by the smokescreens of the "town of Nazareth" and the Hebrew Bible's "Nazirites", Pliny's first century BCE 'Nazerini', the Gospel of John's 19:19 'Nazoraios', and all the other 'Nazoræans',

The Karma Kāgyu "Lineage Tree", Tibet

The Drikung Kāgyu Mahāmudrā "Lineage Tree", Tibet

Reclining Viṣṇu as "Padmanābha", a lotus (padma) arising out of his navel (nābha), Brahmā sitting on it

Reclining Jesse, a "Lineage Tree" arising from his navel
The Basilica of St. Quentin, France
Courtesy of Wikipedia

Reclining Jesse, a "Lineage Tree" arising from his navel
(Ivory panel from Bavaria, c. 1200 – image by Jastrow, 2005)
Courtesy of Wikipedia

Reclining Jesse and his "Lineage Tree"
Capuchin's Bible, c. 1180 – image by Soerfm
Bibliothèque nationale de France, Paris
Courtesy of Wikipedia

⇒

Reclining Jesse, a "Lineage Tree" arising from his navel
(By Simon Bening (1510-1520), tempera colors on parchment)
Courtesy of Wikipedia

'Nazaræans', 'Nasiræans', and 'Notzrim' – all terms derived from N-Z-R or N-S-R – will have to be examined anew, now, as possibly signifying the presence of crypto-Buddhist quasi-Judaic organizations from as early as the 2nd cent., BCE, & crypto-Buddhist quasi-Judaic Christianity from the beginning of the 2nd cent., CE.

Images of scenes from the Hebrew Bible are not too common in Christian churches. However, those illustrating Jesse's "Lineage Tree", because of its connection with Jesus, are the most numerous. It is interesting to note that these images began to appear in Christian art, especially in Europe, around the 11th century CE, the same period when the Buddhist "Lineage Tree" images were also coming into prominence.

In the Basilica of St. Quentin, France, the remarkable carving of the Reclining Jesse with his "Lineage Tree" growing up out of his navel area would immediately make anyone familiar with Indian iconography to think of the images of the Reclining Viṣṇu "Padmanābha"[13] with a lotus flower growing up from his navel, providing a seat for the smaller, sitting image of the creator god (Demiurge) Brahmā! "Christianity" has certainly borrowed from India in the creation of the St. Quentin image! The 'navel' theme of Viṣṇu Padmanābha can be traced back to literary images in the *Ṛig-Vēda* which, long before the prophet Isaiah and the Hebrew Bible, praise the all-encompassing creator-God, Viśvakarma (sometimes identified with Brahmā). For example, in Book 10:

HYMN 82 (Viśvakarma)

(Verse 6) *The waters, they received that germ primæval wherein the gods were gathered altogether. It rested set upon the Unborn's navel, that One wherein abide all things existing.*

Endnotes (ML's)

[1]Mid-third century BCE Rock Edict XIII, at Eṟṟaguḍi, Āndhra Pradēsh; ed. and trans. by D.C. Sircar, in *Aśokan Studies* (Calcutta: India Museum, 1979), p. 35.

[2]*Antiyoka* = Antiochus-II Theos (regnal years 261-246 BCE), Greek ruler of the Seleucid Empire (stretching from Syria to Bactria, in the east), and who was therefore a direct neighbor of Aśōka. His capital city was Antioch, future arena of dramatic incidents in St. Paul's life. . . .

[3]*Tulamāya* = Ptolemy-II Philadelphus (r.y. 285-247 BCE), the Greek ruler of Egypt.

[4]*Antikeni* = Antigonas Gonatas of Macedonia (r.y. 277-239 BCE).

[5]*Maka* = Magas of Cyrene (r.y. ca. 288-258 BCE) [Cyrene is approximately today's Libya.]

[6]*Alikasundara* = Alexander-II of Epirus (r.y. 272-255 BCE) [Epirus, today's Greece and Albania.]

[7]Aśōka's Rock Edict II, at Eṟṟaguḍi, Āndhra Pradēsh (*Aśokan Studies*, ed. and trans. by D.C. Sircar [Calcutta: India Museum, 1979], p. 15). The identifications and dates are after W. Norman Brown's, in his book, *The Indian and Christian Miracles of Walking on the Water* (Chicago: The Open Court Publishing Co., 1928), p. 63.

[8]John J. Collins, "Essenes", *The Anchor Bible Dictionary*, vol. 2 (New York: Doubleday, 1992), p. 619. (Bolding added.)

[9]David T. Runia, *Philo in Early Christian Literature: A Survey* (Minneapolis: Fortress Press, 1993), p. 228. (Bolding added.)

[10]Frank Williams, *The Panarion of Epiphanius of Salamis*, vol. 1 (Leiden: Brill, 1987), p. 115; the bracketed words have been added by ML.

[11]David Winston, *Philo of Alexandria: The Contemplative Life, The Giants, and Selections* (Mahwah, NJ: Paulist Press, 1981), p. 41; the bracketed words have been added by ML.

[12]Winston, *Philo of Alexandria*, pp. 41-42; the bracketed words are added by ML. The reference for Vermes' belief, which is not given in Winston's book, but which was recently communicated personally to ML by him, is: E. Schurer and G. Vermes, *A History of the Jewish People in the Age of Jesus Christ: A New English Version by G. Vermes et al.*, vol. II (Edinburgh 1979), p. 596.

[13]The gold idol of Viṣṇu in his Padmanābha form, pictured above, was discovered along with countless other invaluable treasures, in 2011, in a hidden vault of the Padmanābhaswāmy Temple, Trivandrum, Kerala, South India. The Padmanābha image, solid gold, is said to have weighed in at 30 kilos! – and reported to be valued (only the gold?) at Indian Rupees Five billion – that is, roughly, US$ 100 million!

Second Essay: Two "Divine Engrafters": Isis and Mary

Michael Lockwood

In the previous essay, "Jesse's 'Lineage Tree' and Its Buddhist 'Branch'", the thesis was put forward claiming that primitive Christianity's evangelism was, in fact, the evangelism of crypto-Buddhism masquerading in the form of various Jewish sects – sects which had developed from the third century BCE, spreading throughout Egypt and other countries around the Mediterranean. The previous essay characterized that masquerade as involving an "engraftment" of Buddhism onto the "stem" of Judaism. Leading up to the first century CE, crypto-Buddhism had branched into pre-Christian Gnostic groups and various Essenes/ Jessæans (the Therapeutæ, the Qumranites, and others), and then, around the beginning of the second century CE, some of these were transformed into various Christian sects (those who kept close to Judaism, those who began to pull away from Judaism, and those who radically rejected Judaism).

The thesis that Christianity has developed out of a crypto-Buddhist "branch" originally engrafted, in the third-century BCE, onto the "stem" of Judaism (the idea and significance of this "engraftment" being derived from *Isaiah 11:1*) may seem like a far-fetched theory, but after having finished writing the previous essay, and during a Google search with such terms as '*engraft*', '*engrafting*', '*engraftment*', '*divine engrafters*', I came across, as if by divine confirmation, the thought-provoking article, "A Simile in Christine de Pisan for Christ's Conception", by William Wells, in the *Journal of the Warburg Institute*, Vol. II, No. 1 (July 1938), pp. 68-69. The article's opening is as follows:

> A miniature in MS. Harl. 4431, illustrating the twenty-fifth chapter of Christine de Pisan's moralisation of classical history, *L'Épitre d'Othéa* [a work composed in 1399 CE],[1] shows Isis flying down to graft a new branch on to the barren stem of a tree, growing among other green or leafless trees in a copse (Pl. 13a).[2] The text refers to Isis as the goddess and cultivator of trees. . . .

Wells points out that Pisan exhorts the valiant knight, Hector – and thus the readers – "to imitate this goddess and plant virtues":

> One wonders what particular association of ideas it was that caused the . . . miniaturist . . . to select this particular theme for illustration. But a closer study shows that the artist . . . has given a fuller interpretation of its moral and theological meaning. This can only be appreciated when the nature of the whole book is taken into consideration.
>
> The "Epistle of Othea to Hector," like the more famous *Ovide Moralisé*, belongs to that genre of mediæval literature which subordinates pagan subject matter to a Christian purpose. Christine's method of composition is a particularly rigid example of the sort. Starting with the planets, she works through a hundred stories chiefly drawn from mediæval versions of the Metamorphoses and the Trojan War. There is no variation in her procedure. The theme is introduced by four or five lines of verse; the narrative and moral are explained in a longer 'Gloss' consisting of prose, and an 'Allegory' points out its spiritual meaning.[3]

Wells notes that the spiritual meaning of the 25th chapter of Pisan's work

> is made clear by a few lines, appended to the 'Allegory,' taken from the Latin Vulgate. The Virtues and Vices are followed by the Ten Commandments and the Articles of the Creed. It is significant that it should be the Third Article of the Creed, referring to the Conception of Christ, that is appended to the 25th chapter of her book dealing with Isis. In the 'Allegory' we read: "*La ou il dit que a Isys qui est plantureuse doibt ressembler povons entendre la benoite Conception de Iesucrist par le saint experit en la benoicte Vierge Marie mere de toute grace.*" It seems probable that the miniaturist when he represented Isis in the act of grafting was bearing this 'spiritual' interpretation in mind.[4] . . .
>
> The dry tree of Jesse has become the green tree of the Virgin Mary which has produced the Mystic Apple, Christ.

Pl. 13: a—Isis grafting. Christine de Pisan, *L'Épitre d'Othéa.* British Museum, Harl. 4431 (*p.* 68)

Wells's Notes

[1]English translation by Stephen Scrope. Ed. George F. Warner. The Roxburgh Club. London, 1904. [This note in the original article is footnote '2' on p. 68. – ML]

[2]The ms. was made about 1410-15 for Isabella of Bavaria, wife of Charles VI. Cf. Henry Martin, *La Miniature française du XIII*e *au XV*e *siècle*. Paris et Bruxelles, 1923, pp. 101-102. [This note in the original article is footnote '3' on p. 68. – ML]

[3]The various parts of each chapter appear under these sub-titles. In Jean Pigouchet's edition of the *Épitre d'Othéa*, about 1500, the 'Text' is placed in the centre, the 'Gloss' on the left and the 'Allegory' on the right. [This note in the original article is footnote '5' on p. 68. – ML]

[4]Although the chief emphasis is upon Isis as a 'planter,' there is justification in the text for showing her grafting. The advantage of this form of representation is that it brings out the moral and allegorical meaning, while not being at variance with the rôle of Isis as cultivator. The 'Text' of chapter 25 runs:

Toutes vertus entes et plantes
En toy comme Ysis fait les plantes
Et tous les grains fructifier;
Ainsy doibs tu edifier.

Cf. Campbell, *op. cit.*, p. 125. It is pointed out that the association of Isis and grafting occurs in none of the three works (the *Histoire Ancienne*, the *Ovide Moralisé* and Boccaccio's *De Claris Mulieribus*) which mention this goddess. [This note in the original article is footnote '1' on p. 69. – ML]

The Synoptic Analysis of the Multiple Meta-Narrative Layers of the New Testament

THE FOREGOING TWO ESSAYS have provided a hypothetical framework for now presenting a synoptic analysis of the five major meta-narrative layers in the New Testament, which layers will be identified and studied in the five Sections of this book. Such an analysis will, hopefully, facilitate the achievement of **two** further major **paradigm shifts** (the ***sixth*** and ***seventh***), reaching **two new levels** of understanding: **first**, in comprehending the interrelated nature and *purpose* of the five layers dealt with by Price & Brodie; MacDonald; Pippy & Murdock; Lindtner; and Eisenman – and of other layers in the scriptures of the New Testament; and, **second**, in coming to the realization that "Christianity" was conceived in the minds of Buddhist literary scholars who had been *located in one specific geographical area* – not in Palestine, nor in Antioch, but in the multi-cultural city of ***Alexandria***, Egypt, where the four canonical Gospels, *Acts*, and *Revelation* were conceived. This important fact lies behind one implied meaning of *Matthew 2:15* (with a quotation from *Hosea 11:1*) – "This was to fulfill what the Lord had declared through the prophet: '***I called my son ["Jesus"] out of Egypt***.' "

VI. Metadrama and the New Testament

In India, the visual arts are held to be subordinate to the literary arts. And the dramatic art of India stands at the pinnacle of all this literary 'meta'-business. Classical Indian writers considered drama (*Nāṭaka*) to be the greatest form of literary achievement. The Buddhist narrative panels (painted or sculpted and painted) represent attenuated metadrama (like our comics – and later, cinema).

Looking synoptically at all *four* Gospels and seeking to determine where their authors were coming from – and what they were up to – my suggestion is this: while the Gospels have many clear references (direct and indirect) to the Old Testament (the *Septuagint*) often relating their allegorical, Jewish-born savior of the first century CE to the predictions of the prophets of old, they are introducing these relations as part of their Buddhist *upāya-kauśalyan* stratagem of presenting their Buddhist message in a Jewish form which would be acceptable to both the academic elite and to the common folk ('groundlings'). Thus, the authors are creating their multi-layered allegorical literary work, subtly embodying Buddhism in it, while, at that deeper level, relating it to, and competing with, the scriptures of Judaism (the *Septuagint*), Homer's epics, Egyptian mythology, and the historical writings of Josephus, Philo, and others, with the aim of attracting to the principles of Buddhism persons from varied cultural and religious backgrounds. This *upāya-kauśalyan* multi-layered Buddhist stratagem is even apparent in the missionary, non-academic arena of Paul's frank declaration in *First Corinthians 9:20-22*:

> To the Jews I [*a crypto-Buddhist*] became like a Jew [*an outstanding Pharisee, at that!*], to win the Jews. To those under the law [*of Moses*] I became like one under the law (though I myself [*a crypto-Buddhist*] am not under the law [*of Moses*]), so as to win those under the law. To those not having the law [*the Gentiles – the Egyptians, Greeks, Romans, and the rest*] I became like one not having the law (though I [*a crypto-Buddhist*] am not free from God's law but am under Christ's [*/Buddha's*] law [*Dharma*]), so as to win those not having a law. To the weak I became weak to win the weak. I have become all things to all men so that by all possible means I might save some.

What I am proposing is that all of the themes underlying the surface "Christian" story of the four Gospels – from the Judaic, Buddhist, Egyptian, Astrotheological, and other subset layers, such as the Greek/Roman mythical, Mithraic, Manichæic, etc. – were woven together in different ways in their Gospels by the four Buddhist *literary* scholars, who must have been living in the cosmopolitan setting of the great Alexandrian Library/Sarapæum, and were either active members of the Library/Sarapæum, itself, or in another school of Alexandria. In this setting, it would have been obvious to any academic group that the 'Gospels' were allegorical, fictional works, and their complex multi-layered structure which incorporated comedic, and friendly, morally competitive elements would have had perceptive audiences in this 'university' environment. *These complex works just must have had such knowledgeable audiences in the beginning!* When will our modern professors catch on?

The four Gospels also dealt indirectly with one further underlying meta-narrative layer: the historical antagonism between the crypto-Buddhist missionary movements in Greek-speaking Egypt (continuing the work of the former Therapeutæ) and in Aramaic-speaking Palestine (continuing the work of the former Qumranites and their 'camps'). The so-called anti-Jewish elements in the Gospels should be rather understood as dealing with the profound criticism which the Alexandrians had of their 'Qumranite' colleagues – crypto-Buddhist who, over the span of three centuries from mid-second century BCE, had turned apostate, posing as purer, stricter Jews than even the Pharisees or Sadducees!

Strategy of Assimilation

As Buddhism, during Aśōka's reign, began to spread westward, from India across Persia, toward the Mediterranean kingdoms and Biblical lands, it changed its method of 'propagation' – to use the botanical term! – of its 'Gospel' (The Dharma), and moved from publicly and openly 'planting' its Message (*to evangelion*) and its distinctive institutions (its monasteries and stūpas) in foreign lands, to a strategy of assimilation as camouflage, involving the discrete *upāya-kauśalyan* tactic of '***engraftment***' of the 'Scion' of Buddhism to the 'Jessæan Stock' of Judaism – to put it metaphorically.

As this strategy would have been planned at the highest level of Aśōka's administration, the question must have arisen in the minds of his Buddhist advisors as to which foreign religious group their missionary monks and scholars should assimilate. Since the choice they faced was either assimilating to the dominant Greek polytheism with its idol worship or assimilating to Judaism (a respected alternative) with its abhorrence of idolatry, the decision for them must have been clear cut. For, as I have explained in my earlier work,* from the beginning, Buddhism took an agnostic stance against the widespread polytheism of the Indian masses, and in its art Buddhism reduced the mythical great gods of the Hindu pantheon to mere worshipful attendants, subservient to the *non-divine* human sage, the Buddha! So the **decision** which the Buddhist administrators therefore made was to have their missionary groups assimilate themselves through an '***engraftment***' to Jewish organizations which, **in one sense**, led eventually to success beyond their wildest dreams: Buddhism would, 350 years later, be 'born again' as Christianity, in *Alexandria*, Egypt, around the beginning of the second century CE – yes, *second* century! – and Christianity would, in later centuries, finish the Buddhist task of encircling the globe. But, **in a second sense**, this second century CE re-birth of some of Buddhism's already mutated and diversified sectarian offspring would become unrecognizably different from what the Aśōkan administrators might have envisioned for its crypto-Buddhist "branch".

Furthermore, if aniconicism was not already a practice established in Buddhism before Aśōka's reign, I shall hypothesize that, during his reign, at the highest level of his administration, one other strategic **decision** was taken: no art-work in his dominions would portray either a physical likeness of the young Buddha-to-be or of the enlightened Buddha.

Aniconic Hypothesis

1. We have no known remains of Buddhist art prior to the reign of Aśōka (r.y. 268-232 BCE).
2. In the Buddhist art that does begin with Aśōka's reign, and for between 150 to 250 years thereafter, no physical image of the Buddha appears – though as the young Buddha-to-be or the enlightened Buddha, he very definitely *does* appear everywhere in Buddhist art, but only at a *non-physical* meta-representational level, during its aniconic period.
3. Charles Eliot (in 1921) has suggested that this aniconicism may also have been influenced by Persian traditions (see Third Appendix, p. 178 [Eliot's meta-page 450, footnote 4], for his statement on this). Eliot may be right.
4. In any case, when Aśōka exchanged ambassadors with Ptolemy-II Philadelphus (r.y. 285-247 BCE), the Macedonian pharaoh of Egypt, he did not want the ambassador or any of his entourage or anyone else to claim that in India there were ***idols*** of the Buddha!
5. Solution: a *meta-representational* trick amounting to a *meta-narrative* twist or a *metadramatic* effect!

My 'Aniconic Hypothesis' would also explain the otherwise strange fact that Christian art also had, in its earliest period, works which were 'aniconic'. Early "Christians" (who were, of course, really crypto-Buddhists) were simply continuing the Aśōkan proscription of representing the Buddha (now "Jesus") physically in their narrative art, so as not to unsettle recruited Jewish members, with their ingrained respect for the Mosaic First Commandment. This meta-representational aniconicism creates a sophisticated artefact which is able to represent a physical person without showing that person physically, one which is derivative from India's highly developed meta-narrative and metadramatic literary heritage. To repeat: In India, the visual arts are subordinate to the literary arts. And the dramatic art of India stands at the pinnacle of all this 'meta'-business.

Having an understanding of the terms 'metadrama'/'metatheater' may aid one in seeing how the articles of the five Sections in this book are related and significantly revealing the fictional nature of much of the New Testament. Therefore, on the facing page I reproduce an informative introduction to the term "Metatheatre":

**Buddhism's Relation to Christianity*, p. 169.

"Metatheatre"

Originally created for Stuart Davis' Shakespeare class at Cornell University, Spring 1999.

"meta-" – marked by change or transformation; later in time or development; behind, beyond; transcending, more comprehensive; above, upon, or about. Fr. Greek *meta-*, beside, after.

This painting by the American artist Roy Lichtenstein is entitled "Masterpiece." Why might it be called a "meta-painting"?:

Or consider this potential meta-joke:

A rabbi, a priest, and an imam go into a bar and order a drink. "What is this," asks the bartender, "a joke?" What's the reference of "this" in the two examples? Is it stable or labile? Or "metastable"?

The effect –"Metatheatre" is a convenient name for the quality or force in a play which challenges theatre's claim to be *simply* realistic – to be nothing but a mirror in which we view the actions and sufferings of characters like ourselves, suspending our disbelief in their reality. Metatheatre begins by sharpening our awareness of the *unlikeness* of life to dramatic art; it may end by making us aware of life's uncanny likeness to art or illusion. By calling attention to the strangeness, artificiality, illusoriness, or arbitrariness – in short, the theatricality – of the life we live, it marks those frames and boundaries that conventional dramatic realism would hide. It may present action so alien, improbable, stylized, or absurd that we are forced to acknowledge the estranging frame that encloses a whole play. It may, on the other hand, break the frame of the "fourth wall" of conventional theatre, reaching out to assault the audience or to draw it into the realm of the play. It may – by devices like plays within plays, self-consciously "theatrical" characters, and commentary on the theatre itself – dwell on the boundaries between "illusion" or artifice and "reality" *within* a play, making us speculate on the complex mixture of illusion and reality in our ordinary experience. Any theatrical device can work metatheatrically if we sense in it a certain deliberate reflexiveness, a tendency to refer to itself or to its context in a more general mode: to theatre itself; to art, artifice, and illusion; and perhaps above all to language as such. – *SD*

"M." as genre? – *These remarks by Lionel Abel seek to establish "metatheatre" as a dramatic category or kind. In the context, he mentions such plays as Shakespeare's* Tempest *and Calderón's* Life is a Dream *and works by Genet, Brecht, and Beckett.*

Only certain plays tell us at once that the happenings and characters in them are of the playwright's invention, and that insofar as they were discovered . . . they were found by the playwright's imagining rather than by his observing the world. Such plays have truth in them, not because they convince us of real occurrences or existing persons, but because they show the reality of the dramatic imagination, instanced by the playwright's and also by that of his characters. Of such plays, it may be said: "The play's the thing." Plays of this type, it seems to me, belong to a special genre and deserve a distinctive name. . . . Surely the plays I am referring to should not be described as comedies or tragicomedies. Some of them can, of course, be classified as instances of the play-within-the-play, but this term, also well known, suggests only a device, and not a definite form. Moreover I wish to designate a whole range of plays, some of which do not employ the play-within-a-play, even as a device. [They] have a common character: all of them are theatre pieces about life seen as already theatricalized. By this I mean that the persons appearing on the stage in these plays are there not simply because they were caught by the playwright in dramatic postures as a camera might catch them, but because they themselves knew they were dramatic before the playwright took note of them. What dramatized them originally? Myth, legend, past literature, they themselves. They represent to the playwright the effect of dramatic imagination before he has begun to exercise his own; on the other hand, unlike figures in tragedy, they are aware of their own theatricality. Now, from a certain point of view, only that life which has acknowledged its inherent theatricality can be made interesting on the stage. From the same modern view, events, when interesting, will have the quality of having been thought, rather than of having simply occurred. But then the playwright has the obligation to acknowledge in the very structure of his play that it was his imagination which controlled the event from beginning to end. Plays of the kind I have in mind . . . I call metaplays, works of metatheatre.

– Lionel Abel, *Tragedy and Metatheatre*, ed. Martin Puchner (New York: Holmes and Meier, 2003), 133-35.

VII. "Out of Egypt"

ESSENISM (Jessæanism) is that "Branch" of Buddhism which, in the mid-third century BCE, was engrafted onto the Jewish "Stem of Jesse" (thus forming crypto-Buddhism!) by the Indian missionary monks sent out to the West by King Aśōka.

Two main limbs of this westward-spreading branch were: **first**, the **Essenes who "espoused a life of contemplation"** (the Therapeutæ), headquartered on the shore of Lake Mareotis, outside the city of Alexandria, but to be found, in Philo of Alexandria's day, populating *all* the districts of Egypt, and whose working language was *Greek* and whose Jewish Bible was the Greek *Septuagint*; and **second**, those **Essenes who "cultivated a more active life"** (the strict monastics of Qumran and their less ascetic satellite groups spread throughout Palestine), whose working languages (biblical and sectarian) were *Hebrew* and *Aramaic* – the *Greek* language being present in less than 5% of the Dead Sea Scrolls. We may be in the dark about the three centuries of development which led up to the monastic community of the Therapeutæ which Philo has written about in great detail, but we are incredibly fortunate concerning the history of the monastic community at Qumran, due to the archæological studies of the site and to the serendipitous discovery of the many miraculously preserved Dead Sea Scrolls (whole and in fragments).

We may presume that, by the end of the second century BCE, ***crypto*-Buddhism *masquerading* as Judaic Essenism**, for which we have the Qumranite evidence of it having been established long before then in Palestine, had also been established in other countries around the Mediterranean.

Three Theorems

Concerning the above two limbs of crypto-Buddhism (the Alexandrian and Qumranite), I have formulated three Theorems:

• **1. The Mahāyāna-*Alexandriensis* Theorem (MA Theorem):** which states that *Mahāyāna* Buddhism was primarily conceived and developed, during the last two centuries BCE, ***from Alexandria***, where some of the finest Indian scholars were interacting with some of the finest Western scholars in the great Library/Serapæum of that city.

• **2. The Out-of-Ægypt Two-Stream Theorem (OATS Theorem):** which states that, by the 2nd century BCE, Buddhist scholars, *in Alexandria*, were producing: **1) a stream of Buddhist scriptures**, in Indian languages, which flowed eastward, back to India; and **2),** becoming recognizable in the first century CE, some two hundred years after the first stream began, **a second stream**, in the *Greek* language of the Egyptian diaspora, flowing out around the Mediterranean kingdoms – a ***crypto*-Buddhist-*masquerading*-as-Judaic stream**, the earliest recognizable writings of which are crypto-Buddhist Gnostic works (making no mention of Jesus). We also have, from the first half of the first century CE, Philo's writing in Greek *about* the crypto-Buddhist Essenes in Egypt (the Therapeutæ) and in Palestine (the Qumranites and their scattered "camp" followers). Then, around the beginning of the second century CE, appear the earliest writings, in Greek, of crypto-Buddhist "Gnostic Christians", followed by canonical works of Christianity (in Greek) and non-canonical, in Greek as well as in the Coptic language. Thus, all of the Christian works featuring Jesus (who is the allegorical apotheosis of the 6th-5th century BCE Gautama Buddha) are Buddhist creations through and through!

• **3. The Ultra-Radically-Judaized crypto-Buddhists-of-Qumran Theorem (URJcBoQ Theorem):** which states that when crypto-Buddhism (Essenism/Jessæanism) first entered Palestine in the third century BCE, it followed the general Buddhist practice of adapting itself to the local language/s and customs. At the same time, this limb of Essenism entered into the strong gravitational field of Jerusalem, the religious and cultural center of Judaism, and soon metamorphosed into an apparently exclusive Jewish sect more strict, in many ways, than the other two sects, the Pharisees and Sadducees.

These three Theorems may strike one as preposterous. However, the rock inscriptions of King Aśōka clearly declare that by his scheme of propagating "The Dharma" (= "Paul's" "The Gospel" ["*to evangelion*"]), he *accomplished* – past tense! – the (friendly) "Conquest" of the Seleucid empire of Antiochus-II, and the kingdoms of Ptolemy-II's Egypt, Antigonas Gonatas's Macedonia, Magas's Cyrene, and Alexander-II's Epirus!

If we understand that the spreading of the branchlets of "Gnosticism" and, later, of those of "Christianity" throughout the kingdoms around the Mediterranean was really the spreading of various forms of crypto-Buddhism, we will finally appreciate the full force of King Aśōka's claim. But that the "Conquest" by crypto-Buddhism (in the form of "Christianity") would, then, within about two millennia from Aśōka's reign, continue westward as far as the islands of Hawaii, and would, in the process, spawn a dizzying multitude of various sectarian forms, *seemingly remote from Buddhism*, is something Aśōka could never have imagined and which even modern scholars are having great difficulty realizing!

Thus, we see that the culminating ***seventh paradigm shift*** is illustrated by the following stages of reasoning:

1) There are significant parallels between Buddhism and Christianity.

2) The direction of influence sometimes seems to be from Buddhism to Christianity (very disquieting to Christians) and sometimes from Christianity to Buddhism (most welcomed by Christians!).

3) Christian Lindtner entered the picture, in 1998, and proposed that the evangelists of the New Testament were, in reality, Buddhists who were Sanskrit-fluent and were creating their Greek gospels out of a freewheeling quasi-historical allegorical myth-making (MacDonald's 'Mimesis'): How would the Buddha be imaginatively portrayed, if he were *literarily* reborn in Palestine toward the end of King Herod's reign? According to Lindtner, the gospels incorporate Greek passages which parallel in strange ways specific scattered passages in Buddhist Sanskrit and Pāli scriptures. Lindtner claimed that the direction of influence was from Sanskrit to Greek.

4) Here comes the final **major paradigm shift (No. 7)** which I am proposing: ***The source*** of many of the Buddhist Sanskrit/Pāli scriptures which Lindtner has been dealing with, as well as the New Testament gospels, *Acts*, epistles, and *Revelation*, ***is from the styluses of Sanskrit-and-Greek-fluent Buddhist scholars working in the environs of the Royal Library / Serapæum of Alexandria, Egypt!*** Thus, the Gordian knot of confusion is cut with one stroke.

5) The long-standing debate about direction of influence (Buddhist → Christian or Christian → Buddhist) becomes settled on a single direction: **OUT OF EGYPT**! Scholars have been blind to the tremendous influence which occurred in Alexandria from the creative mixture of Buddhist scholars with Greek, Jewish, and Egyptian scholars. Christianity is the result of three centuries of gestation which took place in Alexandria – in Africa! Christianity is a genuine Indo-Alexandrian – Indo-African – creation! And I would now suggest that Buddhist scholars should reconsider *all of the Buddhist scriptures which Lindtner has been dealing with as to whether many of them would have actually been created or initiated by the crypto-Buddhist scholars* ***in Alexandria*** *– written only during or after King Aśōka's reign!* And such works would have been deeply affected by Alexandrian *literary* interactions between Buddhist scholars and those of other traditions (especially the "Old Testament" [the *Septuagint*], of course).

Aśōka's grandfather, King Chandragupta, patronized Jainism; his father, King Bindusāra, patronized the Ājīvika faith, King Aśōka turned to Buddhism. The evolution of crypto-Buddhism (culminating in Christianity, in Alexandria, in the second century CE) begins with Aśōka.

Examples of Egypt influencing Buddhism

1) King Aśōka adopted certain ***birudas***, royal titles, translated straight from the Pharaonic hieroglyphs. This may also be true of Aśōka's father and grandfather.

2) Aśōka's artisans, now aware in detail of the very long history of rock-cut cave-temples in Egypt, excavated the very first rock-cut architectural caves in India – these, interestingly, were dedicated not to the Buddhists, but to the Ājīvika sect, the sect favored by Aśōka's father, Bindusāra.

3) Aśōka refashioned many of the humble Buddhist stūpas throughout India into magnificent monuments, some of which would, arguably, emulate the Egyptian pyramids, surpassing them in terms of their wealth of ***sculptural*** art.

4) Aśōka introduced into India the Egyptian pharaonic practice of erecting stelæ proclaiming their victories – except, Aśōka differed dramatically from the pharaohs by proclaiming in his Rock Edict XIII and on his "pillars of victory" his "Salvation Army's" (his Buddhist monks' and scholars') *peaceful* "conquest" of the Mediterranean and other kingdoms *by spreading the Buddhist Dharma*, instead of the Egyptian practice of trumpeting on stelæ their bloody victories in war, with the portrayal of numbers of prisoners decapitated or about to be!

5) In India, before the reign of Aśōka, there was **no practice of committing scriptures to writing**. For instance, the four Vēdas, in the priestly language, Vēdic Sanskrit, were not written down, but rather, they were scrupulously memorized and recited by male priests of the Brahmin caste. (The extraordinary feats of memory of these Brahmins – the Ēkavēdīs, Dvivēdīs, Trivēdīs, and Chaturvēdīs – can be gauged by the dominance, today, in the U.S. National Spelling Bee, of their immigrant descendants, the ethnic East Indian children.) The Buddhists, after the death of the Buddha, followed this same practice of memorization with their own scriptures, but with **two** significant differences: **first**, since the Buddha had preached the Dharma in the language of the common people – not in any priestly or learned language – his sayings and the rules of the Buddhist monastic community were memorized by the monastics as canonical works in the common language of the Buddha's day, a *prākrit*, Pāli, the vernacular of that place and time (fifth century BCE); and **second**, groups of monks and groups of nuns, from any caste background *or none*, have, from that time, memorized and recited these Buddhist scriptures on a regularly fortnightly basis. However, wherever Buddhists have preached the Dharma outside of India, it has always been in the language of the common people of that foreign country – a practice, for instance, followed by the Buddhist missionaries to China, around the beginning of the Common Era, and religiously followed, even today, by their crypto-Buddhist-engrafted branch, Christianity. This practice was also evident in first century CE Egypt (land of the crypto-Buddhist Therapeutean Essenes), where the common language of the rulers and the diaspora was Koinē (vernacular = Alexandrian) Greek; and in Palestine (home territory of the crypto-Buddhist Qumranite Essenes and their satellite "camps"), where the common languages were Hebrew and Aramaic.

When the Buddhists finally committed their canonical scriptures to writing in the first century, BCE, it was surely due to their having been in contact with Egypt during Aśōka's reign. For Egyptians, the very act of writing down the sacred accounts of their gods was, itself, a sacred duty. So, if crypto-Buddhists, in Egypt, were going to successfully proselytize the Egyptians (Greeks. Jews, Copts, and others), it would serve them well to follow suit in the common languages, Greek and Coptic, and **adapt the newly written allegorical *literary* works of Buddhist scholars as pseudo-historical *liturgy* for their proto-churches!**

6) After having read through Pippy's book, *Egyptian Origin of the Book of Revelation*, I have become convinced that the development of fervor in India over the relics of the Buddha and other saints arose only during and after Aśōka's reign and was due to Egyptian influence through the crypto-Buddhists' experience in Alexandria! The essence of the Buddha's teaching was to face the reality of death squarely. Quite the opposite of the Egyptian attitude, which supremely valued the idea of bodily resurrection, etc., etc. The Passion, Death, and Resurrection of Jesus was surely introduced into crypto-Buddhist-"Christianity" from Egypt – most likely, in earnest, shortly after 143 CE, when the Church of Alexandria shifted from the leadership of the "bishops of the circumcision" to Gentile (Coptic) bishops. (Can one conceive of Jewish bishops celebrating the Eucharist, imagining they were drinking blood – even divine blood?)

7) Finally, only ***after*** Aśōka's reign, did the development begin, in India, of what was to become the traditional Hindu temple with its highly organized ceremonial customs, much of which is majorly indebted to the Indians' close encounter with **EGYPT** during Aśōka's reign. (I know that many of my Indian friends may be alarmed by this statement.)

FIRST APPENDIX

Pages reproduced from Arthur Drews's book,
The Witnesses to the Historicity of Jesus
(London: Watts & Company, 1912)

[I. NAZARETH.

{p. 200} The historical Jesus is said to have been born in Nazareth. This however, is, in turn, anything but] certain. It may be a matter of chance that neither the Old Testament nor Josephus nor the Talmud mentions the place; and, except in the gospels, the name is unknown until the fourth century (Eusebius, Jerome, and Epiphanius). But the statement of Weiss, that it "cannot be denied that it was firmly believed by the Christians of the first century that Jesus came from Nazareth"* (p. 21), is wholly unjustified, and is based only on the unproved assumption that the gospels already existed then in their present form. On the other hand, it is entirely inadmissible that the sect of the Nazaræans, as the followers of Jesus are first called in *Acts* (xxiv, 3), took their name from the supposed birthplace of their founder, as Nazareth played scarcely any part in the life of Jesus which was known to them. It is true that Matthew (ii, 23) says that Jesus received his epithet "the Nazaraios" from Nazareth, and he appeals to a passage in the prophets. But no such passage is to be found, quite apart from the fact that in that case he ought to be called a "Nazarethene," or else Nazareth, his supposed birthplace, ought to be called Nazara; this is, indeed, found in some of the old manuscripts, and has been affirmed, but merely in order to harmonise it with the name Nazoraios, Nazaraios, or Nazarene, which is given to Jesus in the gospels.

The fact is that the name only occurs in the latest stratum of the gospels (*Matthew* ii, 23; *Luke* iv, 16), whereas the older stratum (*Mark* vi, 1 ; *Matthew* xiii, 54) merely speaks of his "native town." *Mark* i, 9, is clearly only an amplification of the older reading of *Matthew* iii, 13, where it is simply said that Jesus came "from Galilee"; and *Matthew* iv, 13, and xxi, 11, are plainly interpolations, since Nazareth has not previously been mentioned. The same must be said of *Matthew* xxvi, 71, where it is written "Jesus of Nazareth," in accordance with the earlier expression of the evangelist. On the other hand, no theologian will deny that the story of the childhood in Luke is of late date.

*Johannes Weiss, *Das älteste Evangelium: ein Beitrag zum Verständnis des Markus-Evangeliums und der ältesten evangelischen Überlieferung* (Göttingen: Vandenhoek und Ruprecht, 1903). – ML

In Mark Jesus is called "the Nazarene" in i, 24; x, 47; xiv, 67; and xvi, 6, without any statement that this indicates the place of his origin. It may, therefore, just as well have a different meaning, and may be a sect-name.

This is the view of William B. Smith. In his opinion the name can be traced to the ancient root N-Z-R, which means something like watcher, protector, guardian, saviour. Hence Jesus the Nazoræan or Nazarene was Jesus the Protector, just as Jahveh,[1] or the archangel Michael, the "angel-prince," who often takes the place of the Messiah, is known as the "protector of Israel," its spokesman with God, and its deliverer from all its cares (*Daniel* xix, 13, and xii, 1; *Gen.* xlviii, 16); the rabbinical Metatron also plays this part of protector and supporter of the Jewish people, and is regarded as the "angel of redemption," especially of the damned suffering in hell. The followers of Jesus will, therefore, have called themselves Nazoræans because they primarily conceived the expected Messiah in the sense of a Michael or Metatron, a protector; that is, at all events, more probable than that they took their name from the place Nazareth, with which they had no close connection.[2] It is not at all impossible

---

[1]*Psalm* 121. The fact that the protector is here called *schomer*, not *nozer*, has nothing to do with the matter, any more than the fact that the Palestinians of the time about the birth of Christ did not use the Hebrew *nazar* for "the protector," but the Aramaic *ne'tar*: it is well known that the language of a sect tends to preserve antique words, and we are concerned here, not with the word itself, but its meaning.

[2]Smith, *The Pre-Christian Jesus*, 1906. Also see his article on "The Real Ancestry of Jesus" in the Open Court, January, 1910, p. 12, and the article "The Nazarene," by Dr. P. Carus, the editor, in the same number (p. 26). Differently from the German theologians, who cannot speak disdainfully enough of Smith's hypotheses, on philological grounds, Carus admits the possibility of that origin of the name, and regards the existence of a place called Nazareth at the time of Jesus as improbable. Indeed, in his book *The Pleroma: An Essay on the Origins of Christianity* (1910), he says that it is absolutely impossible that the Nazarene could mean the man from Nazareth (p. 46). Moreover, Schmiedel has recently maintained against Weinel in the *Protestantenblatt*, 1910, Nr. 17, p. 438, that Smith's hypothesis is philologically admissible. Hence the charge of "gross ignorance of the Semitic languages" which Weinel brings against Smith is quite unjustified.

that the place Nazareth took its name from the sect of the Nazaræans, instead of the reverse, as is admitted by so distinguished a scholar as W. Nestle.[1] According to the Assyriologist Haupt (of Baltimore), Nazareth was a new name for the older Hethlon (*Ezech.* xlvii, 15), or Hittalon or Hinnathon, which means "protection," and has reference to the protected position of Nazareth among the hills. In that case it would be natural for the evangelist to choose a place called "protection" as the birthplace of the "protector."

According to *Mark* x, 47, the blind Bartimeus, hearing that "Jesus the Nazarene" is passing by, calls out to him, "Jesus, thou son of David." It is possible that we have here another indication of the original meaning of the name. In Isaiah *nazar* is the Hebrew word for the "branch," called *zemah* in Zechariah; and he is called that in Isaiah "a rod from the stem of Jesse" – that is to say, a "son (descendant) of David." May it not be that the expression Nazaræan or Nazarene also contains an allusion to the "branch," as Kobertson suggests?[2] If the figure of Jesus, and even his name, as we have seen, are derived from Isaiah, it is natural to assume that his secondary name "the Nazaræan" may also be traced to the same source, and that in the name of his sect there is a relation to the prophet's branch of David. "He grew up as a tender plant, a *nazar*" (*Isaiah* liii, 2); from this a later age has made him a "Nazarene" and put his birth at Nazareth.[3] This would also afford a simple

[1]*Südwestdeutsche Schulblätter*, 1910, Heft 4 and 5, p. 163. M. Bruckner [in his *Der sterbende und auferstehende Gottheiland in den Orient-Religionen und ihr Verhältniss zum Christentum*, 1908] also says, in regard to Smith's hypothesis: "His proof that the epithet 'Nazaræan' applied to Jesus in *Matthew* ii, 23, cannot have been derived from Nazareth, but was the name of a pre-Christian Jewish sect, especially *deserves attention*" (p. 47). In Hugo Winckler we read: "From the word *neçer* comes the name of the religion of those who believe in the 'Saviour' – the Nazarene-Christians or Nazaræans. Nazareth as the home of Jesus is merely a confirmation of his character as saviour for the symbolising tendency" (*Ex oriente lux*, Band ii, 1906, p. 59, *note*). Cf. also Winckler, *Die babylonische Geisteskultur* (1907), p. 147.

[2]Cf. also Alfred Jeremias, *Das Alte Testament im Lichte des alten Orients*, 2 Aufl., 1906, pp. 353, 577.

[3]Possibly *nazar* also has an astral significance, as the Hyades in Taurus have the

explanation of the curious reference in *Matthew* ii, 23, to some unknown passage in the prophets, and we need not suppose that Nazareth only became the name of a place at a later date; it may have existed already, and have been chosen as the birthplace of Jesus because of its connection with *nazar*.

We are disposed to believe that the sect of the Nazoræans was originally the same as the Nasiræans, the "initiated" or "holy," who were distinguished from the rest of the Jews by their abstinence from oil and wine and the use of the razor, and by the rigour of their lives; and that the Nazoræans were those Nasiræans who conceived the expected Messiah in the sense of the *nazar* of Isaiah. In *Lamentations* (iv, 7) the "pure" are called "Nazarites" [Nazaræans], and Josephus writes Nazaraios in *Antiquities* iv, 4, 4, but Naziraios in xix, 6, 1.

It is admitted that the origin of Jesus from Nazareth is in contradiction to the belief that the Messiah was to be born in Bethlehem as a shoot from David. But it is not a contradiction between the Messianic dogma and a "hard fact of history," as Weiss says (p. 22); it is due simply to the fact that the man of the race of David is called by the prophet a "branch" (*nazar*); and, when men began to make an historical person of Jesus, they found the agreement of the word with Nazareth a very welcome opportunity to conceal the real origin of Jesus in Isaiah. The contradiction gave no more trouble to the early Christians than the circumstance that possibly there was no such place as Nazareth at the time of Jesus. There was also probably no such place as Capernaum, Emmaus, Bethesda, Nain, Gethsemane, or Golgotha. And if our opponents say that, if that were so, the story of Jesus would have betrayed its character as fiction, and a Jew would have seen the defect at once, we may remind them that the massacre of the children at Bethlehem, the wandering about of people to be

---

form of a branch; and Orion, in which we have already suspected the Baptist, seems to bring the "twig" (Fuhrmann).

included in the census, the astronomically impossible eclipse of the sun, which is supposed to have lasted three hours, at the death of Jesus, and many other details, did not give the evangelists the least concern. Even to-day the pious reader of the Bible is not disquieted by these things. Nor was there any fear of Jewish objection to the derivation of Jesus from Nazareth, because the process of the historicisation of the Christ-myth was only completed at a time when no historical evidence whatever of the real origin of Jesus could be adduced, since, as we have seen, the oldest gospel uses the name Nazaræan probably not to indicate the birthplace of Jesus, but as a sect-name with reference to the "protector" or "saviour" and the *nazar* of Isaiah.[1]

II. JERUSALEM.

So far, then, from the name Nazaræan, or Nazoræan, or Nazarene, being derived from the town of Nazareth, we must say that this is the *least probable* of all possible suggestions. The names of places in the gospels, in fact, afford no evidence whatever of the historicity of Jesus, since the whole topography of the life of Jesus is in its main lines borrowed from Isaiah and other prophets. So it was inevitable that, as soon as the process began to be regarded from the historical point of view, the great drama of the suffering and death of the servant of God and the associated redemption of mankind should be located in Jerusalem. As *Luke* says (xiii, 33 – see also *Psalm* cxvi, 14-19): "It cannot be that a prophet perish out of Jerusalem." It is the unvarying theme of the prophets that Jerusalem will be glorified by Jahveh, and become the centre of the world's history (*Isaiah* lxii, 7). In the prophet Zechariah we read of the inhabitants of the city:–

---

[1]Compare Robertson, *Christianity and Mythology*, p. 311, and P. van Dyk's *Krit. Kommentar zu den Evangelien*, pp. 28 and 152.

"An Embarrassment of Riches"

One of the most unusual broadcasts on the internet must surely be Prof. Robert M. Price's podcast, "The Bible Geek". Armed with two Ph.D.s from Drew University (in Systematic Theology and in the New Testament) and an astonishing range of academic and not-so-"academic" reading, a phenomenal memory, and superb command of the English language, delivered in a variety of accents, he sallies forth, often more than twice a week, to wrestle, largely extempore, with questions on the Christian Bible which listeners are welcome to e-mail him. And they do, from around the world.

I count myself as one of his regular listeners, and the two brief excerpts from his podcasts which I have transcribed for this Appendix are offered here as further examples of the multiple layers which underlie the surface meanings of the canonical gospels.

The great problem is this: How do we interpret these multiple layers of meaning, making sense out of them, assuming that we do recognize them as intentional constructs of the authors of the gospels?

If each of these layers steers one in a different direction for identifying the true source of the New Testament gospels, one is left with a bewildering number of sources to pick from. In choosing only one source, the problem becomes accounting for the others.

It is this bewilderment which is expressed by Dr. Price's words, "an embarrassment of riches" in the last paragraph of the second excerpt, "Jesus as the New Sun God". And it is this bewilderment that Dr. Christian Lindtner and I wish to overcome with our crypto-Buddhist solution.

Jesus as the "New Dionysus"

A transcribed extract from Robert M. Price's THE BIBLE GEEK Podcast of September 21, 2011

(Prof. Price reads a written communication from Zoe Butler and responds in asides to it.)

RMP: Zoe Butler says:

ZB: This is a related question to the one on John Barleycorn. We know that Bacchus/Bacchos or Iacchus/Iacchos or Dionysus are all variant forms of the god of the vine. The name standing for different emphases in different cultures. Apologists are quick to claim that this god was never crucified and that the third century amulet depicting him crucified was copied from Christian iconography.

RMP: By the way, he is crucified on an anchor, isn't he. That seems a little odd if it is copied from Christianity. Anyhow:

ZB: I think it is extremely likely that Dionysus was thought of as crucified for the following reason:

Viniculture has always been a major factor of Italian society and was so during the Roman Empire. Now it happens that when vines are grown in vineyards, they are fixed to stakes. . . . The viniculturist takes hold of the vine and divides it into two branches, pulling one branch to the right and the other to the left, binding these parts to stakes. Specifically, the viniculturist calls these the two 'arms' of the vine. The left arm of the vine is bound to the left-hand stake and the right arm of the vine is bound to the right-hand stake. These stakes are, of course, '*stauri*' the very same word translated as 'cross'.

RMP: That's certainly true.

ZB: The process is, literally, crucifixion. The vine is fixed to one stake between two others, like Jesus crucified between two thieves. In a sense, the two stakes on either side of the vine carry away the arms of the vine and could be described as thieves.

Now, it seems to me that there are other correspondences.

Jesus is 'The Truth' or 'The True Vine'. There's a strong association of truth with wine, in Italy. Wine shops often display the Latin motto, '*In vino veritas*' – 'In wine is truth.' Dionysus was associated with wine and the states it induced, one of which was the idea that people who were filled with wine 'give themselves away', so that 'In wine is truth' or 'In Dionysus is truth' is literally true. I also wonder if Jesus was assumed to be Dionysus because of the similarity of 'DION-IESOUS' to Dionysus, so that, perhaps, people connected Dionysus with the 'Follower of Dionysus' – that is, 'IESOUS'. Could Jesus be thought of as 'The New Dionysus' for this reason among the Roman cultists?

Grapes are, of course, pressed, trampled on, and left to ferment in a dark place, a cave or tomb, whereupon the juice turns into wine and could thus be seen as a kind of resurrection.

So I wonder if part of the myth of Jesus, after the destruction of the Temple, might have come from viniculture. And, that aside, doesn't it strongly suggest that crucifixion really was part of the Dionysus myth long before Christianity? – that the crucifixion of Dionysus was as old as wine?

. . .

RMP: . . . I think you've got a real good case for the antiquity of the Dionysus crucifixion motif. That puts a really different light on a lot of things. The name is very interesting. And, of course, something like this is implied if you go as far as saying that the Last Supper's 'words of institution' seem to be borrowed from Dionysus or Osiris, who were identified anyway. 'This wine is my blood' – What does that mean? I mean that has got *nothing* to do with any Passover observance. It just simply has to come from these mystery religions' sacraments. And what you're saying would add more detail to that. And so, yes, this fits in very well with what we already know.

And the 'stakes' are called '*stauri*' – Holy mackerel! Fascinating! This is one to think about a lot.

Thank you, Zoe, very, very interesting!

* * * * * * * * *

Jesus as the New 'Sun God'

A transcribed extract from Robert M. Price's THE BIBLE GEEK Podcast of August 8, 2011

(Prof. Price reads a written communication from Floyd and then comments on it.)

Fl: In my studies of Christianity, I have come across web sites that claim that the gospels contain solar mythology where Jesus is seen as the Sun traveling through the zodiac for a one year period. One web site made the following claims that I thought were quite revealing:

1. The sun enters Capricorn on the winter solstice, a natural place to start the yearly cycle. Then when the sun travels 30 degrees, the sun exits Capricorn and enters Aquarius. Thus an allegorical story of the sun's annual travels could have been the Sun character visiting the Aquarius character, at the age of 30 – that is actually 30º, or about 30 days, but an allegory could imply 30 years instead. And, of course, that would be Jesus visiting John the Baptist (the Aquarius Water Bearer).
2. The Sun begins its journey at age 30 by entering Aquarius. Jesus is said to have begun his ministry at age 30 (*Luke 3:23*). Jesus begins his ministry by visiting John the Baptist (Aquarius) who baptizes him with water.
3. The Sun's annual journey around the zodiac takes one year. Jesus' ministry is said to have lasted one year, at least according to the Synoptics: Matthew, Mark, and Luke. The gospel of John implies Jesus' ministry lasted three years.
4. The temptation to be lazy is a common theme we find expressed near the beginning of a solar myth. The Sun has the temptation to give in to the forces of darkness. But the Sun spurns the temptation. The Sun will not allow cold and darkness to reign. The sun will continue on its journey. Jesus is tempted by the devil (*Matt 4:1-11* etc.).
5. The sun goes on its way, leaving Aquarius behind. Aquarius is figuratively put in prison, that is, below the horizon at sunset. John is put in prison (*Matt 4:12*). Jesus goes on his way (*Matt 4:13-17*).
6. The sun visits Pisces (the Two Fish) – the theme of fishing. Jesus visits Simon Peter and his brother Andrew, Two Fishermen (*Matt 4:18-22*).
7. The Sun visits Aries (the Ram, Sheep, or Lamb) on the vernal equinox, when darkness and cold (the figurative sins of the earth) are overpowered by light and warmth. Jesus is the Lamb of God who takes away the sins of the earth (*John 1:29 & 1:36*).
8. Around roughly 4000 to 2000 BCE, the sun was in Taurus (the Bull) on the vernal equinox, and we find in ancient religions of this period that a bull was worshiped as the One who saves the world from the evils of winter. Due to the earth's precession, this latter became Aries, the Lamb who saves the world. Then, later, when the vernal equinox was in Pisces, the symbol of the Lamb was abandoned and replaced with that of a Fish.
9. The head of Aquarius rises from below the eastern horizon – rises from the dead and appears beheaded by the horizon. In *Matt 14:1-12*, John rises from the dead: "This is John the Baptist, he has risen from the dead" (*Matt 14:2*), and then John is beheaded by Herod, the personification of Night.
10. Right after Taurus (the Bull), lies the Milky Way, that starry band that lies like a lake across the night sky. The sun crosses the Milky Way around May 20th to June 4th. The Sun walks on the water (*Matt 14:25*): "Jesus went out to them walking on the lake."
11. On June 21st we reach the summer solstice, the longest day of the year. Jesus has his transfiguration, his face shone like the sun (*Matt 17:1-13*).
12. In the Babylonian zodiac, the sign for the House of Cancer was the Ass and Foal. Two bright stars in the constellation of Cancer still bear the names, Northern Ass and Southern Ass, with the Southern Ass lying directly on the ecliptic. The Sun, figuratively, rides an Ass and Foal into the middle of summer. Jesus rides an ass and colt into Jerusalem (*Matt 21:7*).
13. On August 23rd, the sun enters the House of Virgo, 'the Virgin'. Virgo is the Virgin that figuratively gives birth to the Sun each year when the sun passes out of Virgo. Even though Virgo gives birth, she remains a virgin, just as Mary is the virgin who gives birth to Jesus and yet remains a virgin. The Sun is born or reborn in four different ways:

i. On Christmas Day, three days after the winter solstice;
ii. by passing out of Virgo, the Virgin;
iii. and at the dawn of every new day, the Sun arises, born again;
iv. and out from a solar eclipse.

14. After the harvest, the sun moves from Virgo into Libra, the Scales, September. These are the Scales of Justice. The harvest has been gathered. It is now time to sell the harvest. The scales are used in buying and selling the harvest.
15. As we enter the season of autumn, the leaves fall from the trees and the trees appear to wither. It is at this point in the story that Jesus is said to curse the fig tree and make it wither, a story which makes no sense if Jesus were a real person, but it makes perfect sense when understood as an allegory. It is simply autumn, and Jesus the 'Sun', who makes the seasons pass, causes the leaves to fall from the trees (*Mark 11:20-25*; *Matt 21:18-22*).
16. In late October, the sun enters Scorpio, the Scorpion. Judas represents Scorpio. It stings the Sun, condemning it to death, just as Judas kisses Jesus, condemning him to death.
17. After the death of Judas, that is, after Scorpio goes below the horizon, Jesus, the 'Sun', is handed over to Pontius Pilate, Sagittarius. Pilate is the last person Jesus encounters in the story before being put to death, only to be resurrected three days later, just as Sagittarius is the last zodiac month of the year through which the Sun passes before dying on the winter solstice, December 22nd, only to be resurrected three days later, and begin anew its journey northward on December 25th, Christmas Day.

The problem I have with these claims is that I am not aware of a critical scholar that has endorsed [this solar myth theory. Are the proponents of this theory] simply reading astrology into the gospels? Or do you think the authors have actually written the gospels this way? Are you aware of any scholars that have endorsed this view or have written books about it?

• • •

RMP: Well, Count Volney wrote a book, back in the 18th century, called *Ruins of Empires*, where he propounded the idea of the solar mythology as the origin of the gospel story. I don't know of any persons associated with the Society of Biblical Literature or the Society for New Testament Study that endorse this. They'd all be chased out as heretics if they did. And I don't think that's because of any inherent implausibility in the story. People like my friend and colleague, Acharya S, uphold this and argue for it eloquently.

I still feel – like . . . let me tell you what my objection – my qualm, let me say, about this – is, in a moment. But I really don't think it's a surprise that no matter how compelling one might find this theory, professional biblical scholars reject it out of hand, because, if this is true, then, of course, you're dealing with a Christ-Myth Theory, and that is an abomination to them. And, forgive me, but I do not think that is nonsense, either. I think – I know somebody's going to say, "Well, this is an example of the *ad hominem* fallacy" (claiming that they cannot bring themselves to entertain this theory because of their religious upbringing and present affiliations). Not that they can't afford to admit what they know is true. I don't mean that. Rather, they cannot bring themselves to *consider* it because it just looms too large in their mind, their life style, their profession, it is simply unthinkable.

Now, I think ultimately that – I am saying that this is in lieu of, instead of, rationally, objectively considering this evidence.

I don't think that I am committing the *ad hominem* fallacy, trying to discount someone's position because of imagined personal factors. No, I am looking at the evidence, namely evidence like you have very concisely and clearly summarized. And considering the other evidence that the gospels are mythical, I have looked at the arguments, and frankly cannot see why scholars reject them. And so I then have to – albeit only by way of speculation – ask myself, "Well, why are they so stubborn? Is the evidence really that stupid?" I don't think it is stupid at all. So I have to ask why they think it is.

Well, ultimately I say, "Look, there's no accounting for how people see things." I'm not a mind reader. But I do have to suspect very seriously that it's because they just can't bring themselves to depart from their deeply ingrained Christian upbringing. . . .

O.K., now what is my qualm about the Solar Myth Theory of the origin of the Gospel Story? Well, I look at the astrotheology theory and I do find it attractive because I am convinced that this kind of thinking reveals several Old Testament characters to have been sun-gods, ultimately just sun-myths: Enoch, Esau, Elijah, Isaac, Moses, and so forth. And, here you've pointed out even more evidence that Jesus would fit the category. So that sounds good. But I have to admit that some of the stuff that Christian Lindtner and others say about a Buddhist origin of the gospels – that is strangely compelling, too. But then there are a lot of different theories, and I have to admit at this point, it's an embarrassment of riches. I don't know that you can combine all of these theories. And it's like I've said before in print, the competing models of a historical Jesus – there's so many of them! – and it can be plausibly argued that they kind of cancel each other out. I'm afraid that may happen with the different versions of the Christ-Myth Theory. Can any of them be all that compelling if too many of them are equally compelling? I wonder about that. The solar-mythologists are making a pretty good case, I think – but since so many others with seemingly incompatible myth theories are doing the same thing, I'm kind of left thinking, "Gee, I don't know!" Well, of course, I said that from the beginning. I'm not a dogmatist. I don't know that there was no historical Jesus – or that there was one. I'm simply trying on the paradigms, imposing them on the evidence tentatively to see what seems to fit. And you've shown it fits pretty well in this case. So I take it as a quite legitimate and powerful scholarly view. But I am not surprised that conventional scholars, many of whom have some kind of conventional Christian affiliation or at least ingrained upbringing, cannot bring themselves to see it that way.

Thanks Floyd for the great summary.

* * * * * * * * *

I

ENGRAFTMENT ON THE "STOCK OF JESSE"

New Testament Narrative as Old Testament Midrash

Robert M. Price (2004, 2005, 2011)

A. Introduction

The line is thin between extrapolating new meanings from ancient scriptures (borrowing the authority of the old) and actually composing new scripture (or quasi-scripture) by extrapolating from the old. By this process of midrashic expansion grew the Jewish *haggadah*, new narrative commenting on old (scriptural) narrative by rewriting it. *Haggadah* is a species of *hypertext*, and thus it cannot be fully understood without reference to the underlying text on which it forms a kind of commentary. The earliest Christians being Jews, it is no surprise that they practiced haggadic expansion of scripture, resulting in new narratives partaking of the authority of the old. The New Testament gospels and the *Acts of the Apostles* can be shown to be Christian haggadah upon Jewish scripture, and these narratives can be neither fully understood nor fully appreciated without tracing them to their underlying sources, the object of the present article.

Christian exegetes have long studied the gospels in light of Rabbinical techniques of biblical interpretation including allegory, midrash, and pesher. The discovery of the Dead Sea Scrolls lent great impetus to the recognition of the widespread use among New Testament writers of the pesher technique whereby prophetic prooftexts for the divine preordination of recent events was sought. Slower (but still steady) in coming has been the realization of the wide extent to which the stories of the gospels and the *Acts of the Apostles* are themselves the result of haggadic midrash upon stories from the Old Testament (as we may call it here in view of the Christian perspective on the Jewish canon that concerns us). The New Testament writers partook of a social and religious environment in which currents of Hellenism and Judaism flowed together and interpenetrated in numerous surprising ways, the result of which was not merely the use of several versions of the Old Testament texts, in various languages, but also the easy switching back and forth between Jewish and Greek sources such as Euripides, Homer, and the Mystery Religion traditions.

Earlier scholars (e.g., John Wick Bowman), as many today (e.g., J. Duncan M. Derrett), saw gospel echoes of the ancient scriptures in secondary coloring here or redactional juxtaposition of traditional Jesus stories there. But the more recent scrutiny of John Dominic Crossan, Randel Helms, Dale and Patricia Miller, and Thomas L. Brodie has made it inescapably clear that virtually the entirety of the gospel narratives and much of the *Acts* are wholly the product of haggadic midrash upon previous scripture. Earl Doherty has clarified the resultant understanding of the gospel writers' methodology. It has been customary to suppose that early Christians began with a set of remarkable facts (whether few or many) and sought after the fact for scriptural predictions for them, the goal being to show that even though the founding events of their religion defied contemporary messianic expectation, they were nonetheless in better accord with prophecy, that recent events clarified ancient prophecy in retrospect. Thus modern scholars might admit that *Hosea 11:1* ("Out of Egypt I have called my son") had to be taken out of context to provide a pedigree for the fact of Jesus' childhood sojourn in Egypt, but that it was the story of the flight into Egypt that made early Christians go searching for the *Hosea* text. Now it is apparent, just to take this example, that the flight into Egypt is midrashic all the way down. That is, the words in *Hosea 11:1* "my son," catching the early Christian eye, generated the whole story, since they assumed such a prophecy about the divine Son must have had its fulfillment. And the more apparent it becomes that most gospel narratives can be adequately accounted for by reference to scriptural prototypes, Doherty suggests, the more natural it is to picture early Christians beginning with a more or less vague savior myth and seeking to lend it color and detail by anchoring it in a particular historical period and clothing it in scriptural garb. We must now envision proto-Christian exegetes "discovering" for the first time what Jesus the Son of God had done and said "according to the scriptures" by decoding the ancient texts. Today's Christian reader learns what Jesus did by reading the gospels; his ancient counterpart learned what Jesus did by reading *Joshua* and *1 Kings*. It was not a question of memory but of creative exegesis. Sometimes the signals that made particular scriptural texts attractive for this purpose are evident (like "my son" in *Hosea 11:1*), sometimes not. But in the end the result is a new perspective according to which we must view the gospels and Acts as analogous with the *Book of Mormon*, an inspiring pastiche of stories derived creatively from previous scriptures by a means of literary extrapolation.

Our purpose here will be to review the bulk of the New Testament narratives, indicating in as brief a compass as possible how each has been derived from previous scripture. *Mark* will receive the most attention, as Matthew and Luke have used *Mark* as the basis of their narratives; there are fewer uniquely Matthean and Lukan items. John's Gospel and the *Acts* will receive more selective treatment, too, as *John* generally cannibalizes the Synoptic Gospels (or their underlying traditions, if one prefers) rather than deriving its material anew directly from scripture. *Acts* likewise draws more from other sources or creates freely. To anticipate, we will see how virtually any scriptural source was fair game, though the favorite tendencies are to draw from the *Exodus* saga and the Elijah and Elisha cycles. For his part, Mark relied about as heavily on the *Iliad* and the *Odyssey* (perhaps seeing the parallel between the adventurous wanderings of both *Exodus* and the *Odyssey* as well as a punning resemblance between their titles, or between Odysseus and the *odoV* of the itinerant Jesus; see Watts, pp. 124-128).

A far greater number of gospel-Old Testament coincidences have been proposed than we will consider here. We will only consider those rendered compelling by the existence of striking parallels at crucial or numerous points, ignoring many, more subtle, suggestions that scholars have proposed as secondary implications of their basic theories. The danger is otherwise great that, in seeking to spot the ancient writers' own exegesis, we may ascribe to them our own creative midrash. What strikes our eye as an irresistible combination of fortuitous texts may not have occurred to them.

B. The Gospel of Mark

1. Introduction (*1:1-3*)

The syncretic flavor of *Mark* is at once evident from his reproduction of a piece of Augustan imperial propaganda and his setting it beside a tailored scripture quote. "The beginning of the gospel of Jesus Christ the Son of God" closely matches the formula found on a monument erected by the Provincial Assembly in Asia Minor (1st century BCE): "Whereas . . . Providence . . . has . . . brought our life to the peak of perfection in giving us Augustus Caesar . . . who, being sent to us and to our descendants as a savior . . . , and whereas . . . the birthday of the god has been for the whole world **the beginning of the gospel (*euaggelion*) concerning him**, let all reckon a new era beginning from the date of his birth" (Helms, p. 24). As is well known, Mark proceeds to introduce as from *Isaiah* a conflation of passages, *Malachi 3:1a*, "Behold, I send my messenger/angel to prepare the way before me," and *Exodus 23:20a*, "Behold, I send a [LXX: my] messenger/angel before you, to guard you on the way," plus *Isaiah 40:3*, "A voice cries: "In the wilderness prepare the way of the LORD; make straight in the desert a highway for our God." The messenger/angel has been made to refer to John the Baptizer, while the speaker seems to be Jesus. The wilderness is no longer, as originally, the place where the way is to be paved, but rather the location of the crying prophetic voice, that of John. The Dead Sea Scrolls sect had used the same *Isaiah* passage to prooftext their own desert witness.

2. Jesus' Baptism (*1:9-11*)

The scene in broad outline may derive from Zoroastrian traditions of the inauguration of Zoroaster's ministry. Son of a Vedic priest, Zoroaster immerses himself in the river for purification, and as he comes up from the water, the archangel Vohu Mana appears to him, proffering a cup, and commissions him to bear the tidings of the one God Ahura Mazda, whereupon the evil one Ahriman tempts him to abandon this call. In any case, the scene has received vivid midrashic coloring. The heavenly voice (*bath qol*) speaks a conflation of three scriptural passages. "You are my beloved son, in whom I am well pleased" (*Mark 1:11*) combines bits and pieces of *Psalm 2:7*, the divine coronation decree, "You are my son. Today I have begotten you;" *Isaiah 42:1*, the blessing on the returning Exiles, "Behold my servant, whom I uphold, my chosen, in whom my soul delights;" and *Genesis 22:12* (LXX), where the heavenly voices bids Abraham to sacrifice his "beloved son." And as William R. Stegner points out, Mark may have in mind a Targumic tradition whereby Isaac, bound on the altar, looks up into heaven and sees the heavens opened with angels and the Shekinah of God, a voice proclaiming, "Behold, two chosen ones, etc." There is even the note that the willingness of Isaac to be slain may serve to atone for Israel's sins. Here is abundant symbolism making Jesus king, servant, and atoning sacrifice.

In view of parallels elsewhere between John and Jesus on the one hand and Elijah and Elisha on the other, some (Miller, p. 48) also see in the Jordan baptism and the endowment with the spirit a repetition of *2 Kings 2*, where, near the Jordan, Elijah bequeaths a double portion of his own miracle-working spirit to Elisha, who henceforth functions as his successor and superior.

3. The Temptations (*Mark 1:12-13*)

The forty days of Jesus in the wilderness recall both Moses' period of forty years in the desert of Midian before returning to Egypt (Bowman, p. 109) and the forty-day retreat of Elijah to the wilderness after the contest with Baal's prophets (*1 Kings 19:5-7*), where Elijah, like Jesus, is ministered unto by angels (Miller, p. 48). The Q tradition shared by *Matthew* (*4:1-11*) and *Luke* (*4:1-13*) and possibly abridged by *Mark*, plays off the *Exodus* tradition in yet another way. Jesus resists the devil's blandishments by citing three texts from *Deuteronomy, 8:3; 6:16; 6:13*, all of which refer to trials of the people of Israel in the wilderness (the manna, Massa, and idolatry), which they failed, but which Jesus, embodying a new Israel, passes with flying colors.

4. Commencement of the Ministry (*1:14-15*)

Only once he has completed the ordeal in the wilderness does Jesus begin his preaching of the near advent of the Kingdom of God. Bowman rightly observes the parallel to Moses leaving the wilderness, with Aaron, to announce to the children of Israel in the house of bondage that liberation would soon be theirs (ibid.).

5. Recruitment of the First Disciples (*1:16-20*)

As Bowman suggests (p. 157), Jesus summons James and John as well as Peter and Andrew, two pairs of brothers, as a gospel counterpart to Moses' recruiting his own unsuspecting brother Aaron at the analogous point in the *Exodus* story (*4:27-28*). But the events, minimal as they are, come from Elijah's recruitment of Elisha in *1 Kings 19:19-21*. Likewise, the calling of Levi in *Mark 2:14*. All are said to have abandoned their family livelihoods on the spot to follow the prophet.

6. Exorcism at Capernaum (*1:21-28*)

Mark has set this first teaching and exorcism of Jesus at the town called Capernaum ("Village of Nahum") to hint at *Nahum 1:15a*, the only passage outside of *Isaiah* to use the term *euaggelizomenou* in a strictly religious sense. "Behold upon the mountains the feet of him that brings glad tidings and publishes peace!" For Mark, that is of course Jesus. And so what better town for him to have begun bearing these gospel tidings than that of Nahum? (Miller, p. 58).

The rude heckling of the local demoniac, "What have we to do with you, Jesus of Nazareth? Have you come to destroy us? I know who you are – the Holy One of God!," comes directly from the defensive alarm of the Zarephath widow in *1 Kings 17:18*: "What have you against me, O man of God? You have come to me to bring my sin to remembrance, and to cause the death of my son!" (Miller, p. 76).

7. Peter's Mother-in-Law (*1:29-31*)

This episode, too, is cut from the cloth of Elijah's mantle. In *1 Kings 17:8-16*, Elijah meets the widow of Zarephath and her son, and delivers them from imminent starvation. As a result she serves the man of God. In *2 Kings 4*, Elisha raises from the dead the son of the Shunammite woman, who had served him. Mark has reshuffled these elements so that this time it is the old woman herself who is raised up from her illness, not her son, who is nonetheless important to the story (Peter), and she serves the man of God, Jesus (Miller, 79).

8. The Healing of a Leper (*1:40-45*)

Bowman (p. 113) has suggested, with some plausibility, that the cleansing of this leper, placed thus early in Mark's story, is meant to recall the credential miracle vouchsafed by God to Moses, whereby he could turn his hand leprous white (*Exodus 4:6-7*). Jesus himself cannot manifest leprosy, even momentarily, perhaps, because he must remain the spotless lamb of God without blemish.

9. Healing the Paralytic (*2:1-12*)

As Roth (p. 56) shows, this story of a paralyzed man's friends tearing the thatch off a roof and lowering him to Jesus amid the crowd seems to be based on an Elijah story in *2 Kings 1:2-17a*, where King Ahaziah gains his affliction by falling from his roof through the lattice and languishes in bed. *Mark's* sufferer is already afflicted when he descends through the roof on his bed (pallet). He rises from his bed because whatever sin of his had earned him the divine judgment of paralysis was now pronounced forgiven on account of his friends' faith, though nothing is said of his own. King Ahaziah is pointedly not healed of his affliction because of his own pronounced lack of faith in the God of Israel: he had sent to the priests of the Philistine oracle god Baal-zebub to inquire as to his prospects. Elijah tells him he is doomed because of unbelief, a dismal situation reversed by Mark, who has Jesus grant forgiveness and salvation because of faith. Mark has preserved the Baal-zebub element for use in a later story (*3:22*).

10. The Withered Hand (*3:1-6*)

Mark borrows the substance of this scene from the miracle of the Judean prophet of *1 Kings 13:1-7 ff.* (Helms, pp. 90-91). There the prophet confronts King Jeroboam in the Bethel temple and predicts Judean King Josiah's destruction of the rival altar. For this blasphemy Jeroboam orders his arrest, with surprising results: "the king stretched forth his hand (*exeteinen . . . thn ceira autou*) from the altar, saying, 'Take hold of him!' and his hand which he stretched forth against him withered (*echraqh*), and he could not draw it back to himself" (*v. 4*). In *Mark*, the man is a nobody, but the authorities are nonetheless present in the house of worship and waiting to pounce. The man's hand is already withered (*echrammenhn*) when Jesus calls him out: " 'Stretch out your hand!' He stretched it out (*thn ceira . . . eceteinen*), and his hand was restored" (*Mark 3:5*). The anonymous prophet, too, heals the sufferer: "And King Jeroboam said to the man of God, 'Entreat the Lord your God, and let my hand be restored to me.' And the man of God entreated the Lord, and he restored the king's hand to him, and it became as before" (*1 Kings 13:6* LXX). Whereas the withering and healing were the aftermath of the villains' attempt to arrest the prophet in *1 Kings*, in *Mark* it is the healing of the withered hand which makes the villains plot to arrest him: "The Pharisees went out and immediately took council with the Herodians against him, how to destroy him" (*3:6*).

11. Choosing the Twelve; Embassy of Relatives (*3:13-35*)

We must imagine that previous to Mark someone had midrashically rewritten the story of Moses heeding Jethro's advice to name subordinates, resulting in a scene in which choosing the twelve disciples was the idea of the Holy Family of Jesus. Note the similarities between *Mark 3* and *Exodus 18*. Just as Moses' father-in-law Jethro hears of Moses' successes and brings Moses' wife and sons to him (*Exodus 18:1-5*), so do the mothers and brothers of Jesus hear reports and journey to meet Jesus (*Mark 3:21*). Moses is constantly surrounded by suppliants (*18:13-18*), just like Jesus (*3:20*). Just as Moses' arriving family is announced ("Lo, your father-in-law Jethro is coming to you with your wife and her two sons with her" *18:6*), so is Jesus' ("Behold, your mother and your brothers are outside looking for you" *3:31-32*). "Moses went out to meet his father-in-law, and bowed down and kissed him; and they asked each other of their welfare, and went into the tent" (*Exodus 18:7*). Originally we would have read of Jesus' welcoming his family. And as Jethro voices his concern for the harried Moses, suggesting he share the burden with a number of helpers (*18:21-22*), so we would have read that James or Mary advised the choice of assistants "that they might be with him, and that he might send them out to preach" (*Mark 3:14*). And Jesus would only then have named the Twelve.

Mark, acting in the interest of a church-political agenda, has broken the story into two and reversed its halves so as to bring dishonor on the relatives of Jesus (representing a contemporary faction claiming their authority) and to take from them the credit for naming the Twelve (which is also why he emphasizes that Jesus "summoned those that he *himself* wanted," i.e., it was all his own idea. As the text now reads, Jesus chooses the disciples, and only subsequently do his interfering relatives arrive harboring doubts about his sanity, and he rebuffs them (*Mark 3:33-35*).

Jesus, however, does not, like Moses, choose seventy (though Luke will restore this number, *Luke 10:1*), but only twelve, based on the choice of the twelve spies in *Deuteronomy 1:23* (Miller, p. 117).

Sandwiched into the middle of this material is a controversy between Jesus and his scribal critics who allege that he performs his exorcisms only by virtue of being in league with Beel-zebul. Some manuscripts read "Beel-zebub," harking back to *2 Kings 1:2, 3*. "Beel-zebul" denotes "Lord of the House," i.e., of the world, a powerful patron of exorcists, while "Beel-zebub" means "Lord of the Flies," denoting an oracle, since the priests would hear a sound like buzzing, the voice of spirits telling the desired fortune. Jesus' reply to the charge seems to come from *Isaiah 49:24* (Watts, pp. 148-149) ("Can the prey be taken from the mighty, or the captives of a tyrant be rescued? Surely thus says the LORD: Even the captives of the mighty shall be taken, and the prey of the tyrant be rescued, for I will contend with those who contend with you, and I will save your children.") and from *1 Samuel 2:25* ("If a man sins against a man, God will mediate for him; but if a man sins against the LORD, who can intercede for him?") (Miller, p. 136).

Matthew and Luke (hence the Q source) make an interesting addition to Jesus' response to the scribes. Luke's, as usual, is probably closer to the Q original: "If I by Beel-zebul cast out demons, by whom do your sons cast them out? Consequently, they shall be your judges. But if I cast out demons by the finger of God, then the kingdom of God has come upon you" (*Luke 11:19-20*). Compressed into these verses is an unmistakeable midrash upon the *Exodus* story of Moses' miracle contest with the magicians of Pharaoh. Initially able to match Moses feat for feat, they prove incapable of copying the miracle of the gnats and warn Pharaoh to give in, since "This is the finger of God" and no mere sorcery like theirs (*Exodus 8:19*). The "sons" of the scribes correspond to the Egyptian magicians and can dispel the scribes' charge against Jesus if they would.

12. The Stilling of the Storm (*4:35-41*)

Helms (pp. 76, 77) demonstrates how this story has been rewritten from Jonah's adventure, with additions from certain of the Psalms. The basis for the story can be recognized in *Jonah 1:4-6*, "But the Lord hurled a great wind upon the sea, and there was a mighty tempest on the sea, so that the ship threatened to break up. Then the mariners were afraid, and each cried to his god. . . . But Jonah had gone down into the inner part of the ship and had lain down, and was fast asleep. So the captain came and said to him, 'What do you mean, you sleeper? Arise, call upon your god! Perhaps the god will give a thought to us, that we do not perish.'" Once Jonah turns out to be the guilty party, they throw him into the maw of the sea, "and the sea ceased from its raging. The men feared the LORD exceedingly" (*1:15b-16a*). See also *Psalm 107:23-29*: "Some went down to the sea in ships, doing business on the great waters; they saw the deeds of the LORD, his wondrous works in the deep. For he commanded, and raised the stormy wind, which lifted up the waves of the sea. They mounted up to the heavens, they went down unto the depths; their courage melted away in their evil plight; they reeled and staggered like drunken men, and were at their wits' end. Then they cried to the LORD in their trouble, and he delivered them from their distress; he made the storm be still, and the waves of the sea were hushed."

Mark was aware of a similar episode in the *Odyssey 10:1-69*, in which Odysseus set sail with his dozen ships from the Isle of Aeolus, the god of winds. Aeolus had given Odysseus a bag containing mighty winds in case he should be stalled in the doldrums. Odysseus falls asleep in the hold, and his men sneak a peek into the bag, letting the winds escape. The ships managed to survive the storm, but Odysseus rebuked his crew for their dangerous folly. MacDonald (pp. 68, 174-175) indicates the origin of Jesus' rebuke to the disciples here (*Mark 1:40*), as well as the puzzling detail in *Mark 1:36* that Jesus and the disciples were accompanied by "other boats." It makes no sense in *Mark* and must be understood as a vestige of the *Odyssey*.

13. The Gerasene Demoniac (*5:1-20*)

Again, Mark has mixed together materials from scripture and from the *Odyssey*. Clearly, as MacDonald shows (pp. 65, 73, 173), the core of the story derives from *Odyssey 9:101-565*. Odysseus and his men come to shore in the land of the hulking Cyclopes, just as Jesus and his disciples arrive by boat in the land of the Gerasenes (or Gergesenes, supposedly the remnant of the ancient Girgashites, hence possibly associated with the mythical Anakim/Rephaim, who were *giants* [Derrett, p. 102]). Goats graze in one landscape, pigs in the other. Leaving their boats, each group immediately encounters a savage man-monster who dwells in a cave. The demoniac is naked, and Polyphemus was usually depicted naked, too. The Cyclops asks Odysseus if he has come with intent to harm him, just as the Gerasene demoniac begs Jesus not to torment him. Polyphemus asks Odysseus his name, and the latter replies "Noman," while Jesus asks the demoniac his name, "Legion," a name reminiscent of the fact that Odysseus' men were soldiers. Jesus expels the legion of demons, sending them into the grazing swine, recalling Circe's earlier transformation of Odysseus' troops into swine. Odysseus contrives to blind the Cyclops, escaping his cave. The heroes depart, and the gloating Odysseus bids Polyphemus to tell others how he has blinded him, just as Jesus tells the cured demoniac to tell how he has exorcised him. As Odysseus' boat retreats, Polyphemus cries out for him to return, but he refuses. As Jesus is about to depart, the man he cured asks to accompany him, but he refuses. As MacDonald notes, sheer copying from the source is about the only way to explain why Jesus should be shown refusing a would-be disciple.

Psalm 107, whence details of the stilling of the storm were borrowed, has also made minor contributions to this story as well. The detail of the demoniac having been chained up seem to come from *Psalm 107's* description of "prisoners in irons" (*v. 10*), who "wandered in desert wastes" (*v. 4*) and "cried to the Lord in their trouble" (*v. 6*), who "broke their chains asunder" (*v. 14*). It is also possible that Mark had in mind the Exodus sequence, and that he has placed the story here to correspond to the drowning of the Egyptian hosts in the Sea.

14. Jairus' Daughter and the Woman with the Issue of Blood (*5:21-24, 35-43*)

Under the long-regnant paradigm of form-criticism this story was considered to be a complex of two prior tradition-units sandwiched together by Mark, and indeed it is easy to divide them into two distinct episodes. The story of Jairus and his daughter (*vv. 21-23, 35-43*, the phrase "while he was still speaking" referring originally to Jairus in *v. 23*) and that of the bleeding woman (*vv. 24b-34*), Mark having to add only *24a* to tape the two together. But the more we recognize Mark's creative sophistication and view him as a real author, not just a scissors-and-paste editor as the form critics did, the more likely it seems that the two anecdotes began life as interdependent parts of a single story, a retelling of that of Elisha and the Shunammite woman (*2 Kings 4*). The Shunammite, a mother, has been replaced by a father, whose name Jairus means "he will awaken," winking to the readers as to the fictive character of the tale. Jairus, like his prototype, approaches the prophet abjectly pleading for help. The prophet, whether Jesus or Elisha, determines to go and raise the child despite the report that the child is already dead. Arriving, he seeks privacy (absolute or relative: Elisha excludes everyone, Jesus the crowd). He touches and speaks to the dead child, and the child rouses. The reaction is verbally almost verbatim. The Shunammite is "ecstatic with all this ecstasy" (*exesthsaV . . . pasan thn ekstasin tauthn*, ***2 Kings 4:31*** LXX), while Jairus and his wife are "ecstatic with great ecstasy" (*exesthsan . . . ekstasei megalh*, ***Mark 5:42***) (Helms, p. 66).

But what about the woman with the hemorrhage? She is the Shunammite, doubled! Jesus heals her of a reproductive problem just as Elisha had miraculously made it possible for the Shunammite to conceive. The woman had been plagued with the bleeding for twelve years, exactly the age of Jairus' daughter, the symbolic implication being that she was the daughter the bleeding woman had never been able to have, now, so to speak, restored to her. Why did Mark break up the story this way? For the most elementary of reasons: to provide narrative suspense, just as in the *2 Kings* original, where we must follow the woman on the journey to Elisha and then endure the failed attempt of Gehazi to raise her son. As we will see, Mark liked the element of the disciple's failure, but instead of using it here, which would have made the story even more like its prototype, he has reserved it till later, in *9:18, 28*.

The element of Jesus' healing energy being released upon contact, even without his say-so, may have been suggested by the story in *2 Kings 13:20-21*, where a corpse, hastily stashed in Elisha's open mausoleum, strikes the bones of the prophet and is restored to life and vigor!

15. Rejection at Home (*6:1-6*)

Miller and Miller (p. 167) point to *1 Samuel 10:1-27* as the likely source of *Mark's* episode of Jesus' frosty reception among his own townsfolk. Saul, newly appointed king of his people, is overcome by the prophetic afflatus and begins to speak in tongues ("prophesy," *v. 10*), whereupon "all who knew him previously" retort, "What has come over the son of Kish? Is Saul, too, among the prophets?" "Who is their father?" (*v. 11*). The upshot is that "it became a proverb, 'Is Saul, too, among the prophets?'" (*v. 12*). Just so, in *Mark* the people who had long known the local boy, now ostensibly a prophet, cannot believe it and raise the issue of Jesus' too-familiar family connections: a prophet must come from out of nowhere, not someone like us (cf. *John 7:27-28*, "'When the Christ appears, no one will know where he comes from.'. . .

'You know me and you know where I come from, but I have not come of my own accord;'" *James 5:17*, "Elijah was a man with a nature like ourselves"). Jesus is merely the son of Mary and brother to James, Joses, Simon and Judas, just as Saul is nothing more than Kish's son. There is even the matching proverb in the case of Jesus: "A prophet is not without honor except in his home town and among his relatives and in his household."

16. Mission Instructions (*6:7-13*)

These marching orders may have been influenced by the practices of Cynic preachers, but in their present form they surely owe something to the Elisha stories. When Jesus forbids the missioners to "take along money nor two cloaks," he is warning them not to repeat Gehazi's fatal error, aggrandizing himself at the expense of those the prophet serves; he had, unauthorized by Elisha, exacted from Naaman "a talent of silver and two cloaks" (*2 Kings 5:22*) (Roth, p. 50; Miller, p. 175). The provision of a staff (*Mark 6:8*) may come from Gehazi's mission for Elisha to the Shunammite's son: "take my staff in your hand and go" (*2 Kings 4:29a*). Luke must have recognized this, since he returned to the same text to add to his own mission charge to the seventy (*Luke 10:4b*) the stipulation "and salute no one on the road," borrowed directly from Elisha's charge to Gehazi in *2 Kings 4:29b*, "If you meet anyone, do not salute him, and if anyone salutes you, do not reply."

17. The Death of the Baptizer (*6:14-29*)

In view of the preceding parallels, it is hardly a surprise that Mark would have people inferring that Jesus is the returned Elijah. Indeed, their opinion is righter than Mark lets on!

Usually scholars allow some core of historical reporting to underlie the story of the Baptizer's death (though any reading of *Mark* must be harmonized with some difficulty with Josephus), recognizing just a bit of biblical embellishment to the narrative. For instance, it is apparent to all that Herod Antipas' words to his step-daughter, "Whatever you ask of me I will give it to you, up to half my kingdom," comes from *Esther 5:3*. Herod's painting himself into the corner of having to order the execution of his favorite prophet may come from Darius' bamboozlement in the case of Daniel (*Daniel 6:6-15*) (Miller, p. 178). But it is possible that the whole tale comes from literary sources.

MacDonald (pp. 80-81, 176) shows how the story of John's martyrdom matches in all essentials the *Odyssey's* story of the murder of Agamemnon (*3:254-308: 4:512-547; 11:404-434*), even to the point that both are told in the form of an analepsis or flashback. Herodias, like Queen Clytemnestra, left her husband, preferring his cousin: Antipas in the one case, Aegisthus in the other. This tryst was threatened, in Clytemnestra's case, by the return of her husband from the Trojan War, in Herodias', by the denunciations of John. In both cases, the wicked adulteress plots the death of the nuisance. Aegisthus hosted a banquet to celebrate Agamemnon's return, just as Herod hosted a feast. During the festivities Agamemnon is slain, sprawling amid the dinner plates, and the Baptizer is beheaded, his head displayed on a serving platter. Homer foreshadows danger awaiting the returning Odysseus with the story of Agamemnon's murder, while Mark anticipates Jesus' own martyrdom with that of John. The only outstanding difference, of course, is that in Mark's version, the role of Agamemnon has been split between Herodias' rightful husband (Philip according to Mark; another Herod according to Josephus) and John the Baptizer.

18. Multiplication of Loaves and Fish (*6:30-44; 8:1-10*)

As all acknowledge, the basis for both the miraculous feeding stories in Mark's gospel is the story of Elisha multiplying the twenty barley loaves for a hundred men in *2 Kings 4:42-44*. There is in all three stories the initial assessment of how much food is available, the prophetic command to divide it among a hopelessly large number, the skeptical objection, puzzled obedience, and the astonishing climax in which not only all are fed, but they had leftovers as well! As Helms notes (p. 76), John has gone back to the source to add a detail. He has made the servant (*paidarion*) of Elisha into a boy (*paidarion*) whose five barley loaves Jesus uses to feed the crowd (*John 6:9*).

But there are more elaborate details in *Mark's* stories which do not come from *2 Kings*. They come from the *Odyssey 3:34-38, 63-68; 4:30, 36, 51, 53-58, 65-68* (MacDonald, pp. 89-90). The reason Mark has two feeding miracles is to emulate Homer, who has Odysseus' son Telemachus attend two feasts, and Mark has borrowed details from both. For the first feast, Telemachus and the disguised Athena sail to Pylos where King Nestor is presiding at a feast in honor of Poseidon. It is a sailors' feast, so only men are present. Four thousand, five hundred of them are seated in nine units of five hundred each. Everyone ate to satiety and there were leftovers. In Mark's first feast story, Jesus and his men also sail to the site of the meal. They encounter a group of five thousand men, *andreV*, males (no explanation is offered for this, a simple vestige of Homer). Jesus has them sit in discrete groups. After the Elisha-style miracle, everyone eats and is filled, and leftovers are gathered.

Homer's second feast witnesses Telemachus going overland to Sparta, just as in Mark's second episode, Jesus and the disciples walk to Galilee, where he meets the crowd of four thousand. This time, in both stories, there is no restriction to males. A servant of King Menelaus bids him send Telemachus and his companion away unfed, but the king will not, just as a disciple urges Jesus to send away the hapless crowd, and he will not. Everyone sits down to eat, in both cases, and in neither is there any mention of the elaborate arrangement of the diners as in the first feast scene. All are filled; leftovers are gathered. Mark has seemingly cast Jesus as Telemachus in both stories until the hero arrives at the banquet scene, whereupon he switches roles, having Jesus take the place of the hosts, Nestor and Menelaus.

19. Walking on the Sea (*6:45-52*)

Though scriptural coloring is again in evidence (*Psalm 107* [LXX: *106*]: *23-30*; *Job 9:8b*, "who . . . trampled the waves of the sea"), the body of the story Mark owes to Homer, this time the *Iliad 24:332, 340-341, 345-346, 351-352* (MacDonald, pp. 148-153). Old King Priam is making the difficult journey to the Greek camp to beg the body of his son Hector. Father Zeus beholds the king's toiling progress and dispatches Hermes, guide to travelers, to aid him. "Under his feet he fastened the supple sandals, never-fading gold, that wing him over the waves and boundless earth with the rush of gusting winds . . . [Hermes] flew, the mighty giant-killer, touching down on Troy and the Hellespont in no time and from there he went on foot." As Hermes approaches Priam and his servant, they fear he is a brigand who will slay them, but he reassures them, takes the reins of their mule cart and speeds them on their way, reaching Achilles' ship in no time flat. Finally he reveals his identity: "Old man, I am a god come down to you. I am immortal Hermes – my Father sent me here to be your escort, but now I will hasten back." Can anyone miss the parallel to Mark's story? The disciples are making poor headway against the storm on their way to the far shore when they see the approaching Jesus, a sight inspiring fear, albeit for different reasons. They see him walking on the water, something Hermes also does to reach Priam, though without the latter seeing him do it. Once their divine visitor reassures them with a declaration ("I am. . . ."), he joins them and they arrive at once at their destination.

Bowman (p. 159) picks up the thread of the *Exodus* story with the mention of the disciples' obtuseness in *Mark 6:52*. They are said not to understand the feat they have just seen – because they had failed to learn anything from the miraculous feeding! The linking of the two would have to imply a reference back to a different but related pair of Moses' miracles, the dry-shod passage over the Sea and the provision of the manna. Despite seeing these, the children of Israel remained obdurate in their unbelief. Likewise the disciples. Their hearts were hardened," just like Pharaoh's. The point is underscored, one might say too broadly, in *8:14-21* (Bowman, p. 180).

20. Jesus versus the Scribes (*7:1-23*)

In debate with the scribes over purity rules, Jesus is made to cite the LXX version of *Isaiah 29:13*, the Hebrew original of which would not really make the required point. Less obviously, there is also a significant reference to Elijah in *v. 14*, "and summoning the multitude again, he said to them, 'Listen to me, all of you, and understand.'" Here we are to discern a reflection of Elijah's gesture in *1 Kings 18: 30*, "Then Elijah said to all the people, 'Come near to me'; and all the people came near to him." Elijah then restored the fallen altar of God and prepared for the miracle which would win the people back from idolatrous compromise with Baalism. We must infer that Mark regards the Judaism of the scribes as on a par with Baalism as a false religion which consistent Christians must shun. His point is much like that of Paul in Galatians, appealing to Christian readers to forswear Torah-observance.

21. The Syro-Phoenician Woman (*7:24-30*)

Jesus meets a foreign woman in the district of Tyre and Sidon, who requests his help for her child, and we find ourselves back with Elijah and the widow of Sidonian Zarephath in *1 Kings 17:8-16*. There the prophet encounters the foreigner and performs a miracle for her and her son. In both cases the miracle is preceded by a tense interchange between the prophet and the woman in which the prophet raises the bar to gauge the woman's faith. The Syro-phoenician parries Jesus' initial dismissal with a clever comeback; the widow of Zarephath is bidden to take her remaining meal and to cook it up for Elijah first, whereupon the meal is indefinitely multiplied (Roth, pp. 51-52; Miller, pp. 196-197).

Why does Jesus call the poor woman and her daughter, by implication, dogs? Mark has taken it from *2 Kings 8:7-15*, where Elisha tells Hazael (a Syrian, like the woman in *Mark*) that he will succeed Ben-Hadad to the throne of Aram. He replies, "What is your servant, the dog, that he should accomplish this great thing?" In *Mark*, the question is whether the great deed shall be done *for* the "dog" (Roth, p. 44).

22. Healing of the Deaf and the Blind (*7:31-37; 8:22-26*)

Bowman (p. 172) makes *Mark 7:31-38* a midrash upon *Isaiah 29:18* ("In that day the deaf shall hear the words of a book, and out of their gloom and darkness the eyes of the blind shall see") and *Isaiah 35:5-6* ("Then the eyes of the blind shall be opened and the ears of the deaf *unstopped*; then shall the lame man leap like a hart, and the tongue of the mute sing for joy"). We probably ought to add the episodes of the blind man of Bethsaida (*8:22-26*) and of Bar-Timaeus (*10:46-52*), who leaped up to follow Jesus, as midrashic fulfillments of the same texts. In the case of the blind man of *Mark 8*, we also have to reckon with influence from *Genesis 19:11-13*, where the angels of God blind the Sodomite welcoming committee and warn Lot and his family to flee the doomed city. The gospel tradition writes off Bethsaida for its lack of responsiveness. In *Matthew 11:24* its fate is likened to Sodom's. The blind man of Bethsaida, then, is healed of the Sodomites' blindness and sent, like Lot, to escape the doomed city's eventual destruction.

Up to the acclamation of the crowd in *v. 37*, "He does all things well," implying he has passed some sort of milestone, Jesus has performed a total of sixteen miracles, meeting the quota set by Elisha, who himself doubled the number ascribed to his master Elijah. Jesus will go on to perform another eight (Roth, pp. 5-7).

23. The Transfiguration (*9:1-13*)

Jesus' ascent of the unnamed mountain and his transfiguration there is, of course, Mark's version of Moses' ascent of Mount Sinai to receive the tablets of the Torah and his shining visage in *Exodus 24* and *34:29*. As Bowman notes (p. 190), the Markan introduction, "And six days later" (*9:2*), must be understood as a pointer to the *Exodus* account. God calls Moses up the mountainside to receive the tablets (*Exodus 24:12*), and he takes Joshua with him (*v. 13*). Once they make the climb, the glory cloud covers the height for six days (*v. 16*), and on the seventh the divine voice calls to Moses from the depth of the cloud. Mark has apparently foreshortened the process.

The glowing apparition of Jesus is most obviously derived from that of Moses in *Exodus 34:29*, but as Derrett (p. 159) points out, we must not miss the influence of *Malachi 3:2*, especially since Elijah, too, appears: "But who can endure the day of his coming, and who can stand when he appears? For he is like a refiner's fire and like fuller's soap." This, then, is the prophesied return of Elijah, and Jesus' garments glow white "like no fuller on earth could have bleached them" (*Mark 9:3*).

Jesus appears like Moses, yet with Moses. He is the predicted prophet like Moses from *Deuteronomy 18:15*: "The LORD your God will raise up for you a prophet like me from among you, from your brothers. Him you shall heed." The heavenly voice reiterates this commandment in *Mark 9:7*, "This is my beloved son; listen to him" (Bowman, p. 193).

Derrett (p. 155) further traces the admonition of Jesus to conceal news of the vision till the Son of Man be raised from the dead (*9:9*) to similar warnings in *Daniel 12:4a* ("But you, Daniel, shut up the words, and seal the book, until the time of the end.") and *Zephaniah 3:8a*, LXX ("Therefore wait upon me, saith the Lord, *until the day when I rise up* as a witness.").

Scholars have puzzled over the intended reference when Mark has Jesus speak in *v. 13* of prophetic writings detailing the sufferings of Elijah in his avatar as John the Baptizer. Does Mark refer to some writing that did not survive in the canon? The pseudepigraphical *Apocalypse of Elijah* gives no help. But we need not search so far afield. By now it is evident that the reference must be to the Elijah (and Elisha) tales of *1 and 2 Kings*, which Mark took as a quarry of information about Jesus and John.

24. The Deaf-Mute Epileptic (*9:14-29*)

Coming as it does following Jesus' descent of the mountain of transfiguration, this episode seems to be intended as an analogue for the Golden Calf incident in *Exodus 32* (Bowman, p. 199; Miller, p. 232). Moses is away with one of his lieutenants, Joshua, leaving Aaron in charge, and when he returns Aaron has completely lost control of the situation, treading the path of least resistance to idolatrous ruin. The conversion of *Exodus'* idol into *Mark's* demon is an easy one, given the later Jewish belief that "what pagans sacrifice they offer to demons and not to God" (*1 Corinthians 10:20a*). So Jesus and his inner circle return from the mountain to find the rest of the disciples making a bad show of things, unable to cast the demon out of a boy and facing the scorn of the crowd and Jesus' enemies.

And yet the conclusion is different, with only a mild rebuke to the unsuccessful disciples. While the punchline instructs early Christian exorcists to make sure they devote ample prayer to such cases in future, the clear lesson is that it takes nothing short of the man of God himself to do the deed, and here Mark connects again with the story of Elisha and the Shunammite (*2 Kings 4*). There Elisha dispatched his disciple Gehazi with his own potent staff to restore the Shunammite's dead son, but he could not (*2 Kings 4:31*). The disciple did nothing wrong; it was just that the ultimate power was required, and Elisha succeeded where Gehazi failed (*2 Kings 4:32-35*), simply because he was Elisha and Gehazi was not. Even so, in *Mark*, Jesus is irreplaceable because he is the divine hero of the story.

25. Jockeying for Position (*9:33-37*)

This passage has long roots reaching back to the Pentateuchal disputes between Moses on the one hand and Aaron and Miriam on the other (*Numbers 12*), or perhaps Dathan and Abiram (*Numbers 16*) (Bowman, p. 205). These others covet Moses' special position before God and make trouble over it, but God himself intervenes to settle the issue in Moses' favor, just as Jesus does here. God preferred Moses as a leader precisely because he did not seek power: he "was very meek, more than all the men that were on the face of the earth" (*Numbers 12:3*) (Miller, p. 239), the same qualification Jesus stipulates for anyone who aims to be a leader among his flock (*Mark 9:35*).

26. The Independent Exorcist, etc. (*9:38-50*)

Mark returns to the same portion of *Numbers* for this story. The man casting out demons outside of Jesus' retinue, intimidating poor John, is based directly on Eldad and Medad, members of the seventy elders who stayed in the camp when the rest followed Moses to the Tent of Meaning to receive prophetic inspiration (*Numbers 11:24-30*). John is a renamed Joshua who protested that "Eldad and Medad are prophesying in the camp," i.e., "not following us" (*Mark 9:38*). Jesus is depicted as being fully as broad-minded as Moses, happy to acknowledge the work of God where ever he hears of it (Bowman, p. 206; Miller, p. 242).

Among other attached preachments, *v. 41*, "For whoever gives you a cup of water to drink because of your name of Christ, truly I say to you, he shall not lose his reward," especially as it is directly followed by a mention of children and their perils, recalls the story of the widow of Zarephath (*1 Kings 17:10*), of whom Elijah requested a drink. The reward? He saved her and her son from starvation (Miller, p. 241).

The warnings of hellfire to come (*vv. 43-48*) depend verbatim on *Isaiah 66:24.*

27. Blessing Children (*10:13-16*)

Jesus is indignant with the well-meaning but insensitive disciples who chase away parents approaching Jesus for his benediction on their infants. ("Don't shove that baby in the Saviour's face!" *Monty Python's*

Life of Brian of Nazareth, p. 124). Is it too much to suggest that Mark modeled the scene on a similar one in *2 Kings 4*, again, the story of Elisha and the Shunammite? "And when she came to the mountain, to the man of God, she caught hold of his feet. And Gehazi came to thrust her away. But the man of God said, 'Let her alone, for she is in bitter distress, and the LORD has hidden it from me and has not told me' " (*v. 27*). The cause of her distress, of course, is the death of her son, and she seeks Elisha's divine blessing to restore him to life. Mark has generalized the scene and, so to speak, lowered the stakes, having matched the urgency and poignancy of the original in his Jairus story back in chapter *5*.

28. The Request of James and John (*10:32-45*)

The whole episode comes right out of that of Elisha's request of Elijah just before his ascension, only Mark's version reflects badly on James and John. The structure is exactly the same (Miller, p. 253). Jesus has just announced for the third time his impending death and resurrection, prompting the brothers to venture, "Teacher, we want you to do for us whatever we may ask of you. . . . Grant that we may sit in your glory, one at your right, one at your left" (*Mark 10:35, 37*). This comes from *2 Kings 2:9*, "Ask what I shall do for you before I am taken from you." Hearing the request, Elijah reflects, "You have asked a hard thing" (*v. 10*), just as Jesus warns James and John, "You do not know what you are asking for." The Elijah-Elisha story cements the "apostolic succession" from one prophet to the other, whereas Mark's rewrite seems to pass over the two disciples to open the possibility of succession to anyone willing to follow Jesus (sacramentally?) along the way of martyrdom.

29. Blind Bar-Timaeus (*10:46-52*)

As already noted, this story puts flesh on the skeleton of LXX *Isaiah 35:5a, 6a, 8a*: "Then the eyes of the blind shall be opened . . . then shall the lame man leap like a hart. . . . And a highway shall be there, and it shall be called the holy way" (Miller, pp. 263-264). Thus Bar-Timaeus leaps up, is given his sight, and follows Jesus on the way. That he is not only blind but a beggar may come from the possible meaning of his name, as Derrett (p. 185) decodes it from Aramaic *Bar-teymah*, "son of poverty." In this, the fictive nature of the story is doubly clear.

MacDonald suggests (pp. 97-99) that Mark has created Bar-Timaeus as a Christian Tiresias, the blind seer of the Odyssey, since Bar-Timaeus distinguishes himself by spiritual insight; he recognizes Jesus as Son of David (*Mark 10:48*).

30. Preparation for the Entry and the Supper (*11:1-6; 14:12-16*)

Both these stories, parallel to one another, alike derive from *1 Samuel* chapter *9* (Miller, p. 325; Derrett, p. 187). Kish sends two men, his son Saul and a servant (*1 Samuel 9:3*), just as Jesus sends two disciples on each of these missions (*Mark 11:1; 14:13*). Saul and his companion were to find some runaway asses (*9:3*), while the disciples are to find a particular ass's colt (*11:2*). When Saul and the servant reach the city they are met by young women coming out to draw water (*9:11*); Jesus' disciples are told to look for a man carrying water (*14:13*). Like Saul and his companion, the two pairs enter the city. Saul and the other are told they will find the man they seek, the prophet Samuel, as soon as they enter the city (*9:13*), as Jesus tells his men they will find the colt tied as soon as they enter the city (*11:2*). All transpires as predicted (*9:6; 11:4; 14:16*). Saul asks "Where is the house of the seer?" (*9:18*). Jesus tells the disciples to ask, "Where is my guest room?" (*14:14*). As in *9:20*, Saul is told the missing asses have been located, so in *11:6* does Jesus say to assure the owner that his borrowed colt will be returned. In *9:19* Samuel oversees the preparation of a feast, and in *14:16* the disciples prepare the Passover.

The upper room of the Last Supper may also hark back to the second-storey rooms provided for Elijah (*1 Kings 17:19*) and Elisha (*2 Kings 4:10*) by benefactors (Miller, p. 331), one of whom Elijah first met by asking a drink of water from a woman God told him would provide for him (*1 Kings 17:9,10*. He met her at the city gate, just as Jesus told the disciples to meet a man carrying water in a vessel as soon as they entered the city.)

31. The Entry into Jerusalem (*11:7-11*)

Though Mark does not make it explicit, it is evident that the scene of Jesus entering the holy city on donkeyback is a fleshing out of *Zechariah 9:9*. The actions and words of the crowd come right from *Psalm 118:26-27*, "Blessed is he who enters in the name of the LORD! . . . Bind the festal procession with branches . . . ." "Hosanna in the highest" comes from the Hebrew or Aramaic of "Save now!" in *Psalm 118:25* and from *Psalm 148* LXX: "Praise him in the highest!" (Helms, p. 104). Of course the *Psalm* offers its blessings on any pilgrim entering the holy city.

32. Cursing the Fig Tree (*11:12-14, 20*)

As anyone can see, the tree is made to stand for unrepentant Jerusalem, and the episode is then seen (Miller, pp. 274-275) to stem from *Psalm 37:35-36*, "I have seen a wicked man overbearing, and towering like a cedar of Lebanon. Again I passed by, and, lo, he was no more; though I sought him, he could not be found." Here is the source of Jesus *seeking* figs on the *tree* but *finding none*, and of the note that it was in *passing the spot again* they discovered the tree blasted.

33. Cleansing the Temple (*1:15-18*)

Jesus' overthrow of the Temple service (not only does he scatter the livestock for offerings but somehow bans anyone carrying sacrificial vessels) is historically impossible as it reads here. The envisioned area is huge, and for Jesus to commandeer it like this would have required a military raid, something of which *Mark's* text seems oblivious. Though it is not unlikely that the story preserves some faded memory of the entry of Simon bar-Gioras into the Temple to clean out the robbers of John of Giscala on the eve of the Temple's destruction, the story may simply conflate various scripture passages, which it seems to do in any case. The "cleansing" must have in view that of *Malachi's* messenger of the covenant who will purify the sons of Levi (*3:1-3*, as hinted by *Mark 1:2* and *9:3*), as well as the oracle of *Zechariah 14:21b*, "And there shall no longer be a trader in the house of the LORD of hosts on that day." The saying of Jesus on that occasion is merely a conflation of *Isaiah 56:7* ("My house shall be called a house of prayer for all the nations") and *Jeremiah 7:11* ("Has this house, which is called by my name, become a den of robbers in your eyes?"). The priests and scribes react to this disturbance by plotting to destroy Jesus, just as the priests, prophets, and people lay hold of Jeremiah and cry out, "You shall die!," when he likewise predicts the destruction of the city and the Temple (*26:8*) (Miller, p. 274).

34. The Parable of the Wicked Tenants (*12:1-12*)

All commentators call attention to the use of *Isaiah 5:1-7* in this parable, and that surely is to account for one of its principal sources. MacDonald (p. 37) identifies another in the *Odyssey*, where we discover the source (here and in other parables) of the absentee owner having left servants in charge of his estate while he is away on a long trip. The servants are not all wicked, but the suitors are, the men who, assuming the long-absent Odysseus is dead, flock to his palace to woo his "widow" Penelope, eating her out of house and home for years. Their complete domination of the estates of Odysseus is threatened by the succession of Prince Telemachus, Odysseus' only son, They plot to kill him and so remove the last obstacle to their squatter's possession. He eludes their scheme. The caution of the Jewish leaders in the face of the veiled threat of the parable comes from the note in the *Odyssey* that the suitors had to tread lightly lest their brazenness finally push the people of Ithaca, Odysseus' subjects, too far and spark their wrath. Mark's result is a hybrid which applies Isaiah's judgment oracle not to the whole people but to their imagined usurping leaders and introduces the plot element of a rejected son.

Mark returned to his recently-used *Psalm 118* for the quotation from *vv. 22-23* in *Mark 12:10-11*.

35. The Olivet Discourse (*13:1-37*)

The whole apocalyptic discourse of *Mark* is a cento of scripture paraphrases and quotations, and it will be sufficient simply to match each major verse to its source. *Mark 13:7* comes from *Daniel 2:28*; *Mark 13:8* from *Isaiah 19:2* and/or *2 Chronicles 15:6*; *Mark 13:12* from *Micah 7:6*; *Mark 13:14* from *Daniel 9:27* and *12:11* and *Genesis 19:17*; *Mark 13:19* from *Daniel 12:1*; *Mark 13:22* from *Deuteronomy 13:2*; *Mark 13:24* from *Isaiah 13:1*; *Mark 13:25* from *Isaiah 34:4*; *Mark 13:26* from *Daniel 7:13*, and *Mark 13:27* from *Zechariah 2:10* and *Deuteronomy 30:4* (Bowman, pp. 241-242; Miller, pp. 300-301).

36. The Anointing at Bethany (*14:3-9*)

Helms (pp. 98-100) is surely correct that the Johannine version of the Bethany anointing (*John 12:1-8*) most clearly reveals its origin in the resurrection mythology of the Egyptian Osiris (Mary and Martha = Isis and Nephthys; Lazarus = Eleazar = El-Osiris; Bethany = Beth-Annu, house of the Sun = Heliopolis). It is apparent that the story even as Mark knew it was already derived from Osiris. Just as Isis restored the slain Osiris to life by anointing him in some versions, the reference here to the unnamed woman anointing Jesus for the day of his death and burial must originally have been set on that day, the day when she raised him from the dead. (The story of Joseph probably came ultimately from the same source, as numerous parallels make clear.)

37. The Last Supper (*14:17-31*)

All critics recognize the seed of the last supper story in *Psalm 41:9*, "Even my bosom friend, in whom I trusted, who ate my bread, has lifted his heel against me." Frank Kermode has traced (pp. 84-85) the logical process whereby the original, entirely and abstractly theological claim that Jesus had been "delivered up" (*paredoqh*, ***Romans 4:25***) has been narratized. From God having "handed over" his son for our sins grew the idea that a human agent had "betrayed" him (same Greek word). For this purpose, in line with anti-Jewish polemic, a betrayer named Judas was created. His epithet "Iscariot" seems to denote either *Ish-karya* (Aramaic for "the false one") or a pun on *Issachar*, "hireling" (Miller, p. 65), thus one paid to hand Jesus over to the authorities. Much of the Last Supper story is taken up with this matter because of the mention of the betrayer eating with his victim in *Psalm 41*.

It is interesting to see how Matthew embellishes the enigmatic figure and fate of Judas. First, he knows the precise amount Judas was paid, 30 silver pieces. He knows this from *Zechariah 11:11b* ("And they weighed out as my wages thirty shekels of silver"). How does he know that Judas returned the money, throwing it into the Temple treasury, and that the priests decided to use it to buy the potter's field? The Syriac version of *Zechariah* reads: "Then the Lord said to me, 'Cast it into the treasury, this lordly price at which I was paid off by them. So I took the thirty shekels of silver and cast them into the treasury in the house of the Lord." The Hebrew of the same verse reads: "Cast it to the *potter*," etc. How does Matthew know Judas hanged himself? That was the fate of David's traitorous counsellor Ahithophel (*2 Samuel 17:23*), whom scribal tradition took to be the subject of *Psalm 41:9*, which the gospels applied to Judas (Helms, p. 106).

Almost secondary in the supper narrative is the bread and cup. Whatever the origin of the sacramental ritual underlying this etiological story, it has been interpreted here in scriptural terms as a covenant renewal. See the unmistakable connection with *Exodus 24:8*, "Behold the blood of the covenant which the LORD has made with you in accordance with these words."

In *v. 26* Jesus and the disciples sing the traditional Passover hymn, which, as we will see, provided Mark the content of Jesus' introspection in the Garden of Gethsemane. *Verse 27's* quotation of *Zechariah 13:7*, "I will strike down the shepherd, and the sheep will be scattered," would seem to be the whole source for the subsequent scene where Jesus' disciples flee from the arresting party.

Peter avers that, no matter what the danger, he will not leave Jesus' side. In this he reminds us, not coincidentally, of Elisha's three avowals that he will not leave Elijah (*2 Kings 2:2, 4, 6*: "As the Lord lives, and as you yourself live, I will not leave you." It seems not too much to suggest, with Roth (p. 17), that Mark has given Peter one such pledge and three betrayals of it. On the other hand (see below), Mark may have had in mind Ittai's loyalty pledge to David, "Wherever my lord the king shall be, whether for death or for life, there also will your servant be" (*1 Samuel 15:21*) (Miller, p. 332).

38. The Garden of Gethsemane (*14:32-52*)

The basis of this whole scene can be found in *2 Samuel* chapters *15-16* (Miller, p. 332). There, a weeping David, fleeing from his usurping son Absalom (a Judas figure), heads up the Mount of Olives and sends three of his allies (Sadoc, Achimaas and Jonathan, *15:27* LXX), back to Jerusalem. Jesus, too, heads up the mountain to the Garden of Gethsemane, where he will be overcome with sorrow. He leaves three disciples behind as he retreats into the recesses of the garden. (Jesus, of course, is moving simultaneously with his betrayer, but, unlike David, he is aiming to converge with him, not to avoid him.)

David finds himself mocked and harassed by one Shimei, a partisan of Saul's dynasty. He curses the fallen king, and David's man Abishai offers to chop the mocker's head off, but David forestalls him, musing that apparently God has bidden Shimei to curse David, given the situation. So as they slink along in silence, Shimei continues to pelt the refugees with rocks. Here we find more elements underlying Mark's story. Abishai is the prototype of the unnamed disciple of Jesus (John fictively identifies him as Peter) who does attempt to behead Malchus in the arresting party. Shimei, another form of Shimeon or Simon, is the prototype for Simon who denies Jesus repeatedly, his stony missiles suggesting "Peter" as well. God having assigned Shimei to utter curses on David has become, in Mark's version, Jesus' prediction of Peter's denials, as well as Peter's calling down curses on himself (or on Jesus) in the high priest's courtyard (*14:71*).

But what of Jesus' prayer? That Mark is creating, not reporting, is evident from the fact that he has eliminated from the scene anyone who might have listened in on it. Mark derived the contents of the prayer from one of the traditional Passover hymns, which he has had Jesus sing at the close of the supper, *Psalm 116:10-15*, "My distress was bitter. In panic I cried, 'How faithless all men are!' . . . I will take in my hand the cup of salvation and invoke the Lord by name. . . . A precious thing in the Lord's eyes is the death of those who die faithful to him" (Helms, p. 111).

Judas' betraying kiss (*14:44-45*) would seem to derive from *2 Samuel 20:7-10*, where Joab, backed up by armed men, greets Amasa as a brother, kisses him, then stabs him (Miller, p. 337). This identification, Helms notes (p. 117), is secured once we realize that Luke has modeled his version of Judas' miserable death upon that of Amasa. In *2 Samuel 20:10* LXX we are told that Amasa's "bowels poured out (*execuqh*) upon the ground," precisely as Luke tells us (*Acts 1:18*) that when Judas died, "he burst open, so that his entrails poured out (*execuqh*)."

Amos 2:16, "And he who is stout of heart among the mighty shall flee away naked in that day," remains the most likely clue to the origin of the fleeing young man who loses his sole garment to escape naked (*Mark 14:51*) (Derrett, p. 252). "That day" sounded like a good reference to the momentous day of Jesus' passion.

Luke adds the element of an angel appearing beside the tormented Jesus to "strengthen" him (*Luke 22:43*), a detail borrowed from *1 Kings 19:7-8* LXX: "And the angel of the Lord returned again and touched [Elijah], and said to him, 'Arise, for the journey is far from thee.' And he arose, and ate and drank, and went in the *strength* of that meat forty days and forty nights to mount Horeb" (Helms, p. 109).

39. The Sanhedrin Trial (*14:53-72*)

Mark borrowed from *Daniel 6:4* LXX the scene of the crossfire of false accusations (Helms, p. 118): "The governors and satraps sought (*ezetoun*) to find (*eurein*) occasion against Daniel, but they found against him no accusation." Of this *Mark* (*14:55*) has made the following: "The chief priests and the whole council sought (*ezetoun*) testimony against Jesus in order to kill him, but they found none (*ouk euriskon*)."

Mark 14:65, where Jesus suffers blows and mockery as a false prophet, comes from *1 Kings 22:24*, "Then Zedekiah the son of Chenaanah came near and struck Micaiah on the cheek, and said, 'How did the spirit of the Lord go from me to speak to you?' And Micaiah said, 'Behold, you shall see on that day when you go into an inner chamber to hide yourself' " (Miller, p. 350).

Mark has used Micaiah's retort, "Behold, you shall see . . ." as the model for Jesus' retort that his accusers/attackers will one day behold Jesus enthroned as the Son of Man from *Daniel 7:13-14*. It is interesting to speculate whether the doctrine of the second coming of Christ did not spring full-blown from Mark's reversal of order between the Son of Man's coming with the clouds and sitting on the throne in *Daniel 7*.

Jesus' silence at both trials before the Sanhedrin and Pilate (*14:60-61; 15:4-5*) comes from *Isaiah 50:7; 53:7* (Crossan, p. 168).

40. The Scapegoat (*15:1-15*)

John Dominic Crossan has drawn attention to the singular importance for early Christian typology of the *Leviticus 16* scapegoat ritual, tracing its development, as it picked up associations from *Zechariah*, on its way to the composition of the gospel narrative of the mocking, abuse, and crucifixion of Jesus. Although Crossan assumes the process began with a vague Christian memory/report of Jesus having been crucified, with no details, his own compelling charting of the midrashic trajectory strongly implies something subtly different, that the process began with something like Doherty's scenario of an even vaguer, ahistorical belief in the savior Jesus becoming progressively historicized by means of progressive biblical coloring, until the final stage of evolution which was a crucifixion.

Crossan describes the scapegoat ritual as it was being practiced in early Christian times by reference to *Yoma 6:2-6*, the *Epistle of Barnabas* chapter *7*, Justin's *Dialogue with Trypho, 40*, and Tertullian's *Against Marcion 3:7*. The goat was led out of the city walls. A crimson thread of wool was divided, half tied to a rock, half between the goat's horns. Along the way, the goat was abused by the crowd shouting, "Bear [sins] and begone! Bear and begone!" The crowd spat at it and goaded it along with pointed reeds till it arrived at the ledge where it was pushed over (Crossan, p. 119). Barnabas implies that in his day the woolen thread was tied onto a thorny bush, no longer a rock, a significant change (no less significant even if this was a misunderstanding, already marking a slippage of the "piercing" motif from the reed-poking to the wool-tying). Even *without reference to a passion narrative of any sort*, Barnabas and the *Sibylline Oracles* (*8:294-301*) apply the ritual in all its details to the death of the savior Jesus. Barnabas and others also attach to it the typology *Zechariah 12:10* ("And I will pour out on the house of David and the inhabitants of Jerusalem a spirit of compassion and supplication, so that when they look on him whom they have pierced, they shall mourn for him as one mourns for an only child, and weep bitterly over him as one weeps over a firstborn") because of the catchword "piercing," derived from the reeds and thorns of the scapegoat ritual. From this it was a natural step to page through *Zechariah* to *3:1-5* and to associate the scapegoat-savior Jesus with the high priest Jesus (Joshua). There Jesus/Joshua is clothed in a crown (turban) and robe, which Barnabas, et al., "recognized" as an expansion of the two bits of crimson wool from the scapegoat ritual. Once this connection was made, it was easy for the wool motif to be segregated to the robe, the crown assimilating to the thorns to which the other thread had been tied, resulting in a crown of thorns (Crossan, p. 128). From these roots, as the passion narrative begins to form, the piercing motif takes several forms. When Jesus becomes a mock king (as in the Roman Saturnalia games or the mockery of Carrabas in Philo, *Flaccus* VI), the reeds that once poked the scapegoat have become the reed sceptre of the mock king (which his mockers seize and use to hit him) as well as the mock crown of thorns and the scraping bits of the scourging whip. Then, in a full-scale crucifixion narrative (involving, of course, the driving of the scapegoat Jesus outside the city walls), the piercing motif takes the form of the nails of crucifixion and finally the piercing lance of Longinus.

41. The Crucifixion (*15:21-41*)

The substructure for the crucifixion in chapter *15* is, as all recognize, *Psalm 22*, from which derive all the major details, including the implicit piercing of hands and feet (*Mark 24//Psalm 22:16b*), the dividing of his garments and casting lots for them (*Mark 15:24//Psalm 22:18*), the "wagging heads" of the mockers (*Mark 15:20//Psalm 22:7*), and of course the cry of dereliction, "My God, my God, why have you forsaken me?" (*Mark 15:34//Psalm 22:1*). Matthew adds another quote, "He trusts in God. Let God deliver him now if he desires him" (*Matthew 27:43//Psalm 22:8*), as well as a strong allusion ("for he said, 'I am the son of God' " *27:43b*) to *Wisdom of Solomon 2:12-20*, which underlies the whole story anyway (Miller, p. 362):

> Let us lie in wait for the righteous man because he is inconvenient to us and opposes our actions; he reproaches us for sins against the law and accuses us of sins against our training. He professes to have knowledge of God, and calls himself a child of the Lord. He became to us a reproof of our thoughts; the very sight of him is a burden to us because his manner of life is unlike that of others, and his ways are strange. We are considered by him as something base, and he avoids our ways as unclean; he calls the last end of the righteous happy, and boasts that God is his father. Let us see if his words are true, and let us test what will happen at the end of his life: for if the righteous man is God's son he will help him and

will deliver him from the hand of his adversaries. Let us test him with insult and torture that we may find out how gentle he is and make trial of his forbearance. Let us condemn him to a shameful death, for, according to what he says, he will be protected.

As for other details, Crossan (p. 198) points out that the darkness at noon comes from *Amos 8:9*, while the vinegar and gall come from *Psalm 69:21*. It is remarkable that Mark does anything but call attention to the scriptural basis for the crucifixion account. There is nothing said of scripture being fulfilled here. It is all simply presented as the events of Jesus' execution. It is we who must ferret out the real sources of the story. This is quite different, e.g., in *John*, where explicit scripture citations are given, e.g., for Jesus' legs not being broken to hasten his death (*John 19:36*), either *Exodus 12:10*, *Numbers 9:12*, or *Psalm 34:19-20* (Crossan, p. 168).

Whence did Mark derive the tearing asunder of the Temple veil, from top to bottom (*Mark 15:38*)? Perhaps from the death of Hector in the *Iliad* (MacDonald, pp. 144-145). Hector dies forsaken by Zeus. The women of Troy watched from afar off (as the Galilean women do in *Mark 15:40*), and the whole of Troy mourned as if their city had already been destroyed "from top to bottom," just as the ripping of the veil seems to be a portent of Jerusalem's eventual doom.

42. Joseph of Arimathea (*15:42-47*)

Joseph is surely a combination of King Priam, who courageously comes to Achilles' camp to beg the body of his son Hector (MacDonald, p. 159) and the Patriarch Joseph who asked Pharaoh's permission to bury the body of Jacob in the cave-tomb Jacob had hewn for himself back beyond the Jordan (*Genesis 50:4-5*) (Miller, p. 373). Whence Joseph's epithet "of Arimathea"? Richard C. Carrier has shown that the apparent place name is wholly a pun (no historical "Arimathea" has ever been identified), meaning "Best (*ari[stoV]*) Disciple (*maqh[thV]*) Town." Thus "the Arimathean" is equivalent to "the Beloved Disciple." He is, accordingly, an ideal, fictive figure.

43. The Empty Tomb (*16:1-8*)

Crossan (p. 274) and Miller and Miller (pp. 219, 377) note that the empty tomb narrative requires no source beyond *Joshua* (= Jesus, remember!) chapter *10*. The five kings have fled from Joshua, taking refuge in the cave at Makkedah. When they are discovered, Joshua orders his men to "Roll great stones against the mouth of the cave and set men by it to guard them" (*10:18*). Once the mopping-up operation of the kings' troops is finished, Joshua directs: "Open the mouth of the cave, and bring those five kings out to me from the cave" (*10:22*). "And afterward Joshua smote them and put them to death, and he hung them on five trees. And they hung upon the trees until evening; but at the time of the going down of the sun, Joshua commanded, and they took them down from the trees, and threw them into the cave where they had hidden themselves, and they set great stones against the mouth of the cave, which remain to this very day" (*10:26-27*). Observe that here it is "Jesus" who plays the role of Pilate, and that Mark needed only to reverse the order of the main narrative moments of this story. *Joshua 10*: first, stone rolled away and kings emerge alive; second, kings die; third, kings are crucified until sundown. *Mark*: Jesus as King of the Jews is crucified, where his body will hang till sundown; second, he dies; third, he emerges alive (Mark implies) from the tomb once the stone is rolled away.

The vigil of the mourning women likely reflects the women's mourning cult of the dying and rising god, long familiar in Israel (*Ezekiel 8:14*, "Behold, there sat women weeping for Tammuz"; *Zechariah 12:11*, "On that day the mourning in Jerusalem will be as great as the mourning for Hadad-Rimmon in the plain of Megiddo"; *Canticles 3:1-4*, "I sought him whom my soul loves; I sought him but found him not; I called him but he gave no answer," etc.).

C. The Gospel of Matthew

1. The Nativity of Jesus

On the whole Matthew seems to have borrowed the birth story of Jesus from Josephus' retelling of the nativity of Moses. Whereas *Exodus* had Pharaoh institute the systematic murder of Hebrew infants simply to prevent a strong Hebrew fifth column in case of future invasion, Josephus makes the planned pogrom a weapon aimed right at Moses, who in Josephus becomes a promised messiah in his own right. Amram and

Jochabed, expecting baby Moses, are alarmed. What should they do? Abort the pregnancy? God speaks in a dream to reassure them:

> One of those sacred scribes, who are very sagacious in foretelling future events truly, told the king that about this time there would be a child borne to the Israelites, who, if he were reared, would bring the Egyptian dominion low, and would raise the Israelites; that he would excel all men in virtue, and obtain a glory that would be remembered through the ages. Which was so feared by the king that, according to this man's opinion, he commanded that they should cast every male child into the river, and destroy it. . . . A man, whose name was Amram, . . . was very uneasy at it, his wife being then with child, and he knew not what to do. . . . Accordingly God had mercy on him, and was moved by his supplication. He stood by him in his sleep, and exhorted him not to despair of his future favours. . . . 'For that child, out of dread for whose nativity the Egyptians have doomed the Israelites' children to destruction, shall be this child of thine . . . he shall deliver the Hebrew nation from the distress they are under from the Egyptians. His memory shall be famous while the world lasts.' (*Antiquities*, II, IX, 2-3)

It is evident that Matthew has had merely to change a few names. Herod the Great takes the role of the baby-killing Pharaoh, and he is warned by his own scribes (along with the Magi) of the impending birth of a savior, whereupon he resolves to kill every child he has to in order to eliminate the child of promise. Joseph takes the place of Amram, though the precise cause of his unease is different. Mary takes the place of Jochabed. A dream from God steels Joseph, like Amram, in his resolve to go through with things.

The rest of Matthew's birth story is woven from a series of formulaic scripture quotations. He makes *Isaiah 7:14* LXX refer to the miraculous virginal conception of Jesus. It is likely that he has in this case found a scripture passage to provide a pedigree for a widespread hagiographical mytheme, the divine paternity of the hero, which had already passed into the Christian tradition, unless of course this is the very door through which it passed.

It is revealing that Matthew's Magi learn from scribal exegesis of *Micah 5:2* that the messiah must be born in Bethlehem. This is the same way Matthew "knew" Jesus was born there – it had to be!

The flight of the Holy Family into Egypt comes equally from exegesis, this time of *Hosea 11:1*, which allows Matthew to draw a parallel between his character Joseph and the Genesis patriarch Joseph, who also went to Egypt. Matthew also seems here to want to foreshadow the death and resurrection of Jesus. Note that *Isaiah 52:9-10* makes the exodus from Egypt into a historical replay of God's primordial victory over the sea dragon Rahab, equating Egypt with Rahab. Matthew also knew that Jonah was swallowed by a sea monster at God's behest, and he saw this as a prefiguration of Jesus' descent into the tomb (*Matthew 12:40*). The flight into Egypt has the child Jesus already going down into Rahab, the belly of the sea beast.

The closest Matthew can come, via punning exegesis, to providing a prooftext for Jesus having become known as "the Nazarene" would seem to be *Judges 13:7*, "The boy shall be a Nazirite to God from birth." He knew Jesus must be born in Bethlehem yet was called "Jesus of Nazareth," so he cobbled together a story whereby Jesus was born in Mary and Joseph's home in Bethlehem, only to relocate in Nazareth (after Egypt) to avoid the wrath of Archelaus (*Matthew 2:22-23*). Luke, on the other hand, working with the same two assumptions, contrived to have Mary and Joseph live in Nazareth but to be in Bethlehem for the census when the time came for Jesus to be born. In both cases, exegesis has produced narrative.

2. The Resurrection of Jesus (*27:62 to 28:20*)

Matthew had before him Mark's empty tomb story and no other source except the *Book of Daniel*, from which he has embellished the Markan original at several points. (Matthew had already repaired to *Daniel* in his Pilate story, where the procurator declared, "I am innocent of the blood of this man," *Matthew 27:24b*, which he derived from *Susanna 46*/*Daniel 13:46* LXX: "I am innocent of the blood of this woman.") (Crossan, p. 97-98). First, Matthew has introduced guards at the tomb and has had the tomb sealed, a reflection of Nebuchadnezzer's sealing the stone rolled to the door of the lion's den with Daniel inside (*6:17*). Mark had a young man (perhaps an angel, but perhaps not) already in the open tomb when the women arrived. Matthew simply calls the character an angel and clothes him in a description reminiscent of the angel of *Daniel* chapter *10* (face like lightning, *Daniel 10:6*) and the Ancient of Days in *Daniel* chapter *7* (snowy white clothing, *Daniel 7:9b*). He rolls the stone aside. The guards faint and become as dead men, particular dead men, as a matter of fact, namely the guards who tossed Shadrach, Meschach, and Abednego into the fiery furnace in (*Daniel 3:22*).

To provide an appearance of the risen Jesus to the women at the tomb (something conspicuously absent from *Mark*), Matthew simply divides *Mark's* young man into the angel and now Jesus himself, who has nothing more to say than a lame reiteration of the angel's words. He appears again on a mountain in Galilee (*Matthew 28:16*) which he now says Jesus had earlier designated, though this is the first the reader learns of it. There he dispenses yet more Danielic pastiche: "All authority in heaven and on earth has been given to me." This is based on a conflation of two Greek versions of *Daniel 7:14*. In the LXX, "to him [the one like a son of man was] . . . given the rule . . . the authority of him [the Ancient of Days]." In Theodotion, he receives "authority to hold all in the heaven and upon the earth." The charge to make all nations his disciples comes from *Daniel 7:14*, too: "that all people, nations, and languages should serve him" (Helms, p. 141).

D. The Gospel of Luke

1. The Nativities of Jesus and John (*1:1 to 2:52*)

The fundamental source of *Luke's* double nativity story is the nativity of Samuel. Eli becomes Simeon (and perhaps also Zachariah), while barren Hannah becomes old Elizabeth (and Mary, too, if we accept the majority of manuscripts' attribution of the Magnificat to her instead of Elizabeth, *Luke 1:46-55*). The Magnificat is clearly a paraphrase of Hannah's song in *1 Samuel 1-10*. The repeated refrain of Jesus' continuing growth in wisdom and favor with God and men (*2:40, 52, cf., 1:80*) comes directly from *1 Samuel 2:26*, "Now the boy Samuel continued to grow both in stature and in favor with the Lord and with men."

The birth annunciation to Mary recalls those of Isaac (*Genesis 17:19*, "Sarah your wife shall bear you a son, and you shall call his name. . ."; *18:9-15*) and Samson (*Judges 13:2-5*, "you shall conceive and bear a son . . . and he shall begin to deliver Israel. . ."). The story also borrows from the commissioning stories of Moses (*Exodus 3:10-12*) and Jeremiah (*Jeremiah 1:4-8*), where the servant of God objects to the divine summons and his objection is overruled (see *Luke 1:18, 34*).

A less familiar source for the Lukan nativity story is the nativity of Moses as told in Pseudo-Philo's *Biblical Antiquities*, where we read that, during Pharaoh's persecution of the Hebrew babies, Amram has determined to defy Pharaoh by having a son. God makes known his will by sending an angel to the virgin Miriam:

> And the Spirit of God came upon Miriam one night, and she saw a dream and told it to her parents in the morning, saying, "I have seen this night, and behold a man in a linen garment stood and said to me, 'Go, and say to your parents, "Behold, he who will be born from you will be cast forth into the water; likewise through him the water will be dried up. And I will work signs through him and save my people, and he will exercise leadership always" ' " (*9:10*).

The angel Gabriel's predictions in *Luke 1:32-33, 35* derive from an Aramaic version of *Daniel*:

> [And when the Spirit] came to rest up[on] him, he fell before the throne. [Then Daniel rose and said,] 'O king, why are you angry; why do you [grind] your teeth? [The G]reat [God] has revealed to you [that which is to come.] . . . [Peoples will make war,] and battles shall multiply among the nations, until [the king of the people of God arises. . . . [All the peoples will serve him,] and he shall become gre[at] upon the earth. . . . He will be called [son of the Gr]eat [God;] by his Name shall he be designated. He will be called the son of God. They will call him son of the Most High. . . . His kingdom will be an eternal kingdom, and he will be righteous in all his ways' (4Q246, *The Son of God*).

When Mary visits her cousin Elizabeth, the latter's unborn child, John the Baptizer, leaps in the womb in greeting acknowledging the greater glory of the unborn Jesus. Here, as G.R. Driver pointed out, Luke refers to *Genesis 25:22* LXX, where Rebecca is in pain because her two rival sons strive within her as a sign of fraternal discord to come: "And the babes leaped within her." This precedent Luke seeks to reverse by having the older cousin, John, already deferring in the womb to his younger cousin. Here he has an eye on the rival John the Baptist sect whom he thus tries to conciliate and coopt.

2. The Centurion's Child and the Son of the Widow of Nain (*7:1-17*)

Luke has used *1 Kings 17* as the basis for the two-miracle sequence here (Brodie, pp. 136-137). The original Elijah version stipulates (*1 Kings 17:1*) how the famine shall be relieved only by the prophetic word, just as the mere word of Jesus is enough to heal the centurion's servant/child at a distance (*Luke 7:7b*). Elijah journeys to the Transjordan where he will meet a Gentile in need, the widow of Zarephath (*1 Kings 17:5, 10a*), just as Jesus arrives in Capernaum to encounter a Roman centurion. Both Gentiles are in dire need, the widow about to succumb to starvation with her son (*17:12*), the centurion desperate to avert his son's/servant's imminent death (*7:2-3*). Once the facts are made known to the miracle worker, there is a series of commands (*1 Kings 17:10c-13*; *Luke 7:8*), and divine deliverance is secured, the multiplication of food in the one case (*17:6*), the return of health in the other (*7:10*).

It appears that Luke has drawn the story of the centurion's son from the wider gospel tradition, as it appears in both *Matthew 8:5-13* (hence in Q) and *John 4:46-54*. It had already been derived from the Elijah story by early Christian scribes. But Luke has decided as well to add a new Jesus tale, unparalleled in other gospels, modeled upon the *1 Kings* sequel to the story of Elijah and the widow. Whereas Elijah later raises from the dead the widow's son, Jesus next comes upon a funeral procession and raises the man about to be buried, again a widow's son, this time from Nain. Luke has decided to reserve one feature from the first Elijah episode to use in his second Jesus episode: the initial meeting with the widow at the city gate of Zarephath, which he makes the gate of Nain (even though historical Ain had no gate!).

But before this, Luke opens his second episode with the same opening from *1 Kings 17:17a*: "And it happened afterward" // "after this . . ." The widow's son is dead (*1 Kings 17:17b*; *Luke 7:12b*). Elijah cried out in anguish (*1 Kings 17:19-20*), unlike Jesus, who, however, tells the widow not to cry (*Luke 7:13*). After a gesture (Elijah prays for the boy's spirit to return, *v. 21*; Jesus commands the boy to rise, *7:14*), the dead rises, proving his reanimation by crying out (*1 Kings 17:22*; *Luke 7:15*). His service rendered, the wonder-worker "gave him to his mother" (*1 Kings 17:24*; *Luke 7:15b*, verbatim identical). Those present glorify the hero (*1 Kings 17:24*; *Luke 7:16-17*).

If Luke himself (as Brodie thinks, pp. 136-152) composed the first episode directly from the first Elijah episode, instead of taking it from Q, he will have also transferred the widow's lament that Elijah has come to punish her sins into the centurion's confession that he is unworthy to have Jesus come under his roof.

3. The Sinful Woman (*7:36-50*)

According to Brodie (pp. 174-184), Luke has created his rather cumbersome story of the sinful woman from a pair of Elisha's miracles, the never-failing cruse of oil (*2 Kings 4:1-7*) and the raising of the Shunammite's son (*2 Kings 4:8-37*). The widow of Elisha's disciple is in financial debt, with her creditors about to take her two children in payment (*2 Kings 4:1*). In Luke's version, her arrears have become a debt of sin (*Luke 7:37, 40-42*). Elisha causes her oil to multiply, becoming enough to pay her debt. Jesus' cancellation of the woman's debt is less material but no less miraculous, as he pronounces her forgiven (*Luke 7:44-50*). As for the oil, it has become the myrrh with which the woman anoints Jesus' feet (*Luke 7:38*). In Luke's version, Simon the Pharisee has invited the itinerant Jesus to dine (*Luke 7:36*), a reflection of the Shunammite's invitation of Elisha to stay and eat with her whenever passing by (*2 Kings 4:8-11*). As a reward, Elisha grants her to conceive a son. Years later, he dies of sunstroke, whereupon she journeys to Elisha for help, falling at his feet (*2 Kings 4:27*), just as the suppliant woman anoints the feet of Jesus (*Luke 7:38*). There is no need to posit Luke's creation of the whole anointing story, the core of which he got from *Mark 14:3-9*, but he has substantially rewritten it in light of *2 Kings*.

4. Appointment in Samaria (*9:51-56*)

The connection between *Luke 9:51-56* and *2 Kings 1:1 to 2:1* is obvious to all in view of the explicit allusion in the one to the other (*Luke 9:54*). But Brodie shows (pp. 207-214) how the Lukan story is simply rewritten from its prototype. Luke has transferred the anticipation of the hero's being taken up into heaven from the end of the section of Elijah's clash with the Samaritan troops (*2 Kings 2:1*) to the beginning of the story of Jesus and the Samaritan village (*Luke 9:51a*). The king of Samaria has sent messengers to inquire of the oracle of Baal-zebub in Philistine Ekron, but Elijah meets them and turns them back (*2 Kings 1:2-5*). In Luke this has become the turning back of Jesus' messengers sent ahead to secure the night's accommodations in Samaria. The Samaritans are no longer those turned back but those who turn others back in their travels. The prophet is now the sender of the messengers, not their interceptor. Once the king of Samaria sends troops to apprehend Elijah, the latter calls down fire from the sky to consume them (*2 Kings 1:9-10*). The scene is repeated (*vv. 1-12*). The third time Elijah relents and comes along quietly (*1 Kings 1:13-15*). James and John want to repeat Elijah's miraculous destruction of the Samaritans (now villagers, not troops), but Jesus will have none of it. Instead he takes the role of the angel of the Lord who bade Elijah show mercy.

5. Calling a Ploughman (*9:59-62*)

The stories of Jesus' calling Peter, Andrew, James, and John (*Mark 1:16-20*) and Levi (*Mark 2:14*) all seem to stem from Elijah summoning Elisha to become his disciple and successor (*1 Kings 19:19-21*). But Luke seems (Brodie, pp. 216-227) to have created another discipleship paradigm which implicitly critiques the prototype. In *Luke 9:59-62*, Jesus forbids what Elijah allows, that the new recruit should delay long enough to pay filial respects. Also, whereas ploughing was for Elisha the worldly pursuit he must abandon for the prophetic ministry, for Luke ploughing becomes the very metaphor for that ministry.

6. The Central Section (*10:1 to 18:14*)

Based on Mark's Transfiguration scene, which both take over directly (*Matthew 17:1-8*; *Luke 9:28-36*), Matthew and Luke depict Jesus as the Prophet like unto Moses, and each has him promulgating a new Torah. Matthew presents a whole new Pentateuch by organizing the teaching of Jesus into five great blocks: the Sermon on the Mount (chapters *5-7*), the Mission Charge (chapter *10*), the Parables chapter (*13*), the Manual of Discipline (chapters *18-19*), and the denunciation on the Pharisees plus the Olivet Discourse (chapters *23-26* – the cramming together of two themes in the fifth section only underlines his determination to squeeze the whole thing into five divisions, no matter how snug the fit!). By contrast, Luke thought it sufficient to have Jesus present a Deutero-Deuteronomy, a "second law" such as Moses offers in the *Book of Deuteronomy*. C.F. Evans ("The Central Section of St. Luke's Gospel," 1967) was the first to point this out. Just as Matthew did, Luke has both simply organized some traditional materials and also created some of his own based on suggestions in the scripture text he was emulating.

a. Sending out Emissaries (*Deuteronomy 1*; *Luke 10:1-3, 17-30*)

Just as Moses had chosen twelve spies to reconnoiter the land which stretched "*before your face*," sending them through the *cities* of the land of Canaan, so does Jesus send a second group, after the twelve, a group of seventy, whose number symbolizes the nations of the earth who are to be conquered, so to speak, with the gospel in the *Acts of the Apostles*. He sends them out "*before his face*" to every city he plans to visit (in Canaan, too, obviously).

To match the image of the spies returning with samples of the fruit of the land (*Deuteronomy 1:25*), Luke has placed here the Q saying (*Luke 10:2*//*Matthew 9:37-38*), "The harvest is plentiful, but the workers are few; therefore beg the Lord of the harvest to send out more workers into his harvest."

And Jesus' emissaries return with a glowing report, just as Moses' did.

b. Judgment for Rejection (*Deuteronomy 2 to 3:22*; *Luke 10:4-16*)

Just as Moses sent messengers to Kings Og of Bashan and Sihon of Heshbon with terms of peace, so does Jesus send his seventy out with the offer of blessing: "Peace be to this house." The Israelite messengers are rebuffed, and God punishes them by sending Israel to decimate them. Jesus warns that in case of rejection (which does not in fact occur), the aloof cities will face divine judgment some time in the future. This mission charge material comes from Q (cf. *Matthew 10*). That it did not originate here with Luke borrowing it directly from *Deuteronomy* is evident from the fact that the hypothetical doom of the unresponsive towns is compared with those of Tyre and Sidon, not of Bashan and Heshbon. Perhaps Luke decided to use the Q material here because it uses the image of the missionaries "shaking the dust" (i.e., the contagion) of the village "from the soles of their feet" (*Luke 10:1*), matching the mention of "the sole of the foot" in *Deuteronomy 2:5*.

c. Praying to the Lord of Heaven and Earth (*Deuteronomy 3:23 to 4:40*; *Luke 10:21-24*)

"At that time" Moses prayed to God, like unto whom there is none "in heaven or on earth" (*Deuteronomy 2:23-24*). In the Q saying *Luke 10:21-24* // *Matthew 11:25-27*, perhaps itself suggested originally by the *Deuteronomy* text, Jesus "at that time" praised his divine Father, "Lord of heaven and earth" (*Luke 10:21*). Jesus thanks God for revealing his wonders to "children," not to the ostensibly "wise." In some measure this reflects the wording of *Deuteronomy 4:6*, where Moses reminds his people to cherish the commandments as their *wisdom* and *4:9*, there he bids them tell what they have seen to their *children*. The Deuteronomic recital of all the wonders their eyes have seen (*4:3, 9, 34, 36*) may have inspired the Q blessing of the disciples for having seen the saving acts the ancient prophets and kings did not live to witness (*Luke 10:23-24*). Only note the antitypological reversal of *Deuteronomy*: for Q it is the ancients who failed to see what their remote heirs did see.

The rest of the Q passage, *Luke 10:22*, may derive from Akhenaten's *Hymn to the Sun*: "O Aten, no man knoweth thee, save for thy son Akhenaten."

d. The Commandments and the Shema (*Deuteronomy 5-6*; *Luke 10:25-27*)

These two chapters of *Deuteronomy* present both the Decalogue and the Shema. *Luke* presents but the tip of the iceberg when Jesus asks a scribe what he considers the gist of the Torah and the man replies with the Shema (adding *Leviticus 19:18*). Here Luke has rewritten *Mark 12:28-34*, which did list some of the Ten Commandments, albeit loosely. Luke's closing comment, "Do this and you will live," comes from *Leviticus 18:5*, "You shall therefore keep my statutes and my ordinances, by doing which a man shall live." It is not a case of Jesus being quoted as quoting the *Leviticus* text; rather it is evident Luke has refashioned the unacknowledged Levitical original into a fictive saying of Jesus.

e. (No) Mercy to the Foreigner (*Deuteronomy 7*; *Luke 10:29-37*)

To *Deuteronomy's* stern charge to eradicate the heathen of Canaan without mercy (*7:2*), itself a piece of long-after-the-fact jingoism, not a historical incitement to genocide, Luke poses this uniquely Lukan parable, that of the Good Samaritan, in which the despised foreigner/heretic is filled with mercy (*Luke 10:33*) for a Jew victimized by thugs. Like all the uniquely Lukan parables, this one is the evangelist's own creation. By contrast, Matthew knew of no such sympathy of Jesus for Samaritans (*Matthew 10:5*). This parable, like the uniquely Lukan narrative of the Samaritan leper (*17:1-19*), reflects Luke's interest in the Samaritan mission (*Acts 8:5-17 ff.*), shared with John (*John 4:1-42*). The parable of the Good Samaritan, like most of Luke's, is a genuine story, no mere extended simile, and it compares two type-characters, in this case the indifferent priest and Levite versus the compassionate Samaritan, just as Luke elsewhere contrasts the Prodigal and his straight-arrow brother, Lazarus and the Rich Man, the Pharisee and the Publican, the Widow and the Unjust Judge, Mary and Martha, the Importunate Friend and his Unresponsive Friend. The contrast with Moses' mercilessness is of a piece with Luke's Elijah/Jesus contrast in *Luke 9:54*, where Jesus shows mercy to Samaritans, unlike his counterpart Elijah who barbecued them (*2 Kings 1:10, 12*).

f. Not by Bread Alone (*Deuteronomy 8:1-3*; *Luke 10:38-42*)

Luke has created the story of Mary and Martha as a commentary on *Deuteronomy 8:3*, "Man does not live by bread alone, but . . . lives by every word that proceeds from the mouth of the LORD." Luke has opposed the contemplative Mary who hungers for Jesus' ("the Lord's") "words" with the harried Martha ("Lady of the House," hence an ideal, fictive character), whose preoccupation with domestic chores, especially cooking and serving, threatens to crowd out spiritual sustenance (cf. *Deuteronomy 8:11-14*). It is not unlikely that the passage is intended to comment in some way on the issue of celibate women and their various roles in the church of Luke's day (cf. *1 Timothy 5:3-16*).

g. Fatherly Provision (*Deuteronomy 8:4-20*; *Luke 11:1-13*)

Deuteronomy compares the discipline meted out to Israel by God with the training a father gives his son, then reminds the reader of the fatherly provision of God for his children in the wilderness and promises security, prosperity, and sufficient food in their new land. Luke matches this with his version of the Q Lord's Prayer, sharing the same general themes of fatherly provision and asking God to spare his children "the test," recalling the "tests" sent upon the people by God in the wilderness. Luke adds the Q material about God giving good gifts to his children (*Luke 11:9-13*//*Matthew 7:7-11*), certainly the point of the *Deuteronomy* text, together with his own parable of the Importunate Friend, which (like its twin, the parable of the Unjust Judge, *18:1-8*, also uniquely Lukan) urges the seeker not to give up praying "How long, O Lord?"

h. Vanquishing Strong Enemies (Deuteronomy *9:1 to 10:11*; *Luke 11:14-26*)

On the eve of Israel's entrance into the land, Moses reviews their fathers' sorry history of rebellion yet promises victory over stronger nations including the half-mythical Anakim, descended from a race of titans. Later haggadah made these Sons of Anak descendants of the miscegenation between the Sons of God understood as fallen angels and the daughters of men (*Genesis 6:1-6*). Thus it is no surprise for Luke to discern a parallel between this text and the Q/*Mark* account of the Beel-zebul controversy, where Jesus exorcises demons (fallen angels?), despoiling Satan, the strong man, of his captives. According to the analogy, the poor hapless demoniacs are like the promised land of Canaan, while the demons possessing the wretches are like the Anakim holding the land until God casts them out because of their wickedness, even though like Satan their chief they are far stronger than any mere mortal.

As noted in the discussion of the Beel-zebul controversy in *Mark* (section **B. 11** above), the Q comparison of Jesus with the "sons" of the Pharisees and his own use of "the finger of God" to cast out demons must derive from a midrash upon the *Exodus* contest between Moses and the priest-magicians of Pharaoh. But Luke anchors it precisely at this point because of the Deuteronomic reference to "the finger of God" writing the commandments upon the stone tables. The "strong man" element of both Markan and Q versions of the Beel-zebul episode also originated elsewhere, in *Isaiah 49:24*, but it seemed to fit the Deuteronomic reference to stronger nations here. That is, though the Beel-zebul controversy does stem from scriptural sources, it was pre-Lukan material which he then placed at a particular point in his sequence because of its perceived analogy to the piece of *Deuteronomy* he needed to parallel.

i. Impartiality and Clear Vision (*Deuteronomy 10:12 to 11:32*; *Luke 11:27-36*)

Again, Luke has done his best to match up previously existing gospel traditions with themes from the next bit of Deuteronomy. To the exaltation of God as impartial to all, no respecter of persons, Luke matches (and, not unlikely, creates on the basis of *Mark 3:31-35*) an anecdote showing that not even the mother of Jesus is higher in God's sight than the average faithful disciple.

Corresponding to the warning for Israel not to repeat the sins of the Canaanites and so repeat their doom, Luke matches the Q material on how even ancient non-Israelites better appreciated the divine witness of their day than did Jesus' contemporaries (*Luke 11:29-32*//*Matthew 12:39-42*).

Finally, Luke places the Q material about the eye being the lamp of the body *(Luke 11:34-36*//*Matthew 6:22-23*) in tandem with *Deuteronomy 11:18's* charge to cherish the commandments in one's heart and to place them as frontlets on one's forehead. Presumably, the unstated middle term of transition from the one image to the other was *Psalm 19:8* ("the precepts of the LORD are right, rejoicing the heart; the commandment of the LORD is pure, enlightening the eyes") or perhaps *Psalm 119:105* ("Your word is a lamp for my feet and a light for my path").

j. Clean and Unclean (*Deuteronomy 12:1-16*; *Luke 11:37 to 12:12*)

The substance of *Deuteronomy 12:1-14's* prohibition of sacrifice on the traditional high places and restriction of worship to the (Jerusalem) Temple, finds no real echo in Luke, who waits to apply roughly parallel material to *Deuteronomy 12:15-16*, which allows for the preparation and eating of meat as a purely secular process at home. (I.e., no longer must every eating of meat be part of a sacrifice, traditionally offered at home.) Here we read that clean and unclean alike may eat meat in this way, and Luke has seized on this rubric to introduce the Q material on the inability of the Pharisees to tell the real difference between clean and unclean (*Luke 11:39-52*//*Matthew 23:4-7, 23-36*, as well as *Mark 7:1-5* (//*Luke 11:37-38*) and the Q material *Matthew 10:26-35*//*Luke 12:2-9*. The connection is merely that of catchwords, as proves also to be the case when we notice that the Q phrase "the blood of all the prophets shed" (*Luke 11:50*//*Matthew 23:35*, "all the righteous blood shed on earth") just barely recalls the Deuteronomic phrase, "you shall not eat the blood; you shall pour it out upon the earth" (*12:16*).

k. Inheritance (*Deuteronomy 12:17-32*; *Luke 12:13-34*)

Approached by someone in the crowd who seeks to have Jesus adjudicate an inheritance dispute, Jesus refuses to play the role of arbiter, one commonly played by itinerant Near Eastern holy men (who, having no earthly connections or interests, the theory went, must be impartial as well as inspired). His retort, "Man, who made me a judge or divider over you?" (*Luke 12:14*), echoes and no doubt derives from *Exodus 2:14a*, "Who made you a prince and a judge over us?" Moses had sought to interfere in his people's worldly troubles, only to be rebuffed. Jesus' intervention is sought, but he rebuffs the request. Here is another Moses-Jesus antitype, at the expense of Moses, since one greater than Moses is ostensibly here.

The ensuing parable, *Luke 12:16-21*, seems to be based on *Ecclesiastes/Qoheleth 6:2*, "a man to whom God gives wealth, possessions, and honor, so that he lacks nothing of all he desires, yet God does not give him the opportunity to enjoy them, but a stranger enjoys them." See also *Ecclesiastes/Qoheleth 2:18-21.*

l. Severe Punishments (*Deuteronomy 13:1-11*; *Luke 12:35-53*)

Deuteronomy takes aim at false prophets, prophets of rival deities, warning Israel not to heed their seductions. It is God who has sent them, and not the deities whom they think themselves to be speaking for. God is in this way testing Israel's fidelity. To match this theme, Luke has chosen to use parable material based on the Markan Apocalypse (*Mark 13:34-37*); note Luke's expansion of *Mark 13:37*, "What I say to you I say to all: watch," into a dialogue between Jesus and Peter: "Peter said, 'Lord, are you telling this parable for us, or for all?' " (*Luke 12:41 ff.*). The Markan parable had the departing master set tasks for his servants; hence they functioned as tests to prove how well they would perform. For Luke, connecting the parable with *Deuteronomy*, the church's job while their Lord is away in heaven is to remain faithful to his name as against the blandishments of other saviors and prophets (*Luke 21:8*).

Since *Deuteronomy* does not exempt even family members who may have fallen under the spell of forbidden gods (*13:6-11*), Luke adds the Q saying *Luke 51-53*// *Matthew 10:34-36*), largely based on an unacknowledged quotation of *Micah 7:6*, "for the son treats the father with contempt, the daughter rises up against her mother, the daughter-in-law against her mother-in-law; a man's enemies are men of his own household."

m. Judgment on this People (*Deuteronomy 13:12-18*; *Luke 12:54 to 13:5*)

Whole cities lapsing into pagan apostasy are to be eliminated, destroyed, *Deuteronomy* mandates, with nothing ever to be rebuilt on the desolation, so seriously does Israel's God take spiritual infidelity. No less gravely does the Lukan Jesus take the lack of repentance on the part of Galileans and Jews. Past tragedies and atrocities will be seen as the mere beginning of the judgments to fall like the headsman's ax on an unrepentant people. Of course, the Lukan Jesus prophesies long after the fact, referring to the bloody triumph of Rome in Galilee and Judea culminating in 73 CE.

n. The Third Year (*Deuteronomy 14:28*; *Luke 13:6-9*)

Luke has seen fit to skip *Deuteronomy 14:1-31*, a list of clean and unclean animals, and *14:22-27*, which repeats *12:17-31*.

Deuteronomy 14 stipulates a tithe of one's produce every three years. Luke uses the law as a springboard for a retrospective parable accounting for the Roman defeat of Judea and Galilee, continuing his discussion from the preceding pericopæ. The people of God are like a barren fig tree which has disappointed its owner three years straight, yielding nothing to offer God. The vinedresser pleads for an extra year's grace period before the fruitless tree should be uprooted. Luke's point: don't say God didn't go the second mile before exacting judgment.

o. Release of the Bondslave (*Deuteronomy 15:1-18*; *Luke 13:10-21*)

Deuteronomy calls for the cancellation of debts in the seventh year, a kind of release from bondage, as well as freedom for bondservants. The last case stipulated is that of the bondwoman (*Deuteronomy 15:17*). From this last, Luke has developed his story of a woman, a bondservant of Satan for eighteen years by virtue of a bent spine, being freed by Jesus.

Luke and Matthew, each using both Q and Mark, have inherited the Markan story of the man with the withered hand (*Mark 3:1-6*), a controversy about healing on the sabbath, and the Q saying "Which of you, having one sheep [*Luke*: 'a son/ass or ox'] that falls into a pit [*Luke*: 'well'] on the sabbath, will not lay hold of it and pull it out?" (*Matthew 12:11*//*Luke 14:5*). Matthew inserted the Q saying into the Markan story, while Luke chose to duplicated Mark's story of the man with the withered hand as the healing of the man with dropsy (*Luke 14:1-6*) and to insert the Q saying into it at the equivalent spot. But he also created the story of the woman with the bent spine, basing it on a paraphrase of the same Q saying, adapted to the case suggested by *Deuteronomy*, the release from a bond, so that the parallel cited becomes *releasing* a farm animal from its *tether* on the sabbath.

p. Go to Jerusalem (*Deuteronomy 16:1 to 17:7*; *Luke 13:22-35*)

Deuteronomy commands thrice-yearly pilgrimage to the Jerusalem Temple, and the Lukan Jesus declares nothing will deflect his inexorable progress to Jerusalem to die there as a prophet must. As the declaration presupposes the Lukan redactional agenda of the Central Section itself, as well as the distinctive Lukan prophet Christology, the saying is itself redactional.

q. Righteous Judges; Remembering the Poor (*Deuteronomy 16:18-20; 17:8-18*; *Luke 14:1-14*)

The fit here is loose, but the connection is nonetheless evident. *Deuteronomy* is concerned with people accepting the oracular verdict of priests and judges, and with limiting the prerogatives of the king. Luke, apparently simply to secure the parallel, has set his scene in the house of a "ruler" and tells the story of the dropsical man to exalt Jesus' judgment over that of the scribes.

The rest of the Lukan passage refers back to the preceding Deuteronomic text, *16:14*, whose ranking of various guests enables Luke to tack on a piece of table etiquette borrowed from *Proverbs 25:6-7* ("Do not put yourself forward in the king's presence or stand in the place of the great; for it is better to be told, 'Come up here,' than to be put lower in the presence of the prince"). The specific inclusion of the widow and the sojourner in *Deuteronomy 16:14* has inspired Luke's admonition to invite the poor, the maimed, the blind, and the lame instead of one's friends and relatives. While the Lukan version may seem a more radical suggestion than *Deuteronomy's* inclusion of the poor alongside one's family, it actually tends toward minimizing the discomfort of the situation: one can bask in playing the benefactor to one's poor clients without having to embarrass one's fellow sophisticates with the crude manners of the poor at the same table (though in *1 Corinthians 11:18-22* we learn some "solved" the problem by segregating the two groups at the same event!).

r. Excuses before Battle (*Deuteronomy 20*; *Luke 14:15-35*)

Luke has omitted *Deuteronomy 19's* discussions of cities of refuge and of false witnesses.

Commentators commonly note the similarity between the excuses offered by those invited to the great supper in Q (*Matthew 22:1-10*//*Luke 14:16-24*), implicitly sneered at by the narrator, and those circumstances exempting an Israelite from serving in holy war in *Deuteronomy 20*, building a new house, planting a new vineyard, getting married. One can only suspect that Q represents a tightening up of what were considered by an enthusiastic sect to be too lax standards, just as the divorce rules were tightened by Christians. (Those standards were now seen to apply, no doubt, to the spiritual crusade of evangelism.)

The parable of the Great Supper is pre-Lukan, as it appears already in Q (*Luke 14:16-24* // *Matthew 22:1-10 ff.*) and the *Gospel of Thomas*, saying *64*. It is very likely an adaptation of the rabbinic story of the tax-collector Bar-Majan, who sought to climb socially by inviting the respectable rich to a great feast. All, refusing to fall for the ploy, begged off, whereupon the tax-collector decided to share the food with the poor that it not go to waste. This act of charity did win him a stately funeral but was not enough to mitigate his punishment in hell (Jerusalem Talmud, *Hagigah*, II, 77d).

The rest of *Luke 14:25-33* has perched here because of the treatment of warfare in the parallel section of *Deuteronomy*, though the connection is really only that of catchwords, as often in the Central Section.

s. Rights of the First-Born Versus Wicked Sons (*Deuteronomy 21:15 to 22:4*; *Luke 15*)

Luke leaves aside *Deuteronomy 21:1-14*, the treatment of corpses and female captives.

The great parable of the Prodigal Son is Luke's own creation, as is evident not only from its juxtaposition of two type-characters, but also from the uniquely Lukan device of character introspection in a tight spot:, "What shall I do? I shall. . . ." The Prodigal, having painted himself into a corner, reflects, "I will arise and go to my father, and I will say to him . . ." (*15:18*), just as the Unjust Judge, exasperated, "said to himself, 'I will vindicate her . . .'" (*Luke 18:4-5*). Similarly, the Dishonest Steward "said to himself, 'What shall I do? . . . I have decided what to do . . .'" (*16:3-4*). And the Rich Fool "thought to himself, 'What shall I do? . . . I will do this . . .'" (*12:17-18*).

The parable's theme was suggested to him by the Deuteronomic treatment of sons and their inheritance in *21:15-21*. Luke has combined the elements of division of property between a pair of sons, the possibility of favoring the wrong one, and the problem of a rebellious son who shames his family. But, typically, Luke replaces the sternness of the original legal provision (no doubt because he writes for a Diaspora audience for whom some of these laws can no longer apply) with an example of mercy. Here the rebellious son is accepted in love, not executed.

Though the basic inspiration of the parable comes thus from *Deuteronomy*, Luke owes the building blocks from another source, the *Odyssey*. The character of the Prodigal was suggested by both the long-absent Odysseus himself and his son Telemachus who returns from his own long quest to find his father. Both the parable's elements of wandering far from home and of the father-son reunion stem from here. The cavorting of the Prodigal with loose women in far lands was suggested by Odysseus' dalliance with Calypso. But the motif of the Prodigal's having "devoured [his father's] estate with loose living" is based on the similar judgment passed more than once by Telemachus and Eumæus on the "gang of profligates" infesting Odysseus' estate during his absence, the suitors.

The Prodigal's taking a job as a swine herder, a galling "transformation" for a Jew, may reflect the transformation of Odysseus' men into swine by Circe, especially since the hungry Prodigal would like to fill his stomach with the pods the pigs eat, i.e., act like a pig. Then again, his working as a swineherd may stem from Eumæus' having been one. The latter's frequent characterization as a "righteous swineherd" may have suggested the depiction of the Prodigal as a repentant swineherd. The return of the Prodigal was suggested by the return of Odysseus, but no less of Telemachus, who together share the same actantial role. The Prodigal hopes to enter his father's household as a mere slave, whereas the returning Odysseus actually disguises himself as a slave on his own estate. The glad reception afforded the Prodigal by his father recalls the reunion of Odysseus and Telemachus, also father and son, but even more the reunion of Telemachus and Eumæus, his father's faithful servant: "The last words were not out of his mouth when his [Odysseus'] own son appeared in the gateway. Eumæus jumped up in amazement, and the bowls in which he had been busy mixing the sparkling wine tumbled out of his grasp. He ran forward to meet his young master. He kissed his lovely eyes and then kissed his right hand and his left, while the tears streamed down his cheeks. Like a fond father welcoming his son after nine years abroad, his only son, the apple of his eye and the centre of all his anxious cares, the admirable swineherd threw his arms around Prince Telemachus and showered kisses on him as though he had just escaped from death."

Next, Luke splits Odysseus into two characters, the two brothers. The elder son also returns from being away, albeit only out in the field (the scene of conflict between another famous pair of brothers, Cain and Abel). Returning, he is dismayed, like Odysseus, to discover a feast in progress. (Here we must note also the echo of *Exodus 32:18*, "It is not the sound of shouting for victory, or the sound of the cry of defeat, but the sound of . . . *singing* that I hear!") It is a feast in honor of a profligate, as the elder brother is quick to point out, just like that of Penelope's suitors. And, just as their feast is predicated upon the assumption of Odysseus' death, the Prodigal's father explains to the elder son that they must feast since the Prodigal was dead and has now returned alive, as Odysseus is about to do.

Deuteronomy 22:1-4 stipulates all manner of lost objects which must be returned if found, just as *Luke 15:3-7* and *8-10* provide examples of lost things zealously sought and found. The first of these is an appropriate Q parable, that of the Lost Sheep (see also *Matthew 18:10-14*), while the second, the parable of the Lost Coin, is presumably Luke's own creation, reminiscent of the uniquely Lukan parable of the Yeast (*3:20-21*) and his story of Martha (*10:38-42*), each with its busy housekeeper.

t. Masters, Slaves, Money, and Divorce (*Deuteronomy 23:15 to 24:4*; *Luke 16:1-18*)

Luke skips *Deuteronomy 22:5 to 23:14*, a catch-all.

Luke appears to have used the *Deuteronomy 23* provision for the welcoming of an escaped slave to live in one's midst as the basis for his parable of the Dishonest Steward, who must soon leave his master's employ and so manipulates his master's accounts as to assure he will be welcomed into his grateful clients' midst after his dismissal.

Luke has nothing particular to say concerning cult prostitutes ("priestitutes," one might call them) and vows, but the Deuteronomic discussion of debts and usury inspires him to accuse the Pharisees of being "lovers of money." Greed like theirs is an "abomination" (*bdelugma*) before God, a word he has borrowed from the same Deuteronomic passage's condemnation of a man remarrying his divorced wife after a second man has also divorced her. On the question of divorce, Luke oddly juxtaposes against the Deuteronomic provision the diametrically opposite Markan rejection of divorce, even while adding that the Torah cannot change!

u. Vindication of the Poor, of Lepers; Fair Judges (*Deuteronomy 24:6 to 25:3*; *Luke 16:19 to 18:8*)

Inspired by *Deuteronomy's* injunctions concerning fair treatment of the poor, Luke has created the parable of the Rich Man and Lazarus, probably basing it upon both the Egyptian Tale of the Two Brothers, where the postmortem fates of two men are disclosed as a lesson for the living, and the rabbinic parable of the tax-collector Bar-Majan (*Hagigah*, II, 77d), whose single act of charity (inviting the poor to a banquet when his invited guests, the respectable rich, did not show up) accounted karmically for his sumptuous funeral, but failed to mitigate his torments in hell afterward.

Luke places the Q saying about the millstone (*Luke 17:1-2*//*Matthew 18:6-7*) to match the Deuteronomic mention of a millstone as the irreplaceable tool of one's trade (24:6), a mere catchword connection.

The provision for a leper's cure and certification (*Deuteronomy 24:8-9*) prompts Luke to create another pro-Samaritan story (with *Deuteronomy 24:14's* counsel to treat the sojourning foreigner fairly also in mind). It is the story of the nine Jewish lepers whom Jesus cures without thanks versus the single Samaritan who returns to thank Jesus. The centrality of the motif of praising/thanking God for a miracle, elsewhere Luke's redactional addition to older miracle stories, brands this one as completely Lukan.

Deuteronomy 24:17-18 and *25:1-3* concern fair judgments rendered on behalf of the poor and fair treatment of widows. Luke required no more inspiration than this to create his parable of the Unjust Judge who delays vindicating a widow too poor to bribe him till she finally wears him out. This he uses to advocate patience in prayer: if even a corrupt judge will at length give in to a just petition, cannot the righteous God be expected to answer just prayers in his own time?

v. Confessing One's Righteousness (*Deuteronomy 26*; *Luke 18:9-14*)

Luke skips *Deuteronomy 25:4-19*, about Levirate marriage, false weights, etc.

Deuteronomy 26:12-15 allows that one who is offering the first-fruits of his crops may confess his own perfect obedience to the commandments, provided one has done so, and thus may rightly claim God's blessing on the land. This must have struck Luke as pretentious and presumptuous, and he satirizes this section in his parable of the Pharisee (whose self-praise in the guise of prayer echoes that of *Deuteronomy*) and the Publican (counted righteous by virtue of his humble self-condemnation).

7. The Ascension (*24:49-53*)

Luke's ascension narrative (the only one in the gospels) is based primarily upon the account of Elijah's ascension in *2 Kings 2* (Brodie, pp. 254-264), though he seems to have added elements of Josephus' story of Moses' ascension as well ("And as soon as they were come to the mountain called Abarim . . ., he was going to embrace Eleazar and Joshua, and was still discoursing with them, [when] a cloud stood over him on the sudden, and he disappeared in a certain valley" *Antiquities* V. 1. 48, Whiston trans.). In *2 Kings 2:9*, Elijah and Elisha agree on the master's bequest to his disciple: Elisha is to receive a double share of Elijah's mighty spirit, i.e., power. Likewise, just before his own ascension, Jesus announces to his disciples his own bequest: "the promise of my father" (*Luke 24:49*). It will be a "clothing" with power, recalling Elijah's miracle of parting the Jordan with his own rolled-up mantle (*1 Kings 2:12*). Both Elijah and Jesus are assumed into heaven (*1 Kings 2:11*; *Luke 24:50-53*; *Acts 1:1-1*), the former with the aid of Apollo's chariot, but both are pointedly separated from their disciples (*2 Kings 2:11*; *Luke 24:51*). After this, the promised spirit comes, empowering the disciples (*2 Kings 2:15*; *Acts 2:4*). And just as Elijah's ascent is witnessed by disciples, whose search failed to turn up his body (*2 Kings 2:16-18*), so is Jesus' after they find only an empty tomb (*Luke 24:3*; *Acts 1:9-11*).

E. The Gospel of John

1. Nathaniel (*1:43-51*)

As all commentators agree, this episode is based on Jacob's dream of the ladder/stairway between heaven and earth, with angels going up and down along it (*Genesis 28:11-17 ff.*). Nathaniel is to be a New Testament Jacob, lacking the shrewd worldliness of his prototype.

2. Water into Wine (*2:1-11*)

Though the central feature of this miracle story, the transformation of one liquid into another, no doubt comes from the lore of Dionysus, the basic outline of the story owes much to the story of Elijah in *1 Kings 17:8-24* LXX (Helms, p. 86). The widow of Zarephath, whose son has just died, upbraids the prophet: "What have I to do with you, O man of God?" (*Ti emoi kai soi,* ***17:18***). John has transferred this brusque address to the mouth of Jesus, rebuking his mother (***2:4***, *Ti emoi kai soi, gunai*). Jesus and Elijah both tell people in need of provisions to take empty pitchers (*udria* in *1 Kings 17:12*, *udriai* in *John 2:6-7*), from which sustenance miraculously emerges. And just as this feat causes the woman to declare her faith in Elijah ("I know that you are a man of God," *v. 24*), so does Jesus' wine miracle cause his disciples to put their faith in him (*v. 11*).

3. The Samaritan Woman (*4:1-44*)

As Robert Alter notes (p. 48), this scene is a variant of the "type scene" which frequently recurs in the Bible of a young man leaving home and coming to a well where he meets young women, one of whom he marries. Other instances and variants include *Genesis 24* (Abraham's servant meets Rebecca), *Genesis 29* (Jacob meets Rachel); *Exodus 2* (Moses meets Zipporah): *Ruth 2* (Ruth meets Boaz); and *1 Samuel 9* (Saul meets the maidens at Zuph). But Helms (pp. 89-90) adds *1 Kings 17*, where, again, Elijah encounters the widow of Zarephath, and it is this story which seems to have supplied the immediate model for John.

4. Elijah and Jesus alike leave home turf for foreign territory.

Each is thirsty and meets a woman of whom he asks a drink of water. In both stories the woman departs from the pattern of the type scene because, though having no husband as in the type scene, she is mature and lacks a husband for other reasons. The woman of Zarephath is a widow, while the Samaritan woman has given up on marriage, having had five previous husbands, now dead or divorced, and is presently just cohabiting. In both stories it is really the woman who stands in need more than the prophet, and the latter offers the boon of a miraculously self-renewing supply of nourishment, Elijah that of physical food, Jesus that of the water of everlasting life. Just as the widow exclaims that Elijah must have come to disclose her past sins ("You have come to me to bring my sin to remembrance," *1 Kings 17:18*), the Samaritan admits Jesus has the goods on her as well ("He told me all that I ever did," *John 4:39*).

5. Jesus Appears to Mary Magdalene (*20:1, 11-18*)

This story owes much to the self-disclosure of the angel Raphael at the climax of the *Book of Tobit* (Helms, pp. 146-147). When Tobias first saw Raphael, he "did not know" he was really an angel (*Tobit 5:5*), just as when Mary, weeping outside the tomb, first saw Jesus there, she "did not know" who he really was (*20:14*). Having delivered Sarah from her curse, Raphael reveals himself to Tobit and his son Tobias and announces, his work being done, that "I am ascending to him who sent me" (*Tobit 12:20*), just as Jesus tells Mary, "I am ascending to my father and your father, to my God and your God" (*John 20:17*). Why does the risen Jesus warn Mary "Touch/hold me not, for I have not yet ascended to the father" (*20:17a*)? This is probably an indication of docetism, that Jesus (at least the risen Jesus) cannot be touched, not having (any longer?) a fleshly body (the story was not originally followed by the Doubting Thomas story with its tactile proofs, hence need not be consistent with it; note that in *20:17b* Jesus seems to anticipate not seeing the disciples again). The reason for seeing docetism here is the parallel it would complete between *John 20* and the Raphael revelation/ascension scene, where the angel explains (in *Tobit 12:19*), "All these days I merely appeared to you and did not eat or drink, but you were seeing a vision" (i.e., a semblance).

F. Acts of the Apostles

1. Pentecost (*2:1-4 ff.*)

The whole scene comes, obviously, from the descent of the Mosaic spirit upon the seventy elders in *Numbers 11:16-17, 24-25*, with an assist from Euripides' *The Bacchæ*, where we read "Flames flickered in their curls and did not burn them" (757-758), just as tongues of fire blazed harmlessly above the heads of the apostles (*Acts 2:3*). Ecstatic speech caused some bystanders to question the sobriety of the disciples, but Peter defends them ("These are not drunk as you suppose" *Acts 2:15a*), as does Pentheus' messenger: "Not, as you think, drunk with wine" (686-687).

2. Ananias and Sapphira; the Martyrdom of Stephen (*5:1-11*; *6:8-15*)

The conspiracy of Ahab and Jezebel to cheat the pious Naboth out of his vineyard (*1 Kings 20:1 to 21:21*) has provided Luke the raw material for two of the most exciting episodes of *Acts*, those of Ananias and Sapphira and of Stephen (Brodie, pp. 271-275). Ahab finds himself obsessed with Naboth's vineyard, which seems more desirable to him, since he cannot possess it, than all his royal possessions. Jezebel advises him to take what he wants by devious means. Luke has punningly made Naboth into the righteous Barnabas, and now it is the latter's donation (rather than possession) of a field that excites a wicked couple's jealousy. Ananias plays Ahab, Sapphira Jezebel. Only they do not conspire to murder anyone. That element Luke reserves for the martyrdom of Stephen. The crime of Ananias and Sapphira is borrowed instead from that of Achan (*Judges 7*), who appropriated for himself treasure ear-marked for God. Ananias and Sapphira have sold a field (wanting to be admired like Barnabas), but they have kept back some of the money while claiming to have donated the full price. They have no business keeping the rest: it is rightfully God's since they have dedicated it as "devoted to the Lord." Peter confronts Ananias and Sapphira, just as Joshua did Achan (*Joshua 7:25*) and as Elijah confronted Ahab (*1 Kings 20:17-18*). Luke takes the earlier note about Ahab's disturbance in spirit (*20:4*) and makes it into the charge that Ananias and Sapphira had lied to the Spirit of God (*Acts 5:3b-4, 9b*). Elijah and Peter pronounce death sentences on the guilty, and those of Ananias and Sapphira (like Achan's) transpire at once (*Acts 5:5a, 10a*), while those of Ahab and Jezebel delay for some time. Fear fell on all who heard of Ananias' and Sapphira's fate, recalling the fear of God sparked in poor indecisive Ahab by Elijah's doom oracle (*1 Kings 20:27-29*). Not long after the Naboth incident we learn that the young men of Israel defeated the greedy Syrians (*21:1-21*), a tale which likely made Luke think of having the young men (never in evidence elsewhere in Acts) carry out and bury the bodies of the greedy couple (*Acts 5:6, 10b*).

Returning to the hapless Naboth, he has become Stephen, *Acts'* proto-martyr. Naboth was railroaded by the schemes of Jezebel. She directed the elders and *freemen* to set up Naboth, condemning him through lying witnesses. Stephen suffers the same at the hands of the Synagogue of *Freedmen*. Stephen, like Naboth, is accused of double blasphemy (Naboth: God and king; Stephen: Moses and God) Both are carried outside the city limits and stoned to death. When Ahab heard of the fruit of his desires, he tore his garments in remorse. Luke has carried this over into the detail that young Saul of Tarsus checked the coats of the stoning mob.

3. The Ethiopian Eunuch (*8:26-40*)

The story of the Ethiopian eunuch and of Philip the evangelist recalls several key features of the story of Elijah and Naaman the Syrian (*2 Kings 5:1-14*) (Brodie, pp. 316-327). The Elijah narrative depicts both healing (from leprosy) and conversion (from Syrian Rimmon-worship), while the *Acts* version tells only of conversion (from Godfearer to Christian). Luke was apparently reluctant to strain plausibility or good taste by having Philip physically restore a eunuch! Both Naaman and the Ethiopian are foreign officials of high status, both close to their monarchs (*2 Kings 5:5*; *Acts 8:27c*). Naaman came to Samaria to ask the king's help in contacting the prophet Elisha. The Ethiopian for his part had journeyed to Jerusalem to seek God in the Temple worship, but the need of his heart remained unmet. This he was to find satisfied on his way home (like those other Lukan characters, the Emmaus disciples, *Luke 24:13 ff.*). The Israelite king fails to grasp the meaning of the letter Naaman presents to him, but a word from the prophet supplies the lack, just as Luke has the Ethiopian fail to grasp the true import of the prophetic scroll he reads till the hitchhiking evangelist offers commentary. In both cases salvation is to be sought by immersion. Naaman initially balks, but his servant persuades him. Luke has this temporizing in mind when he has the Ethiopian ask rhetorically, "What prevents me from being baptized?" (*Acts 8:36*). Healing and/or conversion follow, though in both cases the official must return, alone in his faith, to his heathen court.

4. Paul's Conversion (*9:1-21*)

As the great Tübingen critics already saw, the story of Paul's visionary encounter with the risen Jesus not only has no real basis in the Pauline epistles but has been derived by Luke more or less directly from *2 Maccabees 3's* story of Heliodorus. In it one Benjaminite named Simon (*3:4*) tells Apollonius of Tarsus, governor of Coele-Syria and Phoenicia (*3:5*), that the Jerusalem Temple houses unimaginable wealth that the Seleucid king might want to appropriate for himself. Once the king learns of this, he sends his agent Heliodorus to confiscate the loot. The prospect of such a violation of the Temple causes universal wailing and praying among the Jews. But Heliodorus is miraculously turned back when a shining warrior angel appears on horseback. The stallion's hooves knock Heliodorus to the ground, where two more angels lash him with whips (*25-26*). He is blinded and is unable to help himself, carried to safety on a stretcher. Pious Jews pray for his recovery, lest the people be held responsible for his condition. The angels reappear to Heliodorus, in answer to these prayers, and they announce God's grace to him: Heliodorus will live and must henceforth proclaim the majesty of the true God. Heliodorus offers sacrifice to his Saviour (*3:35*) and departs again for Syria, where he reports all this to the king. In *Acts* the plunder of the Temple has become the persecution of the church by Saul (also called Paulus, an abbreviated form of *Apollonius*), a *Benjaminite* from *Tarsus*. Heliodorus' appointed journey to Jerusalem from Syria has become Saul's journey from Jerusalem to Syria. Saul is stopped in his tracks by a heavenly visitant, goes blind and must be taken into the city, where the prayers of his former enemies avail to raise him up. Just as Heliodorus offers sacrifice, Saul undergoes baptism. Then he is told henceforth to proclaim the risen Christ, which he does.

Luke has again added details from Euripides. In *The Bacchæ*, in a sequence Luke has elsewhere rewritten into the story of Paul in Philippi (Portefaix, p. 170), Dionysus has appeared in Thebes as an apparently mortal missionary for his own sect. He runs afoul of his cousin, King Pentheus who wants the licentious cult (as he views it) to be driven out of the country. He arrests and threatens Dionysus, only to find him freed from prison by an earthquake. Dionysus determines revenge against the proud and foolish king by magically compelling Pentheus to undergo conversion to faith in him ("Though hostile formerly, he now declares a truce and goes with us. You see what you could not when you were blind," 922-924) and sending Pentheus, in woman's guise, to spy upon the Maenads, his female revelers. He does so, is discovered, and is torn limb from limb by the women, led by his own mother. As the hapless Pentheus leaves, unwittingly, to meet his doom, Dionysus comments, "Punish this man. But first distract his wits; bewilder him with madness. . . . After those threats with which he was so fierce, I want him made the laughingstock of Thebes" (850-851, 854-855). "He shall come to know Dionysus, son of Zeus, consummate god, most terrible, and yet most gentle, to mankind" (859-861). Pentheus must be made an example, as must poor Saul, despite himself. His conversion is a punishment, meting out to the persecutor his own medicine. Do we not detect a hint of ironic malice in Christ's words to Ananias about Saul? "I will show him how much *he* must suffer for the sake of my name" (*Acts 9:16*).

5. Peter's Vision (*10:9-16*)

To prime the reluctant apostle for his visit to the dwelling of the Roman Cornelius, God sends Peter a vision, one recycled from the early chapters of Ezekiel (Helms, pp. 20-21). First Peter beholds the heavens open (*thn ouranon anewgmenon*, ***10:11***), just like Ezekiel did (*hnoicqhsan oi ouranoi*, ***Ezekiel 1:1*** LXX).

Peter sees a vast sheet of sailcloth containing every kind of animal, ritually clean and unclean, and the heavenly voice commands him, "Eat!" (*Fagh*, ***Acts 10:13***), just as Ezekiel is shown a scroll and told to "Eat!" (*Fagh*, ***Ezekiel 2:9*** LXX). Peter is not eager to violate kosher laws and so balks at the command. "By no means, Lord!" (*MhdamwV, Kurie*, ***Acts 10:14***), echoing Ezekiel verbatim, *MhdamwV, Kurie* (***Ezekiel 4:14*** LXX), when the latter is commanded to cook his food over a dung fire. Peter protests that he has never eaten anything unclean (*akaqarton*) before (*10:14*), nor has Ezekiel (*akaqarsia*, ***4:14*** LXX).

References

Robert Alter, *The Art of Biblical Narrative*. New York: Basic Books, 1981.

John Bowman, *The Gospel of Mark: The New Christian Jewish Passover Haggadah*. Studia Post-Biblica, 8. Leiden: E.J. Brill, 1965.

Thomas L. Brodie, "Luke the Literary Interpreter: Luke-Acts as a Systematic Rewriting and Updating of the Elijah-Elisha Narrative in 1 and 2 Kings." Ph.D. dissertation presented to the Pontifical University of St. Thomas Aquinas, Rome. 1988.

John Dominic Crossan, *The Cross That Spoke: The Origins of the Passion Narrative*. San Francisco: Harper & Row, Publishers, 1988.

J. Duncan M. Derrett, *The Making of Mark: The Scriptural Bases of the Earliest Gospel*. Volumes 1 and 2. Shipston-on-Stour, Warwickshire: P. Drinkwater, 1985.

Earl Doherty, *The Jesus Puzzle: Did Christianity Begin with a Mythical Christ?* Ottawa: Canadian Humanist Publications, 1999.

C.F. Evans, "The Central Section of St. Luke's Gospel," in D.E. Nineham (ed.), *Studies in the Gospels: Essays in Memory of R.H. Lightfoot*. Oxford: Basil Blackwell, 1967, pp. 37-53.

Randel Helms, *Gospel Fictions*. Buffalo: Prometheus Books, 1989.

Frank Kermode, *The Genesis of Secrecy: On the Interpretation of Narrative*. The Charles Eliot Norton Lectures 1977-1978. Cambridge: Harvard University Press, 1979.

Dennis R. MacDonald, *The Homeric Epics and the Gospel of Mark*. New Haven: Yale University Press, 2000.

Dale Miller and Patricia Miller, *The Gospel of Mark as Midrash on Earlier Jewish and New Testament Literature*. Studies in the Bible and Early Christianity, 21. Lewiston/Queenston/Lampeter: Edwin Mellen Press, 1990.

Lilian Portefaix, *Sisters Rejoice: Paul's Letter to the Philippians and Luke-Acts as Seen by First-Century Philippian Women*. Coniectanea biblica. New Testament series, 20. Stockholm: Almqvist & Wicksell, 1988.

Wolfgang Roth, *Hebrew Gospel: Cracking the Code of Mark*. Oak Park: Meyer-Stone Books, 1988.

William R. Stegner, "The Baptism of Jesus: A Story Modeled on the Binding of Isaac," in Herschel Shanks (ed.), *Abraham & Family: New Insights into the Patriarchal Narratives*. Washington, D.C.: Biblical Archaeology Society, 2001.

Rikki E. Watts, *Isaiah's New Exodus and Mark*. Wissenschaftliche Untersuchungen zum Neuen Testament, 2. Reihe 88. Tübingen: Mohr Siebeck, 1997.

* * * * * * * * *

Jesus as the "New Moses"

A transcribed extract from Robert M. Price's THE BIBLE GEEK Podcast of September 16, 2011

(Prof. Price reads a written communication from David O. Smith and then comments on it.)

DOS: I've continued doing research on The Synoptic Problem, with which I became fascinated a couple of years ago. In my research I've come upon what seems to be a related issue that has puzzled New Testament scholars. It concerns Luke's 'Travel Narrative' which goes from *Luke 9:51-19:48*. For the other Geeks who are not familiar with it, in the Travel Narrative – also called the Central Section – Jesus starts out for Jerusalem and it ends with Jesus entering Jerusalem or clearing the Temple – scholars differ.

In these ten plus chapters, about 2/3 of the double tradition or so-called *Q* material is found. In 1954, professor C.F. Evans proposed that *Luke* used *Deuteronomy* in the construction of the Travel Narrative. In 1974, professor Michael D. Goulder expanded on Evans's idea. Professor George M. Landis wrote in 1996 that this theory has received tentative acceptance, if not whole-hearted acceptance. I have gone through the Travel Narrative and *Deuteronomy* looking for parallels. I found 50, so far – this is 50 parallels in 428 verses of *Luke*. There are 59 verses of *Luke* which seem to have a parallel in *Deuteronomy* (that is, 13.8%). Some of the parallels are phrases, such as 'finger of God' or 'serpents and scorpions'. Others are concepts such as 'divorce', 'recalcitrant sons', or 'bringing fire down on towns and villages'. It looked to me like the passages in *Luke* were roughly in the same order as the parallel passages in *Deuteronomy*. I decided to check it out. I numbered the Lukan passages in *Luke's* order from 1 through 50. Then I numbered the *Deuteronomy* parallels from 1 through 50, in the order in which they are found in *Deuteronomy*. I then did a rank order correlation to see how close Luke followed *Deuteronomy's* order when he wrote the Travel Narrative. I obtained an 87.8% correlation.

This seems to be evidence that Luke constructed his Travel Narrative, at least, partially using *Deuteronomy* as a guide. Certainly he used *Mark* and either *Matthew* or *Q* also. But he could have used *Deuteronomy* for the over-all construction. In the Travel Narrative, Jesus travels from Galilee to Jerusalem. In *Deuteronomy*, the Israelites travel from Egypt to the Levant.

The question remains as to why Luke would do this. But I'm on the trail for an answer.

• • •

RMP: Well, yes, C.F. Evans really lays out the parallels in his great essay, called, "The Central Section of St. Luke's Gospel". And I summarized this in pretty exhaustive detail – though my summary is completely dependent on Evans – in my long piece, "New Testament Narrative as Old Testament Midrash", which appeared in the *Encyclopedia of Midrash* from Brill, and . . . [is] being reprinted in an expanded edition in the book, *The Christ Myth Theory and Its Problems*, that is to come out in about a week, from American Atheist Press. I'd be interested to hear what you think about that. It seems to me, pretty clear, that this is the same sort of thing Matthew is doing having Jesus be a new Moses and promulgating a new Torah – something not uncommon in those days. The *Book of Jubilees* and the *Manual of Discipline* are sectarian new Torahs, as well. But you know what Matthew did, he crammed all sorts of information into five great blocks of text to have Jesus give, and he starts on the Mount with the Sermon on the Mount, just like Moses from Mount Sinai. So he has, in effect, the 'Jesus Pentateuch', in *Matthew*. Now, what does Luke do? Well, he just has a 'Deutero-Deuteronomy', a second version of *Deuteronomy* for the Jesus-Moses to give. I think they are both trying to do the same thing in a slightly different way.

* * * * * * * * *

Thomas Brodie, Mythicist Priest: *Beyond the Quest for the Historical Jesus**

Reviewed by René Salm, March 21, 2013

I have just finished reading Thomas L. Brodie's *Beyond the Quest for the Historical Jesus: Memoir of a Discovery* (Sheffield Phoenix, 2012). A friend gifted me his copy (thanks Alan) and that prompted me to immediately read this important monograph and to delay the rest of the "to read" pile on my desk. Being a painfully slow reader, I spent several weeks on the book and now offer my extended comments on this signal publication in the history of Jesus mythicism.

Beyond the Quest is a mixture of two things: autobiography and historical-theological analysis, all (except Chp. 7) written in an accessible style – like having an extended cup of coffee (p. xv). Jesus mythicists may not be that interested in the autobiographical material, but I find it welcome, for the contemporary assaults on Christianity – from the Catholic Church's sex scandals to the Vati-leaks to the inexorably mounting questions regarding the religion's historical roots – inevitably represent personal challenges to those of faith. Brodie is uniquely well positioned to address the academic challenge of Jesus mythicism for, while he himself is a protagonist attacking the historicity of Jesus, he is also a distinguished man of faith. How he reconciles (or fails to reconcile) these conflicting positions is interesting and perhaps unprecedented.

Thomas Brodie is a 70-year old Dominican priest. He joined the order some four decades ago and, despite pushing the academic envelope throughout his career, he rose in the order to the position of Director of the Dominican Biblical Institute in Limerick, Ireland, an Institute he himself founded. The list of his publications in the Bibliography takes up two full pages and attest to Brodie's longstanding commitment as a researcher into Christian origins. His skeptical views have generally been balanced by a faith which dispenses with the 'letter' in favor of the 'spirit'.** However, the explicitness of Brodie's latest book goes well beyond the pale and, in this regard, stands outside the usual ambit of his oeuvre. Immediately after the book's publication Brodie was (for the first time) forbidden to teach. The book has also caused considerable discussion in Jesus mythicist circles. (Cf. Vridar; Carrier; Salm.)

Dealing with contradictions: the *mythicist* priest

Brodie has long been a closet Jesus mythicist. In the course of his life his views, when made public, have brought him professional grief. He writes (p. 198):

> In Spring of 1975, I produced a manuscript and immediately showed it to a British publisher, and then to a second, but their responses indicated that it was not at all what publishers wanted. What ruled it out above all else was its conclusion that Jesus had not existed. As the first publisher said, 'It's not just that we won't take it. Nobody will take it.' The second publisher said no Christian publishing house would take it. [The] key problem in speaking and writing was that I could never give the full story, I could never say, in crude terms, that Jesus Christ never existed. When I first gave my hand-written manuscript to be typed, in March/April 1975, I made the crucial paragraph on Jesus' existence illegible and typed it in later myself. I could not say it, partly because I would not be believed and would effectively be shut out, and partly because the crude statement of non-existence seemed grossly inadequate. It may be true, but it is so far from the whole truth that it is a radical distortion.

Ironically, Brodie could meet with acceptance from non-academics. He relates (p. 41) how one parishioner accepted his view:

> Our conversation was relaxed until it somehow turned to my work, and she asked what it was that most concerned me about the Bible.
>
> Eventually I said, 'It's just about Jesus.'
>
> Her questions were gentle, but she did want to know more. I was physically holding myself together, and looking down at the carpet. Then looked up.
>
> 'He never really existed.'
>
> 'Oh, that's what I believed since I was a little girl.'

---

*Thomas L. Brodie, *Beyond the Quest for the Historical Jesus* (Sheffield: Sheffield Phoenix Press, 2012); the review reproduced here is Part 1 of a 3-part review – for all 3, see: < mythicistpapers.com/tag/brodie/ >.

**Dealt with in Part 2.

In the academic world Brodie also occasionally encountered a sympathetic ear. The following passage (p. 36) from his book is classic:

> [Everard Johnston took his time in perusing Brodie's page on connections between 1 Corinthians and the Old Testament], then he put it down, muttering, 'In the same order . . . the same order apart from minor modifications.'
>
> We turned to the gospels, discussing the extent to which they too are a product of the rewriting.
>
> Suddenly [Johnston] said, 'So we're back to Bultmann. We know nothing about Jesus.'
>
> I paused a moment.
>
> 'It's worse than that.'
>
> There was a silence.
>
> Then he said, 'He never existed.'
>
> I nodded.
>
> There was another silence, a long one, and then he nodded gently, 'It makes sense.'

And so, for probably the first time in Christian history, one New Testament scholar has persuaded another that Jesus Christ did not exist. Furthermore, to my knowledge Father Brodie is the first active Catholic priest (not "ex-Catholic" priest) with the courage to publicly espouse this ultra-radical position. Thus, he has broken new ground in several ways. In sum, Brodie's book represents a signal step forward for Jesus mythicism and inaugurates mythicism's incursion into 'normative' Christianity.

Shortly before *Beyond the Quest* went to press, Bart Ehrman's *Did Jesus Exist?* appeared (March 2012). Brodie adds a short Epilogue to his book treating Ehrman's tome. Brodie writes here mostly in generalities, but it is clear that – like so many other mythicists – Brodie finds Ehrman wanting. Above all he faults Ehrman for not taking advantage of research since the 1980s and for basing his writing on research of the '50s (229). While Ehrman sees the occasional use of Aramaic in the Gospels as indicating authenticity, Brodie sees it as a technique of archaism which fits in perfectly with biblical literary tradition. The countercultural nature of the crucifixion is for Brodie not suggestive of historicity but "a fresh synthesis of several Old Testament/Septuagintal texts." In any case, as Tom Dykstra writes, *Did Jesus Exist?* "repeats over and over again the assertion that no reputable New Testament scholars deny the historicity of Jesus, and Brodie's book certainly blows that assertion out of the water." Amen.

A digression

While Ehrman is persuaded that what seems plausible on the surface of the ancient Christian texts amounts to authentic history, Brodie is much more skeptical. Underneath such conflicting attitudes, of course, is the burden of proof issue. To be convincing, is it enough for the mythicist to show that Jesus of Nazareth (as set forth in the Gospels) *could not* have existed? *Probably* didn't exist? (Who determines what is 'probable'?) Or does the mythicist have to *prove* that such a Jesus did not exist? (An impossibility.) On the other hand, is it enough for the historicist to merely show that mythicist arguments are imperfect? (Thus arrogating the high ground and placing the entire burden on the mythicist.) Or, does the historicist have to show that Jesus of Nazareth (as set forth in the Gospels) *could have* existed? *Probably* existed? (Again, who determines what is 'probable'?) Or does he have to *prove* it? (An impossibility.) Of course, if nobody really cares any more about the Jesus of Nazareth "as set forth in the Gospels" (as both historicists and mythicists commonly aver), then what, in fact, is at issue?

My answer to the last question is that the existence of Jesus of Nazareth is not at the heart of the matter. Where Jesus of Nazareth does or does not fit in is merely a stepping stone (though a very important one) to the larger historical enterprise – *understanding Christian origins.*

'Deep source criticism' or parallelomania?

Brodie is the quintessential detective-scholar, one who looks below the surface for half-hidden clues. When it comes to early Christian texts he is suspicious of surface appearance. His inveterate digging over the past four decades has led him to embrace numerous controversial theses, not only relating to Jesus.

For example, he is squarely in the camp of the Old Testament minimalists and posits that there was no First Temple: "Solomon builds a splendid temple, of which nothing has yet been found, not a stone" (20). He also questions the conquest model of Israelite origins, noting that "the Jericho site contains no remains from the centuries when the conquest is said to have happened" (121). Evidently, Joshua never did "fit the walls of Jericho." Brodie questions the Documentary Hypothesis; he suggests that the Pentateuch depends on the Prophets (39), dispenses with "Q" (75), and with oral tradition (Chp. 12). By all accounts, this cleric must be deemed in the forefront of skeptics among the latest generation of biblical scholars.

Brodie divides his book into five parts. The first three are devoted to what he calls the three "revolutions" in Jesus studies: (1) historical investigation; (2) literary sources; and (3) literary art, including form/genre. The "literary sources" is the meat of this book, and history will certainly consider Brodie's most enduring contribution to New Testament studies to be his close literary analysis which shows that the canonical gospels – and even the Pauline epistles – represent a "vast phenomenon of rewriting" (86). Already in 1975, his doctoral thesis was entitled "*Luke-Acts as a Systematic Rewriting and Updating of the Elijah-Elisha Narrative in 1 and 2 Kings*" (46). He there announced, among other things, that Deuteronomy "is like Matthew" and that the stoning of Stephen (Acts 6-7) draws systematically on the account of the false accusing and stoning of Naboth (1 Kgs 21). For Brodie, the work of the evangelists was meticulous, sophisticated, and even masterful. Regarding Luke's use of 1 Kgs 19 he writes:

> Like a patient shipbuilder who draws on models of older craft, and who shapes details with the patience and precision of a watch-maker, or like a literary Michelangelo who combines mastery on a grand scale with equal mastery over detail, Luke has made several adaptations. [53]

Regarding the Fourth Gospel, Brodie finds it ahistorical – a text where "history was not required," "imparting a sense of wonder," and a "literary unity that is tightly woven" (84). Lest one suppose that Brodie is out on a limb all by himself, he frequently reminds the reader that his work rests on that of others, e.g., Raymond Brown, Bultmann, Crossan, and Bauckham. Brodie is also conversant with very recent skeptical developments in the field, including Dennis R. McDonald's thesis that the Old Testament drew extensively on Homer (96).

Brodie concludes that the evangelists not only used Old Testament material to fashion their texts, but also used each other – as well as some "Pauline" epistles. "Gradually the pieces of the puzzle began to fall into place," he writes, on p. 32. "Matthew 18 had used first-century materials, including Mark, but it had also absorbed Deuteronomy 15." His source critical literary studies culminated in a seminal 2004 book, *The Birthing of the New Testament: The Intertextual Development of the New Testament Writings.*

Already in 1973 Brodie sketched out a source critical sequence for the canonical gospels – his solution to the Synoptic Problem. It is on p. 33 of his book and merits careful examination:

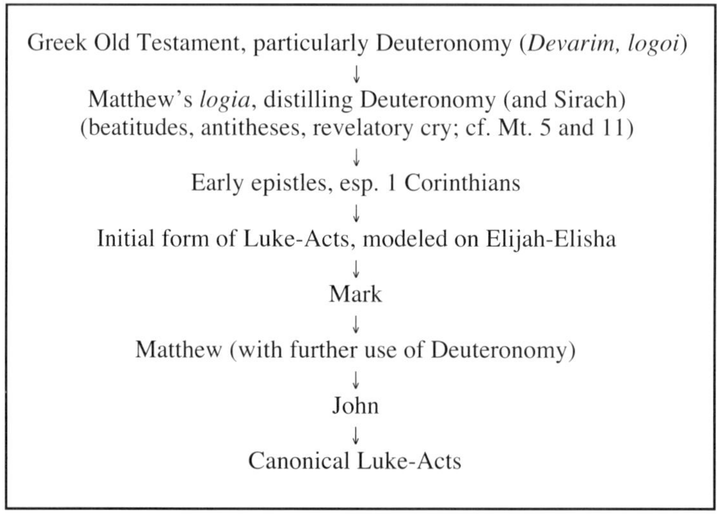

Regarding the Pauline epistles, Brodie has offered several significant insights during his long research career:

> Many epistles had transformed the great Old Testament narratives, especially the Pentateuch, and – apart from building on one another (itself a huge phenomenon) – they in turn had been transformed into one component of the Gospels and Acts. The process was particularly decisive in 1 Corinthians. Despite its distinctive first-century content, it was pervaded by the Old Testament, especially the Pentateuch, including Deuteronomy, and it had contributed decisively to the early shorter version of Luke-Acts, the proto-gospel modeled on Elijah-Elisha, what might be called Proto-Luke.

In the New Testament, some thought that Jesus was Elijah "come back to life" (Mt 11:14; 16:14; 17:10-13). In fact, the Elijah-Elisha narrative is Brodie's special object of study. For him, Chapter 7 (1 Kgs 19) encapsulates much of the Old Testament as well as provides much of the basis for the New Testament:

> [T]he Elijah-Elisha narrative is a ready-made synthesis of the Old Testament's foundational epic (Genesis-Kings), of its narrative and theology. If you were writing a narrative about Jesus, and wanted to ground that narrative in the older scriptures, you could scarcely find a more suitable foundation than the ready-made synthesis, the Elijah-Elisha narrative. [93]

Brodie devotes Chapter 7 – the longest chapter in the book – to the technical aspects of his source critical arguments. The chapter extends to twenty-five pages and includes much small print. In a sense this is the core of the book, where Brodie argues the actual evidence for his OT-NT parallels. It's doubtful, however, that many readers will do more than skim this very dry chapter. Nevertheless, Brodie did well to include it, for his book is something of a compendium of his life's work and would not be complete without this academic foundation of his overall thesis. In a sense, Chapter 7 is a frontal assault on the inerrancy of scripture, or at least on its originality. It is the antipode to his Chapter 21 (the next longest chapter) which assuages his more traditionalist readers on the other extreme – the many non-academic people of faith. So, *Beyond the Quest* tries valiantly to offer something to everyone.

And therein lies the book's – and its author's – dilemma. Brodie's life has been, as it were, not only a journey *to* the edge but a journey *on* the edge – on the knife-edge of heresy/inclusion, respectability/exclusion. Outwardly, he has fulfilled the assignments given him by the Dominican order – teaching in South Africa, Trinidad, and Ireland, all the while muting his more controversial discoveries as necessary.

No oral tradition

In the short but important Chapter 12, "The Funeral," Brodie categorically debunks oral tradition. "Why impose an oral model on a literary phenomenon?" he asks (115). "The core presumption is that Jesus Christ was a specific historical person, and within that theory, something is needed to bridge the gap between the death of Jesus (generally placed around 30 CE) and the composition of the Gospels (generally placed around 70-100)." Brodie gives a pithy account from his own experience of how direct memory remains vibrant for at least a century – being no more than one person removed from the source ("My friend told me that when he was young he heard . . ."). Brodie logically concludes: "It would make elementary sense, if the evangelists wanted to bridge a gap of several decades, that they would speak directly to those who had been present" (117).

Richard Bauckham claimed to have found evidence of formal transmission and eyewitnesses in the New Testament (1 Cor. 11:23; 15:1-8; Lk. 1:1-4; Jn. 21:24-25; cf. 19:35-37; 20:30-31). But Brodie notes problems with Bauckham's proposal and sees no reason to go beyond purely literary processes. He cites Collins in this regard (122) and notes that what is merely "history-like" is not necessarily "history" but could well be "literature." Brodie's detailed analyses, which often reveal unsuspected sources of texts, rest on the conviction that literary dependence is a more natural explanation than "history." Thus, Brodie can write that "it is impossible to make a historical claim about John 1-4 without first examining its dependence on Acts 1-8" (124). For him, this is one more straw added to the "mimesis model" (below). Where traditionalists see history, Brodie sees textual imitation and rewriting – going all the way back to Jewish scripture. The growth of the tradition is entirely literary.

Brodie terms the thesis of an oral tradition, so long a staple in Jesus studies, "convenient" and "incomparably easier" than the hard work of trying to "follow the retrievable but complex processes of literary transformation and genius" (117). He notes: "[W]hen an undefined oral tradition is combined with an undefined link to the Synoptics, then all bases seem to be covered. But the result is a world of vagueness where, despite fine erudition, logic is lost." For Brodie, the positing of an oral tradition stage has introduced a "fog of confusion" and "blocked progress on central issues." He concludes Chp. 12 thus:

> Oral tradition is like a theory of ether that has has clouded form-history ('form criticism') and created a vast vague world, often of simple isolated people or communities telling developing stories, a theory that by its very vagueness is evocative and engaging. It is time that this theory be laid to rest, time to free the study of forms from unnecessary complications and to bring it to a new level of maturity. We need a gentle funeral. [119]

The mimesis model of Christian origins

In Chapter 14 Brodie expands on "A Key Practice: Transforming Texts beyond Immediate Recognition." He claims that "the hidden connections are vast" between texts whose association is not readily apparent. Brodie exhorts biblical scholars "to move out into the deep," that is, beyond the superficial appearance of the primary texts (130). His next section is entitled, "Dealing with a Strange World: Criteria for Recognizing the Presence of Transformed Texts." Brodie's summation is on p. 134:

> This new world is not a passive place. The New Testament authors did not just lie back and, in a process of hearing or re-reading, simply let the Old Testament flow over them. Far more than readers, they are writers, holding sensitive instruments in their hands. They bring to the older text the full apparatus of their sophisticated wide-awake craft, and they generally bring that craft not to isolated quotes but to the texts in their entirety. They are proactive. Some texts they swallow whole, almost; others they distill; or reverse; or adapt in ways that are strange – so that the old cloth becomes a new thread. And having thus produced something new – the new thread – the active writer does not cease. In a highly complex process, the thread is interwoven with other threads to produce a new text, literally a new *textus*, 'woven' (Latin *textere*, 'to weave'), and the pattern of the weaving can open up a new country. So when the twenty-seven countries are placed together – the twenty-seven books of the New Testament – a whole new continent lies open.

Though Brodie's *Beyond the Quest* does not attempt a thoroughgoing academic argument for the mimesis model (excepting perhaps Chapter 7), the book contains numerous 'points of argument' in its favor, including the following observations: "the Pauline writings are engaging large narratives from the Old Testament" (135); Galatians "contains a rehearsed literary adaptation of ancient Jeremiah" (141); and the book of *Acts* borrows extensively from the Old Testament (142, 144). For a more rigorous substantiation of Brodie's view, one must of course refer to his numerous published articles and to his 2004 book, *The Birthing of the New Testament*.

Brodie's source critical summation is on p. 160: "[D]ependence on the Old Testament pervades all the Gospels and Acts. It will take decades to spell out all the details, but sufficient evidence is already in place that it is no longer plausible to base claims to the historical Jesus on the Gospels or Acts."

* * * * * * * * *

II

IMPLANTED IN HELLENISTIC SOIL

Mimesis Criticism

From Wikipedia

en.wikipedia.org/wiki/Mimesis_Criticism

Criteria

In order to circumvent the capriciousness of subjectivity, MacDonald suggests six criteria for determining whether a claim for a mimetic connection between texts is reasonable: accessibility, analogy, density, order, distinctive traits, and interpretability. The first two criteria concern the status of the text used as a model ("ante-text"); the final four concern the later text that may have used the antetext.

- **Accessibility**: One must demonstrate that the author of the later text would have been reasonably able to access a copy of the text being imitated. Was the antetext well known or obscure at the time of the later text's composition?
- **Analogy**: If one text is discovered to imitate a certain antetext, it is probable that other texts have also done so. Are there examples of other authors using this antetext as a literary model?
- **Density**: The greater number of parallels one can induce between the two texts, the stronger one's case will be for a mimetic relationship between them.
- **Order**: The more frequently the parallels between the two texts follow the same order, the less likely it becomes that the parallels are just coincidental.
- **Distinctive Traits**: If there are parallels between two texts, but none of the parallels are anything but one would expect in their respective contexts, then it becomes difficult to argue for a mimetic connection. Especially helpful are non sequitur or other unusual elements present in the later text which parallel the proposed model. It is also typical for authors to use significant names to alert the reader to the textual interplay.
- **Interpretability**: A common motivation for imitating an earlier text is to rival that text, whether philosophically, theologically, politically, or otherwise. If one can determine such a motivation in a compelling fashion, then there is a stronger case for imitation.

Mimesis in Early Christianity

New Testament

Two examples of imitation within the New Testament will be outlined. The first pertains to Luke's use of 1 Kings 17 as a literary model. The second outlines Luke's imitation of Homer's *Odyssey* 10-12 in Acts 20.

1 Kings 17:9-24	Luke 7:11-16
Elijah went to Sarepta.	Jesus went to Nain.
Elijah saw a widow after approaching the city gate. Her son later becomes sick and dies.	Jesus saw a widow's dead son after approaching the city gate being carried out on a bier.
Elijah told the widow, "Give me your son."	Jesus told the widow, "Do not weep."
Elijah took the corpse and reproached God.	Jesus took the corpse and spoke directly to him.
The dead son revived and cried out (lxx).	The dead son sat up and began to speak.
"And he gave him to his mother."	"And he gave him to his mother."
The widow praised Elijah as "a man of God."	The crowd glorified God, calling Jesus "a great prophet."

One can justifiably argue that Luke used 1 Kings 17:9-24 as a model for Luke 7:11-16 because it meets the criteria of **mimesis criticism**. **Criterion 1** (**Accessibility**): Luke cites this very story in Luke 4:25-26. **Criterion 2** (**Analogy**): Mark provides an analogous imitation of 1 Kings 17 with his story about the raising of Jairus' daughter (Mark 5:35-43). **Criteria 3** (**Density**), **4** (**Order**), and **5** (**Distinctive Traits**) can be identified in the above table. The most important aspect for **criterion 5** is the identical Greek wording for "And he gave him to his mother." **Criterion 6** (**Interpretability**): Luke improves upon his model in the following ways. In 1 Kings, the widow initiates the miracle by castigating Elijah for causing her son's death; in Luke, Jesus is the one to initiate the miracle. In 1 Kings, Elijah then reproaches God, asking if God has "brought calamity even upon the widow with whom I am staying, by killing her son" (17:20); in Luke, Jesus does not blame God for the boy's death but instead has compassion for her. In 1 Kings, it is the Lord who raises the boy, not Elijah; in Luke, it is Jesus himself. In 1 Kings, only the widow responds to the miracle; in Luke, a "large crowd" responds positively.

Odyssey 10-12	Acts 20:5-12
Odysseus and his crew left Troy and sailed back to Achaea.	Paul and his crew arrive at Troas en route to Jerusalem from Achaea.
The account is narrated in the first-person plural.	The account is narrated in the first-person plural.
After a sojourn, Odysseus and his crew ate a meal.	After a sojourn, Paul and the believers there ate a meal.
Disaster came at night.	Disaster came at midnight.
The crew slept in Circe's "darkened halls."	"There were many lamps in the room upstairs where they were meeting."
The narrator switches to the third person.	The narrator switches to the third person.
"There was a man, Elpenor, the youngest..."	"A young man named Eutychus, who was sitting in the window."
Elpenor fell into "sweet sleep."	Eutychus fell into a "deep sleep."
"[He] fell down from the roof. His neck / broke from the spine, and his soul went down to the house of Hades."	"He fell to the ground three floors below and was picked up dead. But Paul went down,...and said, 'Do not be alarmed, for his soul is in him.'"
Associates fetched the body, dead.	Associates took up the body, alive.
Elpenor was not buried until dawn.	Eutychus was not raised alive until dawn.

In the same way, one can justifiably argue that Luke has used the story of Elpenor from *Odyssey* 10-12 as a model for his account of Eutychus in Acts 20:5-12 using the criteria. **Criterion 1** (**Accessibility**): Books 10-12 of *Odyssey* were among the most popular in antiquity. **Criterion 2** (**Analogy**): Among the many imitations of these books in antiquity, Virgil's *Aeneid* contains two, the stories about Palinurus and Misenus. **Criteria 3** (**Density**), **4** (**Order**), and **5** (**Distinctive Traits**) can be seen to be met by referring to the above table. Of particular significance is Luke's name choice: Homer often called Elpenor "unlucky" (*Odyssey* 11.61, 76, 80); Luke's Eutychus literally means "good fortune." Furthermore, the raising of Luke's Eutychus occurs in the Troad, the site of the Trojan War. **Criterion 6** (**Interpretability**): Luke emulates Homer in the following ways. Elpenor fell to his death because he was in a drunken stupor; Eutychus appeared to die after falling asleep (out a window) while listening to Paul preach deep into the night. Odysseus was unaware of Elpenor's misfortune; Paul knew immediately about Eutychus' fall and also that "his soul [was] still in him." Later in Homer's story, Elpenor's body was buried at dawn; at dawn, the other believers lifted up Eutychus alive.

In addition to imitating the Septuagint and Homer's *Odyssey*, MacDonald proposes that Mark's Gospel and Luke-Acts used the following literary models: Homer's *Iliad*, several *Homeric Hymns*, Euripides' *Bacchae* and *Madness of Heracles*, and dialogues by Plato and Xenophon about Socrates.

The Homeric Epics and the Gospel of Mark

Dennis R. MacDonald; Yale University, 2000

Reviewed by Richard Carrier

An Incredible Book

This is an incredible book that must be read by everyone with an interest in Christianity. MacDonald's shocking thesis is that the *Gospel of Mark* is a deliberate and conscious anti-epic, an inversion of the Greek "Bible" of Homer's *Iliad* and *Odyssey*, which in a sense "updates" and Judaizes the outdated heroic values presented by Homer, in the figure of a new hero, Jesus (whose name, of course, means "Savior").

When I first heard of this I assumed it would be yet another intriguing but only barely defensible search for parallels, stretching the evidence a little too far – tantalizing, but inconclusive. What I found was exactly the opposite. MacDonald's case is thorough, and though many of his points are not as conclusive as he makes them out to be, when taken as a cumulative whole the evidence is so abundant and clear it cannot be denied. And being a skeptic to the thick, I would never say this lightly. Several scholars who reviewed or commented on it have said this book will revolutionize the field of Gospel studies and profoundly affect our understanding of the origins of Christianity, and though I had taken this for hype, after reading the book, I now echo that very sentiment myself.

Background and Purpose of *Mark*

MacDonald begins by describing what scholars of antiquity take for granted: anyone who learned to write Greek in the ancient world learned from Homer. Homer was the textbook. Students were taught to imitate Homer, even when writing on other subjects, or to rewrite passages of Homer in prose, using different vocabulary. Thus, we can know for certain that the author of Mark's Gospel was thoroughly familiar with the works of Homer and well-trained in recasting Homeric verse into new prose tales. The status of Homer in basic education remained throughout antiquity, despite the fact that popular and intellectual sentiment had been sternly against the ethics and theology of his epics since the age of Classical Greece. Authors from Plato (c. 400 BCE) to Plutarch (c. 100 CE) sought to resolve this problem by "reinterpreting" Homer as allegory, or by expunging or avoiding offensive passages, neither of which was a perfect solution.

For the Latin language, the opportunity was afforded for Virgil to solve this problem by recasting the Homeric epic into Roman form, exhibiting Roman ideals and creating more virtuous heroes and gods. Likewise, borrowing and recasting from Homer is evident in numerous works of fiction, which often had a religious flavor, and were proliferating in the very same period as the Gospels. One prominent example (mentioned but not emphasized by MacDonald) is the *Satyricon* of Petronius, which can be decisively dated prior to 66 CE, and thus is most likely earlier than any known Gospel, and since this novel was in Latin (and a satire), it is almost certain that many undatable Greek novels, which surely originated the form, long precede this. So rewriting Homer to depict new religious ideas and values was a standard phenomenon. In MacDonald's words, "Homer was in the air that Mark's readers breathed" (p. 8), and all the more so among Mark's Gentile audience. But to smartly recast Homer into a new Greek form, reflecting contemporary Græco-Jewish ideals, was a task simply waiting to be done. If MacDonald is right, this is what Mark set out to do. So much is clear: the motive, ability, and inspiration were certainly present, and MacDonald rapidly presents all the evidence, backing it up with copious and scholarly endnotes in chapter 1.

Why? In MacDonald's words, Mark "thoroughly, cleverly, and strategically emulated" stories in Homer and the Old Testament, merging two great cultural classics, in order "to depict Jesus as more compassionate, powerful, noble, and inured to suffering than Odysseus" (p. 6), and hence "the earliest evangelist was not writing a historical biography, as many interpreters suppose, but a novel, a prose anti-epic of sorts" (p. 7). In particular, the differences between Mark and Homer need no explanation: the differences are the point, the very objective of the later author. Some of those differences are also the obvious result of a change of scene from the ancient Mediterranean to near-contemporary, Roman-occupied Judæa, or of literary borrowing from Jewish texts. Some may reflect some sort of traditional or historical core story, though it is almost impossible to tell when. Instead, it is the similarities that "cry out for explanation," and contemporary apologists must now begin to address this issue.

Of particular use, for all those who want to develop (or attack) theories of literary borrowing – in the Gospels or elsewhere – is the set of six criteria for identifying textual influence outlined by MacDonald at the end of his first chapter, though based on the previous work of Thomas Brodie, and demonstrated quite effectively on a passage in *Acts*, which MacDonald has subsequently expanded in *Does the New Testament Imitate Homer? Four Cases from the Acts of the Apostles* (Yale University Press 2003). Though no one of these criteria alone carries very much weight, the more criteria that are met in a single instance, the stronger the case. However, one caveat MacDonald does not provide is in regard to his criterion of order. In many cases, matching sequences of passages or themes is indeed significant. However, some cases of matching sequence are such that any other sequence would be logically impossible. Therefore, correlation of this kind can in some cases be coincidence. Nevertheless, even engaging this caution, the sequential evidence MacDonald presents is very often, taken as a whole, not coincidental. Likewise, it should be known that much of Mark's use of Homer is to shape and detail an otherwise non-Homeric story, and the task of deciding what that core story is, or whether this core story in any given case is a Biblical emulation, or a historical fact, or a legend, or something of the author's deliberate creation, or any combination thereof, is not something MacDonald even intends to undertake in this book, although he makes some suggestions in his concluding paragraphs.

Modeling Odysseus

The *Odyssey* is rife with the theme of the suffering hero, and MacDonald builds a solid case in chapter 2 for the philosophical veneration of Odysseus as the best example of a man. If Jesus could be made to one-up and even replace Odysseus, Mark would achieve a literary and moral coup. And there are in the overall story obvious if not overly-telling similarities: "Both [men] faced supernatural opposition. . . . Each traveled with companions unable to endure the hardships of the journey, and each returned to a home infested with rivals who would attempt to kill him as soon as they recognized him," and "both heroes returned from Hades alive" (p. 17). Some parallels are a little more startling but less significant to the historian than to the literary critic: the parable of the Wicked Tenants (*Mk. 12:1-12*), and the passage capturing the famous phrase "for you do not know when the master of the house will come" (*Mk. 13:34-35*), both evoke the image of Odysseus returning in disguise to surprise the suitors who have turned his house into a den of sin (MacDonald develops this theme further in chapter 5, and again in chapter 14, and in the conclusion). Do not be like them, Mark is saying to his readers. But of course Jesus himself could have said that, intending the very same allusion. Examples like these can make good material for sermons, and serve well the connoisseurs of visionary prose, yet don't really prove whether Mark has himself deliberately crafted the story. But in conjunction with what follows, this becomes part of a cumulative case for Mark's inversion of Homer.

How many knew, for instance, that Odysseus was also a carpenter? The companions are another general link with the *Odyssey*. MacDonald points out how Mark is the harshest evangelist in his treatment of the disciples, while the others sometimes go out of their way to omit or alter this disparagement when they borrow from Mark. Why were the disciples such embarrassing nitwits, "greedy, cowardly, potentially treacherous, and above all foolish" (p. 20)? As history, it is hardly credible. As a play on Homer, it makes perfect sense: for the companions of Odysseus were exactly like this. Homer cleverly employed the ineptitudes of the crew to highlight the virtues of Odysseus, making him appear even more the hero, enhancing his "wisdom, courage, and self-control" (p. 23). MacDonald briefly explores five other general similarities between the two "entourages" in chapter 3, including the fact that in the one story we have sailors, while in the other, fishermen – who do a lot of going about in boats, even though the vast majority of Judæa is dry land (and the whole of Galilee is landlocked).

Chief among these similarities is the comparison between Peter and Eurylochus. Both spoke on behalf of all the followers, both challenged the "doomsday predictions" of their master to their own peril, both were accused by their leader of being under the influence of an evil demon, and both "broke their vows to the hero in the face of suffering" – in effect, both "represent[ed] the craven attitude toward life" (pp. 22-23). Again, this could be a mere veneer woven through an otherwise true story by Mark, and some of MacDonald's ideas (such as developed in chapter 4) are intriguing but too weak to do much with. But it is true that both epics announce from the start a focus on a single individual, both center on a king and his son reestablishing authority over a kingdom, both involve an inordinate amount of events and travel at sea. Both works begin by summoning their own Muse: Homer, the Muse herself; Mark, the prophet Isaiah. In both stories, the son's patrimony is confirmed by a god in the form of a bird, and this confirmation prepares the hero to face an enemy in the very next scene: Telemachus, the suitors; Jesus, Satan. And eventually the odd links keep accumulating, and compel one to question the whole thing.

Stark Examples

"Once the evangelist linked the sufferings of Jesus to those of Odysseus, he found in the epic a reservoir of landscapes, characterizations, type-scenes, and plot devices useful for crafting his narrative" (p. 19). Of course, all throughout, MacDonald points out coinciding parallels with the Old Testament and other Jewish literature, a project he has since expanded in *Two Shipwrecked Gospels* (SBL 2012), but even these parallels have been molded according to a Homeric model in every case he examines. Consider two of the many mysteries MacDonald's theory explains, and these are even among the weakest parallels that he identifies in the book:

- Why do the chief priests need Judas to identify Jesus in order to arrest him? This makes absolutely no sense, since many of their number had debated him in person, and his face, after a triumphal entry and a violent tirade in the temple square, could hardly have been more public. But MacDonald's theory that Judas is a type of Melanthius solves this puzzle: Melanthius is the servant who betrays Odysseus and even fetches arms for the suitors to fight Odysseus – just as Judas brings armed guards to arrest Jesus – and since none of the suitors knew Odysseus, it required Melanthius to finally identify him. MacDonald also develops several points of comparison between the suitors and the Jewish authorities. Thus, this theme of "recognition" stayed in the story even at the cost of self-contradiction. Of note is the fact that Homer names Melanthius with a literary point in mind: for his name means "The Black One," whereas Mark seems to be maligning the Jews by associating Melanthius with Judas, whose name is simply "Judah," i.e. the kingdom of the Jews, after which the Jews as a people, and the region of Judæa, were named.
- Why does Pilate agree to free a prisoner as if it were a tradition to do so? Such a practice could hardly have been approved by Rome, since any popular rebel leader who happened to be in custody during the festival would always escape justice. And given Pilate's reputation for callous ruthlessness and disregard for Jewish interests, it is most implausible to have him participating in such a self-defeating tradition – a tradition for which there is no other evidence of any kind, not even a precedent or similar practice elsewhere. But if Barabbas is understood as the type of Irus, Odysseus' panhandling competitor in the hall of the suitors, the story makes sense as a clever fiction. Both Irus and Barabbas were scoundrels, both were competing with the story's hero for the attention of the enemy (the suitors in one case, the Jews in the other), and both are symbolic of the enemy's culpability.

Of course, Barabbas means "son of the father," and thus is an obvious pun on Christ himself. Barabbas also represents the violent revolutionary, as opposed to the very different kind of savior in Jesus (the real "Savior", the literal meaning of the name 'Jesus'). On the other hand, Irus was a nickname derived from a goddess (Iris), and MacDonald fails to point out that her name means "rainbow," which to Mark would have meant the sign from God that there would never again be a flood (*Ge. 9:12-13*). Moreover, Irus' real name was Arnæus, "the Lamb." What more perfect model for Mark? The Jews thus choose the wrong "son of the father" who represents the Old Covenant (symbolized by the rainbow, and represented by the ideal of the military messiah freeing Israel), as well as the scapegoat (the lamb) sent off, bearing the people's sins into the wilderness, while its twin is sacrificed (*Lev. 16:8-10, 23:27-32, Heb. 8-9*). MacDonald's own analysis is actually confirmed by this additional parallel that he missed, and that is impressive.

MacDonald goes on to develop many similar points that not only scream of Homer's being on Mark's mind, but also explain strange features of *Mark*. The list is surprisingly long:

Why did Jesus, who taught openly and performed miracles everywhere, nevertheless try to keep everything a secret?

Why did Jesus stay asleep in a boat during a deadly storm?

Why did Jesus drown two thousand pigs?

Why does Mark invent a false story about John the Baptist's execution, one that implicates women?

Why are the disciples surprised that Jesus can multiply food even when they had already seen him do it before?

Why does Jesus curse a fig tree for not bearing fruit out of season?

How does Mark know what Jesus said when he was alone at Gethsemane?

What is the meaning of the mysterious naked boy at Jesus' arrest?

Why does Jesus, knowing full well God's plan, still ask why God has forsaken him on the cross?

Why does Mark never once mention Mary Magdalene or the other two women at the crucifixion, or even Joseph of Arimathea, until after Jesus has died?

Why is the temple veil specifically torn "top to bottom" at Jesus' death?

Why is Joseph of Arimathea able to procure the body of a convict so soon from Pilate?

Why do we never hear of Joseph of Arimathea again?

Why does Jesus die so quickly?

Why do the women go to anoint Jesus after he is buried?

Why do they go at dawn, rather than the previous night when the Sabbath had already ended?

All these mysteries are explained by the same, single thesis. This is a sign of a good theory. With one theoretical concept, not only countless parallels are identified, but numerous oddities are explained. That is very unlikely to be due to chance. And there is evidence of so many plausible connections, that even though any one of them could perhaps with effort be argued away, the fact that there are *so many more* makes it increasingly unlikely that MacDonald is seeing an illusion. Finally, his entire theory is plausible within the context of what we can deduce to have been Mark's cultural and educational background.

Crescendo of Doom

MacDonald's book is built like a crescendo: as one reads on, the cases not only accumulate, they actually get better and better, clearer and clearer. In the story of the Gerasene swine (*Mk. 5:1ff.*) MacDonald finds that 18 verses have thematic parallels in the *Odyssey*, 13 of those in exactly the same order! And even with some of those out of order, the order is not random but is inverted, and thus a connection remains evident. In the story of Salome and the execution of John, MacDonald finds seven thematic parallels with the Murder of Agamemnon, all of them in the same order, and on top of that he details two other general parallels. And the two food miracles, forming a doublet in *Mark*, contain details that match a similar doublet of feasts in the *Odyssey*, and contain them in the same respective order: "Details in the [first] story of Nestor's feast not found in the [second] story of Menelaus appear in the [first] feeding of the five thousand and not in its twin," while, "details in the [second] story of Menelaus not found in the [first] story of Nestor appear in the [second] feeding of the four thousand and not in the first story," so that "the chances of these correspondences deriving from accident are slim" (p. 85).

These examples of a connection between Mark and Homer are far more dense than the two examples I detailed earlier, and cannot be explained away even by the most agile of thinkers. Consider the last case, which even has the fewest parallels relative to the other two: in the first feasts, the main characters go by sea, but in the second, by land; in the first, only men attend (even though there is no explanation in *Mark* of why this should be), but in the second there is no distinction; in the first, the masses assemble into smaller groups, and lie on soft spots, but not in the second; more attend the first than the second (and the numbers are about the same: 5000 in *Mark*, 4500 in Homer). On the other hand, in the second feasts, unlike the first, someone asks the host a discouraging question and yet the host shows compassion anyway – in *Mark*, this is particularly strange, since after the first miracle the disciples have no excuse to be surprised that Jesus can multiply food, so the doubting question can only be explained by the Homeric parallel; finally, in the second feasts, as opposed to the first, there are two sequential courses – bread, then meat. In both authors, the feasts serve an overt educational role: in the one case to educate the hero's son about hospitality, in the other to educate the disciples about Jesus' power and compassion, drawing attention to the difference in each story's moral values. There are even linguistic parallels – Homer's feasts were called "symposia" (drinking parties) even though that word usually referred to smaller gatherings; likewise, Mark writes that the first feast was organized by "symposia," despite the fact that only food is mentioned, not water or wine. Several of these details in *Mark*, as noted, are simply odd by themselves, yet make perfect sense when we see the Homeric model, and therein again lies the power of MacDonald's thesis.

MacDonald does similar work illuminating the Transfiguration, the healing of Bartimæus, the Hydropatesis (water-walk), the Marcan Apocalypse, the Triumphal Entry, the Anointing, the Passover Feast (including a definite connection with cannibalism that offers a possible ideological origin for the Eucharist as a transvaluation of Homer), the Prayer and Arrest at Gethsemane, the Crucifixion, the Burial, and some details of the Empty Tomb narrative. His theory provides an excellent reason to suppose that the naked boy at Jesus' arrest is the same as the boy the women find in the empty tomb – and he is a marker of resurrection: a type of the ill-fated Elpenor. Likewise, his theory puts a serious damper on the historicity of Joseph of Arimathea and the burial account in *Mark*: Joseph is a type of Priam, who rescued the body of Hector for burial in a similar way.

What I found additionally worthwhile is how MacDonald's theory illuminates the theme of "reversal of expectation" which so thoroughly characterizes the Gospels – not only in the parables of Jesus, where the theme is obvious, but in the very story itself. Though MacDonald himself does not pursue this in any detail, his book helped me to see it even more clearly. James and John, who ask to sit at the right and left of Jesus in his glory, are replaced by the two thieves at Jesus' crucifixion; Simon Peter, Jesus's right-hand man who was told he had to "deny himself and take up his cross and follow" (*Mk.8:34*), is replaced by Simon of Cyrene when it comes time to truly bear the cross; Jesus is anointed for burial *before* he dies; and when the women go to anoint him after his death, their expectations are reversed in finding his body missing. Later Gospels added even more of these reversals: for instance in Matthew Jesus' father, Joseph, is replaced by Joseph of Arimathea when the duty of burial arose – a duty that should have been fulfilled by the father; likewise, contrary to expectation, the Mary who laments his death and visits his tomb is not Mary his mother, but a prostitute; and while the Jews attack Jesus for healing and doing good on the Sabbath, they in turn hold an illegal meeting, set an illegal guard, and plot evil on the Sabbath, and then break the ninth commandment the next day. This theme occurs far too often to have been in every case historical, and its didactic meaning is made clear in the very parables of reversal told by Jesus himself, as well as, for instance, his teachings about family, or hypocrisy, and so on. These stories were crafted to show that what Jesus preached applied to the real world, real events, "the word made flesh."

Death and Resurrection

MacDonald's book concludes with an analysis of how Jesus as a character in *Mark* is also an inversion of Hector and Achilles in the *Iliad*. Both Jesus and Achilles knew they were fated to die and spoke of this fate often, but whereas Achilles chose his fate in exchange for "eternal fame," and for himself alone, Jesus chose it in exchange for "eternal life," for all humankind. This is one among many examples of how Mark has updated the values in Homer, highlighting this fact by crafting his narrative in deliberate imitation of Homer's epics. In a similar fashion, while the death of Hector doomed Troy to destruction, Jesus' death doomed the Temple to destruction. According to MacDonald, these themes and others guide Mark's construction of the passion narrative, and though borrowing from the Old Testament and other Jewish texts in the passion account is far more prevalent than anywhere else in his Gospel, there is still a play on the *Iliad* evident in various details.

For example, MacDonald finds more than 11 parallels between Mark's account of the crucifixion and the death of Hector, all but one of those in the same order (and that one exception is in inverted order), and 11 more parallels between Mark's account of the burial of Jesus and Homer's account of the burial of Hector, all in the same order. It is notable that resurrection, *anastasia*, was a theme in the *Iliad*: the concept appears three times, twice in declarations of its impossibility, once in a metaphor for Hector's survival of certain death. It thus contained a fitting challenge that Mark was happy to answer with a simple prose epic that everywhere flaunted the fact that *anastasia* was indeed possible, and real. While Hector, Elpenor, and Patroclus were all burned and buried at dawn, the tomb of Jesus was empty at dawn; while the *Iliad* and *Odyssey* were epics about mortality, the Gospel was an epic about immortality.

The Ending of *Mark*

I have one point of criticism for chapter 21, where MacDonald diverges from his central thesis to explain why Mark ends his Gospel as he does. MacDonald proposes an explanation from the historical context of the author. It is quite likely that many Christians were killed, and the original Jerusalem church destroyed, in the Jewish War of 66-70 CE. MacDonald in several places relates how Mark most likely wrote his Gospel after the conclusion of the war (there are, to be sure, ample references that assume this, as well as that the world would end soon thereafter – cf. especially MacDonald's third appendix). So Mark, MacDonald argues, was faced with explaining why Jesus had not forewarned his disciples to evacuate Judæa. Mark's explanation, so the theory goes, is that Jesus did warn them, but they never heard the warning – in particular, they were supposed to go to Galilee after the resurrection to see Jesus, but the women failed to report this to the disciples and so they never went (and this tactic also allows the disciples to get off the hook: those at fault were mere fickle women).

The problem with this theory should be obvious: it is not the fact that it fails to explain how Mark could know the story if no one told it – for this did not stop him from relating what Jesus said in private when no witnesses were at hand, nor did it stop Matthew from relating secret conversations of the Jews – rather, the problem is that it fails to explain how Christianity started. Even assuming Mark is inventing this account apologetically, how did Mark imagine that the resurrection ever began to be preached if no one was ever told about the empty tomb and no one saw the risen Jesus, even in visions or dreams? Since the earliest accounts, in Paul, clearly suggest *post mortem* sightings of Jesus, and even tie these to the origin of the Gospel itself (and I have in mind the revelation to Paul mentioned in Galatians, and the visions to Peter and the others mentioned in *1 Corinthians*), it does not seem plausible for Mark to expect his readers to reject this tradition, as would be required for his alleged hidden point even to be noticed, much less understood. I thus cannot buy MacDonald's theory on this point.

My own hypothesis is that Mark ended the Gospel thus in order to set up a pretext for why little of *his* particular story had been heard in the Christian community until he wrote it down. If we suppose that the resurrection as preached by Paul was of a spiritual nature, and therefore had nothing to do with empty tombs, then to suddenly disseminate such a story would raise eyebrows unless the author were ready with an explanation. And by building an explanation into his story he essentially covers himself. It is possible that Mark originally concluded his tale with an assertion that the women later reported the story to him, an ending that would be struck out and replaced to suit the new physicalist Christology that would follow, as well as in support of the new reliance on apostolic authority which seems never to have been a concern for Mark. But it is also possible that this would not have mattered. The faithful would not necessarily be too bothered about Mark's sources, since Revelation itself could always provide a source (in his letter to the Galatians, Paul himself claimed he learned the Gospel through direct revelation from God). Even if they were to ask, Mark or the sellers of his story could easily have provided persuasive oral explanations to satisfy any believer, who would be more than ready to believe anything that agreed with their values and doctrine and which glorified and magnified the power of their beloved Lord. Ultimately, if Mark invented the empty tomb, he may also have inadvertently caused the invention of a physical resurrection – since an empty tomb, though meant as a symbol, if taken as a fact could imply a physical resurrection, leaving room for future evangelists to spin the yarn further still.

Conclusion

What is especially impressive is the vast quantity of cases of direct and indirect borrowing from Homer that can be found in *Mark*. One or two would be interesting, several would be significant. But we are presented with countless examples, and this is as cumulative as a case can get. In the end, I came away from this book with a new appreciation for Mark, whose Gospel tends to be derided as the work of a rather poor, simple

Greek author. Though Mark's Greek is extremely colloquial, not at all in high literary style, this itself is surely a grand and ingenious transvaluation of Homer: whereas the great epics were archaic and difficult, only to be mastered by the educated elites, only to be understood completely by those with access to glossaries and commentaries and marked-up critical editions, Mark not only updated Homer's values and theology, but inverted its entire character as an elite masterpiece, by making his own epic simple, thoroughly understandable by the common, the poor, the masses, and lacking in the overt pretension and cleverness of poetic verse, written in plain, ordinary language. The scope of genius evident in Mark's reconstruction of Homeric motifs is undeniable and has convinced me that Mark was no simpleton: he was a literary master, whose achievement is all the greater in his choice of idiom – his "poor Greek" was deliberate and artful, as was his story.

Another theme that becomes apparent throughout this book is how quickly Christians lost touch with this allegorical meaning. Even the other Evangelists, when borrowing from *Mark*, stripped out the key and telling details and thus obviously missed the point; and only one other author, that of the *Acts of Andrew*, did anything overtly comparable in comprehensively recrafting Homer. By itself, this might be evidence against such a meaning actually being in *Mark*. But the evidence that this meaning is present is overwhelming on its own terms, and we can only conclude of early Christian ignorance, instead, that the real origins and message of the earliest Christians was all but lost even to the second or third generation. By the time there was a church in any significant sense, Christianity had been radically changed by the throngs of its converts, and, amidst the din of outsiders who stole the reigns, the very essence of that original Church of Jerusalem faded, powerless to survive under the mass of superstition and arrogance.

Having read this book, I am now certain that the historicity of the Gospels and *Acts* is almost impossible to establish. The didactic objectives and methods of the authors have so clouded any historical truth with literary motifs and allusions and parabolic tales that we cannot know what is fact and what fiction. I do not believe that this entails that Jesus was a myth, however – and MacDonald himself is not a mythicist, but assumes that something of a historical Jesus lies behind the fictions of *Mark*. Although MacDonald's book could be used to contribute to a mythicist's case, everything this book proves about *Mark* is still compatible with there having been a real man, a teacher, even a real "miracle worker" in a subjective sense, or a real event that inspired belief in some kind of resurrection, and so on, which was then suitably dressed up in allegory and symbol.

Nevertheless, the inevitable conclusion is that we have all but lost this history forever. The Gospels can no longer support a rational belief in anything they allege to have occurred, at least not without external, unbiased corroboration, which we do not have for any of the essential, much less supernatural details of the story. And if Alvar Ellegård is right (*Jesus One Hundred Years Before Christ* [Overlook Press 1999]), *Mark* was almost entirely fiction, written after the sack of Jerusalem to freeze in symbolic prose the metaphorical message of Christianity, a faith which began with a Jesus executed long before the Roman conquest, who then appeared in visions (like that which converted Paul) a century later, in the time of Pilate, to inspire the new creed. What is important is not that this can be decisively proven – nothing can, as our information is too thin, too scarce, too unreliable to decisively prove anything about the origins of Christianity. What is important is that theories like Ellegård's can't be disproven, either – it is one among many distinctly possible accounts of what really happened at the dawn of Christianity, which MacDonald's book now makes even more plausible. And so long as it remains possible, even plausible, that the bulk of *Mark* is fiction, the contrary belief that it is fact can never be secure.

* * * * * * * * *

Osiris, Isis Lactans, and Horus
Hermitage Museum, St. Petersburg, Russia
Courtesy Wikipedia

III

NOURISHED UNDER EGYPTIAN SUN

Mary Lactans and Jesus

Amesbury Psalter, c. 1250 CE

Courtesy Wikipedia

Parallelomania*

by Samuel Sandmel

I encountered the term parallelomania, as I recall, in a French book of about 1830, whose title and author I have forgotten, in a context in which there were being examined certain passages in the Pauline epistles and in the *Book of Wisdom* that seem to have some resemblance, and a consequent view that when Paul wrote the *Epistle to the Romans*, a copy of the *Book of Wisdom* lay open before him, and that Paul in *Romans* copied generously from it. Three items are to be noted. One, that some passages are allegedly parallel; two, that a direct organic literary connection is assumed to have provided the parallels; and three, that the conclusion is drawn that the flow is in a particular direction, namely from *Wisdom* to Paul, and not from Paul to *Wisdom*. Our French author disputes all three points: he denies that the passages cited are true parallels; he denies that a direct literary connection exists; he denies that Paul copied directly from *Wisdom*, and he calls the citations and the inferences parallelomania. We might for our purposes define parallelomania as that extravagance among scholars which first overdoes the supposed similarity in passages and then proceeds to describe source and derivation as if implying literary connection flowing in an inevitable or predetermined direction.

---

*The opening paragraph of Samuel Sandmel's article, "Parallelomania", in the *Journal of Biblical Literature* 81 (1962): pp. 1-13. In a note on Sandmel's passing, Hershal Shanks wrote:

> Samuel Sandmel, a member of *Biblical Archaeology Review's* editorial advisory board and one of the world's leading Biblical scholars, died on November 4, 1979, at the age of 68.
>
> At the time of his death Sandmel was Professor of Religion at the University of Chicago Divinity School. He had just moved to Chicago earlier in the year. Previously he had taught for more than 26 years at Hebrew Union College in Cincinnati, Ohio.
>
> Professor Sandmel's scholarly interests and competence covered an enormous range. He is best known for his commentary entitled *The Hebrew Scriptures* (Oxford University Press, 1978). He served as general editor of the Oxford University Press Study Edition of the *New English Bible*.

* * * * * * * * *

Observations on John H.C. Pippy's *Egyptian Origin of the Book of Revelation**

Michael Lockwood

Samuel Sandmel's warning (see facing page) of "that extravagance among scholars which first overdoes the supposed similarity in passages and then proceeds to describe source and derivation as if implying literary connection flowing in an inevitable or predetermined direction" has, unfortunately, been taken by emboxed traditionalists as a warrant to summarily dismiss the work of any scholar who uses parallelisms in arguments which go against their traditionalism. This dismissiveness is apparent in the lack of scholarly reaction to Pippy's book, *Egyptian Origin of the Book of Revelation*, first published in 2009, revised in 2010, and issued in a second edition, 2011 – with no observable academic response!

Here are some of those parallels:

1. The opening scene in Egypt's *Book of the Dead*** (Chp. 30B) is extremely similar to the opening scene of *Rev. 1-2*. Practically all the main elements (knowledge of people's deeds, rebellious activities, etc.) in the letters to the seven churches (*Rev. 3-4*) are present in a group of six consecutive chapters in the Egyptian *Book of the Dead* plus one in the *Book of Caverns*. The structure of two of the letters has the same form as Egyptian sources. [ref. Pippy, p. 568]
2. The entire middle section of the 6th Division of ancient Egypt's *Amduat* is similar to the one describing the opening of the scroll in *Rev. 5:1-9*. Almost all characters and events follow the same order in both sources. [ref. p. 197]
3. The unusual scene describing the cries of the souls those slain in *Rev. 6:9-11* is remarkably similar to that depicting the cries of the souls slain in the 8th Division of the *Amduat*. [ref. p. 223]
4. Egyptian names with similar meanings as those of the tribes of Israel in *Rev. 7:4-8* are present in a single group of 24 characters in the *Amduat*. Also, most of the individual groups in the two sources have similar physical characteristics. [ref. pp. 125-126]
5. The scene describing the four angels and the four winds in *Rev. 7:1-3* bears an extraordinary resemblance to a scene prominently displayed on the wall of a tomb in Egypt's Valley of the Kings. [ref. p. 556]
6. Multitudes with palm branches in their hands described in *Rev. 7:9* are also shown in the 7th and 9th Divisions of the *Amduat*. [ref. p. 144]
7. Apocalyptic events in the *Book of Revelation*, taken as a whole, are those normally associated with an eruption of an island volcano. A number of events in Egyptian sources also describe a volcanic eruption which conforms with modern knowledge of an eruption in the Aegean Sea in the 17th century BCE [ref. p. 279]
8. In what is possibly the most remarkable grouping of parallels found, the 1st beast, 2nd beast and the image of the 1st beast in *Rev. 13* are not only clearly identified in the 4th Division of *Amduat*, but the order in which they appear and the events in which they are involved are in the same order in both sources. Even *Revelation's* use of the most enigmatic number, "666," for the name of the 1st beast has a very simple explanation when viewed from an ancient Egyptian perspective. [ref. pp. 391-393]
9. The capture of Apophis, the ancient serpent, illustrated in the 10th Division of the *Book of Gates* conforms with those described in the capture of Satan, the "ancient serpent" in *Rev. 20:1-3*. [ref. p. 475]
10. The 10th Division of Egypt's *Book of Gates* refers to the reign of the Lamb (the juvenile form of the sun-god Re) for a thousand year period, just as we find in *Rev. 20:2*. Similarities include martyrs (as in *Rev. 20:4-5*), the resurrected made priests (as in *Rev. 20:6*) and Satan's release from prison and his subsequent recapture (as in *Rev. 20:7-10*). [ref. pp. 475-493]
11. The judgment of the dead (*Rev. 20:11-15*) (including the great and the small), the opening of the **scrolls** (with an emphasis on those who had died by drowning), and of the resurrection and punishment of the wicked are all emphasized in Egypt's *Book of Night*. [ref. pp. 512 ff.]
12. The final picture in the *Book of Gates* contains practically all the elements of *Rev. 21:1-8*. For example: a new creation including a new heaven and earth, the arrival of a new holy city and the dwelling place of God and his faithful followers. *Revelation's* bride is readily identifiable as Egypt's "holy city". [ref. p. 517]
13. The physical description of the holy city in *Rev. 21:10* to *22:5* conforms with ancient Egypt's heavenly city – including the functions of its walls, the number of guarded gates and the river which runs through it with banks where various kinds of plants grow. [ref. pp. 529 ff.]

**Egyptian Origin of the Book of Revelation*, second edition (Raleigh, NC: J.H.C.P., Lulu Enterprises Inc., 2011).

Note**: The word 'book' can be misleading: *Revelation* speaks of a ***scroll and the Egyptian 'books' are ***not codices***.

I leave to accredited Egyptologists the critiquing of these thirteen groups of parallelisms and the many, many others which Pippy has indefatigably brought to our attention in his book. Instead, I aim to support Pippy's main proposal that *Revelation* was, indeed, in large part mimetically modeled on ancient Egyptian written works. And if this is so, then what are some interesting **H**ypothetico-**D**eductive **C**onsequences (**HDC**s) which can be drawn from his approach?

First HDC: Like the four canonical gospels, *Revelation* is also a meta-parable – a *literary* work – which has assumed the combined forms of 1) an apocalypse, 2) a multi-fold epistle, and 3) a multi-fold prophetic work. We shouldn't be fooled by the references to the historical cities, Ephesus, Smyrna, Pergamum, Thyatira, Sardis, Philadelphia, and Laodicea, or by references to historical groups, such as the Nicolaitans. These are merely part of a historical meta-narrative layer. As we have seen with the gospels, the "historical" meta-narrative layer is often not truly historical, and, in any case, it is swamped by the other, purely fictive meta-narrative layers.

Second HDC: Like the four canonical gospels, *Revelation* also has the following five major meta-narrative layers: [1] the Egyptian (from various ancient written sources), [2] the Judaic (*Septuagint*), [3] the Greek (Homer's epics), [4] the Buddhist (various Sanskrit, Pāli, and Chinese written works), and [5] the quasi- or pseudo-historical, often the imaginative reworking of assorted passage, lifted randomly from such historical writings as those of Philo of Alexandria or Flavius Josephus. Because this multi-layered style of literary creation would have required an exceedingly broad knowledge of different languages and cultures, we are led to conclude that *Revelation*, like the canonical gospels, was a product of Alexandria, Egypt, and that the author, "John", was not recording his "visions" on the island of Patmos, Greece – but, rather, we should look for a 'Patmos' somewhere in Egypt, and understand that the author was – or had been – a crypto-Buddhist ("Christian") literary scholar in the great Library / Serapæum of Alexandria.

The Second HDC's inference that there is a Buddhist meta-narrative layer in *Revelation* will, undoubtedly, be met with great skepticism by most readers of this book.

However, Edward Conze (1904-1979), who was one of the greatest translators of Buddhist works,[1] had, in 1959, noted "close verbal coincidences" between passages in *Revelation* and the great Mahāyāna work, the *Aṣṭasāhasrikā-Prajñāpāramitā-Sūtra* (*The Perfection of Wisdom in 8,000 Lines*):

> Occasionally we find close verbal coincidences between the Christian and the Mahāyāna scriptures. Just one instance must suffice. At the time when *The Revelation of St John* was written down in Greek in the Eastern Mediterranean, the Mahāyānists produced in the South of India one of their most revered books, *The Perfection of Wisdom in 8,000 Lines*. *Revelation* (v. 1 [*Rev. 5:1*]) refers to a book "closely sealed" with seven seals, and likewise *The Perfection of Wisdom* is called a book "sealed with seven seals". It is shown to a Bodhisattva by the name of "Everweeping" (*Sadāpradrudita*), and St John "weeps bitterly" (v. 4) because he sees no one worthy to open the book and to break its seals. This can be done by the Lamb alone, slaughtered in sacrifice (v. 9). In the same way, chapters 30 and 31 of the Mahāyāna book describe in detail how Everweeping slaughtered himself in sacrifice, and how he thereby became worthy of the 'Perfection of Wisdom' (see pp. 302-303). This parallel is remarkable not only for the similarities of the religious logic, but also for the fact that both the number seven and the whole notion of a "book with seven seals" point to the Judaeo-Mediterranean rather than to the Indian tradition. Here is a fruitful field for further study. [R.C. Zaehner (ed.), *Encyclopedia of the World's Religions*, London 1959, p. 293.]

Now, what may a parallelomaniac conclude from Conze's observation of "close verbal coincidences" between the "Christian" *Revelation* and the Buddhist *Perfection of Wisdom*? Sandmel's first requirement is certainly present (an alleged parallelism). But what of his second (a direct organic literary connection)? And what about the third (a conclusion that the direct flow is in a particular direction)? Conze concludes that the direction is from the Judæo-("Christian")-Mediterranean to the South Indian (Buddhist) tradition, rather than the other way around. Conze was clearly correct about the geographical direction of the flow of literary influence (from the eastern Mediterranean to Southern India). But what Conze did not realize was that the eastern Mediterranean source was from a *Buddhist* Sanskrit literary scholar who was – or had been – in Alexandria, and that it was in this sense 'flowing from Egypt back to South India'! In what sense was this scholar a crypto-Buddhist? Well, from the mid-third century BCE, the Buddhist communities in the West (peri-Mediterranean) had assimilated themselves to quasi-Judaic forms of organization. The Essenes in Palestine were considered by Josephus and others as forming one of the three prominent sects of Judaism. But we have seen how this so-called Jewish sect had actually evolved out of crypto-Buddhism. In fact, the Qumranites may have considered themselves, from the second century BCE, to be a reformed sect of Judaism rather than "crypto-Buddhists", though they prayed in the morning facing the rising sun, *with their backs to Jerusalem!* That is, they may have deliberately suppressed, in their own minds, their Buddhist heritage by the second or first centuries BCE. And they certainly kept it hidden from others.

The first century, CE, Egyptian Therapeutæ, however, had certainly not rejected or forgotten their Buddhist heritage. The proof of this is that their later fellow crypto-Buddhists, the four authors of the canonical gospels, were adept Sankritists! We can thus be certain that the Greek speaking Egyptian Therapeutæ, forerunners of the second century, CE, "Christian" evangelists, knew precisely their own Buddhist background!

An Even Earlier Story Mentioning a Scroll Sealed with Seven Seals

It may come as a surprise to learn that, even predating the *Revelation* and *The Perfection of Wisdom*, there is among the Dead Sea Scrolls a story involving a scroll which is sealed with seven seals. In *The Dead Sea Scrolls – Revised Edition: A New Translation* (2005), by Michael O. Wise, Martin G. Abegg, and Edward M. Cook, there is discussed an interesting passage in one of the "Dead Sea Scroll" Aramaic fragments of 4Q550 (line 5) which mentions "a scroll sealed with seven seals with the signet of Darius his father." This passage is part of "The Tale of Patireza and Bagasraw", a tale the authors say (p. 552) belongs to a genre called "court stories",

> tales set within the royal court of a foreign land in which members of a despised ethnic group (usually the ones telling the story) prove their worth or cleverness. Such is the tale of Joseph in the court of Pharaoh (*Gen. 38-50*) and also the stories about Daniel and his friends in the time of Nebuchadnezzar and his successors (*Dan. 1-6*; ca. 600-543 B.C.E.). The entire book of Esther is devoted to the story of how the pious Esther and her uncle Mordecai foil the plans of the evil Haman and save the Jews from genocidal destruction in the court of Ahasuerus (Xerxes) in the time of the Persian Empire (fifth century B.C.E.).

The authors go on to suggest:

> These tales do not exhaust the supply of court stories from the ancient Near East; other cultures had them too. But it also appears that Jews produced more tales of this sort than are preserved in the Bible, and one of them is The Tale of Patireza and Bagasraw. It takes place, like Esther, in the Persian court, and the king whose court provides the setting is also Xerxes. But what happen in this tale is not clear. Two main figures appear, Patireza and Bagasraw. Both names are Persian, and both men are rewarded by the Persian king for unspecified services, but it is not clear what their relationship is or even whether they belong to the same story. However, the following summary, though largely hypothetical, is consistent with the extant fragments and resembles the kind of plot that is normal in the court story.
>
> Patireza was in charge of making the royal garments for King Darius; at some point, Patireza was able to help Darius in some way, and the king recorded this favor in his records. When his son Xerxes learned of the episode, he decided to show favor to Patireza's son.
>
> The next paragraph is highly hypothetical, ending with this statement: "The king commands all to honor Bagasraw and to revere his God."

The whole passage (beginning on p. 553) which mentions the "scroll sealed with seven seals" is given below (with bolding added) after this heading:

> "*The Persian king discovers the service Patireza performed for his father.*"
>
> **4Q550**
>
> 3 . . . *At that very time*
>
> 4 *the king was patient and read all the records of his father. They were read before him, and among*
>
> 5 *the books was found* **a scroll sealed with seven seals with the signet of Darius his father**. *On the outside it said*
>
> 6 . . . *"Darius the king to those who exercise authority in the land, greeting."*
>
> 7 *It was opened and read, and the following was found written in it: "Darius the king*
>
> 8 *to the kings who will reign after me and to those who exercise authority, greeting.*
> *Let it be known to you that all oppression and deceit. . . ."*

The king decides to reward the family of Patireza. "Ushai king of Tamar" is not known elsewhere, but the name Ushai appears in several ancient inscriptions.

4Q550a

1 *. . . a man, therefore the king knows if there is . . .*

2 *and his good name will not perish and his loyalty will be rewarded . . .*

3 *the king asked, "Does Patireza have a son?" And they said . . .*

4 *the fear of the house of . . . fell on him . . .*

5 *Ushai king of Tamar and it will be given . . .*

6 *my house and my possessions to whatever may be given . . .*

7 *are you able to take upon yourself your father's business? . . .*

4Q550b

1 *. . . Ushai king of Tamar to Sharhata his wife . . .*

2 *. . . Patireza your father from the day that he stood over the work from before the king . . .*

3 *. . . with him and he served honestly and reliably before him . . .*

4 *. . . and Ushai said . . .*

5 *. . . clothe him in purple . . .*

Bagasraw promises to serve Bagoshi. A story of some kind of procession of gifts follows. In the end, Bagasraw receives all the benefits that were rightfully his.

4Q550c Col. 1

1 *For you know . . . in the sins of my fathers*

2 *that the committed before you . . . and I spent a long time . . . a man,*

3 *a Jew from the princes of the kingdom . . ., standing before him and* [[p. 554]] *asking . . . a good deed*

4 *the good man has done . . . what shall I do for you, since you know . . . What is possible*

5 *for a man like me to answer a man like you, standing in the place where you stand? . . .*

6 *However, whatever you want, command me, and you die, I will bury you . . .*

7 *dwelling in everything, it may be that you would bring my work before . . . all that . . .*

Col. 2

1 *. . . decreed . . . and the second ones passed . . .*

2 *. . . the plagues, and the third ones passed . . . in the clothing of the kingdom . . .*

3 *. . . a crown of gold on his head; and the fifth ones passed . . .*

4 *. . . he alone . . . and the sixth ones passed . . .*

5 *. . . all silver and all gold, all the possessions that belonged to Bagoshi, in double measure . . .*

6 *and the seventh ones passed . . . then Bagoshi came in peace to the court of the king . . .*

7 *. . . Bagoshi . . . was killed, then Bagasraw entered the court of the king . . .*

8 *so he took him by the hand . . . on his head . . . and he kissed him.*
He raised his voice and said, "Bagasraw, Bagasraw, from . . ."

The king recommends to his court and people the worship and respect of Bagasraw's God.

Col. 3

1 *. . . the Most High that you all revere and worship; He rules over all the earth. All who will, draw near in honor to . . .*

2 *. . . everyone who says anything bad about Bagasraw . . . shall be killed, so that there may be no . . .*

3 *. . . I forever . . . everything that is proper . . . twice. And the king said, "Let it be written . . .*

4 *. . . ruler . . . they are in the great court of the king . . .*

5 *. . . those who arise after Bagasraw will read in this book . . .*

6 *. . . who says anything bad, the bad shall come upon his head . . .*

– Edward M. Cook

* * * * * * * * *

With reference to *Revelation*, what may we learn from this Dead Sea Scroll "court story"?

As Edward Cook has noted, above:

1. This DSS story, like those of Joseph, Daniel, and Esther, is set within a royal court of a foreign land.
2. It involves members of a captured group of Jewish people, not free to return to their "homeland".
3. At times, the heroes of such stories are threatened with execution.
4. These heroes, however, through their wisdom, righteousness, and the divine assistance of their 'Most High' God, escape personal death as well as prevent the genocidal destruction of their fellow captives.
5. The kings, who were generally impressed with these Jewish leaders (in *Esther*, the king makes her his chief queen!), end up endorsing the Hebrew God as *the* supreme deity.

Revelation as a Grandiose 'Court Story'

Is *Revelation*, in fact, a grandiose 'Court Story'? *Revelation's* "foreign court" is the greatest of all courts, the court of 'The Most High' God, who sits on a heavenly throne, surrounded by twenty-four enthroned "elders" (Pippy, 90ff. & 58ff.) and "four living creatures" (*Rev. 4:2, 4, 6-7*):

> *2*There in heaven stood a throne, and on the throne sat one whose appearance was like the gleam of jasper
> and cornelian. . . . *4*In a circle about this throne were twenty-four other thrones, and on them sat twenty-
> four elders, robed in white and wearing crowns of gold. . . . *6*In the centre, round the throne itself were
> four living creatures, covered with eyes, in front and behind. *7*The first creature was like a lion, the
> second like an ox, the third had a human face, the fourth was like an eagle in flight. *8*The four living
> creatures, each of them with six wings, had eyes all over. . . .
>
> – *The New English Bible*

Where did John get his idea for this court scene? For one source, consider Ezekiel's vision of an enthroned heavenly figure together with "four living creatures":

> *5*In the fire was the semblance of four living creatures in human form. *6*Each had four faces and each four
> wings. . . . *10*Their faces were like this: all four had the face of a man [facing front] and the face of a lion
> on the right, on the left the face of an ox and [facing back] the face of an eagle.
>
> *Ezekiel 1:5-6, 10 – NEB*

Ezekiel's "four living creatures in human form" seem to be indebted to Egyptian images of the four sons of Horus appearing together just in front of the enthroned Osiris. One famous vignette, in chp. 30B of Ani's *Book of the Dead*[2] (the actual scroll was created c. 1250 BCE!), shows the miniature figures of Horus's sons standing in a line on a lotus flower, just in front of a large seated image of Osiris 'Lord of Eternity'. Their names, from the foremost, backward: 1) Imsety, in human form; 2) Hapi, with a human body and a baboon's head; 3) Duamutef, with a human body and a jackal's head; 4) Qebehsenuef, with a human body and a hawk's head. Ezekiel transformed these 'four living creatures' (Egyptian godlings) into four identical twins, each having four faces: a man's facing forward; a lion's, to the right; an ox's, to the left, and an eagle's, facing backwards. Each of these 4 faces (or the whole creature), in Christian times, became emblematic of one of the four evangelists. One among other combinations is: *man* (Matt); *lion* (Mark); *ox* (Luke); *eagle* (John).

Metropolitan Museum of Art, Ivory plaque, 11th century, southern Italy.

Depicting, in the center, Lamb of God;

Matthew, winged *man*;

Mark, winged *lion*;

Luke, winged *ox*;

John, an *eagle*.

This is the central medallion on the face of a *rhipidium* (Lat.) / *ripida* (Ital.), a fan-like decorative gold and silver head of a staff. Matthew's emblem, in the center, is an anthropomorphic angel/seraph having four wings (closer to Ezekiel's six-winged 'living creature' than the ivory plaque's two-winged 'living creatures'). A lion's head and one of its wings is to the angel's right; and an ox's head and one of its wings is to the angel's left. On the reverse side of this central medallion there is an image of John's eagle.

Rhipidium, gold & silver, dt. 1497 A.D., Patna Monastery, Romania

Just as Joseph, Daniel, and Esther are seen as suffering internment in a foreign land, the author of *Revelation* views followers of Christ as living in a 'foreign land' – in this, our earthly, evil world. (As Jesus said: "My kingdom is not of this world" – *John 18:36*.) All humans on earth are, in a sense, "imprisoned" (à la Gnosticism, Plato). Those who turn away from the 'dark' ways of the world (selfishness, hatred, pride, greed, lust, etc.) and devote themselves to 'enlightened' righteousness (Dharma), will be resurrected and, on the final 'Judgment Day', attain heaven. While those who have wallowed in the 'dark' ways of the world will, on that dreadful day, be condemned to 'second death' in the 'Lake of Fire' (two truly Egyptian concepts!):

> *6*'A draught from the water-springs of life will be my free gift to the thirsty. *7*All this is the victor's heritage; and I will be his God and he shall be my son. *8*But as for the cowardly, the faithless, and the vile, murderers, fornicators, sorcerers, idolaters, and liars of every kind, their lot will be the second death, in the lake that burns with sulphurous flames.' – *Rev. 21:6-8, NEB*

Keep in mind that, for Buddhists, hell and heaven are merely temporary way stations between rebirths. Their ultimate goal is Nirvāṇa – freedom from rebirth. By the second century, CE, however, some crypto-Buddhist "Christians" had dropped the belief in rebirth and had, thus, ended up with the prospect of either eternal heaven or eternal hell. No 'way stations', these!

Now, what other ways can we tie *Revelation* to Egyptian religious views? Well, consider the following propositions which I think no Egyptologist would call false:

1) The Egyptian god Osiris, at times, is identified with the waters of the Nile.

2) His wife, the goddess Isis causes the annual flood out of the abundance of the tears that she sheds at the death of her husband, Osiris, killed by his evil brother, Seth.

We have, here, in this Egyptian meta-mythology, a very simple explanation of the strange and otherwise inexplicable name, 'Everweeping' (Sanskrit, '*Sadāprarudita*'), of the main character of the *Aṣṭasāhasrikā-Prajñāpāramitā-Sūtra* (*The Perfection of Wisdom in 8,000 Lines*), together with the description of the profuse weeping of John, in *Revelation 5:6*. The Nile river (Isis' "weeping") is an ever-flowing river, even in its lowest level and driest season.

3) Osiris, at times, is identified with the Sun (Re).[3]

4) Osiris, at other times, together with Isis, is identified with the Moon.

Which is it, then? Both. First, let us agree that Isis is the Moon. But the light of the Moon is the Sun's! A resolution of this conundrum is to consider that the Moon together with its Light is *androgynous* (like the Indian deity Ardhanārīśvara):

5) The Moon (Isis/Osiris) has a 14th of Osiris's light-body sliced off, every day, for fourteen days (the waning fortnight), by brother Seth, the 'Prince of Darkness and Desert Aridity', before Osiris's light-body is totally lost to darkness. Fortunately, sister/wife Isis finds and restores, every day, a 14th of his light-body, for fourteen days (the waxing fortnight), until we see, again, the full light (Osiris) of the Moon (Isis). However, there is a dark blotch even on the full Moon – which, according to the mythology, is due to Osiris's missing phallus (when that 14th-part of Osiris was thrown into the Nile river by brother Seth, it was, unfortunately swallowed by a fish and lost forever).

The basis of *Revelation's* heptamania should be traced back to the Egyptian time-keeping importance of the moon with its 4 x 7 rhythm – as expressed in the above mythology – long, long antedating the Hebrew Bible and, of course, *Revelation*.

In the Chronicle Books' 2005 edition of Ani's *Book of the Dead*, Ogden Goelet, in his commentary on the illustration of the enthroned Osiris (Plate 4) notes the following (p. 156):

> The pattern on the garment which Osiris wears may represent fish scales, a possible reference to the way in which Osiris drowns and gets eaten by a fish.

For logical reasons, I beg to differ with the distinguished Egyptologist. In the preceding paragraph (same page) he also says that:

> Osiris's audience chamber is surmounted by the recumbent mummiform figure of the hawk-headed god Sokar, originally the chief god of the vast Old Kingdom necropolis at Saqqara and a major deity of the Egyptian afterlife. During the New Kingdom, Sokar plays an important role . . . illustrating the nighttime journey of the sun. . . .

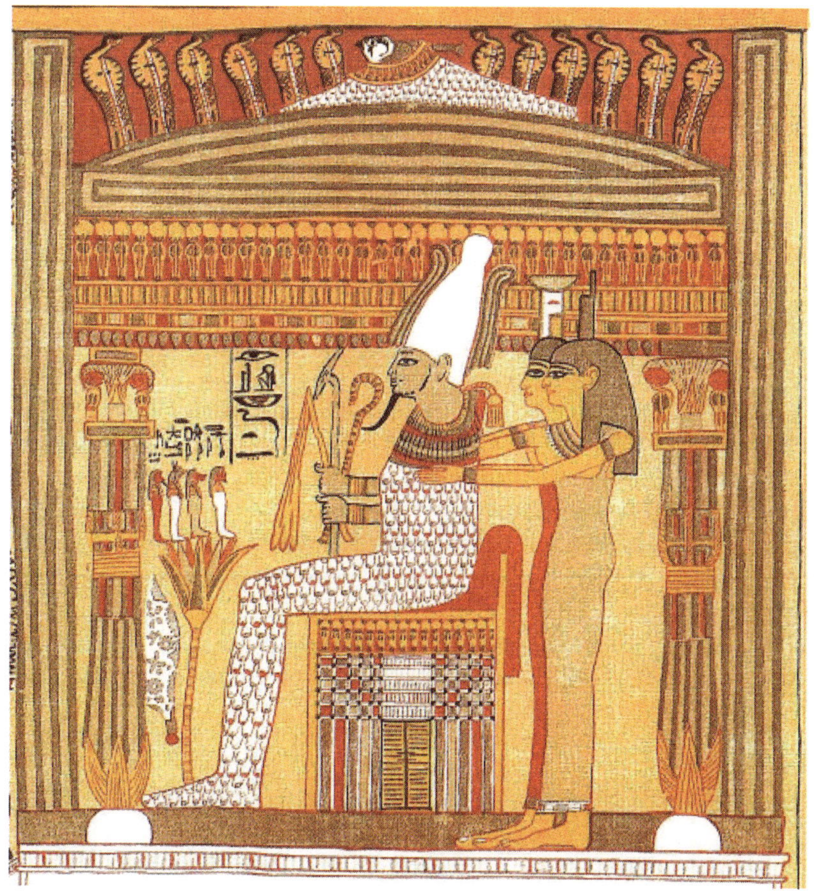

Osiris in his audience chamber – detail of Plate 4 – Ani's Book of the Dead

This mummiform figure of Sokar (in Plate 4) is shown enwrapped in exactly the same pattern which Goelet would interpret as fish scales. But what does Sokar have to do with fish scales? My suggestion is to turn to *Revelation 4:6*, to discover the real meaning of this pattern (emphasis added):

> 6 In the centre, round the throne itself were four living creatures, *covered with eyes, in front and behind.*

The pattern on Osiris's garment and Sokar's enwrapped body certainly looks more like myriad eyes than fish scales. Furthermore, it would be more appropriate to cover these two embodiments of the 'All-Seeing" sun-god with a multitude of eyes, than with fish scales.

This interpretation strengthens the connection between *Revelation* and Egyptian mythology.

Rivka Ulmer, in *The Evil Eye in the Bible and in Rabbinic Literature* (Hoboken, NJ: KTAV Publishing House, 1994), p. 23, writes:

> [T]he angel of death . . ., covered with eyes, is mentioned only once in the Talmud. The Hekhalot literature, however, contains numerous references to angelic princes whose bodies are completely covered with eyes.

The Jewish Encyclopedia (1906), under the heading 'ANGEL OF DEATH', mentions passages in the Koran (suras xxxii. 11, lxxix. 1), which describe the Angel of Death, Azrael, 'his whole body covered with eyes' (see 'Ab. Zarah 20b). When any of the living creatures on earth dies, "the corresponding eye bulges forth".

The 'eyes' covering Osiris and Sokar do look as though they were all "bulging forth"!

Endnotes

[1]The Buddhist scholar, Jan Nattier, has recently called Conze "the foremost Western scholar of the *Prajñāpāramitā* literature", in her article, "The Heart Sūtra: A Chinese Apocryphal Text?", *Journal of the International Association of Buddhist Studies*, Vol. 15, No. 2 (1992), p. 166.

[2]*The Egyptian Book of the Dead: The Book of Going Forth by Day: Being The Papyrus of Ani (Royal Scribe of the Divine Offerings)*, ed. Eva von Dassow, trans. Raymond O. Faulkner & Ogden Goelet, Jr. (San Francisco, CA: Chronicle Books LLC, 2nd ed. 2005 / 1998 / 1st ed. 1994).

[3]*Ibid.*, p. 132: (chp. 181 of *The Theban Recension of The Book of Going Forth by Day*, translated by Raymond O. Faulkner): "Hail to you [Osiris], Foremost of the Westerners, Wennefer, Lord of the Sacred Land! You have appeared in glory like Re, and behold, he has come to see you and to rejoice at seeing your beauty.

His sun-disk is your sun-disk;
His rays are your rays;
His crown is your crown;
His greatness is your greatness;
His appearings are your appearings;
His beauty is your beauty;
His majesty is you majesty;
His savor is your savor;
His extent is your extent;
His seat is your seat;
His throne is your throne;
His heritage is your heritage;
His panoply is your panoply;
His destiny is you destiny;
His West is your West;
His goods are your goods; . . ."

* * * * * * * * *

Observations on D.M. Murdock's *Christ in Egypt**

Michael Lockwood

Whereas John H.C. Pippy has concentrated on the influence of ancient Egyptian religious writings on the last book of the New Testament, *Revelation*, D.M. Murdock has, in the main, addressed the influence of ancient Egyptian religious writings on the four canonical gospels and on a number of apocryphal stories which imaginatively invent events involving various characters of the gospels.

According to Murdock, the 'Nativity Scene at the Temple of Luxor' can be seen as a precursor to the nativity stories in the gospels; and the Virgin Mary is Isis/Mery Redux. This latter view has the support of two very important scholarly books. The first book is classicist Dr. Reginald E. Witt's *Isis in the Graeco-Roman World*, published by two university presses: Cornell (1971) and Johns Hopkins (1997)! Witt's erudite book is, in effect, a monograph revealing that the extremely long list of titles and virtues of St. Mary were actually transferred to her from the Egyptian goddess Isis. The second scholarly book is art historian Dr. James Stevens Curl's *The Egyptian Revival* (2005), which solidly supports Witt's treatment of the goddess Isis as *the* significant forerunner of St. Mary.

Murdock, of course, a 'Mythicist', therefore, claims that the evangelists and Christian legend-makers were simply creating their Christian myths by taking (usurping! according to Murdock) some of their building blocks from Egyptian mythology.

Murdock covers such topics as the Egyptian background of the 'Star in the East and Three Kings', 'Horus at the Age of 12 and 30', 'Anup the Baptizer', 'The Twelve Followers', various miracles as 'Walking on Water, Healing the Sick and Raising the Dead', the 'Sacred Meal' (Eucharist), 'The Good Shepherd', 'Crucifixion'(of Horus), 'Burial, Resurrection, and Ascension', and 'Heaven and Hell'.

Murdock's next to last chapter, "The Alexandrian Roots of Christianity", is very informative indeed. Throughout her work, she has substantiated her arguments with direct quotes from acknowledged experts in their fields. What follows here, is a taste of her indefatigable research – and, in what follows, **please note:** *CIE = Christ in Egypt.*

**Christ in Egypt: The Horus-Jesus Connection* (Seattle: Stellar House Publishers, LLC, 2009).

• Swiss Prof. **Erik Hornung** (Egyptologist), *The Valley of the Kings*[1] (1990), p. 9, wrote:

> [I]t is not improbable that even early Christian texts were influenced by ideas and images from the New Kingdom religious books. [Quoted in *CIE*, p. 7]

---

[1]In English, *The Valley of the Kings: Horizon of Eternity* (New York, New York: Timken Publishers, 1990); in German, *Das Tal der König* (München: C.H. Beck, 2002).

• **Hornung**, in his book, *Akhenaten and the Religion of Light*[2] (1999), pp. 13-14, discussing earlier renowned Egyptologist James H. Breasted and amateur Egyptologist Sir Arthur Weigall, remarked:

> [Breasted] noted the modernity of Akhenaten's teaching and its anticipation of Christian attitudes and beliefs. . . .
>
> Arthur Weigall, the first biographer of this religious innovator, [said of Akhenaten that] he established a "religion so pure that we must compare it to Christianity in order to discover its faults."[3] Weigall otherwise stresses that *no other religion so closely resembles Christianity*. . . .[4] [Emphasis added]

---

[2]*Akhenaten and the Religion of Light* (Ithaca: Cornell University Press, 1999; German original, *Echnaton: Die Religion des Lichtes* [Düsseldorf and Zürich: Artemis & Winkler Verlag, 1995]).

[3]Weigall, *The Life and Times of Akhnaton Pharaoh of Egypt* (London: Thornton Butterworth, 1922),p. 62.

[4]Weigall, p. 147.

• **Hornung**, in *The Secret Lore of Egypt: Its Impact on the West*[5] (2001), p. 73, summarized:

> Notwithstanding its superficial rejection of everything pagan, *early Christianity was deeply indebted to ancient Egypt*. In particular, the lively picture of the ancient Egyptian afterlife left traces in Christian texts; thus, among the Copts, and later in Islam, we encounter a fiery hell quite like that of the Egyptians. The descensus [descent into hell] of Jesus, which played no role in the early church, was adopted into the official Credo after 359, thanks to apocryphal legends that again involved Egypt. *Christ became the sun in the realm of the dead, for his descent into the netherworld had its ultimate precursor in the nightly journey of the ancient Egyptian sun god Re*. . . . [Quoted in *CIE*, p. 429; emphasis added]

---

[5]English translation (Ithaca, NY: Cornell University Press, 2001); German original edition, *Das esoterische Ägypten* (München: C.H. Beck, 1999).

• **Hornung** (*The Secret Lore of Egypt*, p. 70) discussed the Egyptian religion's inroads into the highest strata of Roman society during the time of the Christian effort:

> Claudius was also positively disposed toward Egyptian religion, and Nero expressed interest in the sources of the Nile. Nero also had an Egyptian teacher, Chaeromon, who saw to the dissemination of Egyptian knowledge at Rome. According to Suetonius, Otho (69 C.E.) was the first Roman emperor to participate publicly in the cult of Isis. Notwithstanding his well-known stinginess, Vespasian dedicated a large statue of the Nile to Rome, after a Nile miracle occurred during his visit to Alexandria in the year 69. Together with his son Titus, he spent the night before their triumph over Judea (71 C.E.) in the temple of the Roman Isis, which was first depicted on Roman coins that year. Titus is probably the anonymous "pharaoh" depicted in front of the Apis bull in the catacombs of Kom el-Shuqafa in Alexandria. From the reign of Domitian on, Apis was represented on imperial coins. [Quoted in *CIE*, p. 463]

Murdock has cited Hornung's book, *The Secret Lore of Egypt*, in her book, *Christ in Egypt*, over 40 times – she says that there is much in it about the relationship between Christianity and the Egyptian religion. Note the subtitle of Hornung's book: *Its Impact on the West* – the entire book is designed to demonstrate how Egypt influenced "the West", i.e., Christendom.

• On p. 60 of *The Secret Lore of Egypt*, **Hornung** stated:

> There was an obvious analogy between the Horus child and the baby Jesus and the care they received from their sacred mothers; long before Christianity, Isis had borne the epithet "mother of the god."
> [Quoted in *CIE*, p. 124]

• On p. 75 of *The Secret Lore of Egypt*, **Hornung** wrote:

> . . . there was a smooth transition from the image of the nursing Isis, Isis lactans, to that of Maria lactans. The miraculous birth of Jesus could be viewed as analogous to that of Horus, whom Isis conceived posthumously from Osiris, and Mary was closely connected with Isis by many other share characteristics. . . .
> [Quoted in *CIE*, p. 120]
>
> Devotion to the folk god Bes was especially tenacious. Amulets bearing his image have been found in Christian graves, and Bes and Christ are equated in a Coptic magical papyrus. . . .
>
> On another amulet, one side depicts the head of Christ and scenes from the New Testament, and the other a winged, youthful god (Horus-Shed). . . . *There was also an association of the passion of Jesus with traditions regarding Osiris*, especially in the Gospel of Nicodemus, with its detailed description of a descent into Hades.
> [Quoted in *CIE*, p. 385; emphasis added]

• On pp. 75, 76, 78 of *The Secret Lore of Egypt*, **Hornung** commented:

> Many legends grew up around the sojourn of Jesus and his parents in Egypt. . . . He was greeted by dragons and lindworms, whom He affectionately caressed. He caused His mother to wade through a stream without getting her feet wet, commanded a salted fish to leap back into the water, healed the sick with the touch of his diaper, bade graven images to fall from their columns, and so forth. Entirely "ancient Egyptian" was the miracle of the tree, in which a palm bowed down before Mary and her child, so that they might conveniently eat of its fruits, just as the goddess in tombs of the New Kingdom had offered her gifts to the deceased. These legends lie outside of the "canonical" gospels, but they were often illustrated in Christian art of the late Middle Ages. . . .
>
> Naturally enough, Coptic Christians had many legends about Jesus' stay in their land. . . .
>
> As early as Origen's *Contra Celsus* (I, 28), we encounter the claim that it was in Egypt, and specifically as an adult laborer, that Jesus had learned all the magical arts with which he worked miracles and on which he based his divinity. This tradition also occurred in early rabbinic literature, but it was of course suppressed in official Christianity, and it was Morton Smith who did the service of shedding fresh light on this "Egyptian" background of Jesus' deeds through his careful research. In his book *Jesus the Magician* (1978), he demonstrated how motifs from Graeco-Egyptian magical texts are to be found in the Gospels.

• German Egyptologist **Dr. Siegfried Morenz**, in *Egyptian Religion*[6] (1973), p. 251, stated:

> The influence of Egyptian religion on posterity is mainly felt through Christianity and its antecedents.
> [Quoted in *CIE*, p. 506]

---

[6]English translation (Ithaca, NY: Cornell University Press, 1973); original German edition, *Ägyptische Religion* (Stuttgart: W. Koblhammer GmbH.,1960).

• German Egyptologist Prof. **Jan Assmann,** in *Death and Salvation in Ancient Egypt*[7] (2001), pp. 115-116, remarked:

> "Salvation" and "eternal life" are Christian concepts, and we might think that the Egyptian myth can all too easily be viewed through the lens of Christian tradition. Quite the contrary, in my opinion, *Christian myth is itself thoroughly stamped by Egyptian tradition*, by the myth of Isis and Osiris, which from the very beginning had to do with salvation and eternal life. It thus seems legitimate to me to reconstruct the Egyptian symbolism with the help of Christian concepts. As with Orpheus and Eurydice, the constellation of Isis and Osiris can also be compared with Mary and Jesus. The scene of the Pietà, in which Mary holds the corpse of the crucified Jesus on her lap and mourns, is a comparable depiction of the body-centered intensity of female grief, in which Mary is assisted by Mary Magdalene, just as Isis is assisted by Nephthys. Jesus also descended into the realm of death, though he did not remain there. . . . Osiris remained in the netherworld, but he was resurrected and alive. [Emphasis added]

---

[7]English translation (Ithaca, NY: Cornell University Press, 2005); original German edition, *Tod und Jenseits im alten Ägypten* (München: C.H. Beck, 2001).

• Egyptologist Dr. **Ogden Goelet, Jr.**, translator, along with Dr. Raymond O. Faulkner, in the sumptuous book, *The Egyptian Book of the Dead*[8] (1998), p. 18, stated:

> The *Book of the Dead* promised resurrection to all mankind, as a reward for righteous living, long before Judaism and Christianity embraced that concept. [Quoted in *CIE*, p. 376]

[8]*The Egyptian Book of the Dead* , 2nd edition (San Francisco, CA: Chronicle Books LLC, 1998).

• Egyptologist Dr. **Bojana Mojsov**, in her book, *Osiris: Death and Afterlife of a God*[9] (2005), p. xii, "summarized the Christian effort nicely, bringing it all back to Alexandria, . . . the crucible of Christianity":

> When the Greeks established themselves as rulers in Alexandria (332-30 BC), they continued to worship Osiris as Sarapis and passed his cult on to the Romans. Through the Greeks the Hellenized version of the Osiris myth endured in Western culture. [. . .] It was in Roman Alexandria (30 BC - AD 394) that the new Christian religion blossomed, inspired by the writings of the Egyptian, Greek and Jewish philosophers.
> [Quoted in *CIE*, p. 431]

[9]Malden, MA: Blackwell Publishing Ltd., 2005.

• In his article, "The Baptism of the Pharaoh," *The Journal of Egyptian Archaeology*, vol. 36 (1950), p. 6, British Egyptologist Sir Dr. **Alan H. Gardiner** stated:

> The analogy of [the Egyptian] rite to that of Christian baptism is close enough to justify the title given to this article. In both cases a symbolic cleansing by means of water serves as initiation into a properly legitimated religious life. [Quoted in *CIE*, pp. 244-245]

• The British Classicist Dr. **Reginald E. Witt**, in his book, *Isis in the Graeco-Roman World*[10] (1971), p. 272, stated:

> In Hopfner's invaluable collection of the literary sources, Isis needs more pages of the Index than any other name. A brief glance at her attributes as there listed reveals her sharing titles with the Blessed Virgin whom Catholic Christianity has ever revered as Mother of God. Some of these resemblances may be set aside at once as commonplace. Yet so many are the parallels that an unprejudiced mind must be struck with the thought that cumulatively the portraits are alike. Indeed, one of the standard encyclopedias of classical mythology specifically deals with 'Isis identified with the Virgin Mary'.
>
> Let us observe a few of the resemblances. Isis and Osiris, as we have so often seen, are mythologically interfused. In the language of the Roman Church the Blessed Virgin Mary is 'sister and spouse of God: sister of Christ'. Christian writers identify Sarapis with Joseph and then make Isis 'wife of Joseph'. Like her heathen forebear the Catholic Madonna wears a diadem. She too is linked with agricultural fertility. . . .
> [Quoted in *CIE*, p. 166]

Murdock notes that "Witt continues with a long list of comparisons between Mary and not only Isis but also other goddesses, such as Juno and Minerva. The list of parallels, in fact, goes on for several pages. . . ."

[10]*Isis in the Graeco-Roman World* (Ithaca, NY: Cornell University Press, 1971); republished under the title, *Isis in the Ancient World* (Baltimore, MD: The Johns Hopkins University Press, 1997). [This is peer approval! – ML]

• **Witt**, on p. 273, *Isis in the Graeco-Roman World*, stated:

> The Egyptian goddess who was equally 'the Great Virgin' (*hwnt*) and 'Mother of the God' was the object of the very same praise bestowed upon her successor. Mary, Virgin Mother of Jesus, could gradually (and silently [*upāya kauśalyanly*! – ML]) replace the Graeco-Roman Isis-Sophia. [Quoted in *CIE*, p. 120]

• **Witt** , on pp. 216-217, *Isis in the Graeco-Roman World*, further remarked:

> Convincing examples can be found of the influence on Christian iconography of the figure of Horus/Harpocrates, both in his mother's company and on his own. The most obvious parallels appear when we compare the ways in which the sacred Mother and Child of Egypt are portrayed and the types of the Theotokos/Madonna together with the infant Jesus in Byzantine and Italian ecclesiastical art. . . . [Quoted in *CIE*, p. 167]

• Dr. **James Stevens Curl**, a professor at the Queen's University of Belfast, remarked in his book, *The Egyptian Revival*[11] (2005), p. 66:

> *The Christian religion, it might be proposed, owes as much to the Nile as it does to the Jordan*, and for the Church Alexandria should be at least as important as Jerusalem (whereas Rome absorbed influences from both cities). In both Western and Eastern iconography the attributes of Isis survived. Coptic stelai show the Mother and Child, identified as Christian by the Greek crosses on either side of the head, but the basic iconography of the image is that of Isis and Horus, translated into Mary and Jesus. . . . [Quoted in *CIE*, p. 431; emphasis added]

---

[11]*The Egyptian Revival* (London: Routledge, 2005).

From an earlier generation, "Sir Dr. **E.A. Wallis Budge** was a well-respected Egyptologist who ran the Department of Egyptian and Assyrian Antiquities at the British Museum. . . . [His] work was voluminous, and his tackling of the Egyptian religion remains quite valuable. He is one of the scholars who was so astonished by the Egypto-Christian parallels that he thought the Christian religion was the fulfillment of the Egyptian promise" – D.M. Murdock.

• In his book, *Egyptian Ideas of the Future Life*[12] (1900), p. 48, **Budge** wrote:

> In Osiris the Christian Egyptians found the prototype of Christ, and in the pictures and statues of Isis suckling her son Horus, they perceived the prototype of the Virgin Mary and her Child. Never did Christianity find elsewhere in the world a people whose minds were so thoroughly well prepared to receive its doctrines as the Egyptians. [Quoted in *CIE*, p. 28]

---

[12]*Egyptian Ideas of the Future Life* (London: Kegan Paul, Trench, Trübner & Co., Ltd., 1900).

• Another quote by **Budge**, *Egyptian Tales and Romances*[13] (1931), p. 12:

> The Christian Trinity ousted the old triads of gods, *Osiris and Horus were represented by our Lord Jesus Christ, Isis by the Virgin Mary, Set the god of evil by Diabolus* [Satan] . . . and the various Companies of the Gods by the Archangels, and so on. [Quoted in *CIE*, p. 67; emphasis added]

---

[13]*Egyptian Tales and Romances* (London: Thornton Butterworth, 1931).

• Again, **Budge**, *The Gods of the Egyptians*[14] (1904), I, xv-xvi, stated (emphasis added):

> . . . at the last, when [Osiris's] cult disappeared before the religion of the Man Christ, *the Egyptians who embraced Christianity found that the moral system of the old cult and that of the new religion were so similar, and the promises of resurrection and immortality in each so much alike, that they transferred their allegiance from Osiris to Jesus of Nazareth without difficulty. Moreover, Isis and the child Horus were straightway identified with Mary the Virgin and her Son*, and in the apocryphal literature of the first few centuries which followed the evangelization of Egypt, several of the legends about Isis and her sorrowful wanderings were made to centre round the Mother of Christ. Certain of the attributes of the sister goddesses of Isis were also ascribed to her, and, like the goddess Neith of Sais, she was declared to possess perpetual virginity. Certain of the Egyptian Christian Fathers gave to the Virgin the title 'Theotokos', or 'Mother of God', forgetting, apparently, that it was an exact translation of *neter mut*, a very old and common title of Isis. [Quoted in *CIE*, p. 120]

---

[14]*The Gods of the Egyptians* (London: Methuen & Co., 1904).

• **Budge's** Egyptoparallelomania continues in "The Cult of Isis and the Worship of the Virgin Mary compared", *Legends of Our Lady Mary*[15] (1922), p. 1:

> It has been well said that the Egyptians were better prepared to receive and accept Christianity than any of the nations round about them. *For thousands of years before St. Mark came to Alexandria to preach the Gospel of his Master Christ, the Egyptians believed in Osiris the Man-god who raised himself from the dead.* He was held to possess the power of bestowing immortality on his followers because he had triumphed over Death, and had vanquished the Powers of Darkness. He was the Judge of souls and the supreme lord of the Judgment of the Dead; he was all-wise, all-knowing, all-just, and his decrees were final and absolute. No man could hope to dwell with him in his kingdom unless he had lived a life of moral excellence upon earth, and the only passports to his favour were truth-speaking, honest intent, and the observation of the commands of the Law (Maāt), coupled with charity, alms-giving and humane actions. . . . [Quoted in *CIE*, p. 431; emphasis added]

---

[15]*Legends of Our Lady Mary* (London: The Medici Society, Ltd., 1922).

IV

THE BUDDHIST “GRAFT” (“SCION”)

Meditating Buddha, Polonnaruwa, Śrī Laṅkā

“She will give birth to a son” (*Matthew 1:22*)

Christian Lindtner: “News Bulletin”, March 15, 2012

The first seven syllables of *Matthew 1: 22* are a direct translation from the Sanskrit of the *SBV* [*Saṁgha-**B**heda-**V**astu*] I, p. 40. The Greek runs: ***teksetai de huion***, which is as close to the original Sanskrit as one can possibly come: *putraṁ janayiṣyati*.

More precisely, “Matthew” here combines the famous Old Testament passage (*Isaiah 7:14*) quoted in *1:23*: “***idou hê parthenos en gastri heksei kai teksetai huion . . .***”, with the Buddhist one just quoted. In *1:22* he adds a ***de*** in order to match the seven syllables of the Sanskrit.

To be sure, when I here write “Matthew”, I mean the unknown author or authors, who copied the *SBV* (a part of the *MSV* [***M**ūla-**S**arvāstivāda-**V**inaya*]) in which “Matthew” is mentioned as a disciple of the Buddha, as I have pointed out elsewhere long ago (cf. Michael Lockwood, *Buddhism's Relation to Christianity*, Chennai 2010, p. 232).

This method of combining two or more otherwise quite different passages with one or more words (or numbers) in common, is very typical of “Matthew” and the other evangelists. You have two or more different texts with a few words in common; on that basis you create a third. It is easy – and fun – to do, but difficult to trace since the sources are not mentioned.

The situation in the *SBV* is this:

The mother of the Bodhisattva is called Mahāmāyā, which becomes ***hê Mariam***, also four syllables. She “sees” four dreams. In the first dream, a white “elephant” (i.e. a white cloud) enters her womb, Sanskrit *kukṣim*. The Sanskrit *kukṣi-* becomes the Greek synonym ***gastri*** (locative), in the womb. She informs the king of her dreams. The king calls upon some Brahmin priests skilled in the interpretation of dreams.

They say: *deva, yathā śāstre dṛṣṭaṁ – putraṁ janayiṣyati . . .* “Sir, as seen from the book [on astrology] she will give birth to a son . . .”. In *Matthew* these priests are transformed into an angel of the Lord (***aggelos kuriou***), an OT motif. Just as the priests refer to the authority of a book, the angel in *Matthew* also refers to the authority of a book (viz. the OT, in its LXX version). This angel says to Joseph: “Son of David . . .”, the Sanskrit *deva*, ‘Sir’, ‘God’, becomes ***Daueid***. A few lines later (p. 41), we have the Sanskrit *deva-putras*, the source for the ***huios Daueid*** in *Mt 1:20*.

In the *SBV* the Brahmin priests predict that the child will either become a (worldly) king or leave his home in order to become a *Tathāgata*, a famous saviour of mankind. The Bodhisattva was carried down from heaven (where there are many other god-sons, *deva-putra*) like a cloud driven by the power of the wind (*māruta*) into the womb. The wind becomes the holy ***pneuma*** of *Matthew 1:18* and *1:20*. There is nothing mysterious about a cloud being driven by the wind.

By leaving out the cloud, “Matthew” creates a great mystery. Easy for him, difficult for us. The Bodhisattva was born as the king of the Śākyas. Jesus was born as the king of the Jews. Both descended from heaven for exactly the same purpose – to teach us about righteousness and immortality.

A little later, we hear about the various names of the Bodhisattva – Greek ***to paidion***, the boy (*SBV*, I, p. 17-18). *Śākya-munis* is one of them; *Devāti-devas*, God above Gods, is another. Even the gods fall down at the feet of the prince (*kumāra*), and “let therefore the name of the prince be *Devātideva* (p. 48), for he is a god above (all other) gods.” The OT source of *Matthew* spoke of his name as ***Emmanouêl***, which means, when translated, “With us is the God” – ***meth' hêmôn ho theos***. The name ***Em-manuo-êl*** is unique in the OT and NT. The source is Buddhist in both cases. The ***-manou-*** contains a pun on the Buddhist *-munis*, in *Śākya-munis*. (Yet another pun on *Śākya-munis* is found in the ***suka-minos*** of *Luke 17:6*.) The motive of the king, Herod, who, hearing this, becomes agitated, and all Jerusalem with him, is also inspired by the *SBV*, where we hear about the anxiety of the king (p. 67). The king was afraid that his son would leave the palace. He did. Jesus left for a foreign country, Egypt. Eventually, both of them returned.

In the original, the king is called *Śuddhodanas*. One of the teachers of the Bodhisattva is *Ārādas* (p. 97). Thus king Herod, ***Hêrôdês***, is a combination of the king and the teacher.

What about the mother of *Śākyamuni(s)* – was she a ***parthenos***, a virgin? This question is also taken up in the *SBV* (p. 34): When she was still an unmarried young girl, a *dārikā*, she was given the name *Mahā-māyā*, explained as “Great-beauty”. Already when she was still an unmarried virgin, it was said that she would one day “give birth to a son” – *putraṁ janayiṣyati*. The Sanskrit *dārikā* means “a young girl”, but from the context we can infer for sure that she was also a virgin. An unmarried girl who was not a virgin would have been an absolute scandal in the Buddhist/Indian context, as in the Jewish, of course. But once the Bodhisattva has entered her womb, she is no longer spoken of as a *dārikā*, only as the mother or as Mahāmāyā. She is never a mother and a *dārikā* at the same time. It is quite clear from the *SBV* that the *dārikā* had intercourse with the king before she gave birth to the Bodhisattva. But after she had given birth she no longer longed for any man, *SBV*, p. 43. She was then “like a virgin”, if you wish.

So, to sum up so far: The idea in the *SBV* and in Isaiah is the same. There is a young girl of whom it is predicted that she one day will become the mother of an extraordinary son. There is no suggestion whatsoever that she remains a virgin. ***The Buddhist and the OT sources know nothing of parthenogenesis.*** The Greek ***parthenos***, the Sanskrit *dārikā*, and the Hebrew ***haalmah*** are synonyms. They refer to a young woman, a virgin, who later on becomes a mother in exactly the same way that all other girls may become mothers. She is ***never*** a virgin and a mother at the same time.

But when we come back to "Matthew", the situation is quite different. It has changed. There can be no doubt that "Matthew" introduces the concept of parthenogenesis.

Thus we have to look for yet another source. It was not "Matthew" who invented the paradox of a woman who was at the same time a virgin and a mother. Any Greek schoolboy would immediately be able to answer the question: Who is famous for being at the same time a virgin and a mother?

The answer is, of course: Athena. Did you never hear of the Parthenon?

I have previously made the point that the Greek text of the NT often works on two levels at the same time. What appears as a paradox on the surface, is perfectly logical on the deeper or geometrical level.

This rule also works here.

On the surface it is a paradox that a virgin is the mother of the Messiah. But not so once you look at the statement in terms of geometry:

First you draw a circle with the circumference 515, which is the number of Greek ***parthenos*** (80+1+100+9+5+50+70+200 = 515). The inscribed square is 464, which is the number of the mother, ***hê mêtêr***. The double solar cross inscribed in the 515 circle (= the square containing the 515 circle) is 656, the number of ***Messias***.

So this nice drawing – which also looks like the sun – tells you that a virgin (515) is the mother (464) of the ***Messias*** (656). Since 656 is also the number of Mary, the mother (***Mariam hê mêtêr*** = 192 + 8 + 456 = 656), the same drawing also tells you, that the Mother Mary is a virgin who is also at the same time the mother – of the ***Messias*** (if yet another square is drawn). Since ***Nazaret*** is also 464, you can go on and on.

The diameter in the 515 circle is 164, which is the famous ***Athênê Nikê*** (76+88 = 164), known to all from coins and from the Acropolis.

So, for the Greek readers of *Matthew* it must have been obvious, that the mother of Jesus was Athena. In the *SBV* the Bodhisattva is said to be a "boy-sun", *bāla-sūrya*. It is, also in *Matthew*, the Sun that is being born in the form of a man, Jesus.

Athena is his mother.

The idea that Athena was the mother of the Sun-god is not at all original with "Matthew". For instance, Cicero, in his *De natura deorum* 3, 55, refers to an old myth according to which Minerva (= Athena) gave birth to Apollo, the Sun-god. This myth was also known to some of the Christian authors. It can be traced back to Aristotle (see e.g. the references in Arthur Stanley Pease (ed.), *M. Tvlli Ciceronis De natura deorum*, Cambridge, Mass., p. 1105).

If Athena is the mother of Jesus – who, then, is his father? The answer is simple, when you look at how Jesus elsewhere identifies his heavenly father. It is Zeus. When the Greeks spoke of the God, ***ho theos***, they meant Zeus. Jesus, the son of God, is thus the son of Zeus and his beloved daughter (Homer), Athena. The God is identified with the ***pneuma*** in *John*. Zeus was also identified with ***pneuma*** by the Stoic philosophers. So, again, Zeus is the father of Jesus. More about Zeus, the true father of Jesus later. To Leda he came as a white swan. To Māyā, Zeus came as a white cloud etc. etc.

All this has provided us with a glimpse into the workshop of "Matthew": His intention is to create a myth about a Jewish king. He already is familiar with the *MSV* which contains the myth of the king of the Śākyas. He was also familiar with the OT, and he was very much familiar with Greek mythology and geometry. He uses and "translates" his Buddhists sources as if they had already been present in the OT. He does exactly the same with his Greek sources. The readers he first had in mind must therefore primarily have been Jews. The gospel of "Matthew" is an extreme but also typical case of Hellenistic syncretism.

* * * * * * * * *

To Fulfill All Righteousness (*Matthew 3:15*)

Christian Lindtner, "News Bulletin": March 18, 2012

The noun ***dikaiosun***, righteousness, has been used by Matthew seven times, and has, in recent years, given rise to numerous discussions and interpretations by theologians. There is, as always, an Old Testament and Jewish background, but there is also a Buddhist one, which seems to have escaped notice.

The Buddhist source is not just important for a better understanding of Matthew 3:15, but also because it allows us to identify yet another of Matthew's sources – the *Prajñā-Pāramitā* (*PP*), still available in several Sanskrit recensions. The most important versions of the *PP* have been translated into English by the late Edward Conze.

The idea in *Matthew* is puzzling, if not hilarious: Take a quick dive in a river, and all righteousness will have been fulfilled! Jesus says to John that baptism is more or less the same as "quickly fulfilling all righteousness".

How so? – we do not know from Matthew alone! Obviously, he does not want us to know. It remains his own secret. The *PP* known as *Suvikrāntavikrāmi-paripṛcchā* (ed. by Ryusho Hikata, Kyoto 1958, p. 4, line 5) provides us with the direct source:

The situation is this: a Bodhisattva by the name of Suvikrāntavikrām asks the Lord (Bhagavān) about the "perfection of wisdom", *prajñā-pāramitā*. How does a Bodhisattva quickly attain the fulfillment of the dharma(s) of all-knowledge? That is the question.

The ideal of the *PP* is to attain knowledge of all dharmas (concepts, things, principles, laws etc.). That knowledge, we learn from the Lord, is to see that all things (*dharma*) are empty. This is, in brief, the message of all the recensions of the *PP*.

The knowledge that sees all dharmas as being empty is the same as enlightenment, or *sambodhi*. A Bodhisattva who has attained *sambodhi* is a *sambuddhas* – "fully baptized". (The ***baptistheis*** in *Mt 3:16* therefore translates the Sanskrit *sambuddhas*.

Matthew's ten syllables: ***plêrôsai pasan dikaiosunên*** is a direct translation of the Sanskrit (*loc. cit.*): *sarva-jñatā-dharma-paripūrim*. Sanskrit *paripūrim* becomes Greek ***plêrôsai***. Sanskrit *sarva-jña-tā-dharma* means "the concept (*dharma*) of the state (*-tā-*) of knowing (*-jña-*) all (*sarva-*), in short, omniscience.

In the *PP*, therefore, it is a question about the highest kind of knowledge, not about "righteousness" in any moral or practical sense of the word. (We are dealing with Buddhist "gnosticism".)

In the *PP* (*ibid.*) it is a question of the Bodhisattva living (*caran*) "in the *prajñā-parāmitā*", the locative form of which is the heptasyllabic: (*prajñā-pāramitāyām*). The seven syllables (***prepon estin hêmin***) of *Matthew 3:15* contains an obvious pun on the Sanskrit compound.

Thus Jesus identifies *PP* with omniscience. He can do so as a *sambuddhas*.

A few lines later, *PP* is defined as being *sarvadharmānāṁ grāhikā*, 'She (as a goddess) grasps all dharmas'.

This identification allows us to make yet another identification: *Matthew*'s *3:15* (8 + 5 = 13 syllables): ***apokritheis de ho 'Iêsous eipen pros auton*** is an echo of *PP* (*ibid.* p. 4, line 7-8 = 14 syllables): *evam ukte Bhagavān . . . bodhisat(t)vam avocat.*

I have already pointed out in my book *Geheimnisse* (p. 357 for ref.) that the Greek: ***khreian (ekhô) hypo (sou) baptisthênai*** in *Matthew 3:14* is a direct rendering of the Sanskrit: *upasampādayitavya(ḥ).*

A teacher may then accept the novice and say to him: 'go forth!' – *pravrājetu*. (This imperative, *pravrājetu*, accounts nicely for the otherwise quite obscure ***aphes arti*** in *Matthew 3:15*.)

As known, it is only Matthew who places an ***arti*** after a verb. The reason, we now see, is that he imitates the Sanskrit.

On the whole, we here have a picture of a student coming to a teacher for initiation and enlightenment. This is Buddhist, and this is what some early Christians understood by baptism.

I hope these observations have established a historical link between the New Testament and the Buddhist *PP*. *Matthew 13:54* asks from where, ***pothen***, Jesus has this wisdom, ***sophia***. He does not reveal the source of this unusual ***sophia***. A good question, indeed: The Greek ***hê sophia hautê*** probably renders the Sanskrit *prajñā-pāramitā*.

Matthew goes on to ask: Is the name of his mother not Mary? This fits very nicely with what we learn from the *PP-sūtras*: Typically, *PP* is depicted (also in Buddhist art) as the Mother of Buddhas and Bodhisattvas, and She is identified with Māyā, "Illusion". Thus *Māyā*, or *PP*, is the Mother of Jesus, the *Sambuddhas*.

Note, finally, that *Mt 13:53-58* forms a textual unit that consists of exactly 108 words – the "holy Buddhist number" (cf. my observations reprinted in Lockwood, *op. cit.*, pp. 148-156; see also *Lalitavistara*, Chp. 4, on the 108 "Doors of Dharma"). It is thereby suggested that ***sophia*** has to do with counting (words, syllables etc.), as in *Revelation 13:18* (***arithmosgar anthrôpou estin*** = *Sad-dharma-puṇḍarīka-sūtram*).

This is also the right place to recall that in all the *PP* (Sanskrit) texts, the number of syllables has been carefully counted, as reflected in the various titles of *PP*. Perfection of wisdom has, for sure, something to do with counting words and syllables. It is a feature that the New Testament shares with many Buddhist scriptures. It is a fact that should never be ignored.

Matthew 13:55 provides a wonderful example of this "wisdom of numbers". Jesus is identified by a question – Is he the son of the carpenter? ***estin ho tou tektonos huios***, which is 565 + 70 + 770 + 1015 + 680 = 3100 = ***ho huios ho tou anthrôpou*** = 'The Son of Man'. You have to count in order to identify "the son of the carpenter". That Matthew should use the *PP* is, in itself, not surprising. One of his other main Mahāyāna sources is the *Sad-Dharma-Puṇḍarīka-sūtra*, and the *SDP* also refers, briefly, to the *PP*. It may here be recalled that Edward Conze, comparing John's *Revelation* with the *PP* in 1959, called attention to "close verbal coincidences" (see Michael Lockwood, *Buddhism's Relation to Christianity*, p. 260).

For the Lord taking a bath in the river, and for baptism in the original sense of initiation (*upasampadā*) there are other Buddhist sources (mainly the *Catuṣ-Pariṣat-Sūtra*), not to be found in the *PP* (but presupposed). Typically, Matthew combined various Buddhist sources.

Before I forget: The ***Oratio montana*** (*Mt 5-7*) is a sermon on ***dikaiosunê*** (*Mt 5:6 &10* etc.), a *Dharma-deśanā* (Sanskrit *deśanā* becomes Greek ***didakhê*** in *Mt 7:28*). The ***hoiptôkhoi tô pneumati*** in *5:3* has always been difficult. In the *PP* (Hikata, p. 5, line 4), we have the compound *daridra-cittas*, a person of poor mind, poor-minded. The Greek ***ptôkhos pneumati*** would be a perfect rendering of that Sanskrit compound.

In line 5, we have the Sanskrit compound *hīnādhimuktikas*, which would account well for the Greek ***oligo-pistos***, *Matthew 6:30* etc., a person of little faith. Normally, ***oligopistos*** translates *alpotsukas*, for sure.

* * * * * * * * *

Walking on Water and Peter's Faith (*Matthew 14:28-33* par)

Christian Lindtner, "News Bulletin": March 21, 2012

According to Buddhist lore, a Buddha is in possession of supernatural faculties allowing him, the "God above the Gods", to fly like a bird in the sky, to pass unhindered through walls, to walk on water as if on solid ground etc. – to mention just a few of many similar miracles.

According to Greek mythology, Hercules could also walk on water. Like Jesus, Hercules is a son of the God, i.e. of Zeus.

The Jews of the Old Testament said the same of their Lord, the God, ***kurios ho theos***, whose proper name we are not allowed to mention.

Thus, in the Greek words of *Job 9:8*, God may be seen "walking around on the sea as on firm ground". Here, the Greek (but not the Hebrew, which is quite different!) runs: ***peripatôn hôs ep' edaphous epi thalassês***.

This is almost a literal translation of the Pāli: *udake pi (abhijjamāno) gacchati sayyathā pi pathaviyam* (*cit.* Derrett, *The Bible and the Buddhists*, p. 70).

Matthew, in his usual way, combined the OT passage with this and other Buddhist passages when he composed his version of Jesus walking on water (*Mt 14:22-33* par). *Mt 14:25* replaces the genitive of *Job* by writing: ***peripatôn epi tên thalassan***. But *Luke 6:48* retains the genitive of *Job 9:8*: ***peripatôn epi tês thalassês***.

The German scholar Norbert Klatt has argued (1982 and 1990) – quite convincingly – that Matthew's text must have been based on the Buddhist text, not vice versa (as Derrett had argued against Klatt 1982).

Comparing the Christian and Buddhist (mythical) reports, Klatt's literary analysis revealed that they were congruent in the following points (Klatt, 1990, p. 29):

1. A person (the Lord, C.L.) is alone in a place of solitude.
2. This person (the Lord, C.L.) is performing spiritual exercises (prayer/meditation).
3. Some time later this person walks about, on or in the water (***peripatein***, *cankami, cankramati*).
4. The waters are depicted as rough or powerfully rapid.
5. The story changes its focus of attention and turns to another set of persons (disciples or Kassapa).
6. On the water is/comes a boat with several persons aboard.
7. Those aboard the boat are astounded at the sight of the person walking on the water.
8. They do not know who the person walking on the water is (and therefore ask him).
9. The person walking on the water identifies himself with the words "It is I."
10. Those in the boat wish to take the person walking on the water aboard.
11. The person walking on the water enters the boat.

The concordance is obvious, and Klatt finds that the only way to explain it is to assume that the story of the walking on the water found its way "from one culture into another" (p. 30). The "borrowing is from the Buddhist source into the Christian gospels" (*ibid.*). Derrett, ten years later (*BB*, p. 70), wrote that already Martin Dibelius, the German theologian, in 1933, had "rightly divined foreign influence". His own view is that the Buddhist and the Christian stories may here have "gained reciprocally". They are somehow historically related.

The main Sanskrit source is, to be sure, to be found in the *Catuspariṣatsūtra* (part of the *MSV*), chapter 24. This source escaped Klatt. The Buddha performs no less than 18 miracles, the purpose of which is to convert the famous teacher, Kāśyapa(s)/Kassapa and his 500 disciples. Miracle 18 gives the story of a great flood that arose in the river Nairañjanā. The Lord is now surrounded by water. He walks to and fro on a firm sandy spot (in the middle of the flood waters). The ascetic, Kāśyapas, finding the Lord to be gracious, fears that he may be carried away by the flood. So he takes a boat made of tree and goes in search of the Lord. He sees the Lord surrounded by water of more than the height of a full-grown man, walking around on a sandy spot. He asks: "Are you alive, great ascetic?" – "I am alive, Kāśyapa!" "Come aboard, great ascetic! Will you come into the boat made of one tree, great ascetic?" – "I come aboard, Kāśyapa." – And the Lord accomplished such a performance of magic power that he, (his) mind concentrated, rose up to the boat made of one tree, as water arises. Then Urubilvā-Kāśyapa thought: "It is marvellous, the extent to which the great ascetic possesses great supernatural power and authority. But I too am an Arhat."

The purpose in *Matthew* is the same as in the *Catuṣ-Pariṣat-Sūtra* (*CPS*): If you have faith in the teacher, as a son of God, you will be saved. The number 5000, mentioned in *Matthew 14:21* links up with the 500 in the original. The 5000 are also found in another Buddhist source, the *Sad-Dharma-Puṇḍarīka-sūtra* (see my essay from June 2010, reprinted in Michael Lockwood, *Buddhism's Relation to Christianity*, Chennai 2010, p. 283).

Kāśyapas with his 500 disciples turn up again in Paul, *1 Corinthians 15:5-6*, as Kêphas and more than 500 brothers. (The "more than" ***epanô***, from yet another Buddhist source, *MPS*.) A "structural concordance" may well be sufficient to establish a historical relationship, but to be on firm ground the broader context must also be taken into consideration, if possible.

What is decisive here, is that the Greek text of *Matthew* contains some **Sanskritisms** that can, of course, only be accounted for by assuming that the Sanskrit text enjoys the relative (chronological) priority.

These Sanskritisms in *Matthew* provide "Buddhist fingerprints", as it were:

1. In the Greek of *Matthew*, two sentences are introduced by an ***euthus*** or ***eutheôs*** (*Mt 14:27 & 31*). According to our Greek dictionaries ***euthus* / *eutheôs*** means "at once, immediately" – which does not make good sense here. In the Buddhist original *atha* introduces a new sentence, and means: then, and then. Hence the Greek has the sense of the Sanskrit. Here we have Sanskrit fingerprints.
2. The Greek ***kat' idean*** in *14:23* renders the Sanskrit *ekānte*, "aside", often said of the Lord.
3. In *14:28 & 29*, the ***epi tên thalassan* / *epi thalassês*** of Job has been replaced by ***epi tahudata***, on the waters. This is highly revealing, for it reflects the Sanskrit *udake*, "on water". This noun was **not** derived from the quotation from Job! The Sanskrit and the Pāli had *pi* (from *api*) which in the Greek becomes ***epi***.
4. Kāśyapas who had not yet been converted by the Buddha – the great ascetic – is transformed into Peter, who had little faith. Now we understand why Peter is also called Kêphas (*John 1:42*; *1 Cor 15:5* etc.). Behind Kēphas = Petros we have the Buddhist Kāśyapa(s). The consonants are similar.
5. The compound ***oligopistos*** in *14:31* is most revealing. It only occurs a few times in *Matthew*, and once in *Luke*. Otherwise, it is not attested in Greek before the New Testament. It is derived from the Sanskrit *alpotsukas*, used in exactly the same context, when the Lord rebukes someone (esp. Māra, the "Devil"). Sanskrit *alpas* becomes Greek ***oligos***, synonyms, and Sanskrit *utsukas* becomes ***pistos***. – The corresponding abstract noun, ***oligopistia***, *Mt 17:20* only, pentasyllabic, is a precise rendering of the Sanskrit compound *hīnādhimuktitā*, "little faith" (common in Mahāyāna scriptures; see the Sanskrit dictionaries for ref. to the Buddhist sources: *MSV* etc.).

The episode originally took place near Urubilvā near the river Nairañjanā, where the Bodhisattva (not yet a *sa-buddha*) attained perfect enlightenment as Buddha. Being one, he multiplied himself; being multiplied, he became one, the *CPS* says.

The authors of the gospels did exactly the same: one became many, many became one. This literary device of turning one into many and many into one is absolutely fundamental for the "Buddhist" authors of the gospel. There can be several originals behind one "person", and one "person" can appear as several "persons". One must never ask for one source only. Otherwise one will sink into the water!

Matthew 14:22-36 forms a numerical unit. It consists of 222 words, i.e. one quarter of the most basic of all numbers, 888 – the number of Jesus. Matthew always has to serve several masters at the same time: The Buddhist sources, the Jewish sources (OT), sound and sense, and the Pythagorean requirements of textual geometry (called gematria by the Jews).

* * * * * * * * *

Some Sanskritisms in the New Testament Gospels

Christian Lindtner, Archive (2001)

When Dr. Kunjunni Raja visited me here in Denmark in May 1999, we not only had the occasion to read and discuss the Sanskrit text of Bhavya's *Madhyamakahṛdayam*, but I also availed myself of the opportunity to share with my old friend some of the discoveries I had made in regard to the New Testament Gospels and their Sanskrit sources.

Dr. Raja immediately recognized that if merely one convincing example of the Greek text being based on the Sanskrit could be pointed out and convincingly accounted for in this light, then this would be sufficient to establish a historical relationship.

If more cases could be pointed out, where the Greek could be explained in the light of the Sanskrit, so much the better, of course.

Here I would like to draw the reader's attention to some cases of "Sanskritisms", where old and still unsolved difficulties in the Greek of the Gospels are convincingly solved once it is recognized that they are translated from the Sanskrit.

The main Buddhist source of the NT Gospels is the *Mūla-Sarvāstivāda-Vinaya* (*MSV*), a huge collection of texts which also include the celebrated *Catuṣ-Pariṣat-Sūtra* (*CPS*) and the *Mahā-Parinirvāṇa-Sūtra* (MPS). *CPS* and *MPS* were edited in Sanskrit and Tibetan by the German scholar Ernst Waldschmidt, Berlin 1952-1962 & 1950-1951, respectively. The *CPS* also forms a part of the Saṁghabhedavastu (*SBV*), the Sanskrit text of which (from Gilgit) was edited by Raniero Gnoli, Rome 1977-1978. Full references to these and other relevant sources may be found in the indispensable *Sanskrit-Wörterbuch der buddhistischen Texte aus den Turfan-Funden*, Göttingen 1973 – and in my monograph *Comparative Gospel Studies* (forthcoming). My thesis is simply that there is not much in the NT Gospels that cannot be traced back to the *MSV*. The NT Gospels are translated – in a prima facie very strange fashion, to be sure – directly from the Sanskrit of the *MSV*. This novel thesis of mine was first presented to an international public in Sarnath, November 1998. My paper was subsequently expanded and published as a pamphlet by the Ananda Buddha Vihara Trust under the title *Buddhism in Relation to Science and World Religions*, Secunderabad 1999.

Currently I am preparing, inter alia, a running commentary on *Matthew*, pointing out, chapter by chapter, the Buddhist sources of the first of the four Gospels. For references to the Greek sources and modern commentaries on the Gospels etc., I shall have to refer the interested readers to that book. Here, I shall have to assume my reader to be familiar with the Greek and Sanskrit texts, and their philological problems.

1. *Matthew 17: 5.* Jesus takes Peter et al. up on a high mountain, where a transfiguration takes place. Peter offers to set up three shelters (Greek ***skênê***). From the context one does not understand why Peter would want to set up such shelters. Candidly, *Luke 9:33* admits that Peter did not know what he was saying. While he was still speaking, a bright (Greek ***nephelê phōteinê***) cloud envelops them. The Buddhist source solving the problems is *CPS* 6. Bhagavat [the Buddha] is staying with Mucilindas, the *nāgarāja*. Then a *saptāhikôkālameghaḥ samupāgataḥ* ['seven-day-unseasonal-(raining)-cloud arrives'], *CPS* 6:2. To protect Bhagavat from the rain of the *a-kāla-megha*, lasting seven days, Mucilindas offers his hood (*phana*) as a shelter. Matthew, clearly, has inverted the order of events. Also, he has "mistranslated" *a-kāla*, which either means "out of season", or "bright". To make sense he should, as in the *CPS*, first have mentioned the dark rain cloud, and then Peter's offer to put up shelters (Sanskrit *phana* becoming Greek ***skênê***). He confuses his reader by translating *a-kāla* as "bright", though the sense required here is "out of season". All the other details are also in the Buddhist source: The seven days become six days in *Matthew* and *Mark*, about eight days in *Luke*. Muci-lindas inspires to Moses and Elias; the description of Jesus is based on that of the Buddha in *CPS* 10; Peter (Greek ***Petros***) etc. were originally *Tripusa* etc., *CPS* 2 (***p-t-r-s***/*t-r-p-s*, same numerical value and consonants).

2. ***Mark 6:39-40.*** No satisfactory explanation for the two Greek expressions ***symposia symposia***, "companies companies", and ***prasiai prasiai***, "groups groups", has ever been offered. Both are translations of the frequent *saṁghāt saṁgham pūgāt pūgam*, "from group to group, from multitude to multitude", which occurs in the same sense, e.g. *MPS* 26:5. The Greek gives the original sense, and at the same time it attempts to reproduce the sounds and the order of the original Sanskrit. Since this is the only place where the four words occur as such in the Gospels, this also proves that "Mark" had direct and independent access to the Sanskrit original.

3. ***Matthew 16:17.*** Again, no satisfactory explanation has been given why Simon Peter is called ***Bar-Iôna***. Now, ***Simon Petros*** is, as a rule, no other than *Śāri-Putras*. *Śāri-Putras* is often addressed in Buddhist sources (Mahāyāna only?) as a *jina-putras*, "son of Jina".[1] ***Bar-Iôna*** means son (***bar***) of ***Iôna***, and so it is easy to see that ***bar*** translates *putras* whereas ***Iôna*** imitates the sound of *Jina(s)*. So ***Bar-Iôna*** was simply *Śāri-Putras*. Puns on the name of this important disciple – in both sources – are quite frequent. In *Matthew 16:18* Jesus says: ***sy ei Petros***, "You are Peter". The Greek ***sy ei*** contains a pun on *Śāri*. The "missing ***r***" can, according to a general rule, be taken from *putras*. In *John 1:47* the noun Israelite, Greek ***Israêlitês*** – the disciple in whom there is no guile – contains another pun on *Śāri-Putras*. The word means "son of Israel", which means that first the ***s-r*** represent the original two consonants of *Śāri*, whereas *putras* is represented by its original meaning in Israelite as a whole. By means of a simple pun, *Śāri-Putras* has become a son of Israel. In the Gospels "Israelite" only occurs here. To be sure, the other disciples mentioned by *John 1* can all be traced back to the Buddhist sources. As I point out in my forthcoming book, *Aniruddhas* thus becomes ***Andreas***, *Pippalas* becomes ***Philippos***, and *Nālandā* becomes ***Nathanael***. The Gospels always try to retain the number and nature of the consonants (guttural, palatal, lingual, dental, labial, semivowel, sibilant) of the names of persons and places in the Sanskrit original.

4. ***Matthew 14:34 & 15:39.*** Jesus, who has just been addressed as "son of God", Greek ***theou huios*** – which of course is a direct translation of Sanskrit *deva-putras*, as is the hybrid "son of David (Greek ***huios Daueid***)" – now "and crossing over came to land Gennesaret".

Here the Greek ***kai diaperasantes êlthon epi tên gên (eis) Gennêsaret*** is a direct rendering of Sanskrit (*māgadhakā manuṣyā*) *nadīṁ Gaṅgām uttaranty api pratyuttaranti*, *MPS* 7:5. Some editors of the NT add an ***eis***, "to", to avoid the difficult reading ***gên Gennêsaret***, "to land G.". But wrongly so, for Greek ***gên Gen-*** is an attempt to render the *Gaṅgām* of the original, retaining all the original consonants (viz. *g-n-g-[m=**n**]*). The Sanskrit *uttaranty api* has been inverted so as to become Greek ***kai*** (= *api*) ***diaperasantes*** (= *uttaranti*), the sense being thus preserved. The second Sanskrit verb, *pratyuttaranti*, is represented by the five syllables, and consonants, of ***êlthon epi tên*** (NB: ***l*** counts as *r*, as often).

For Sanskrit *māgadhakā*, meaning "(men) from the land of Magadha" (cf. Tibetan: *yul ma ga dha'i mi rnams*, "men of Magadha land"), we have to consult *Matthew 15:39*, which says that Jesus went into the boat and came "into the borders of Magadha", Greek ***eis ta oria Magadan***.

All modern commentators agree that this strange location "Magadan" is quite unknown from other sources. Equally puzzling is the variant given in *Mark 8:10*: "to the parts Dalmanutha", Greek ***eis ta merê Dalmanoutha***. Neither "Magadan" nor "Dalman(o)utha" are to be found on the map.

In the light of the original source, *MPS* 7:5, all the old problems are now finally solved. One only has to look at a map of Buddhist India!

It was originally the Buddha who crossed the Ganges in the land of Magadha. This famous episode is not only known from *MPS*, but even from Buddhist art. The earliest artistic representation of this episode is already to be found in Sanchi, see Dieter Schlingloff, "Die wunderbare Überquerung der Gaṅgā", in N. Balbir & J.K. Bautze (eds.), *Festschrift Klaus Bruhn zur Vollendung des 65. Lebensjahres*, Reinbek 1994, pp. 571-584. To be sure, this proves the chronological priority of the Buddhist source.

MPS 7:5 also provides us with the clue to the mysterious location "Dalmanoutha". Immediately after the words *uttaranty-api*, the Sanskrit says that some of the Magadha people crossed the river (*nadī*) Gaṅgā in *salmani-phaleṣu* (Tibetan *sin sal ma la'i span leb*, "boards of the *salmani* tree"), i.e. on rafts. Here there can hardly be any doubt that ***dalman*** imitates *salman*. In all likelihood, the Greek ***outha*** is intended to imitate Sanskrit *atha*, the first word in the following sentence, *MPS* 7:6.

Speaking of *atha*, this common word is usually translated by Greek ***eutheôs*** or ***euthus***, in all the four Gospels. This literal translation creates confusion, because the Greek words means "at once", "immediately", whereas Sanskrit *atha* simply means, "(and) then". By translating Greek ***eutheôs*** or ***euthus*** in the sense of Sanskrit *atha* the reader can suddenly make natural sense of virtually all the passages in the Gospels where *atha* occurs in Greek disguise.

A similar observation applies to Greek ***apo tote*** in *Matthew 4:17* and *16:21*. Some scholars have suggested that this strange expression "from then on" may mark a turning point in the life of Jesus. The reader familiar with the style of *SBV*, however, will have no problems in recognizing the Greek ***apo tote*** as an inverted translation of Sanskrit *tatôpi*, "and then". As a rule, Greek ***tote*** likewise translates Sanskrit *tato/tataḥ/tatas*, a synonym of *atha*.

In other words: To understand the Greek one must know the Sanskrit behind it. This is a general rule that – so I maintain – applies to all the "Sanskritisms" of the four Gospels as a whole.

These are just a few typical examples of how the unknown authors of the Gospels "translated" the Sanskrit into Greek. The puns on the sounds of the original Sanskrit are sufficient to show that there was no "Aramaic" (or any other) intermediate.

The strange way of "translating" may come as a surprise to modern readers. But if things are seen in their proper historical context there is but little cause for surprise. Indian readers familiar with the norms of *alaṁkāraśāstra* – the *śabda-* and the *arthālaṁkāras* – will easily recognize the various kinds of puns on the sound and meaning of the original.

Jewish readers familiar with the rules (middoth) that are employed in the exegesis of their sacred scriptures, will have even less cause for surprise. A convenient survey of rabbinic hermeneutics is provided by Hermann L. Strack, *Introduction to the Talmud and Midrash*, New York 1959.

The Gospels, with odd results, have been translated "according to the book". The main rules (Hebrew middoth) at work when the Sanskrit was translated into Greek, were:

1. **Neged**, corresponding significant number, as when the seven days of the original become six, six, and about eight.
2. **Ma'al**, paronomasia, a playing on words which sound alike, Sanskrit *anuprāsa*, alliteration, or *yamaka*, as in the case of *Nālandā* and *Gaṅgām* becoming ***Nathanael*** and ***gên Gên-***.
3. **Gematria**, from Greek grammateia, computation of the numeric value of letters, and metathesis of the letters, e.g. when *putras* and *Tripusa(s)* both become ***Petros***.
4. **Notarikon**, when a word is broken into two or more, as when *gaṇikā* becomes ***gynê ekh-*** or ***gynê êtis***. Gematria is often seen as a subdivision of Notarikon.
5. *Mukdam shehu'meuhar ba-'inyan*, when something that precedes is placed second, ***hysteron proteron***, as when the shelters are mentioned before the *a-kāla-megha*, though they should have been mentioned after the rainy cloud.

These and many other middoth are extremely common in Haggadah literature, i.e. in Hebrew stories of the Passover.

The common technical term for translation or interpretation is Targum. It may either be Peshat (literal), or a free haggadic translation with midrashic passages, or commentaries. The Gospels should thus be seen as Targum belonging to Haggadah, done according to the middoth current among learned Jews about two thousand years ago. Often, one cannot fail to suspect that ancient Hebrew hermeneutics were somehow indebted to Indian sources to a much higher extent than generally assumed. Not just in Greek but also in Hebrew there are many "Sanskritisms". This interesting issue I hope to take up on another occasion.

Endnote (by ML)

[1]To spell out the significance of this title: the term, *Jina*, is an honorific title signifying the 'Victorious One' and was applied to the Buddha and to the chief arhats of Jainism, among others. Remember that the Buddha had said: "Were it to be said of anyone: 'He is the son of the Blessed One [the Buddha] . . .', it is of my follower Sāriputta [Śāriputra] that this should be said" (*Majjhima-Nikāya 111:22-23*). Thus, just replace the Buddha's title, the 'Blessed One', with his title, the 'Victorious One' (*Jina*), and one will appreciate Lindtner's equation of *jina-putras* (son of Jina = Śāriputra) with ***Bar-Iôna*** (son of Jona = Peter)!

* * * * * * * * *

http://www.jesusisbuddha.com/archive.html

The Washing of Feet (*John 13*)

Christian Lindtner: "News Bulletin": April 24, 2012

Some days ago the world was witness to Benedict XVI washing the feet of twelve priests. This strange ritual is based on what *John 13:1-17* has to report about the behaviour of Jesus.

As far as I am aware, there are no Jewish or pagan sources for the odd notion of a master washing the feet of his disciples. But there is a Buddhist source. It is the Pāli version of the *Mahā-Parinirvāṇa-Sūtra* (*MPS*), i.e. the *Mahā-parinibbāna-suttanta* of the *Dīgha-Nikāya* (*D.* xvi. 1.22). It runs:

> Then the Lord dressed, took his bowl and garb (*pātra-cīvaram*) and went with the group of monks to the rest-house, washed his feet, entered the hall, and took a seat against the centre pillar, with his face towards the East. The group of monks also, after washing their feet, entered the hall, and took seats around the Lord, against the western wall, and facing the East. And the Pāṭali-village laymen (*upāsaka*) too, after washing their feet, entered the hall, and took their seats opposite the Lord against the eastern wall, and facing to the West.

Then follows what in *Matthew 25:1-13* becomes the parable of the ten virgins. (This has been reprinted in Michael Lockwood's *Buddhism's Relation to Christianity*, pp. 230-31). Our episode, in Pāli, is not to be found in the Sanskrit version of the *MPS*.

Before they entered the rest-house etc., a 'water-pot' and an 'oil-lamp' had been placed there. This transcreates into the multiple lamps and the oil in Matthew. A single 'oil-lamp' becomes 'oil' and 'multiple lamps'. (In Sanskrit you cannot determine the grammatical number from the compound 'oil-lamp' itself!)

John uses two very rare nouns, namely ***niptêr*** and ***lention*** to render the Sanskrit *pātra(m)* and *cīvaram* respectively. So when Jesus was taking (***labôn***) the ***lention*** it was originally the Lord who took (*ādāya*) the *cīvaram* (robe). Jesus, in John's uninhibited imagination, uses the *pātram* or ***niptêr*** for water for washing the feet of his disciples. The Sanskrit word for the bowl, *pātram*, also becomes the Greek ***Petron*** (***p-t-r-m/n***). This is why Peter comes into the picture.

In the original, three different groups wash their (own) feet. They do so before entering the hall, and that is quite natural. In John, the Lord washes the feet of his disciples, but the disciples are also asked to wash the feet of one another. Not their own. That is not very natural.

So here we have a picture of quite a few people busy washing other peoples feet – but not their own!

Certainly, John had a sense of humor! Would he not have had a good laugh had he seen the Pope washing the feet of the twelve priests in 2012?

In a learned paper, "*Domine, tu mihi lavas pedes*?" (Studio su Giovanni 13, 1-30), Dr. Derrett (in Italian, reprinted in his *Studies in the New Testament*, Vol. III, Leiden 1982, pp. 130-160) has discussed most of the different interpretations of this curious incident where a teacher washes the feet of his students.

Why do theologians always tend to take for granted that the New Testament gospels are written by people with little or no sense of humor? Imagine a famous professor washing the feet of his students in class!

John also refers to Judas, the famous "traitor". But we now know that this Judas was concocted by combining various words etc. from the *MPS* having to do with Çundas, the last meal, the theft, and with the unknown monk who was a traitor (see Lockwood, *op. cit.*, p. 203).

All these events took place shortly before the death and resurrection of the Lord – in the Buddhist and in the Christian gospels. The Christian account of Easter is, in other words, an imaginative combination of Jewish and Buddhist elements.

* * * * * * * * * *

Mary Magdalene and the Empty Tomb (*John 20*)

Christian Lindtner: "News Bulletin": April 25, 2012

This is a Christian legend based, as so often, on two or more different Buddhist sources, the *Sad-Dharma-Puṇḍarīka-sūtram* (*SDP*) and the *Saṁgha-Bheda-Vastu* (*SBV*) of the *Mūla-Sarvāstivāda-Vinaya* (*MSV*).

From the *SDP* we have the motif of the empty *stūpa(s)* that contained the Lord. The Sanskrit *stūpas* becomes the Greek ***taphos***, "grave". In *John 20:7*, the Sanskrit *stūpas* also becomes Greek ***topos***, '(empty) place', where the body of the Lord used to be located. The sense and sound (consonants) of the original Sanskrit have been preserved well. The "translation" is faithful to sound and sense at the same time, as so often.

The purpose of the legend is to "prove" the Resurrection of Jesus. All the New Testament "proofs" have, as I have shown by now, been taken from Buddhists sources. They do not, therefore, prove any historical event, but they do prove that the New Testament to a large extent is a "pirate copy" of Buddhist sources. Things take place, not "out there", but "in here" – in the imagination of the authors. We are, to be sure, not dealing with mere parallels, but with a direct literary dependence – as can be seen from the following observations:

John 20:1 starts out with the odd Greek phrase:

tê de mia tôn sabbatôn,

which is a DIRECT RENDERING of the eight syllables of the very common introductory Sanskrit:

ekasmin khalu samaye

with the frequent variant:

tena khalu samayena

'reportedly (*khalu*), on one occasion'/ 'they say, on that occasion'/ 'once upon a time'.

Note how nicely *eka-* becomes ***mia***, how *tena* becomes ***tê de***, how the final *samaye / samayena* becomes ***sabbatôn***. Even the Greek ***de*** retains some of the force of the Sanskrit *khalu*. The Sanskrit *khalu* indicates, in Mahāyāna usage, that this is something that is supposed to have taken place: 'it is said, for sure, reportedly'.

The legend of the woman who in the early morning sees the empty bed of *Yaśāḥ* is reported in the *SBV* (I, p. 141) in these words:

1. *adrakṣīd* – '(she) saw';
2. *anyatamāvaruddhikā* – 'a certain harem woman';
3. *sarātram eva* – 'while it was still night';
4. *suptapratibuddhā* – '(when she) had woken up from sleep';
5. *Yaśāḥ kumāro* – 'prince *Yaśās*';
6. *mahāśayane* – 'on the great bed';
7. *na dṛśyate* – 'is not seen';
8. *iti* – 'thus (she saw, or said)'.

John renders as follows, as a rule, with the same number of syllables, respecting the word order:

0. The Greek ***tê de mia tôn sabbatôn*** was, as said, based on a combination of the Sanskrit *tena khalu samayena / ekasmin khalu samaye*.
1. *adrakṣīd*, the Sanskrit verb, becomes Greek ***erkhetai***, 'she came'; but the sense is retained in the ***blepei***.
2. *anyatamāvaruddhikā*, 'a certain harem woman', becomes ***Maria hê Magdalênê***; but the *anyatama-* is also to be seen in the ***ho allos mathêtês***, *John 20:3, 8*.
3. *sarātram eva* becomes ***prôi skotias***, 'while still quite dark'; the ***eti ousês*** renders the force of the emphatic Sanskrit *eva*.
4. This is applied to Jesus – *Yaśāḥ* – who was now raised, not from the bed, but from the dead, *John 20:11*. John refers to the ***graphê***, 'scripture', i.e. the *SBV*, I, p. 141. (Likewise, "Paul", in *1 Cor. 15*.)
5. Sanskrit *kumāras* becomes Greek ***kurios***, and *Yaśās* becomes ***Jesus***.
6. *mahāśayane* becomes ***eis to mnêmeion***, 'to the tomb'.
7. The *na dṛśyate*, 'he (*kumāras* / ***kurios*** = Jesus) is not seen'. This is the main motif.
8. The *iti* reflected in the ref. to ***graphê***, *John 20:9*.

The story goes on: The woman runs to the father of *Yaśāḥ* (the counterpart to 'Simon Peter'), who suspects that his son may have been taken away by robbers and, therefore, sends out his men to look for him, etc. In the end, the prince (*kumāras*) turns up again – safe and sound. There is a sermon about rebirth in heaven – *svarga-kathā*. There is a teaching that is like a pure cloth, *suddhaṁ vastram* – the **sudarion**, linen cloths, in *John 20:7*. Jesus refers to his "brothers", *John 20:17*, and the original also refers to the four brothers of Yaśās (I, p. 146). Jesus refers to his father, who, in the original, is the father of Yaśās. The wife and the mother of Yaśās are also converted (I, p. 144), as are his four brothers (I, p. 146).

What Matthew, Mark and Luke have to report about the alleged resurrection can easily be traced, with several nice details, to the same Buddhist sources, above all to the *MPS* in the *MSV*.

The strange mother of Joses, *Mark 15:47*, was the counterpart to the mother of Yaśās. The Jesus from Nazareth of *Mark 16:6* was here Yaśās from the town (*nagarī*) of Vārāṇasī (I, p. 146). The FOUR brothers of Yaśās account for the FOUR brothers of Jesus, *Matthew 13:55*. Their names are listed in *SBV*, I, p. 146. Each of them is – as Yaśās is – described as an *agra-kulika-putras*, i.e., as a 'son', *putras*, of an *agra-kulika*, 'belonging to a prominent (*agra-*) family (*-kulika*)' – 'the nobility' / 'the chief family'. It is because of this relationship, that Yaśās is called a *kumāras*, 'prince'. Here, in *Matthew 13:55*, Jesus himself is described as "the carpenter's son", ***ho tou tektonos huios*** – a direct rendering of the Sanskrit used for Yaśās and his brothers: *agra-kulika-putras* – seven syllables in the original and in the copy.

What went on in the mind of "Matthew" when he chose to render the Sanskrit *agra-kulika-putras* by ***ho tou tektonos huios***? Well, first of all, the *putras* at the end of the compound was no problem: *putras* becomes Greek ***huios***, 'son'. Then he faced the five syllables *agra-kulika*. According to our dictionaries, *kulika-* means not only 'of a good family', but also refers to the chief or head of a guild, even an artist of high birth. Now, the father of Jesus was certainly of high birth, being "the son of David", *Matthew 1:20*. Moreover, the Greek ***tektôn*** can mean a craftsman or workman of almost any sort, a master in any art. The Greek ***tektôn*** can, therefore, be accepted as a fine rendering of the Sanskrit *agrakulikas*.

A summary will make all this come out more clearly: The main person is Yaśās, a *kumāras*, the son of an *agrakulikas* in Vārāṇasī (Benares). Yaśās becomes sick and tired of life in the palace. One night he wakes up, sees the harem women, and leaves his 'great' bed.

A little later, one of the concubines wakes up and sees the empty bed. She runs to the father of Yaśās, who suspects that his son may have been kidnapped by robbers in order to collect a ransom. He sends out two groups of men to seek for his son. The son is found in the company of the Bhagavān (Lord [Buddha]), who, by way of a miracle, makes Yaśās invisible so that his father cannot recognize him. John follows this story, but faces certain problems. John cannot give any natural explanation for the tomb of Jesus suddenly being empty. Why would ***kurios*** want to leave the grave?

Mary Magdalene faces the same problem. She suspects that "they" may have stolen the body of her Lord – but why would "they" want to do that? Certainly not to collect ransom money – for who would want to buy the dead body of Jesus? She then suspects the gardener – the counterpart to the *unrecognizable* Kumāras – to have removed the body. But what would his motive have been? Perhaps to sell the grave to another? We do not know.

John then resorts to a supernatural explanation: resurrection. But even this notion is taken by combining two different Buddhist motifs. On the one hand we often hear that humans can stay in hell for some time, and then come up again. Such a person, in Sanskrit, is called a *nārakas* – which becomes the Greek ***nekros***, 'dead'. The other idea is that of a human being who wakes up from his / her sleep. The compound is *supta-pratibuddhas*, being awake again after having slept. By "transcreating" from one to the other of these two entirely different notions, John and the early Christians (crypto-Buddhists) bring about the resurrection of Jesus from the dead.

The authors of the gospels have combined the motif of the empty bed of *kumāras* (prince) Yaśās with the motif of the empty *stūpa(s)* of a Tathāgata(s) (Buddha). Nearly all the other events having to do with Easter can be traced back to these Buddhist sources – above all, to the *MPS*.

The empty grave has, of course, often been discussed by theologians. Here, I will only mention the rare and learned book by J. Duncan M. Derrett, *The Anastasis: The Resurrection of Jesus as an Historical Event* (published by P. Drinkwater, 56 Church Street, Shipston-on-Stour, Warwickshire, England, 1982).

In 1982, Derrett took it for granted that we were here dealing with an account of a Palestinian historical event. But later on, in 2001, in his important book, *The Bible and the Buddhists*, Derrett was much more open to the account being a crypto-Buddhist allegory.

Faith as Small (or as Big) as a Mustard Seed

Christian Lindtner: "News Bulletin": April 29, 2012

It is a great pity that New Testament theologians still have the chutzpah of ignoring the numerous Buddhist sources of almost all the parables of the mythical Jesus.

The German New Testament scholar Heinrich Weinel in his book on the parables of Jesus (*Die Gleichnisse Jesu*, 1903 & 1910), was willing to admit that Jesus had been influenced by Indian parables, above all in the Parable of the Talents (*Matthew 25:14-30* and *Luke 19:12-27*). It was the German Indologist Hermann Jacobi who first translated it (from the Uttarādhyayana 7:14-21[*]), and it runs:

> Three merchants set out on their travels, each with his capital; one of them gained there much, the second returned with his capital, and the third merchant came home after having lost his capital. This parable[**] is taken from common life; learn (to apply it) to the Law [the Dharma]. The capital is human life, the gain is heaven; through the loss of that capital man must be born as a denizen of hell or brute animal. . . . He who brings back his capital is (to be compared to) one who is born again as a man. . . . But he who increases his capital is (to be compared to) one who practises eminent virtues; the virtuous, excellent man cheerfully attains the state of gods.
>
> (Quoted in the English translation of Richard Garbe's *Indien und das Christentum*, Tübingen, 1914, p. 42; reprinted Süderbrarup 2004 [English trans.: *India and Christendom* (Open Court Publishing Company, 1959), pp. 42-43])

Weinel admitted that Jesus may have been influenced by this Indian parable, but found that Jesus changed it so that it became more profound, more original, more poetical.

The reader may judge the poetical originality of Jesus for himself!

Let us now look at the celebrated Parable of the Mustard Seed! It is about the power of faith.

> According to *Matthew 17:20*, if you have faith (***pistis***) as small (or as big?) as a mustard seed (***kokkos sinapeôs***), you can order a mountain to go from here to there, and it will do so.
>
> According to *Luke 17:6*, if you have faith as small as a mustard seed, you can order a mulberry tree (***suka-minos***) to pull itself up by the roots and plant itself in the sea, and it will.
>
> According to *Mark 11:20-23*, Jesus cursed a fig tree (***sukê***). He then said, that if you have faith in God, you can tell this mountain to get up and throw itself in the sea, and it will.

All this is about "little faith" – ***oligo-pistia*** – the word (a compound) only appears here (*Matthew 17:20*), and, as I have pointed out elsewhere, translates the noun corresponding to the Sanskrit adjective *alpotsukas*, from *alpa(s)* + *utsukas* (= *alpotsukas*, "having little faith"). As a rule, it is used by the Lord only.

Jesus speaks of '**faith**', of a '**mustard seed**', of a '**mountain**', of the '**sea**' ('**ocean**'), and of a '**mulberry tree**', or a '**fig tree**'.

The Buddhist source of all these is to be found – as to be expected by now – in the usual source, the *Mūla-Sarvāstivāda-Vinaya* (*MSV*), I, pp. 186-87.

The Buddhist legend, in brief, is this:

Udāyī (nom.) has faith (*prasādas*) in the Śākya monk, i.e. *Śākya-munis* (the Buddha from Kapilavastu). Udāyī goes to the king, the father of *Śākyamunis*. The king is impressed by the peaceful state of mind (*upasamas*) of Udāyī. He asks Udāyī if *Śākyamunis* has also attained such a peaceful state of mind?

Udāyī confirms that this is so, but that the peaceful state of mind of *Śākyamunis* is very different. Udāyī's is small like that of a mustard seed (*sarsapa-vat*) whereas that of *Śākyamunis* is huge like the Sumeru mountain. Or, again, his own is small like that of the amount of water in the hoof-print of a cow (*gospada-vat*), whereas that of the teacher in whom he has faith is as profound as the ocean (*samudra*).

---

[*]In Lecture 7 of Jacobi's translation of the Uttarādhyayana-Sūtra, in Part 2 of *Jain Sūtras*, Vol. 45 of *Sacred Books of the East* (Oxford 1895). – ML

[**]Jacobi's footnote, here, states: "This parable closely corresponds to Matt xxv:14 & Luke xix:11." – ML

I have already pointed out how the *MSV* has served as a source for numerous passages and ideas found in the New Testament Gospels. Hence there can be no room for doubt that the parables of Udāyī served as a source of the parables of Jesus.

I have also already pointed out elsewhere (Lockwood 2010, pp. 230-31), that if Jesus was responsible for the Parable of the Ten Virgins in *Matthew 25:1-13*, then Jesus **must** have been a great Sanskrit scholar. Only a Sanskrit scholar could have rendered it into Greek. This parable is to be found in the *Mahā-Parinirvāṇa-Sūtra* (*MPS*, a part of the *MSV*; only in Sanskrit, not in the Pāli version).

The Parable of the Mustard Seed presupposes a direct knowledge of the Sanskrit:

The version of Udāyī is so plain and rational that no further comments are needed. His own faith in *Śākyamunis* has given him peace of mind, but his own peace of mind is very small compared to that of his Lord.

Comparing the original to the "transcreation" in the New Testament Gospels (cf. also the Gospel of Thomas 20), we learn a lot about the "poetical originality" of "Jesus". We are dealing with wild and irrational exaggerations. All is mixed up. The pirate copy is by no means more "profound" than the original, but – deliberately so – highly paradoxical. The intention of "Jesus" is to puzzle and thereby also to attract his readers.

Accordingly, his obscure parables have puzzled his readers ever since.

It is now easy to identify the ***suka-minos*** in *Luke* (and the ***sukê*** in *Mark*). The ***suka-minos*** is a pun on *Śākya-munis*. The mulberry tree as well as the fig tree refer to *Śākya-munis*.

He was cursed by Jesus, he was thrown into the ocean by the new faith.

The Indian 'King of Dharma' has thus been replaced by the Jewish 'King of Righteousness'.

That trick of transcreation is a part of what – quite understandably – had to remain the Secret of the Christ. Behind Jesus we find the Buddha. Early "insiders" must have been aware of the true identity.

And it is still a question of faith, and the old Buddhist ideal of heaven remains the same.

* * * * * * * * *

The Lord from Nagara/Nyagrodha

Christian Lindtner: "Communication": May 20, 2012

On Jesus from ***Nazaret*** and ***Kaphar-naum*** etc.:

As usual, a given New Testament passage can be accounted for as a combination of Old Testament and Buddhist sources combined according to the demands of gematria (not discussed here).

The initial sentence of the *Saṁgha-Bheda-Vastu* (*SBV*) in the *Mūla-Sarvāstivāda-Vinaya* (*MSV*) (p. 5) provides most of the Buddhist materials.

It says: The Lord is staying in *Kapila-vastu*, in the *Nyagrodha*-garden. Many of the inhabitants of *Kapila-vastu* are assembled in the *saṁsthā-āgāra* (locative – *ārāmē*), an assembly-hall. They invite the Lord to tell the story of their own old family genesis (*paurāṇa-kula-vaṁśas* = the two initial words, "***Biblos geneseôs***", of Matthew 1:1).

We hear of events that once took place in the town (*nagarē*), of *Kapila-vastu-ni* (locative again) (*ibid.*, p. 23).

Behind the various forms ***Nazara***, ***Nazareth***, ***Nazaret***, we thus have *Nyagrodha* and *nagara* (above).

The Lord himself is called ***Nazarênos*** and ***Nazô-raios***. These are combinations of Buddhist and Old Testament sources (known), spelled so as to meet gematria requirements (about which later). ***Nazô-raios*** also contains a pun on the common *Nāga-rājas* (King of the serpents). (So, here a *z* is allowed to replace an original *g*.) In his former lives, the Lord was once a *nāga-rājas*, as known.

Ha, ha! Jesus ***Nazô-raios*** as an Indian *Nāga-rājas*!!

The Lord Buddha teaches to the gods etc. in the *saṁsthāgārē* (loc.) in *Kapila-vastu*. The Sanskrit *saṁsthāgārē* is behind the ***sunagogê*** (cf. Old Testament usage with another meaning!), likewise four syllables, a synonym used in precisely the same context. The Sanskrit inspires to a new meaning of ***sunagogê***! Cf. e.g. new meaning of ***doxa*** in the New Testament compared to classical Greek, retaining the meaning of the original Hebrew!

Behind ***Kaphar-naoum***, the place of the strange ***Kaphar***, we obviously have *Kapila-vastu*, the place (***naoum*** = *vastu*) of the famous sage Kapila(s). *Kapila-vastu* was the place of the father of *Śākyamunis* (the Buddha).

Several miracles, e.g. that of the boy falling into fire and water etc., originally took place in *Kapila-vastu*. This was the Lord, up in the air, emitting water and fire!

Conclusion: Jesus teaching in the synagogue of ***Kaphar-naoum*** was originally the Lord teaching in the *saṁsthāgārē*, "***sunagogê***", of *Kapila-vastu*. The Lord was staying in this *nagarē* (loc.), or just outside in the *Nyagrodha*-garden etc.

So, behind *nagarē* and *nyagrodha*, we have a good deal of the background source for ***Nazara***, ***Nazareth***, ***Nazaret***. From now on, no scholarly book about Jesus from Nazareth should forget to make it clear that this is the Lord from *Nagara*, or the Lord from *Nyagrodha*, etc.

There is more about the compound *Kapila-vastavas*, the inhabitants of *Kapilavastu*, in my book *Geheimnisse um Jesus Christus*. Looking at those passages, you will see that the pirate copying cannot possibly have worked the other way around.

I consider this identification, not probable, but certain.

One can have fun finding a Buddhist image/sculpture of a *Nāga-rājas*, if one wants to illustrate the original ***Nazô-raios***. So, please, don't say that we do not know what Jesus looked like or could have looked like!

Reminder: As you know, my general rule says: When you have to account for a given passage in the New Testament gospels, you need to start out with the working-hypothesis that this passage consists of a combination of materials from *Q* (= *MSV*, *SDP* [*Sad-Dharma-Puṇḍarīka-sūtra*], etc.) + Old Testament + demands of gematria. We can then add a small box with "other sources":

Q (= *MSV*, *SDP* etc.) + OT + demands of gematria + "other sources".

* * * * * * * * *

Was He a Man or Was He a God?

Christian Lindtner: "Note", May 30, 2012

Commenting upon *1 Cor. 9:19*, Porphyry (ca. 232 - ca. 305 C.E.) wrote: "Ah! the asinine nature of all this. Such scenes are used in the theater in order to get a laugh. Jugglers give exhibitions like this! For how can a free man be everyone's slave?" (quoted from R. Joseph Hoffmann, ed. & trans., *Porphyry's* Against the Christians, 1994, p. 59).

In order to understand and resolve the paradox of how a free man can be everyone's slave, one may well ask for the sources of *1 Cor.*, traditionally ascribed to the foremost of the apostles, Paulos, or Saulos.

The idea of a free man being everyone's slave is typical of Mahāyāna Buddhism. A Bodhisattva – the Mahāyāna hero – is expected to sacrifice even his own flesh and blood for the sake of other living beings. By doing so, he may – let us hope! – become a Buddha – the highest ideal of Mahāyāna.

As I have repeatedly pointed out, the *Mahā-Parinirvāṇa-Sūtra* (*MPS*) and *Sad-Dharma-Puṇḍarīka-sūtra* (*SDP*) are among the main Buddhists sources of the New Testament. The *MPS* is a part of the *Mūla-Sarvāstivāda-Vinaya* (*MSV*). Along with other Buddhist texts in Sanskrit and Pāli, they are to be identified with "Q".

The *SDP* is the source of numerous episodes familiar to us from the New Testament gospels – e.g. the Secret of the Christ, the identity of **Simôn Petros**, the Saints arising from their Graves, numerous parables, etc. It would therefore also be natural to expect the *MPS* and *SDP* to have served as sources for the fabrication of the foremost among the apostles – Paulos, or Saulos, the "slave" of the Lord.

Chapter VIII of the *SDP* introduces us to a certain apostle called Pūrṇas and the future destiny of the five hundred monks. Pūrṇas has a mind that is free, and he is said to have been and to have become "the foremost among the preachers of the law" (*agryo dharmakathikānām*) and "the keeper of the true Law" (*saddharmaparigrāhakas*) (Sanskrit ed. Kern, p. 201; trans. Kern, p. 193). Pūrṇas is the only disciple in the *SDP* to be described in such terms.

The Lord has much to say about Pūrṇas:

> He is the man to excite, arouse, and stimulate the four classes of the audience; unwearied in the preaching of the law (*dharmas*); capable to preach the law as to oblige his fellow-followers of the course of duty. The Tathāgata excepted, monks, there is no one able to equal Pūrṇa(s), son of Maitrāyanī, either essentially or in accessories. Now, monks, do you suppose that he keeps my true law only? No, monks, you must not think so. For I remember, monks, that in the past, in the time of the ninety-nine Buddhas, the same Pūrṇa(s) kept the true law under the mastership of those Buddhas. Even as he is now with me, so he has, in all periods, been the foremost of the preachers of the law; he has in all periods been a consummate knower of Voidness (*śūnyatā*); has in all periods acquired the (four) distinctive qualifications of an Arhat; has in all periods reached mastership in the transcendent wisdom of the Bodhisattvas. He has been a strongly convinced (*su-viniścitas*) preacher of the law, exempt from doubt, and quite pure. Under the mastership of those Buddhas he has during his whole existence observed a spiritual life, and everywhere they termed him 'the Disciple' (*śrāvakas*).

The "monks" to whom the Lord is speaking, are identified as the twelve-hundred self-controlled (*vaśī-bhūtas*) ones (Sanskrit ed. Kern, p. 206; tr. Kern, p. 198). Among these are the Great Kāśyapas (*ibid.*).

The Lord goes on (Sanskrit ed. Kern, p. 209; tr. Kern, p. 200):

> Thus, Kāśyapa, keep now in view here these (twelve-hundred) apostles (*vaśī-bhūtas*), no less than five hundred (in number), as well as my other disciples, and speak of this matter to the other disciples.

The anonymous authors of the *SDP* were, of course, familiar with the "canonical" version of the Buddhist gospel.

In a sense, the *SDP* is, itself, a "new testament", compared to the old one. The "new" idea is that faith is sufficient for salvation – to put it very briefly. It is the duty of the Bodhisattva to use all sorts of tricks (*upāya*) to make common people believe in the eternal Tathāgata. These "tricks" include parables, puns, arguments, etc. In this way, Bodhisattvas, as apostles, freely give their lives for others.

The Buddhist background of Paul's paradox is beginning to become more clear, I hope. Typically, the authors of the New Testament combined materials from the *MSV* (including the *MPS*) with materials from the *SDP*.

This, as expected, is also the case here: *1 Cor.* is essentially based on a combination of materials from the *MPS* and *SDP*.

How so?

Gods and Heroes in Disguise.

The idea of a god or a hero who appears in disguise, or as a ***metabolê***, as a human being or even as an animal, is not only a common Buddhist motif, but in fact a typical Hellenistic or Greek idea that can be traced all the way back to Homer.

Have we forgotten that Zeus appeared as a swan when he approached Leda? The idea that gods may appear disguised as human beings is also familiar to us even from *Acts 14:12*: They called Barnabas Zeus, and Paulos they called Hermes. So some people must have been familiar with the ancient idea of gods appearing as human beings. They shouted: "The gods have become like men and have come down to us", *Acts 14:11*. One may also recall the very first lines of Ovid's *Metamorphoses*.

As I have tried to point out in my book *Geheimnisse um Jesus Christus* (2005), even the New Testament remains a book closed with seven seals, if we are not aware of this motif. Jesus is the Buddha or a Bodhisattva in the disguise of a Jewish king. Śāri-Putras is disguised as ***Simôn Petros***, Mahā-Maudgalyāyanas is disguised as ***Matthaios legomenos***, Maitreyas as ***Messias***, Kumāras as ***Markos***, etc.

If we wish to understand *1 Cor.*, we must go back to the blueprint found in the *SDP* VIII, where we first are introduced to Pūrṇas and the five hundred monks.

Clearly, keeping the context in mind, Pūrṇas is then disguised as Paulos, and in *1 Cor. 15:5-6*, the 1200 apostles have been reduced to 12 apostles, Kāśyapas has become **Kêphas**, and the 500 monks have now become 500 brothers.

The five hundred also appear several times in the *MPS*, as I have already pointed out elsewhere (Lockwood 2010, pp. 278-79). In one passage we hear about the more than 500 followers who have passed away, and in another about the 500 monks present at the cremation (along with Kāśyapas a.k.a. **Kêphas**) at the cremation of the Lord. The context remains the same.

The 500 brothers of *1 Cor.* are thus a combination of three different Buddhist sources to be found in *SDP* and *MPS*. Now we finally understand what Paulos – Pūrṇas – had in mind when he referred to "the scriptures" in *1 Cor. 15:3*. To this day, theologians have failed to identify these "scriptures" for the simple reason that they have not been looking in the right place, viz. the *SDP* and *MPS*.

It is a fundamental idea of the *SDP* that the "historical Buddha" – Śākyamunis – is a mere apparition or image of an eternal Tathāgatas. There have, in fact, been numerous such "historical Buddhas" – all of them mere empty apparitions. The same goes, of course, for the endless number of Bodhisattvas, or Great-beings, *Mahāsattva(s)*.

While rather typical of Mahāyāna, this motif can be traced back to the *MPS*.

In *MPS 23:4-7* (Sanskrit) the Lord tells his disciple Ānanda how a Tathāgata miraculously has appeared in numerous assemblies, in different bodies and speaking different languages.

This passage is available in Sanskrit and Tibetan (almost identical), as well as in Chinese and Pāli (ed. Ernst Waldschmidt, Berlin 1951, pp. 234- 237).

The Pāli version is to be found in the Dīgha Nikāya, Vol. 2 (publ. by the Pali Text Society 1903, p. 109 = 3:22-23). In the translation of Trevor Ling (1981), *The Buddha's Philosophy of Man*, p. 169, it runs:

> "Now I call to mind, Ānanda, how when I used to enter into an assembly of many hundred nobles, before I had seated myself there or talked to them or started a conversation with them, I used to become like them in colour, and in voice. Then with religious discourse I used to instruct and exhort, and liven them, and fill them with gladness. But they did not know me when I spoke and they would say: 'Who can this be who speaks in such a way – a man or god?' [cf. *Acts 14:11*, *supra* – CL]. Then having instructed, exhorted, livened and gladdened them with religious discourse. I would vanish. But they did not know me even when I vanished, and would say: 'Who can this be who has just vanished away? a man or a god?'" – In the same words the Master spoke of how he had been used to enter into assemblies of each of the other eight kinds [priests etc. – CL], and of how he had not been made known to them either in speaking or in vanishing.

The other versions contain minor variants, but the basic idea is the same: The Lord recalls how he has, in numerous previous lives, been able to transform himself into many different forms, speaking with many different voices, or "languages". The sole purpose of these transformations – ***metabolê*** in Greek – was to please other people with discourse about the Dharma – the teachings about good and bad karma, heaven and hell, etc. Once he had achieved this aim he would vanish, leaving the various assemblies deeply puzzled: Was he a man or was he a god?

The *SDP* then takes up this old idea: The Lords – the "historical" Buddhas – are mere apparitions. They appear in different forms, speaking different languages. The sole purpose is to save "all beings" by teaching a Dharma based on Faith, *śraddhā*, the Greek ***pistis*** of Paulos, a.k.a. Pūrṇas.

His true identity remains a mystery that is only revealed to insiders – the Secret of the Tathāgata is also the Secret of the Christ.

The *SDP* as well as the New Testament conveys a message of faith to all people, the great masses. The *SDP* and the New Testament are thus typical Mahāyāna scriptures. But at the same time, both the *SDP* and the New Testament have a secret message, a mystical meaning, only available to a small group of insiders. Now and then the Lords allude to "secrets" and to "mysteries" – but they do not provide us with the "keys to the kingdom of the heavens". These secrets were only to be revealed to the closest disciples.

Porphyry asked a perfectly reasonable question: How can a free man be everyone's slave?

The answer is, as we have seen, quite as logical: Because the free man only appears to be a slave.

It is among these mysterious disciples, who must have known both Greek and Sanskrit, that we have to look for the authors of the Buddhist and Christian gospels.

References

Hoffmann, R. Joseph, ed. & trans. (1994), *Porphyry's* Against the Christians*: The Literary Remains* (Amherst, NY: Prometheus Books).

Kern, Hendrik, & Bunyiu Nanjio, eds. (1908-1912), *Saddharmapuṇḍarīka* (St. Petersburg; reprint Osnabrück 1970).

Kern, Hendrik, trans. (1884), *Saddharma-Puṇḍarīka* or *The Lotus of the True Law* (Oxford: Clarendon Press; reprint New York: Dover, 1963).

Lindtner, Christian (2005), *Geheimnisses um Jesus Christus: Das Neue Testament ist Buddhas Testament* (Süderbrarup: Lühe-Verlag), being the German translation of the Danish original: *Hemmligheden om Kristus: Det Nye Testamente er Buddhas Testamente* (2003).

Ling, Trevor (1981), *The Buddha's Philosophy of Man: Early Indian Buddhist Dialogues* (London: J.M. Dent Publishers).

Lockwood, Michael (2010), *Buddhism's Relation to Christianity* (Chennai: Tambaram Research Associates).

Waldschmidt, Ernst, ed. (1950-1951), *Mahāparinirvāṇasūtra*, in 3 Parts (Berlin: Akademie-Verlag).

* * * * * * * * *

Gematria of the 'Lotus' (*Saddharmapuṇḍarīkasūtram*)

Christian Lindtner, "News": May 31, 2010

In order to understand the Greek of the New Testament, one must be able to read Sanskrit, and, likewise, in order to understand the Sanskrit of several Buddhist texts composed in that language, one must know ancient Greek. The reason for this is simple: Just as the New Testament often depends on Buddhist sources, the Buddhist texts often depend on Greek sources. These scholars were bilingual, they knew both Greek and Sanskrit.

Here is a passage from the ***Sad-Dharma-Puṇḍarīka-sūtram*** (***SDP***), or '*Lotus-sūtra*' (Kern ed. p. 391; Wogihara ed., pp. 331 ff.; Vaidya ed. pp. 231 ff.). In the translation of Kern (p. 367), with a few additions:

> Therefore, young men of good family (*kula-putras*), you should after the complete extinction (*parinirvāṇa*) of the Tathāgata, with reverence keep, read, promulgate, cherish, worship it [the *Dharma-paryāya* (the Dharma-parable)]. And wherever on earth, [to] young men of good family, this *Dharmaparyāya* shall be made known, read, written, meditated, expounded, studied or collected into a volume, be it in a monastery or at home, in the wilderness or in a town, at the foot of a tree or in a palace, in a building or in a cavern, on that spot one should erect a shrine (*caityam*) in dedication to the Tathāgata. For such a spot must be regarded as a terrace of enlightenment (*bodhi-maṇḍas*); such a spot must be regarded as one where all Tathāgatas &c. have arrived at supreme, perfect enlightenment; on that spot have all Tathāgatas moved forward the wheel of the law (*dharma-cakram*); on that spot one may hold that all Tathāgatas have reached complete extinction (*parinirvāṇa*).

The idea, in brief, is this: The *SDP* is a dharma-parable. It may be recited, written (or drawn, Sanskrit *likhyeta*), considered, copied, explained etc. on a given spot of earth, in a given place. A *caityam*, or sanctuary, shrine, should then be made in honour of the Lord – *Tathāgatam* (accusative), for this spot is the bodhi-temple (*maṇḍas*) of ALL the Tathāgatas. They have been enlightened in that spot of earth. Moreover, all the Tathāgatas have turned the Wheel of Dharma, the *dharma-cakram*, in that place.

To understand this curious passage, it will be helpful to visualize the situation as a whole. First, it says that the *SDP* is a dharma-parable. The Sanskrit for 'parable' is *paryāyas*, and, as I have pointed out elsewhere, Sanskrit *paryāyas* is translated in the New Testament by the Greek ***parabolê***. Greek ***parabol*** means, in geometry, application. In other words: the *SDP* is being drawn on a spot of earth, in the learned sand, as the Greek scholar would say.

The numerical value (***psêphos***) of 'Saddharma-puṇḍarīka-sūtram' is, according to the Greek mode of calculation, 352+666+1041 = 2059. The diameter of a 2059 circle is 656, and the radius, of course, 328. The numerical value of *dharma-cakram* is 146+182 = 328; and the numerical value of *Tathāgatam* (the accusative case as found in the text above) is 656. (For the Christians 656 is ***Messias*** = 40+5+200+200+10+1+200).

To sum up: The passage invites the *kula-putras*, son of good family, i.e., the educated reader, to draw a 2059 circle with the 656 diameter of *Tathāgatam*, and the 328 radius of *dharma-cakram*. The Sanskrit *cakram* (here the neuter, also attested in earlier Sanskrit masculine: *cakras*) clearly represents Greek ***kuklos***, circle. Once we know Greek, we easily see that *dharma-cakram* is 328, that *Tathāgatam* is 656, that *Saddharma-puṇḍarīka-sūtram* is 352+666+1041 = 2059. Furthermore, it is said that all Tathāgatas have turned the *dharma-cakram* on that spot of earth. This means that the 656 diameter of *Tathāgatam* has turned, i.e. has drawn the 2059 circle of *Saddharmapuṇḍarīkasūtram*.

What, then, about the two words *caityam* and *bodhimaṇḍas* (nominative case)? It will be observed that the numerical value of *caityam* is 20+1+10+300+10+1+40 = 382. Likewise, the number of *bodhi-maṇḍas* is 86+296 = 382. The number 382 must, therefore, be significant in the present context, i.e. in connection with the drawing – the 2059 circle of *SDP* – before our eyes. If we draw *Tathāgatas*, which is 816, as a circle, the inscribed pentagon measures 763.62 . . . or 764, which is the sum of the numerical values of *caityam* and *bodhimaṇḍas* (i.e. 382 + 382 = 764). The 816 circle with the inscribed 764 pentagon thus tells us that the *caityam* which is the *bodhimaṇḍas*, is contained in *Tathāgatas*. Or, to the same effect: *Tathāgatas* contains the *caityam* and (or: which is) the *bodhimaṇḍas*.

But how do we go from the initial 328 radius in 2059 *SDP* circle to the 382 of *caityam* and *bodhimaṇḍas*? First, 328 is the 2 x 164 solar cross in the 514.95 = 515 circle. Four such circles amount to 514.96 = 2059.84, which, taken as 2059 was, as demonstrated, the number of *SDP*. The 515 circle contains the inscribed 464 square. When we subtract one half of 164, i.e. 82, from 464, we arrive at 382, the value of *caityam* as well as *bodhimaṇḍas*. We can now easily see how the author, who must have known the Greek language as well as the Greek mode of ***psêphos***, went about: He started out with 328 – *dharmacakram*. From that he derived the figure 382. This figure he divided by five, giving him the image of the 382 pentagon inscribed in the 408.20, or 408 circle. Two such circles gave him 816 for Tathāgatas.

The words of the *SDP*, in this passage, to sum up, thus operate – as the text itself often states when it refers to "hidden or symbolic language (*saṁdhā-bhāṣya*)" – on two levels. There is a hidden message. There are, as always in Mahāyāna, two truths. On the superficial level of words one can translate from one language into another language. On a deeper level, one must know the numerical value of each Sanskrit word according to the Greek mode of calculation (***psêphos***).

All this was, as I hope to have shown by numerous examples, also known to the authors of the New Testament. Let me therefore, briefly repeat what I have pointed out elsewhere:

Revelation 13:18 refers to the number 666, saying that "it is, in fact, the number of a man" – ***a-rith-mos gar an-thrô-pou es-tin***. These nine syllables of the Greek represent the nine original syllables of the Sanskrit of the title: *sad-dhar-ma-puṇ-ḍa-rī-ka-sūt-ram*. The total number of syllables, as said, is, in both cases, nine. Moreover, the number of letters is, in both cases, 23. Each phrase consists of four different words. The Sanskrit counts nine vowels, but the Greek has ten.

Revelation 13:18 does not explicitly identify the man whose number is said to be 666. This omission has, unfortunately, given rise to endless speculations. In our view, philological problems must, if possible, be solved in the light of their sources. The Greek for "man" is ***anthrôpos*** (nominative form). His number is said to be 666. But 666 is the number of Sanskrit *puṇḍarīka*: 80+400+50+4+1+100+10+20+1 = 666. The "man" in *Revelation 13:18*, is, therefore, the Lotus, the *puṇḍarīka*. Something is missing! The man has not been fully identified from the New Testament point of view. The Greek ***anthrôpos***, man, is 1310. When we subtract 666 from *puṇḍarīka*, we are left with 644. We would expect, from the context, that 644 somehow refers to the hero of the New Testament, i.e. to Jesus or Christ (888 or 1480).

According to the Old Testament quotation in *Matthew 1:23*, Jesus will be called ***Emmanouêl*** – but, strangely, the New Testament never mentions him by that name. We must thus look for our ***Emmanouêl*** on some deeper level, i.e. on the numerical level. Now ***Emmanouêl*** is 5+40+40+1+50+70+400+8+30 = 644. The 1310 "man" that *Revelation 13:18* refers to, is, therefore, *puṇḍarīka* as ***Emmanouêl***, for 666 + 644 = 1310.

To put it simply: The Christian saviour (known as Jesus etc.) is identified with the Buddhist saviour (known as *Śākyamuni(s)* etc.). The great hero of the *SDP* is, of course, *Śākyamunis*, whose number is 932. The Lotus is his symbol. Since ***Emmanouêl*** was identified with this Lotus, we would expect that Jesus also was identified with the Lotus, for ***Emmanouêl*** is one of the names of Jesus.

When we look closer at various passages of the New Testament, we shall find that our suspicions are fully confirmed: During the Last Supper, Jesus refers to his body, Greek ***sôma***, and to his blood, ***to haima mou***. The ***sôma*** is 1041, and 1041 is also Sanskrit *sūtram*. And "the blood of mine", ***to haima mou***, is 932, and 932 is *Śākyamunis*. The ***tês diathêkês***, of the covenant, that follows (*Matthew 26:28*) contains a clear pun on Sanskrit *Tathāgatasya*, 'of the Tathāgata', i.e. of *Śākyamuni[s]*, both pentasyllabic. Jesus thus identifies himself with *Śākyamuni(s)*, the main Tathāgata of the *SDP*. Jesus is an embodiment of the *SDP*.

There is more to the very same effect: When we draw a circle that measures 888 for Jesus (***Iêsous***), the inscribed Lotus (the Star of David, the *hexagram*) measures 1470, but 1470 is the number of the Greek word for the Lotus, viz. ***ho lôtos*** = 70+30+800+300+70+200 = 1470. So we see Jesus as the Lotus, the Star of David.

Did the authors of the *SDP* already have this drawing in mind – the drawing of the Lotus inscribed in a circle? The answer is: yes, they did: The ***psêphos*** of *SDP* was, as will be recalled, 2059 (or 2059.84). If one draws a Lotus (as the Buddhists often did) measuring 2059, the circle in which this hexagram is inscribed measures ca. 1244. To be quite precise: the inscribed hexagram measures 6 x 343.306666666..... suggesting the number of man: 666. If we add 816, the number of Tathāgatas (above), we arrive at 2060 or 2059, which is the number of 'Saddharmapuṇḍarīkasūtram'. This Buddhist drawing, therefore, also identifies Tathāgatas on the basis of a drawing of a hexagram showing us the stylized image of a Lotus.

Jesus, was, therefore, in several ways born from a Buddhist lotus.

A final point: In the *SDP*, the Lord Śākyamuni(s) encourages his disciples to spread the message in writing etc. His disciples are called Bodhisattvas, Mahāsattvas etc., and *kula-putras*, i.e. "family-sons" (often translated freely as "sons of good family"). The passage from the *SDP* quoted above read:

> Therefore, young men of good family, you should after the complete extinction of the Tathāgata, with reverence, keep, read, promulgate, cherish, worship it.

In other words: Once *Śākyamuni(s)* has passed away, it is up to the *kula-putras* to spread the *SDP* in various ways. The *kula-putras* is thus one of the many synonyms of a Buddhist missionary. The ***psêphos*** of Sanskrit *kula-putras* is 451+1081 = 1532. I have already pointed out, again and again, that Jesus is such a Buddhist missionary in disguise.

The truth of this observation can now be established from yet another point of view. The number of Jesus is 888, and the number of ***Emmanouêl*** is 644. Thus Jesus ***Emmanouêl*** is 888 + 644 = 1532. But 1532 is also the number of *kula-putras*, a missionary of the Lotus. It was stated clearly, that the *kula-putras* was expected to become active AFTER the extinction of *Śākyamunis*.

Jesus ***Emmanouêl***, therefore, was such a *kula-putras*, who propagated the message of the *SDP* – in disguise as the son of God, the son of David etc. etc. He was, indeed, born in or from a lotus, for all Bodhisattvas are, as students of Buddhist art are aware, born in a lotus.

Jesus was also known as ***Messias***, and ***Messias*** is 40+5+200+200+10+1+200 = 656. But, as we have seen, 656 is the diameter of the 2059 circle of 'Saddharmapuṇḍarīkasūtram'. Thus, ***Messias***, alias Jesus ***Emmanouêl***, was also born from the Lotus. In various places, the New Testament would like to have us believe that Jesus is identical with the ***Messias*** mentioned in the Old Testament.

We can now prove that this belief is, in a strange and unexpected way, quite true, for since the *SDP* circle is 2059, and since Jesus is 888, and since ***Messias*** is 656, and since 515 was also established above, it follows that:

Jesus is ***Messias*** – in Greek: ***Iêsous esti Messias*** = 888+515+656 = 2059.

Moonstone Step, Anurādhapura, Śrī Laṅkā

Courtesy Wikipedia

Moonstone Step, Polonnaruwa, Śrī Laṅkā

V

THE GRAFT'S "HISTORICAL" JUDAIC ROOTS

Mythicist Recalibration

Mythicists, of course, will not agree with Robert Eisenman when he assumes, in his books, *James the Brother of Jesus* (1997) and *The New Testament Code* (2006), that the gospels' Jesus and his brothers/disciples are historical persons.

However, from the Mythicist position, the importance of Eisenman's research can be clarified and strengthened by realizing that the allegorical 'Christian' characters of the canonical gospels (second century CE works) have been imaginatively placed back in a first century setting and correlated haphazardly with both pre-Christian crypto-Buddhists (the real forerunners of Christianity) and with other highly sensational historical figures, such as Jesus ben Ananias! (Is this evidence of black humor?)

The New Testament Code
The Cup of the Lord, the Damascus Covenant, and the Blood of Christ

by Robert Eisenman; Watkins Publishing, 2006

Reviewed by Robert M. Price

Readers of my earlier reviews in this series will not find themselves altogether unprepared for the arguments of this massive sequel to Professor Eisenman's great opus *James the Brother of Jesus* (1998). But they will still find plenty of surprises. Before we give attention to some of them, let us observe that the book is a very great challenge to read. Those who found *James the Brother of Jesus* too long, too redundant, too circuitous, will only find those sins magnified here. One almost feels Eisenman, like an apocalyptic scribe, wants to make his readers prove their mettle by working for the pay-off. Reading the book, despite its very fascinating revelations, must frankly be called an ordeal. One is inevitably put in mind of one's adolescent determination to embark on reading the Bible straight through, only to get bogged down in *Numbers* or *Deuteronomy*. But you are just going to have to soldier on. It is worth the time. Whether Eisenman is correct in his apparent conviction that it is necessary to cover every relevant document, surveying all possible cross references, and doing it again every time he comes to the same item in the next document, I cannot say. But he does make his case that there is an inescapable commonality of terminology and conceptuality, sometimes used ironically or satirically, between a mass of texts which need to be placed together on a mental map if one is to grasp the shape of the religious world in which they all float as continents.

And the first achievement of *The New Testament Code* hard won through this methodology, is the realization that the Dead Sea Scrolls stem from the mid to late first century CE (equivocal Carbon dating results no longer even being relevant), and that they represent the sectarian baptizing *Schwärmerei* known variously as the Essenes, Zealots, Nasoreans, Masbotheans, Sabaeans – *and Jewish Christians headed by James the Just*. Endless references to the armies of the Kittim and "the kings of the Peoples" make the date clear even before we get to the catalogue of terminological and conceptual links between the Scrolls, the New Testament, and the Pseudo-Clementines. I should say that in all these comparisons Eisenman has established a system of correspondences fully as convincing, and for the same reasons, as the Preterist interpretation of the Book of Revelation by R.H. Charles and others. I just do not see any room for serious doubt any more. Teichner was right; Eisenman is right: the Scrolls are the legacy of the Jerusalem Christians led by the Heirs of Jesus: James the Just, Simeon bar Cleophas, and Judas Thomas. The Teacher of Righteousness was James the Just (though Arthur E. Palumbo, Jr., *The Dead Sea Scrolls and the Personages of Earliest Christianity*, 2004, may be right: as per Barbara Thiering, John the Baptist may have been the first to hold that office, with James as his successor). The Spouter of Lies who "repudiated the Torah in the midst of the congregation" was Paul. It was he who "founded a congregation on lies," namely the tragically misled "Simple of Ephraim," converts from among the Gentile God-fearers who knew no better. The Wicked Priest was Ananus ben Ananus, whom Josephus credits with lynching James on the Day of Atonement.

Granted, Eisenman indulges in overkill, flooding the reader with so many convergences of language and basic concepts that the unsympathetic reader may dismiss him as simply documenting a common atmosphere of belief and language characteristic, not of specific sects (or factions of sects), but of the period in general. But there is a smaller set of correspondences which are sharp enough to persuade us that, e.g., *1 Corinthians 10* is using a specific portion of the *Covenant of Damascus* (a well-known ancient document, as its presence in the Cairo Genizah as well as Qumran suggests), namely column III, 2-7 (p. 919), or that the Habakkuk Pesher means to refute Paul's use of the famous *Habakkuk 2:4* (see pp. 903-904). These comparisons are as telling as that which persuades us that *James 2:14-24* means to refute *Romans 3:27* to *4:5 ff.*

Ironically, all these correspondences serve as collateral evidence for a much clearer basis for identifying early Christianity with the sect of the Scrolls. Have you ever read the truism that the Scrolls neglect to name their parent body? And yet their sect is again and again called both "the Poor" (*Ebionim*, Ebionites) and "the Way." These, of course, are the earliest known self-designations of Christians, as *Acts* tells us, long before they were called "Christians" – by outsiders. The refusal to recognize the identity of the nomenclature, and therefore of the groups behind them, is astonishing and attests a simple unwillingness to factor the Scrolls into Christian Origins on such an integral level. Even so, Eisenman's reading of the Scrolls tells us much about the dawn era of Christianity, certainly more than some will want to know. But with *The New Testament Code* we have reached a crossroads. Will we begin to take into account all this new data and move forward along the indicated lines? Or will we continue to temporize and find new excuses to isolate our conventional assumptions and play in the pool of Eusebian apologetics? '

Eisenman recapitulates the basic outlines of his discoveries about James' role as obscured by *Acts*. The election of Matthias to replace Judas Iscariot is a mask for the election of James the Just to replace the absent Jesus as his *caliph* (the root reference behind the epithets of both "James of *Alphaeus*" and "Simeon bar-*Cleophas*," both meaning the same thing). James' name, à la Noth's redundancy principle, remains in the text, albeit shouldered aside, in the guise of the other nominee for the job, "Joseph bar-Sabbas *Justus*." (Why even retain the name, unless there is another purpose?)

James bar-Zebedee is another fictive double for James the Just, and his elimination in *Acts 12:2* is merely the dropping of the mask before James the Just can appear in his own name in chapter 15.

James was a rainmaker like Elijah, Honi the Circle-maker, and Hanan the Wise. Nathanael is another mask for James. Jesus finds him, conspicuously, sitting beneath a fig tree, the posture of rain-makers, as they waited (in a gesture of anticipative, imitative magic) for their prayers to be answered. And Jesus tells him he will, *like the Genesis Jacob*, witness heaven open, revealing the Son of Man, which Nathanael does not see in John but which James does see, at his martyrdom, according to Hegesippus.

James' stoning to death after proclaiming his vision of the Son of Man standing in heaven has been (as Hans-Joachim Schoeps first noted) changed into Stephen's martyrdom after announcing the same vision.

But Eisenman adds more. For instance, he argues that the resurrection appearance of Jesus to James the Just in the *Gospel according to the Hebrews* is the origin of both *Luke's* Emmaus Road story and *John's* Doubting Thomas tale. Here is the ostensible original:

> *Now the Lord, when he had given the linen cloth to the servant of the priest, went to James and appeared to him, for James had sworn that he would not eat bread from that hour wherein he had drunk the Lord's cup until he should see him risen again from among those who sleep. And he said to him, "Hail!" And he called to the servants, who were greatly amazed. "Bring," said the Lord, "a table and bread." He took bread and blessed and broke and gave it to James the Just and said to him, "My brother, eat your bread, for the Son of man has risen from those who sleep."*

In the Emmaus story, Jesus appears to a pair of disciples who are pointedly not among the twelve. One is named Cleopas and is therefore to be identified as Simeon bar-Cleophas. He is, of course, one of the brothers/ Heirs of Jesus, as is James. And then who must his companion be? James himself! His name and Simon's (deferred till *Luke 24:34*, so as to make him into Simon *Peter*) have been changed because of the factional rivalry between the Heirs and the Twelve. The climactic detail of Jesus being recognized in the act of breaking bread echoes the same gesture in the Gospel according to the *Hebrews* version, in which the risen Christ calls for bread to break the fast James had sworn not to break till Jesus should rise again. In the Thomas story (*John 20:24-29*), Jesus appears to a figure who is listed among the twelve, as we now read it, but it is obvious that he is not one of them, as the narrator has just said Jesus previously appeared to the twelve with no hint that any of them but Judas Iscariot was absent. Thomas, though subsequently counted as one of the twelve, is only one of many doublets in that group, his namesake being another of the Pillars, Judas Thomas. And like James in *Hebrews*, Thomas has made a vow that is satisfied by the appearance of the risen Jesus ("Until I place my hand in his side and my finger in the wounds. . .").

Given the rapid succession of events involved, it would certainly appear that James' execution was the trigger for Jesus ben Ananias, the mad prophet predicting Jerusalem's demise, to begin his doom-crying. We already knew Origen read a text of Josephus which said the people blamed the fall of Jerusalem on the death of James. It is ironic that Origen piously harrumphs that they should have traced the disaster to the execution of Jesus instead, because, as Theodore J. Weeden has shown beyond reasonable doubt (*The Two Jesuses*, a monograph published as *Foundations and Facets Forum* New Series 6/2, Fall 2003), Mark and John both based their gospel passion narratives on Josephus' account of Jesus ben Ananias. Eisenman similarly suggests that Mark has replaced Jesus ben Ananias' prophecy with one attributed to Jesus Christ, the Olivet Discourse, which was the signal for several of the "Essene" groups, including the Church of the Pillars, to flee Jerusalem while they had the chance, leading to their fanning out through Pella to farther fields.

Eisenman's broadest goal is to show how the Greek gospels are products of a Paulinized, Hellenized, completely non-Jewish retrofitting of the tradition. The underlying reality must be speculatively pieced together by comparisons between gospel materials and apparently related texts from the Mishnah and Talmud, the Dead Sea Scrolls, Josephus, and Ebionite sources. Very often, all we may find is a series of sets of motifs that seem to have, as he puts it, "reverberated" between documents and traditions, forming very different stories as the motifs gradually combined into various "multicellular organisms" of different sorts. Eisenman spends the first several hundred pages trying to reel in these minnows and to reconstruct the schools of fish they used to swim in.

The most straightforward set of cases cluster about the gospel transformation of stories of neo-Joshua prophets and Samaritan messiahs leading their flocks of four hundred or four thousand or five thousand into the wilderness to witness a miracle which will commence the liberation of the messianic age. When Jesus is shown multiplying food for such crowds in the wilderness, we certainly have gospel reworkings of these stories originally recounted of Theudas the Magician, the unnamed Egyptian prophet, and the Samaritan messiah whose followers Pilate ambushed on Mount Gerizim. The secondary nature of the gospel versions is evident from the fact that Palestine contained no genuine deserts such as the stories require. But the connection is even more manifest from the fact that John's version pointedly raises the question of whether Jesus should be made king by force – only to dismiss it (*6:15*). Thus also Paul is asked whether he is not the Egyptian who led the Sicarii out into the desert (*Acts 21:38*), to give him the opportunity to deny it.

And remember, "Theudas," as in the Nag Hammadi *Apocalypses of James*, is another version of Thaddeus. Eisenman also makes Theudas a version of Judas Thomas. Was it he who promised to make Jerusalem's walls collapse? As for the Samaritan whom Pilate killed, he must have thought himself the Restorer (*Taheb*), and Eisenman sees a refracted glimmer of this hero when Peter resurrects *Tabitha* in Lydda, all the more since the Samaritan messiah's followers rallied at *Tirathaba*. Speaking of Lydda, Rabbinic tradition tells us of the crucifixion there of a Messiah ben Joseph who was named either *Doetus* or *Dortas* (originally perhaps the messianic *Dositheus* of Samaria), who shows up cross-dressing at Lydda as *Dorcas*, Tabitha's other name!

All this represents a bowdlerizing of precisely such traditions, "cleaned up" for the gospels, i.e., for Gentile consumption. Much less straightforward (which is perhaps why Eisenman takes so incredibly long tying the ends together, and that pretty loosely) is another set of stories sharing DNA, and not necessarily dominant strands). Hang on. First there is the story in *Mark 7:24-30* and *Matthew 15:21-28* in which a Syro-Phoenician woman (a Gentile) begs a reluctant Jesus to heal her devil-possessed daughter back home. Demon exorcism is the ostensible topic, but the story turns on the issue of dining at table and of the proper dinner guests' food falling off the table to the dogs. Eisenman implies that the story means to deal not just generally with the Gentile Mission (true enough as far as that goes), but specifically with the issue of Jewish-Christian table fellowship with Gentiles. The reader is to think of how "what Gentiles sacrifice, they sacrifice to demons, not to God" (*1 Corinthians 10:20*). But Jesus, allowing that Gentile "dogs" may eat what falls from (Jewish-) Christian tables, seems to resolve the issue in a manner acceptable to the author of *1 Cor. 10:25*: "Eat whatever is sold in the meat market without raising questions of conscience."

That would also seem to be the/an underlying issue in Luke's version of the same story, the parable of the Rich Man and Lazarus. Here the dogs that greedily devoured crumbs falling off the table in *Mark* and *Matthew* have become those who lick the wounds of the skeletal Lazarus, who wishes he might eat the scraps from the rich man's table. He has taken the place of both the dogs and the daughter. Luke derives his canines from the dogs who came to the Rich Man ben Kalba Sabu'a's door but always went away *not* "wanting to be filled" as in Luke's substitution, but rather the opposite: *always* "filled." Especially in view of Scott Morshauer's exegesis of the parable in a recent issue of this periodical, it is evident that the Gentile taint of the Syro-Phoenician mother has become the Idumaean taint of Dives, since he patently stands for the faux-Jewish scofflaw Herod Antipas. (She has also become the sinful woman in *Luke 7:36-50*, whom Jesus defends against "Simon the Pharisee," i.e., the historical Simon Peter as depicted in *Galatians 2:11 ff.* and *Acts 10:14.*)

Lazarus will meet us again in *John 12*, at a feast served by his sisters Miriam and Martha, at which Miriam anoints Jesus with perfume, as did the sinful woman of *Luke 7*. And these two ladies stand for a pair of supremely wealthy daughters in Talmudic tradition. One of these was Miriam, daughter of the rain-maker Nakdimon, the other Martha, daughter of the Sadducee Boethus. Miriam was so spoiled that she required a daily budget of 400 dinarii just for perfume. Whenever she walked to synagogue, her servants laid a path of richly embroidered cushions for her to tread upon so that her dainty feet might never touch the dirty ground. (The cushions were then given to the poor.) The expensive perfume has become that "wasted" upon Jesus (instead of being sold for the poor) by the unnamed woman (Mary Magdalene) in *Mark* and *Matthew*, *Luke's* "sinful woman," and Mary in *John*. The cushions have become the clothing spread in his donkey's path by Jesus' fans on Palm Sunday. Nakdimon is Nicodemus who joins Joseph of Arimathea to bury Jesus, smearing him in a fantastically huge amount of funeral *perfume* (*John 19:39*).

The anticipated stench of Lazarus, thought to be dead (or actually dead but soon-to-be-revived) derives from another reek arising from a tale of Johanon ben Zakkai, who made his escape from Jerusalem, being passed through the Roman lines as a corpse in a coffin. To simulate the stench of decomposition, the Rabbi had to carry a mouthful of dung. But, despite the stench, he sprang alive from the coffin. The filthy smell reminds us of Paul's reckoning his former, spotless record of Torah-observance as mere dung (*Philippians 3:8*) when compared to Christian devotion without the Jewish Law. The latter would be symbolized by the perfume with which Jesus is anointed, and which fills the "house" (i.e., the inhabited world) with the anointer's fame. And of course, unenlightened Jews can be expected to recoil at the sweet savor of gospel preaching as if it were the stench of decomposing flesh (*2 Cor. 2:14-16*). Again, when we read of Jesus filling the pallid Jewish ablution jars with heady Christian wine in *John 2:6-11*, we are to think of the many cisterns filled in a time of drought by the rain-making prayers of the hasid Nakdimon. Not bad, but not wine.

Whence the black comedy in *Matthew 27:3-10*, in which the pious hypocrites of the Sanhedrin, having just delivered the Son of God to death, scruple over what to do with Judas' returned bounty money? Hmmm, they cannot put it back into the treasury, but there's nothing stopping them from putting it toward a cemetery for indigents! Eisenman traces this one to a Rabbinic report to the effect that Eliezer ben Hyrcanus approved of a legal opinion ascribed to Jesus that, should a pious Jewish prostitute donate her evening's wages to the temple, they might, instead of being rejected outright, be used to buy a new commode for the High Priest! (Think of *Mark 7:18-19*, "Whatever goes into a man from outside cannot defile him, since it enters not his heart but his stomach and so lands in the toilet, which renders all things clean," as well as *1 Cor. 6:12-19*, which uses the same motifs a bit differently.) Judas Iscariot corresponds to the harlot with her hire, which he casts back into the temple just as she donated it (implying that she had been paid the same money by the priest whose privy it will now buy – just as it rented her private parts!). And think of *John 13:29-30*, where Judas leaves to collude with the Sanhedrin and some think he is off to make a holiday contribution to the poor. He *is*, since the money he has received from his evil masters is going to end up paying for a burial place for the poor!

The utter transformation of Jamesian Torah-Christianity into a Gentile mystery religion is epitomized by the subtitle of this book. It represents a Pauline esoteric reinterpretation of the judgment language of the Scrolls, paralleled in *Revelation 14:9*: "Whoever worships the Beast and his statue and allows a mark to be imprinted on his forehead or his hand, he shall choke on the wine of the fury of God, mixed full strength in the cup of his rage!" (cf. *Isaiah 51:17*; *Jeremiah 25:15-16; 49:12; 51:7*), plus the Qumran jargon of "the New Covenant in the Land of Damascus." Paul employs a homophonic pun between the Hebrew "*Dam-Chos*," or Blood-Cup (or *Dam-mashek*, "giving blood to drink") and "Damascus" (the retreat of the James community). In his communion meal he administers the "New Covenant of the Cup of Blood" of the Christ. If one fails to discern this allegorical reference to the saving, sacramental body and blood of Christ (thinking obliviously only of "Damascus" as Jamesian Christians would), one winds up instead drinking of the cup of the wrath of God, the classic fate of the enemies of God.

The New Testament Code enables us to see not only how wholesale a Hellenization overtook Christianity, far beyond anything Harnack ever envisioned, but also the absolute rage of Torah-Christians who understood Paul as Antichrist and apostate. For the first time, they are not made to look like horned villains and sinister opponents of a noble Pauline gospel. Eisenman's monumental work stands as a new milestone in the progress of New Testament research. As much as some might wish it otherwise, we can now never turn back from his revelations, great and small, any more than we dare retreat from the ground gained by Strauss, Baur, and Bultmann. Indeed, it is among the ranks of these scholarly titans that we must now enroll Robert Eisenman.

* * * * * * * * *

www.robertmprice.mindvendor.com/

Meroitic inscription on a king's votive plaque, Sudan, Africa. c. 100 BCE
Walters Art Museum, Baltimore
Via Wikipedia

MISCELLANEOUS CONCLUDING REMARKS

Michael Lockwood

IF, AS CHRISTIAN LINDTNER HAS CLEARLY SHOWN, all four authors of the canonical gospels had a command of Sanskrit, and many of the passages in all four gospels are demonstrated to be in a mimetic relation to passages in Buddhist scriptures, then one may conclude that the "evangelists" – all four of them – were Buddhists, and that "Jesus" is an allegorical apotheosis of the Buddha. It can be shown that Buddhism has adapted its gospel in other mission fields, such as China. And it is certain that the Jews, the Greeks, the Egyptians, or others, were not adapting their religious views to Buddhism, mastering the intricacies of Sanskrit.

Indian Polysemy

As the articles in this book have jointly shown, the gospel writers have conveyed a multi-fold Dharmic message – a message simultaneously assimilating itself, on different major levels, to: **(1)** select passages of scripture in the *Septuagint*, appealing to the Jews, **(2)** major literary elements of the *Iliad* and *Odyssey*, appealing to the Greeks, **(3)** important aspects of Egyptian mythology, appealing to the Egyptians, and **(4)**, in general, presenting a competitive version of an adapted Buddhist heritage to other Buddhist communities (e.g., various Gnostics groups, ex-Therapeutæ and ex-Qumranites and their followers). I have mentioned only four major levels here, but as illustrated in this book, there are also other levels.

This multi-level approach is thoroughly Indian. Nothing in the Western languages of those early centuries equals Sanskrit and Prākrit in this. Consider the extreme complexity of polysemy which was attained in the work of an Indian poet, in the 11th century AD, which was recently announced as a publication of the French Institute, Pondicherry, India:

> *La geste de Rāma: poème à double sens de Sandhyākaranandin* (Introduction, texte, traduction, analyses)
> Editor and translator: Sylvain Brocquet, Collection Indologie n° 110, IFP/EFEO, 2010, vii, 523 pp.
> Language: French.
> ISBN (IFP): 978-81-8470-174-6.
> ISBN (EFEO): 978-2-85539-676-7.
>
> The *Rāmacaritam* by Sandhyākaranandin, a narrative poem of 215 stanzas (of which 215 survive), is a perfect example of poetry with two meanings: by constant use of śleṣa, it contrives to summarize the plot of the Rāmāyana and to relate the recovery of Eastern Bengal, during the eleventh century AD, by Rāmapāla, a ruler of the Pāla dynasty. The last chapter extends beyond the martial story and deals with the succession of the epic hero and of the historical king. Some thirty stanzas add a third meaning, of theological character, to the two main ones.
>
> This book provides the transliterated Sanskrit text (the transliteration is duplicated to reveal the different morphological analyses), a separate translation of each meaning, and a close analysis of polysemous sequences. An introduction sheds light on the literary and historical context on the one hand, on the linguistic and rhetorical devices which generate polysemy on the other hand. The book is complemented with several appendices containing: another famous literary example of double entendre, a list of known inscriptions issued by the rulers who are referred to in the poem, and the text and the translation of one of the main epigraphs. Two indices record all the polysemous words and all those of historical or geographical purport.

Writers of no other country have ever matched the level of polysemy attained in India. And four hundred years before Sandhyākaranandin, an even greater poet, Daṇḍin, who hailed from the Pallava country of South India, composed a famous poem which could be read through from beginning to end recounting the epic of the *Rāmāyana* – or by varying the divisions of the *same* compound Sanskrit expressions throughout, it was turned into a recounting of the epic of the *Mahābhārata*!

Comedic Domains

Let us meditate for a moment on the complexity of the canonical gospels. Were not the four authors radically different from the usual religious conception of them? For instance, quite overlooked by most scholars is the presence, in the gospels and in their multiple meta-narrative levels, of comedic domains containing great irony and humor: puns, parodies, and the like. **Please note:** Price, Brodie, MacDonald, Pippy, Lindtner, and Eisenman – *all six* – have stressed the use of these comedic literary devices in the New Testament. Matthew and Luke trace Jesus' genealogy back to King David. Jesus, who is portrayed in the gospels as being strictly against divorce was thus a descendant of a king who, desiring another man's wife, commits adultery and then murders her husband! Is there not great irony here? Or in the name of 'Jesus/Joshua' shared with one of the Bible's bloodiest militarists?

Or take the well known passage in *John 3:1-4*:

> *1* There was one of the Pharisees named Nicodemus, a member of the Jewish Council, *2* who came to Jesus by night.
> 'Rabbi', he said, 'we know that you are a teacher sent by God; no one could perform these signs of yours unless God
> were with him.' *3* Jesus answered, 'In truth, in very truth I tell you, unless a man has been born over again he cannot
> see the kingdom of God.' *4* 'But how is it possible', said Nicodemus, 'for a man to be born when he is old? Can
> he enter his mother's womb a second time and be born?' – *The New English Bible*

"John, the evangelist" (who is a Buddhist literary scholar) has fashioned a pun on the Greek expression generally translated in English as 'born again' (*gennēthē anōthen*). There is a vulgar element in the pun (fourth verse) which is put in the mouth of Nicodemus:

> *4* "What do you mean?" exclaimed Nicodemus. "How can an old man go back into his mother's womb and be born again?" – *Holy Bible: The New Living Translation*

To really grasp the pun one must turn to the Greek and understand that '*anōthen*' has, among other meanings, two which can be expressed in English as (1) 'from above' and (2) 'again'. The *NEB* scholars tried to sneak the 'from above' sense into their translation by using the word 'over'. But 'over', which can, of course, convey the meaning of 'above' is neutralized, here, and merely stresses the repetitiveness of 'again'.

Jesus, in the Greek, is simply conveying both the idea that a man must be 'born' *metaphorically* 'from above' (from the realm of the kingdom of God) and ('again') experience a second non-physical, *spiritual* rebirth. However, Nicodemus, the great teacher of Israel, misunderstands '*gennēthē anōthen*' as Jesus' demand that he, an old man, should (physically) be 'born again', and he crudely expresses his shock.

Now, the Jewish Christians of Palestine, the ex-Qumran crypto-Buddhist colleagues of the Alexandrian Buddhist gospel writers, would have been absolutely horrified by this kind of almost obscene punning in *John 3*. To demonstrate the attitude of the Qumran monastics toward sexuality and especially the sexual organs of the female body, I quote from Lawrence H. Schiffman's book, *Reclaiming the Dead Sea Scrolls*, pp. 150-51:

> According to the sectarian view, the human being is a lowly creature made of clay (or dust) and molded with water. This idea is especially emphasized in *Thanksgiving Hymns* and may reflect to a great extent the personal experience of the author, who many scholars have surmised was the Teacher of Righteousness.
>
> Just one example from the text (*Thanksgiving Hymns* 12:24-26) will bring together those dominant motifs:
>
> But I have been ta[ken] from dust [and] form[ed from clay],
> into a fount of impurity and the nakedness of shame,
> a source of dust and knea[ded with water,
> a place of gui]lt and a dwelling of darkness.
> And a return to dust is (the destiny) of a creature of clay,
> at the time which is [appointed for it,
> and] its [end] is in the dust,
> to the place from which it was taken.
>
> Over and over the author stresses his own feelings of inadequacy when standing before God. But the author goes even further: the terms translated "fount" and "nakedness" refer to female reproductive organs. The language of this and many other passages makes clear that the author of *Thanksgiving Hymns* regarded those organs as always impure, even during birth.

Schiffman states clearly (p. 150) that "this image of human beings is . . . exceptional in Jewish teachings, and probably exerted its influence more fertilely on early Christianity." (The Qumranites being the crypto-Buddhist forerunners of "Judaizing" groups of Christians, of course.) This kind of DSS 'image' has appeared so alien, today, to dominant Jewish values, especially to women, that a prominent Israeli scholar, Rachel Elior, has even disputed that the Essenes ever existed at all!:

> "I think that Philo invented the Essenes as an ideal society and Josephus was much influenced by him, and the fact that no Jewish source written in Hebrew or Aramaic before or after the Common Era knows anything about a group called Essenes or mentions any group known as celibates denouncing private property and family life raises severe questions about their historical existence in the Land of Israel." < paleojudaica.blogspot.com/2009_04_26_archive.html >

In the Torah, the 'backbone' of Jewish blessings – holding together all other blessings – is expressed again and again as a mind-boggling reproduction of descendants (through myriad sexual copulations, of course), often coupled together with the promise of the possession of cities of enemies. I give below a summary of what the Torah has to say on fecundity (all passages are quoted from *The New English Bible*):

Genesis 15:5

'Look up in into the sky, and count the stars if you can. So many', [God] said [to Abraham], 'shall your descendants be.'

Genesis 17:2

'I am God Almighty. Live always in my presence and be perfect, so that I may set my covenant between myself and you [Abraham] and multiply your descendants.'

Genesis 22:17-18

'[I]n as much as you [Abraham] have done this and have not withheld your son, your only son, I will bless you abundantly and greatly multiply your descendants until they are as numerous as the stars in the sky and the grains of sand on the sea-shore. Your descendants shall possess the cities of their enemies. All nations shall pray to be blessed, and this because you have obeyed me.'

Genesis 26:2-4

The Lord appeared to Isaac and said, . . . 'I will make your descendants as many as the stars in the sky; I will give them all these lands, and all the nations of the earth will pray to be blessed as they are blessed. . . .'

Genesis 28:3

[Isaac blessing Jacob:] 'God Almighty bless you, make you fruitful and increase your descendants until they become a host of nations.'

Genesis 28:12-14

[Jacob] dreamt that he saw a ladder, which rested on the ground with its top reaching to heaven, and angels of God were going up and down upon it. The Lord was standing beside him and said, 'I am the Lord, the God of your father Abraham and the God of Isaac. This land on which you are lying I will give to you and your descendants. They shall be countless as the dust upon the earth. . . . All the families of the earth shall pray to be blessed as you and your descendants are blessed.'

Genesis 32:11-12

[Jacob prays to God:] 'Save me, I pray, from my brother Esau, for I am afraid that he may come and destroy me, sparing neither mother nor child. But thou didst say, "I will prosper you and will make your descendants like the sand of the sea, which is beyond all counting."'

Genesis 48:4

[Jacob said to Joseph:] 'God Almighty appeared to me at Luz in Canaan and blessed me. He said to me, "I will make you fruitful and increase your descendants until they become a host of nations. I will give this land to your descendants after you as a perpetual possession."'

Exodus 32:11, 13-14

. . . Moses set himself to placate the Lord his God; 'O Lord,' he said, . . . 'Remember Abraham, Isaac and Israel [Jacob], thy servants, to whom thou didst swear by thy own self: "I will make your posterity countless as the stars in the sky, and all this land, of which I have spoken, I will give to them. . . ."' So the Lord relented and spared his people the evil with which he had threatened them.

Deuteronomy 1:10-11

[Moses said to the Israelites:] 'The Lord your God has increased you so that today you are as numerous as the stars in the sky. May the Lord the God of your fathers increase your number a thousand times and may he bless you as he promised.'

Deuteronomy 10:22

[Moses said to the Israelites:] 'When your forefathers went down into Egypt they were only seventy strong, but now the Lord your God has made you countless as the stars in the sky.

With the above declarations by the God of Israel in mind, we might certainly empathize with Elior's refusal to believe that such groups of "celibates denouncing private property and family life" as the monastics, in Qumran, and the Therapeutæ, in Egypt, ever existed. But she is mistaken. Does one think that Eusebius of Cæsarea, in his *Church History*, firmly maintaining that Philo's report of the Therapeutean monasticism was describing the "first heralds of the Gospel" (proto-Christianity!), is being duped by an imaginary utopia, set so challengeably smack next to Alexandria?:

> 23 Philo describes the order of dignities which exists among those [the Therapeutæ] who carry on the services of the church [the monastery on Lake Mareotis], mentioning the diaconate, and the office of bishop, which takes the precedence over all the others. But whosoever desires a more accurate knowledge of these matters may get it from the history already cited. 24 But that Philo, when he wrote these things, had in view the first heralds of the Gospel and the customs handed down from the beginning by the apostles, is clear to every one.*

And why on earth would this be pure imagination on Philo's part, spinning out a description of a monastic organization so similar to what "Christian" monastic organizations would actually turn out to be, around Alexandria and in Egypt, a century or so later? The arguments in the present book, together with those, in *Buddhism's Relation to Christianity*, would go, on the contrary, to support the strong likelihood of monasticism, of the kind we read about in Philo's, Josephus's, and others' accounts of it in Egypt and Palestine, having developed over the centuries from the Buddhist monasticism introduced in kingdoms around the Mediterranean by King Aśōka's missionary monks and scholars, in the mid-third century BCE – and the likelihood that there was a continuous development of such monasticism in these lands thereafter – though we may, at present, have little evidence to confirm this. Elior is evidently not aware of this possible source.

The practices of eschewing both private property and family life (where the latter's fundamental purpose is sexual procreation) were, indeed, practices which were introduced by the Buddhist monks into the Mediterranean kingdoms. In later centuries, these missionary monks were followed by their "descendants", cenobitic ascetic groups living near the shores of the Dead Sea (Palestine) and Lake Mareotis (Egypt). And, still later, ca. early 2nd century CE, these ascetic groups were similarly followed by *their* "offspring", the earliest Christian communes. Thus, it was from India that Egypt and Palestine received their cenobitic monasticism. In India, its earliest appearance, there, had been in the development of the Buddhist saṅghas, in the 5th century BCE.

Let us return to the topic of 'female reproductive organs' and the negative attitude toward them which was shared by Buddhists, Qumranites, Therapeutæ, and members of the early Christian communes. Of these groups, it is only Buddhism which provides us with a philosophical psychoanalysis of its reasons for taking a strong negative stance against the powerful attractions of sexuality. These reasons are to be found spelled out in detail in the very heart of Buddhist doctrine, in the **Four Noble Truths** (see the facing page for a summary of these).

To appreciate the distinct character of the original Buddhist stance against sexuality – distinct, that is, from the positions taken by the later crypto-Buddhist organizations: the Qumran, Therapeutean, and early Christian – one must take into account the distinct cultural background of the rise of Buddhism in India, with its assumptions: 1) a general belief in reincarnation, 2) a belief in the implacable operation of the Law of Karma, and 3) a widespread desire of religiously minded persons to escape from the seemingly endless cycle of deaths and rebirths by attaining '*mōkṣa*' ('liberation', one version being the absorption of their souls into a panentheistic state of Being, free from the ever-flowing stream of '*saṁsāra*'). What is peculiar about this analysis by Buddhism is its pointed criticism of the very nature/structure of the world we live in – and *this* was the reasoning which, when launched in the West, led to the demotion of the Jewish God Most High to a bungling 'Demiurge', in the minds of some of the crypto-Buddhists groups which were attempting to assimilate themselves to Judaism.

Sexuality is but one – though a very powerful one – among the many urges and "thirsts" in life, all of which have suffering imbedded in them. George Boeree's comment (facing p.) on the **Second Noble Truth**, makes this clear: "When we fail to recognize that all things are imperfect, impermanent, and insubstantial, we cling to them in the delusion that they are indeed perfect, permanent, and substantial. . . ." This is very, very different from the optimistic declaration in *Genesis 1:31* that "God saw all that he had made, and it was very good," and, in *Genesis 1:28*, that "God said to [Adam and Eve], 'Be [sexually] fruitful and increase, fill the earth and subdue it. . . ."

When Buddhism set out, in Egypt and other Mediterranean countries, to spread the Good News of the Dharma (how to achieve liberation from the sufferings of earthly life with its cycle of deaths and rebirths), it would have faced inevitable difficulty in communicating certain aspects of its doctrine in the West, the intelligibility of which was dependent more or less on the basic assumptions of reincarnation, with its ever-turning cycle of deaths and rebirths, the Law of Karma, and the ultimate goal of *Mōkṣa*.

---

*From Vol. 1, Bk. II, of the *Nicene and Post-Nicene Fathers of the Christian Church*, 2nd Series, ed. & trans. Philip Schaff (Grand Rapids, MI: Wm. B. Eerdmans Publishing Co., 1890), p. 119.

Excerpted from C. George Boeree's, "Towards a Buddhist Psychotherapy", *BRC*, pp. 164-167:

SUMMARY

The **Four Noble Truths** sound like the basics of any theory with therapeutic roots:

1. **Life is suffering.** Life is at very least full of suffering, and it can easily be argued that suffering is an inevitable aspect of life. If I have senses, I can feel pain; if I have feelings, I can feel distress; if I have a capacity for love, I will have the capacity for grief. Such is life.

   Duḥkha, the Sanskrit word for suffering, is also translated as stress, anguish, and imperfection. The Buddha wanted us to understand suffering as a foundation for improvement. One key to understanding suffering is understanding ***anitya***, which means that all things, including living things, our loved ones, and ourselves, are impermanent. Another key concept is ***anātman***, which means that all things – even we – have no "soul" or eternal substance. With no substance, nothing stands alone, and no one has a separate existence. We are all interconnected, not just with our human world, but with the universe.

2. **Suffering is due to attachment.** We might say that at least much of the suffering we experience comes out of ourselves, out of our desire to make pleasure, happiness, and love last forever and to make pain, distress, and grief disappear from life altogether.

   My [Boeree's] feeling, not quite in line with some Buddhist interpretations, is that we are not therefore to avoid pleasure, happiness, and love. Nor are we to believe that all suffering comes from ourselves. It's just that it is not necessary, being shot once with an arrow, to shoot ourselves again, as the Buddha put it.

   Attachment is one translation of the word ***tṛishṇa***, which can also be translated as thirst, desire, lust, craving, or clinging. When we fail to recognize that all things are imperfect, impermanent, and insubstantial, we cling to them in the delusion that they are indeed perfect, permanent, and substantial, and that by clinging to them, we, too, will be perfect, permanent, and substantial.

   Another aspect of attachment is ***dvesha***, which means avoidance or hatred. To the Buddha, hatred was every bit as much an attachment as clinging. Only by giving those things which cause us pain permanence and substance do we give them the power to hurt us more. We wind up fearing, not that which can harm us, but our fears themselves.

   A third aspect of attachment is ***avidyā***, meaning ignorance. At one level, it refers to the ignorance of these Four Noble Truths – not understanding the truth of imperfection and so on. At a deeper level, it also means "not seeing," i.e. not directly experiencing reality, but instead seeing our personal interpretation of it. More than that, we take our interpretation of reality as more real than reality itself, and interpret any direct experiences of reality itself as illusions or "mere appearances"!

3. **Suffering can be extinguished.** At least that suffering we add to the inevitable suffering of life can be extinguished. Or, if we want to be even more modest in our claims, suffering can at least be diminished.

4. **And there is a Way to extinguish suffering.** This is what all therapists believe – each in his or her own way. But this time we are looking at what the Buddha's theory – dharma – has to say: He called it the **Eightfold Path**:

   1) **Right view** – understanding the Four Noble Truths, especially the nature of all things as imperfect, impermanent, and insubstantial and our self-inflicted suffering as founded in clinging, hate, and ignorance.

   2) **Right aspiration** – having the true desire to free oneself from attachment, hatefulness, and ignorance.

   3) **Right speech** – abstaining from lying, gossiping, and hurtful speech generally. Speech is often our ignorance made manifest, and is the most common way in which we harm others.

   4) **Right action** – behaving oneself, abstaining from actions that hurt others (and, by implication, oneself) such as killing, stealing, and irresponsible sex.

   5) **Right livelihood** – making one's living in an honest, non-hurtful way.

   6) **Right effort** – taking control of your mind and the contents thereof.

   7) **Right mindfulness** – mindfulness refers to a kind of meditation involving an acceptance of thoughts and perceptions, a "bare attention" to these events without attachment.

   8) **Right concentration** – meditating in such a way as to empty our natures of attachments, avoidances, and ignorance, so that we may accept the imperfection, impermanence, and insubstantiality of life.

Though the Buddha is portrayed in scripture as preaching the duty of physically helping the sick and the dying, not being put off by various types of impurity, Buddhism did considered anything having to do with sexuality as something negative and impure. When, in Indian literature and art, the Buddha-to-be is shown in the form of a little white elephant-'cloud' descending with the wind (Spirit) into his mother's womb, we see that the Bodhisattva enters it through his mother's 'pure' right side (by a miraculous, bloodless reverse cæsarean), avoiding any approach to her sexualized birth canal. And again, when he is born, he exits through his mother's right side (a miraculous, bloodless cæsarean), once again avoiding that organ of lust, and as a preternatural child, he is immediately able to stand, walk, and declare his wonderful destiny on earth!

As for the crypto-Buddhist Qumranites, they had, over the 300 years following their founders' arrival in the West, lost their moorings in Buddhism (and in the Indian context of reincarnation, 'Karma', and panentheism) and, being swept back into apostasy, were afloat in a sea of Jewish beliefs concerning 'purity' and 'impurity', ritual and otherwise. Thus, we read in Josephus, *The Jewish Wars* (Bk. 2 §150), that "so far are the junior [members of the Essene monastics] inferior to the seniors that if the seniors should be touched by the juniors, they must wash themselves. . ."! (Whiston & Maier, 738). Their Alexandrian crypto-Buddhist colleagues, the evangelists, make absolutely clear their disagreement with this behavior in their allegorical pericope of 'Jesus Healing the Bleeding Woman' (*Mark 5:21-43*; *Matt. 9:18-26*; *Luke 8:40-56*).

The Book of Esther and the Qumran Monks

That there is only one book of the Hebrew Bible which is missing in the Qumran collection of the Dead Sea Scrolls – *The Book of Esther* – raises the question, 'why?':

> Why *Esther* has so far not been found at Qumran has been debated. Since this genre of literature has now been found at Qumran, there most probably was an ideological antagonism to it. Previously one might not have thought so. This objection can best be understood in terms of the militant xenophobia and apocalyptic nationalism of the Community, as well as its condemnation of precisely the kind of 'fornication' Esther indulges in. That Esther could marry and enter the harem of a foreign potentate, even in order to save her people, as the book posits, would have been anathema to a Community or movement such as this.
>
> On the other hand, if *Esther* is to be considered highly mythologized, and if the anti-Herodian animus of the group responsible for many of these writings is confirmed, then a book like *Esther* would, no doubt, have been looked upon as 'a stalking horse' for Herodian pretensions. Herodian princesses like the infamous Berenice and Drusilla (not to mention their aunt Herodias in the previous generation) were making precisely the same kind of marital and extra-marital arrangements with people no less despised than Nero's freedman Felix and the destroyer of Jerusalem and emperor to be Titus. Presumably they, too, were making the same excuse, 'to save their people'.
>
> Therefore *Esther* would have been seen as particularly repugnant in a way that these tales – containing no hint of illicit activity or sexual impropriety – were not. For their part, the Maccabee books present 'the day of Mordechai' as preceded by a feast day they call 'the day of Nicanor'.*

'Queen Esther', painting by Edwin Long (1878) – detail
Courtesy of Wikipedia

*Robert H. Eisenman and Michael O. White (editors), *The Dead Sea Scrolls Uncovered: The First Complete Translation and Interpretation of 50 Key Documents Withheld for Over 35 Years* (Shaftesbury, Dorset: Element Books Ltd., 1992), pp. 100-101.

To Eisenman and White's list of reasons why *The Book of Esther* is missing in the Qumran collection, I would only add to those reasons a note of generalization of, and emphasis on, that particular repugnance with which they claim the Qumranite monastics would have held Esther's "fornication". It was not just fornication that was repugnant to them, but *all* sex, and this attitude, I maintain, was grounded in their un-Judaic antipathy (the type of binding and blinding attachment the Buddhists call ***dvēsha***) toward sexuality – an attitude which had, over a period of more than 200 or so years, mutated from the calm Buddhist detachment pursued by their forebears when they arrived in the West.

* * * * * * * * *

A MODERN PARABLE

'Saints' and 'Widows'

A Teenager and her Morfar's Biblical Research on the Internet

Our teenage granddaughter recently came and asked me to clarify a Bible passage which she and her classmates had been reading in Sunday School. It was *Acts 9:36-42*, the pericope wherein we are told that a disciple of Jesus, a widow named Tabitha (which name is said to translate into the Greek language as 'Dorcas') lay dying. She is surrounded by a group of widows, disciples of Jesus. The apostle Simon Peter, who happens to be in a nearby town is quickly sent for. Before Peter comes, Dorcas dies, and her body is moved to an upper room. When Peter arrives, he is taken to the upper room. He has all of the widows leave the room. He prays, and then says to her, 'Tabitha, arise.' He takes her hand and raises her up from the dead.

Acts 9:36-42 (King James version)**:**

> *36* Now there was at Joppa a certain disciple named Tabitha ['Tabitha', translated
> into Greek, is 'Dorcas', meaning a gazelle]: this woman was full of good works and
> almsdeeds which she did. *37* And it came to pass in those days, that she was sick, and
> died: whom when they had washed, they laid her in an upper chamber. *38* And
> forasmuch as Lydda was nigh to Joppa, and the disciples had heard that Peter was
> there, they sent unto him two men, desiring him that he would not delay to come to
> them. *39* Then Peter arose and went with them. When he had come, they brought him
> into the upper chamber: and all the widows stood by him weeping, and showing the
> coats and garments which Dorcas made, while she was with them. *40* But Peter put
> them all forth, and kneeled down, and prayed; and turning him to the body said,
> Tabitha, arise. And she opened her eyes: and when she saw Peter, she sat up. *41* And
> he gave her his hand, and lifted her up, and when he had called the **saints** and
> **widows**, presented her alive. *42* And it was known throughout all Joppa; and many
> believed in the Lord.

Having been raised in a multi-generational spirit of the Women's Liberation movement, granddaughter's questions did not touch on the miracle of raising someone from the dead, but rather in asking about the meaning of the word 'saints' – and were the saints men? Were widows saints, too?

Not knowing how to answer her, I suggested that we try first to find answers on the internet. We went to the very informative website (< biblehub.com/ >) and found the appropriate passage, chapter 9, verse 41 of *Acts* (< biblehub.com/acts/9-41.htm >). I asked granddaughter to click on the Greek tab. Up came the 'Text Analysis' page sporting five columns. From left to right they are: **(1)** the first column which gives Strong's Concordance analyses and numbers for each and every word in the verse (and when a number is clicked upon, another page comes up with the word's part of speech; its transliteration; phonetic spelling and definitions); **(2)** the second column gives the transliterations of each and every Greek word in the verse; **(3)** the third column gives each and every Greek word in the Greek script; **(4)** the fourth column gives an English translation of each word; **(5)** and, finally, the fifth column lists in code the grammatical morphology of each word – click on the code of any word and one gets a page of explanation of the elements of the code.

Granddaughter and I were primarily interested in what 'Strong' had to say about the various possible meanings of the original Greek words that were translated as 'saints' and 'widows' – and which of those meanings might be most suitable for interpreting verse 41.

The Greek word which has been translated by 'saints' is (in transliteration) the noun *hagious* (Strong's No. 40 [e]). Clicking on the number 40, we read that the 'original word' from which the noun *hagious* is derived is the adjective *hagios*, that its phonetic spelling is (*hag'-ee-os*), and that the definition of *hagios* (adjective) is "set apart by (or for) God, holy, sacred". And from the 5th column, we learned that *hagious* (noun) is masculine gender (though, of course, it could also stand for 'saints' of mixed gender). From the knowledge that I have that early "Christians" were crypto-Buddhists, I could assure granddaughter that the word 'saints' (as used in verse 41), is referring only to men who have been 'set apart by (or for) God, holy, sacred'.

Granddaughter's first two questions had now been answered by our internet research and my background knowledge: (1) what the meaning of 'saints' in verse 41 was, and (2) that they were men. We then went back to the Bible Hub for help in answering her third question, "Were widows saints, too?"

The Greek word which has been translated by 'widows' is (in transliteration) the noun *chēras* (Strong's No. 5503 [e]). Clicking on the number 5503. we read that a shorter 'original word' noun-form is *chēra*, that its phonetic spelling is (*khay'-rah*), and that its short definition is simply: "widow". This one word definition was certainly not helpful in giving us other possible meanings of *chēra*. Fortunately, a well-read friend sent us the following note:

> The standard Greek lexicon lists an adjective 'bereaved', *chêros*, which comes from the same verbal root as the word for *widow*. In the entry, the variant meaning 'bereft' is listed, along with examples that include 'a thicket bereft [of men]' and 'to live bereft of women' [highlighted in bold below].
>
> **δρυμοὶ χ. bereft of men, AP9.84 (Antiphan.)**: c. gen., Il.6.408; φάρσος . . . στελεοῦ χῆρον ἐλαϊνέου AP6.297 (Phanias), cf. Vett. Val. 117.6; **χήρους γυναικῶν οἰκεῖν Str.7.3.4**; τὰ χῆρα φρονήσεως Ph. 1.601; ναῦς ὕδατος χ. Ael.NA13.28. (Cf. χωρίς, χατίζω, Skt. jáhāti 'abandon, renounce'.)

Armed with the above information from this lexicon entry, I could now confirm for granddaughter that Dorcas and her fellow 'widows' were indeed 'saints', like the men who were called back to the upper room by Peter to witness the miracle of his having raised Dorcas from the dead.

Confirming this for granddaughter is one thing. Explaining it in depth to her is another. That will have to wait a few years. So I did some further preparatory searching on the internet and came across three very informative and interesting entries in *The Catholic Encyclopedia* (**'Widow'**, in vol. 15 [1912], **'Double Monasteries'**, in vol. 10 [1911], and **'Deaconesses'**, in vol. 4 [1908]) which greatly illuminate the nature of these saints, male and female. I have reproduced these three articles in the Fourth Appendix of this book so that when granddaughter is older she may then read them and attain a deeper understanding of what type of special people – "set apart by (or for) God, holy, sacred" – these 'saints' and 'widows' of early Christianity really were.

* * * * * * * * *

Comment: Leaving the realm of 21st century Sunday School, I took a cue from the above Greek lexicon entry and applied "being bereft of women" to our 'saints' and "being bereft of men" to our 'widows', and then followed the entry's concluding note that another possible meaning besides 'bereft' could be 'abandonment, renunciation', as suggested by the related Sanskrit word, *jáhāti*. Thus, in the Dorcas pericope, 'saints' could be understood as "men who have *abandoned* or *renounced* women" and 'widows', as "women who have *abandoned* or *renounced* men"– but only in the limited sense that the actual object of *abandonment* or *renouncing* for both groups is specifically with reference to *all sexual passions and sexual relationships*.

Let me note that the earliest (mid-first century CE) proto-Christian type female ascetics that we have knowledge of are the Therapeutrides of Mareotis. Philo, their contemporary, praises them begrudgingly in his work, *De Vita Contemplativa*, betraying, at times, his rather misogynistic attitude toward these female monastics, labeling (most of) them 'aged virgins'. Early Christians followed Philo's use of the term 'virgin', meaning a celibate woman living in a monastic type of community. But soon 'virgin' (*parthenos*) was to be overtaken by the term 'widow' (*chēra*), which became, for these Christians, a usefully ambiguous term: **(1)** ordinary 'widow' (a woman whose husband has died) or **(2)** a 'female ascetic' (a religious 'sister' or 'nun'). It has been suggested that Christian female ascetics (whether having lost a husband or not) may have taken to dressing as widows when they went out in the world so as to deflect unwanted attention.

The promotion of this ascetic goal of renouncing one's sexuality is a motif, largely unnoticed by most scholars, which runs throughout the gospels. The Norwegian theologian, Prof. Halvor Moxnes' book, *Putting Jesus in His Place: A Radical Vision of Household and Kingdom*, published in 2003, has rectified this neglect with a rather startling, frank treatment of the subject. Moxnes takes *Matt 19:12* (the verse on eunuchs) as a foundational passage for his elaboration of this total-sexual-abstinence motif in the book's chapter 4 (dealing with eunuchs) and chapter 5 (dealing with, barren women, and children).

Eunuchs

Matt. 19:10-12 (*New International Version*):

> *10*The disciples said to him {Jesus}, "If this is the situation between a husband and wife, it is better not to
> marry." *11*Jesus replied, "Not everyone can accept this word, but only those to whom it has been given.
> *12*For there are eunuchs who were born that way, and there are eunuchs who have been made eunuchs by
> others – and there are those who choose to live like eunuchs for the sake of the kingdom of heaven.
> The one who can accept this should accept it.'

Commenting on *Matt 19:12*, Moxnes states (pp. 84-85):

> There is one early Christian writer Tertullian (d. ca. 220 C.E.) . . . {who}* did not attempt to distance Jesus and his saying from "real," castrated eunuchs as did other early Christian writers. . . . Tertullian stands out also because of the terminology that he uses. He rarely employs the Latin transliteration *eunuchus* of the Greek term, but prefers the Latin *spado*. This was a common Latin word for eunuch, whether by nature or by castration, and it could also be used of any impotent male. Tertullian uses *spado* for the first category of eunuchs (by nature) in Matt. 19:12, but it is more remarkable that he also uses it for the last category, eunuchs for the kingdom of heaven. This must have given his writings on the topic a shock effect, particularly when he identifies Jesus as *spado*: "For the Lord Himself opened the Kingdom of Heaven to eunuchs and He Himself lived as a eunuch [or he himself being a eunuch, *ut et apse spadone*]. The Apostle {Paul} also, following His example, made himself a eunuch [*ipse castratus*] and indicated that continence is what he himself prefers" (*De Monogamia* 3.1). Not only does Tertullian use the coarse word *spado* about Jesus, he even speaks of Paul as "castrated" a shockingly strong term if what Tertullian meant was {only} a continent lifestyle.

And again, on p. 88:

> Eunuch is a term used of a man, but of a man who lacks many of the characteristics of a "real Man." Therefore eunuchs were unfit for marriage. This affected a broad spectrum of the rule of a man. Jesus' saying should be read in the context of masculinity as it was constructed through role models, demands, and expectations for men in Jewish society. One aspect was, of course, sexuality. Another was power, and a third was place, to be integrated as husband and father in a household. All these aspects of male identification were challenged by the figure of the eunuch.
>
> With the figure of the eunuch Jesus held on to a metaphor that violated masculine identity. It was a metaphor that moved those men that experienced castration, either literally or figuratively (e.g., by slander), out from a secure male place into an uncertain zone of ambiguity and suspicion.

---

*Words within these {} brackets are my interpolations; straight bracketed expressions are Moxnes'. – ML.

On p. 92:

> To compare Jesus' saying about eunuchs with those about barren women and children may not be so strange as it sounds. There are parallels in other ancient religions. These religions also describe a similarity between the eunuch, the child, and the virgin, particularly in relation to fertility cults. It seems a paradox that the infertile served a goddess of fertility, but the cult required ritual purity, and eunuchs, virgins, and children represented the chastity that was needed.

Barren Women

On p. 93, Moxnes discusses barren women:

> Sayings about barren women constitute another group of sayings that are attributed to Jesus and associated with the eunuch saying. The primary text is the blessing of women who never bore children, which is found in slightly different versions in Luke 23:29 and *Gos. Thom.* 79:
>
> > For behold the days are surely coming when they will say, "Blessed are the barren, and the wombs that have never bore, and the breasts that never gave suck." (Luke 23:29)
> >
> > A woman from the crowd said to him {Jesus}, "Blessed are the womb which bore you and the breasts which nourished you." He said to [her], "Blessed are those who have heard the word of the Father and have truly kept it. For there will be days when you will say, 'Blessed are the womb which has not conceived and the the breasts which have not given milk.'" (*Gos. Thom.* 79)
>
> The Lukan version adds, "Blessed are the barren," and emphasizes even more the motif of a reversal of status for women who do not have children. Throughout Jewish Scriptures the barren woman was pitied. Since childbirth and procreation were part of God's promise to Israel, her fate was described as a punishment, which only God could lift. Her position was one of social shame, parallel to that of the eunuch.

Children

On pp. 92-93, Moxnes discusses children:

> Matthew's Gospel explicitly combines the eunuch saying (19:12) with a saying about children (19:13-15). In the story we hear about the lack of esteem that children suffered; the disciples tried to prevent the mothers from bringing their children to Jesus. The logion itself says: "Let the children come to me, and do not hinder them; for to such belongs the kingdom of heaven" (Matt. 19:14). The same logion is found also in Mark 10:14 and Luke 18:16. In an act of reversal, the kingdom is ascribed not to adults but to children. In Matthew this logion stands by itself. In Mark and Luke it is followed by another logion that employs the children as good examples for the disciples to follow, that is, the logion receives a moralistic interpretation (Mark 10:15; Luke 18:17).
>
> *Gospel of Thomas* 22:1-3 has a different version of the saying: "Jesus saw infants being suckled. He said to his disciples: 'These infants being suckled are like those who enter the kingdom.' They said to him: 'Shall we, then, as children enter the kingdom?'" *Thomas* . . . speaks about the identity of those who will enter the kingdom. The list is characterized by the typical *Thomas* idea of making "two into one"; for instance, "when you make the male and the female one and the same, so that the male be not male, nor the female female" (22:5). Here the idea seems to be that celibate asceticism negates sexual and other differentiations. And the child serves as a metaphor for those entering the kingdom, because it is considered "asexual or presexual or nonsexual."

Prof. Moxnes has advanced strong arguments for his interpretation of the *Matt 19:12* verse on eunuchs and of other passages in the synoptic gospels which deal similarly with 'barren women' and 'little children'. I thoroughly endorse and admire Moxnes' interpretation. But, as for his assumptions about **(1)** the historicity of Jesus, **(2)** the type of men the authors of the gospels were, and **(3)** the historical origin of the Jesus' sayings, I must respectfully disagree with him.

First, as one who is supporting Mythicism, my view of Moxnes' assumption that the Jesus of the gospels is a historical person (which is, of course, the overwhelming majority view of scholars) is that this assumption is profoundly mistaken. When academics carefully review the research by the various scholars whose works have been reproduced or reviewed in this volume they may experience the "paradigm shifts" necessary to become aware of Tradition's multiple veils of blinding illusion.

The most doggedly blinding of these veils is, of course, the common belief that there was a historical person, Jesus, who, with a band of celibate male disciples, was moving around the Palestine countryside, preaching the "Good News" of the coming of the "Kingdom of Heaven".

I have argued that this common belief turns the literary fiction of the four gospels into supposed 1st century CE Palestinian "historical" accounts, and creates serious difficulty in reconciling events within and without the gospels. These difficulties evaporate if one considers the original texts as literary fiction.

Second, Moxnes makes no mention of things Buddhist in his work. It is a limited number of scholars who hold that the authors of the canonical gospels were Buddhist literary scholars with a command of the Sanskrit language, but if this claim is proved to be correct, then current scholars will find rich new veins of material for description and analysis of the Gospel narrative.

In the statement of his 2012 Academic Interests (< http://www.tf.uio.no/english/people/aca/perm/hmoxnes/ >), Moxnes tells us:

> For many years I have been interested in studying the New Testament and Early Christianity with the use of social anthropology and other social science methods. The main thematic focus over the last years have been the historical Jesus and gender studies, especially masculinity. Another area of interest is the cultural presuppositions for our interpretations. . . . Both areas raise the issue of hermeneutics and the use of the Bible in a multi-cultural and multi-religious context.

In *Buddhism's Relation to Christianity*, I (ML) have discussed the nearly two hundred years of numerous scholarly writings describing the influence of Buddhism on Christianity and have cataloged a good many of the parallels between them. No other two 'religions' have such a great number of close parallels. (See the Fifth Appendix for a selection of 49 from among the many more parallels dealt with in *BRC*.) Especially noteworthy are the similarities between the forms of Buddhist and Christian monasticism. It is therefore a little surprising that Moxnes did not include in his multi-cultural and multi-religious orbit the otherwise obvious example of Buddhism.

Third, as for the historical origin of the Jesus' sayings, it will prove to be beyond the imagination of anyone to get close to a true answer who does not connect the origin of Jesus' sayings with the initial spread of Buddhism throughout the Mediterranean world during the reign of the Indian king, Aśōka, mid-third century BCE. Aśōka's missionary effort in the West had gone "underground", its organizations masquerading as Jewish groups, spawning, in time, the Therapeutæ of Egypt, headquartered on Lake Mareotis, and the Qumran monastics and their 'camps' in Palestine. We read of the Therapeutean and Qumranite 1st century CE "descendants" in the historical works of their contemporaries, Philo and Josephus. These "descendants" must have been scattered after the destruction of the Jerusalem Temple. I suggest that the ensuing periods of chaos led to their survival in "voluntary associations" and private homes, which eventually led to the quasi-monastic, semi-secularized synagogues/churches of earliest "Christianity", around the beginning of the 2nd century CE, when the literary "birth" of Jesus took place in Alexandria, Egypt, with the writing of the four gospels. Amazingly, the gospels became historicized and adopted as the foundational scriptures of a "new" religion, Christianity – in truth, but a reshaped crypto-Buddhism – sprung Phœnix-like from the purely literary events, which occurred creatively in the minds of four Buddhist scholars who were studying in the environs of the famous Alexandrian Royal Library/Sarapæum.

I suggest that Buddhism was operating in Alexandria and, perhaps, at a few outstations at **two different levels**. The **first**, **higher level** was that of 'university' life in the environs of the Royal Library/Sarapæum. There must have been nothing 'crypto' about the Buddhist scholars. They were recognized there as Buddhists. This is not to say that their writing was not "hiding" things. As a matter of fact, we should read the four gospels as, indeed, basically poetic, suggestive material, in the sense that the evangelists intended to create puzzlement in the minds of their readers due to the literary ambiguity produced by the multiple layers of meaning in given passages. The evangelists' non-Buddhist academic colleagues would have had pleasure reading the gospels, figuring out these various levels of meaning. This is what I mean by the term '**higher level**'. This was '**literary mimesis**' and '**emulation**' pursued by clearly identified Buddhist scholars.

This means that the gospel writers' 2nd-century colleague, Clement of Alexandria (c. 150-215 CE), a truly great scholar, knew very well the Buddhist origin of Christianity. But when he was writing for the crypto-Buddhist quasi-Judaic "Christian Church" – for those secularized, lapsed monastics bishops, presbyters, deacons, and ordinary church members – he was then operating at a **second**, **lower level**, the crypto-Buddhist mission level. In Book I, Chapter 15, of his *Stromata*, Clement lets slip a hint that **Indian ascetics might be the forerunners of the Encratites**. Such a hint about a rival sect of "Christianity", opens up the possibility of acknowledging that Indian ascetics – Buddhists – were the forerunners of *all* "Christian" sects:

> [P]hilosophy, a thing of the highest utility, flourished in antiquity among the barbarians, shedding its light over the nations. . . . The Indian gymnosophists are also in the number. . . . And of these there are two classes, some of them called Sarmanæ [Sanskrit: *Śramaṇa* (ascetics) – ML], and others Brahmins. And those of the Sarmanæ who are called Hylobii neither inhabit cities, nor have roofs over them, but are clothed in the bark of trees, feed on nuts, and drink water in their hands. Like those called Encratites in the present day, they know not marriage nor begetting of children.
>
> Some, too, of the Indians obey the precepts of Buddha; whom, on account of his extraordinary sanctity, they have raised to divine honours.
>
> – *Stromata* 1.15 (*Ante-Nicene Fathers*)

Buddhism's **second**, **lower level** of operation was at the **non-academic level** of its monastic organizations spread around Alexandria and *throughout* Egypt. This is where crypto-Buddhism existed. Philo, in mid-1st century CE, tells us that the Therapeutæ were members of a world-wide movement, and that the Therapeutean Essenes/Jessæans had, beside the Hebrew Bible [in the Septuagint's Greek translation – ML], certain ancient works [Sanskrit – ML] of their ancient progenitors. Josephus also tells us that the Palestinian Essenes/Jessæans had certain ancient works, which they required their new recruits, under solemn oaths, to keep secret. As reviewed earlier, above, Dennis MacDonald's book showed us how the fictional *Gospel of Mark* is extensively mimetically dependent on Homer's epics. MacDonald has emphasized how Mark has Jesus emulating Odysseus – surpassing the Greek hero in qualities of character and righteousness. But it is Christian Lindtner, also featured above, who has shown us how this Jesus of the gospels, is really a stand-in for the Buddha, whose domain, now, is an imaginary setting placed in 1st century CE Palestine – nearly a century earlier than when Mark was writing. This literary "conception" of Jesus and the world in which he lived, preached, suffered, died, and was resurrected was a creation in the minds of the Buddhist scholars who wrote the four canonical gospels.

Furthermore, it is almost certain that Alexandria, Egypt, with its great library and university, was the only place on earth where these evangelists, fluent in Sanskrit, could also have become well acquainted with the Septuagint version of the Hebrew Bible, thoroughly knowledgeable about the Egyptian world, its myths and religion, and acquainted with the other amazingly numerous and varied realms of knowledge which have been revealed in the multiple meta-narrative layers of the gospels. This is the hallmark of the greatest university in the Western world, in the early centuries of the Common Era. Mark's Gospel, seemingly simple on the surface, surpasses even the complexity of the poetic works of a T.S. Eliot.

The Buddhist/Christian 'Organic Connection' Demonstrated

Consider, again, the *Luke* and *Gospel of Thomas* passages quoted by Moxnes on p. 93 of his book:

> For behold the days are surely coming when they will say, "Blessed are the barren, and the wombs that have never bore, and the breasts that never gave suck." (*Luke 23:29*)
>
> A woman from the crowd said to him {Jesus}, "Blessed are the womb which bore you and the breasts which nourished you." He said to [her], "Blessed are those who have heard the word of the Father and have truly kept it. For there will be days when you will say, 'Blessed are the womb which has not conceived and the the breasts which have not given milk.' " (*Gos. Thom.* 79)

Here follows a sample of comments by traditional scholars on the *Gospel of Thomas* passage, quoted from the 'Gospel of Thomas' page at Early Christian Writings (www.earlychristianwritings.com/thomas/gospelthomas79.html):

Robert M. Grant and David Noel Freedman write: "The first part of this saying comes from *Luke 11:27-28*, though the word 'nourished' is derived from *Luke 23:29*, which Thomas uses as the second part of the saying. The word of the Father, then, is that sterility is better than pregnancy. Just so, in the *Gospel of the Egyptians*, Salome says to Jesus, 'I did well, then, by not bearing [children]' (Clement of Alexandria, *Strom.*, 3, 66, 2). For Jesus really came 'to destroy the works of the female' (*Strom.*, 3, 63, 2)." (*The Secret Sayings of Jesus* [1960], p. 179)

F.F. Bruce writes: "Two quite independent sayings are conflated here. Jesus's reply to the woman who says how wonderful it must be to be his mother indicates that to do the will of God is more wonderful still (*Luke 11.27 f.*), but this is merged with his words to the weeping woman on the Via Dolorosa (*Luke 23.29*). The two sayings are linked by the common theme of bearing and suckling children, but the historical perspective of the second (the impending siege and capture of Jerusalem in A.D. 70) is here replaced by a suggestion that motherhood is incompatible with 'hearing the Father's word and keeping it in truth'. As regularly (except in Saying 100), 'God' in the canonical text is here replaced by 'the Father'." (*Jesus and Christian Origins Outside the New Testament* [1974], p. 143)

Funk and Hoover write: "*Thom* 79:3, which has a parallel in *Luke 23:29*, has possibly been retained by Thomas because of its ascetic interest: the procreation of the race is not necessarily a good thing. This kind of asceticism seems to have been shared by the Qumran community, which some scholars believe was celibate, although it must be noted that not all Essenes were celibate." (*The Five Gospels* [1996], p. 516)

Gerd Ludemann writes: "The basis of these verses is *Luke 11.27-28*, as *v. 28* derives from Lukan redaction and 'word of the Father' (*v. 2*) clearly derives from the redaction of Thomas. 'Word of the Father' is typical of Thomas, as he avoids the term 'God'. 'Truth' (*v. 2*) picks up the same word from 78.3." (*Jesus After 2000 Years* [2001], p. 630)

It is the Harvard trained scholar, Henry Clarke Warren (1854-1899), the translator from Buddhist Pāli scriptures of a passage which describes a key incident in the life of Prince Siddhārtha (the Buddha-to-be), who, in his translation and commentary, has, without realizing it himself, thrown a flood of explanatory light on the New Testament and apocryphal passages which we – and the scholars above – have been analyzing. This incident is the event which leads the future Buddha to his momentous decision to quit the life of a 'householder' and take up the life of an ascetic sage. The excerpt of Warren's translation* and footnote commentary, which I reproduce on the next page, is taken from his book, *Buddhism In Translations*, Harvard Oriental Series, vol. 3, ed. Charles R. Lanman (Cambridge, MA: Harvard University, 1896), pp. 59-61:

---

*You will note, on the next page, that Warren's analysis of the incident which leads Prince Siddhārtha to resolve to quit the life of a 'householder' and become a homeless ascetic turns on a very sophisticated pun. One must have a command of Pāli and Sanskrit to appreciate the depth of it. It is at this point I would like to suggest that this punning – in essence the presenting of a puzzling situation, which is in want of a solution – is the heart of the 'Parable' form of teaching which both the Buddha and Jesus are described as widely employing. To follow the sophistication of the punning, next page, one must be able to recognize the double layered meaning of the Pāli. (I would therefore suggest that this Jātaka was composed sometime after Aśōka's Buddhist scholarly monks had reached Alexandria. It could have been written near the 2nd century CE, since we have the parallel versions in *Luke* and the *Gospel of Thomas*. That Luke fragments the Buddhist story and interjects one sherd (*Luke 11:27-28*) rather randomly into a moment when Jesus was teaching a crowd, on the one hand, and then introduces the other sherd (*Luke 23:29*) when Jesus is on his way to be crucified, should make obvious the fact that we are not dealing with history, here, but rather with literary imagination.

This brings me, following Anthony Barry, to stating another Theorem:

• **The Theorem that the 'Kōan Derives from the Parable' (KDP Theorem)**

The translation is from the Introduction to the (*Nidānakathā*) Jātaka i.60:

[T]he Future Buddha in his splendid chariot entered the city with a pomp and magnificence of glory that enraptured all minds. At the same moment Kisā Gotamī, a virgin of the warrior [Kṣatriya]* caste, ascended to the roof of her palace, and beheld the beauty and majesty of the Future Buddha, as he circumambulated the city; and in her pleasure and satisfaction at the sight, she burst forth into this song of joy:–

271. "Full happy now that mother is,
Full happy now that father is,
Full happy now that woman is,
[Whose lord so glorious this is]!"

On hearing this, the Future Buddha thought, "In beholding a handsome figure the heart of a mother attains Nirvāṇa, the heart of a father attains Nirvāṇa, the heart of a wife attains Nirvāṇa. This is what she [means]. But wherein does Nirvāṇa [really] consist?" And to him, whose mind was already averse to passion, the answer came: "When the fire of lust is extinct, that is Nirvāṇa; when the fires of hatred and infatuation are extinct, that is Nirvāṇa; when pride, false belief, and all other passions and torments are extinct, that is Nirvāṇa. She has taught me a good lesson. Certainly, Nirvāṇa is what I am looking for. It behooves me this very day to quit the household life, and to retire from the world in quest of Nirvāṇa.[1] I will send this lady a teacher's fee." And loosening from his neck a pearl necklace worth a hundred thousand pieces of money, he sent it to Kisā Gotamī. And great was her satisfaction at this, for she thought, "Prince Siddhattha has fallen in love with me, and has sent me a present."

---

[1]The Future Buddha puns upon the word "happy" in Kisā Gotamī's verses. The word in Pāli is *nibbuta*, and is in form a past passive participle of a verb which perhaps does not occur in Pāli in any finite form, but which appears in Sanskrit as *nirvr*. Now there is a Pāli verb of which the third person singular present indicative is *nibbāyati*, and from this verb is formed the verbal noun *nibbāna* (Sanskrit, *Nirvāṇa*). *Nibbuta* is constantly made to do duty as past passive participle to this verb, so that what would be the true form (*nibbāta*) is never found. The Future Buddha therefore puns when he pretends that Kisā Gotamī was using *nibbuta* as the participle of *nibbāyati*, and was urging him to Nirvāṇa.

The verb *nibbāyati* means "to be extinguished," as the flame of a candle; and, when used as a metaphysical term, [the flame] refers to the fires of lust, desire, etc. And as when fire is extinguished coolness results (a consummation devoutly to be wished in a hot climate like India), the verb acquires the further meaning of "be assuaged," "become happy." And in like manner the verbal noun Nirvāṇa (in Pāli *nibbāna*), meaning both literally and metaphorically "becoming extinguished," comes to stand for the *summum bonum*.

I [Warren] add a retranslation of the passage, to show the punning meanings given by the Future Buddha to the words, *nibbuta*, *nibbāyati*, and Nirvāṇa:–

"Nirvāṇa hath that mother gained,
Nirvāṇa hath that father gained,
Nirvāṇa hath that woman gained,
[Whose lord so glorious this is]!"

On hearing this, the Future Buddha thought, "In beholding a handsome form the heart of a mother is made happy (*nibbāyati*), the heart of a father is made happy, the heart of a wife is made happy. This is what she [means]. But wherein does happiness (*nibbuta*) consist?" And to him whose mind was already averse to passion, the answer came: "When the fire of lust is assuaged (*nibbuta*), that is happiness (*nibbuta*); when the fires of hatred and infatuation are assuaged, that is happiness; when pride, false belief, and all other passions and torments are assuaged, that is happiness. She has taught me a good lesson. Certainly, happiness (Nirvāṇa) is what I am looking for. It behooves me this very day to quit the household life and to retire from the world in quest of [that] happiness. I will send this lady a teacher's fee."

*All square-bracketed expressions interpolated by ML. The footnote (1), above, is Henry Clarke Warren's.

Confession and Absolution

The Buddhist Confession and Absolution of Monks/Nuns

From Buddhist scripture, we learn of the Buddha's establishment of a fortnightly service (on the full moon and new moon) of 'confession and absolution' (*prātimōkṣa*, Sanskrit; *pātimōkkha*, Pāli):

> Now it happened to The Blessed One [The Buddha], being in seclusion and plunged in meditation, that a consideration presented itself to his mind, as follows:
>
> "What if I now prescribe that the monks recite a confession [*pātimokkha*] of all those precepts which have been laid down by me; and this shall be for them a fast-day duty?"
>
> Then The Blessed One, in the evening of the day, rose from his meditation, and on this occasion and in this connection, after he had delivered a doctrinal discourse, addressed the monks:
>
> "O monks, it happened to me, as I was just now seated in seclusion and plunged in meditation, that a consideration presented itself to my mind, as follows: 'What if now I prescribe that the monks recite a confession of all those precepts which have been laid down by me; and this shall be for them a fast-day duty?' I prescribe, O monks, that ye recite a confession. And after this manner, O monks, is it to be recited:
>
> "Let a learned and competent monk make announcement to the congregation, saying, 'Let the reverend congregation hear me. To-day is the fast-day of the fifteenth day of the half-month. If the congregation be ready, let the congregation keep fast-day, and recite the confession. What is the first business before the congregation? Venerable sirs, the proclaiming of your innocency. I will recite the confession, and let as many of us as are here present listen carefully and pay strict attention. If anyone have sinned, let him reveal the fact; if he have not sinned, let him remain silent; by your silence I shall know that your reverences are innocent. But now, in assemblages like this, proclamation is made up to the third time, and each one must make confession as if individually asked. But if, when proclamation up to the third time has been made, any monk shall remember a sin and not reveal it, it will be a conscious falsehood. But a conscious falsehood, reverend sirs, has been declared by The Blessed One to be a deadly sin. Therefore, if a monk remember having committed a sin, and desire again to be pure, let him reveal the sin he committed, and when it has been revealed, it shall be well for him.' "*

In Buddhism, this ritual of what Christians call 'Confession and Absolution' is called *Prātimōkṣa*'. (See my coverage of these Buddhist and Christian rituals in *BRC*, pp. 111-115, and Lindtner's perceptive analysis of the Buddhist-Johannine equation of Sanskrit, '*Prātimōkṣa*' = Greek '***Paraklêtos***', in *BRC*, p. 285.) For Buddhists, this was a ritual *strictly for the monks and nuns* – not for laypersons. In Buddhism there are 227 precepts (rules) for monks and 311 for nuns. The ritual of the *Prātimōkṣa*' involved group chanting (from memory) of these precepts, stopping after each precept to repeat three times the exhortation that if any monk/nun had knowingly failed to follow that precept, it would be well to confess it. If, after the third exhortation, anyone failed to confess such a lapse, it would constitute the committing of a 'deadly sin' by that person. Compare this elaborate and lengthy *monastic* Buddhist ritual with Catholicism's abbreviated versions including *lay congregations* and individual *laypersons*. And Protestantism has reduced 'Confession and Absolution' to a mere shadow of the Buddhist original.

---

*Translated from the *Mahāvagga*, ii. 2-3, by Henry Clarke Warren, in *Buddhism In Translations*, Harvard Oriental Series, vol. 3, ed. Charles R. Lanman (Cambridge, MA: Harvard University Press, 1896), pp. 404-405. I have taken the liberty of replacing Warren's translation, 'priest/s', with the more acceptable term, 'monk/s'. The square bracketed [*pātimokkha*] is Warren's. – ML

Although the Buddha is said to have arrived at his idea of the ritual of 'confession and absolution' while "plunged in meditation", this is not to say that he was not at the same time reformulating certain ancient Indian practices. William Norman Brown, for instance, writes of such an ancient practice under the section heading of 'Act of Truth':

> In very early times in India the speaking of truth became invested with magic power. The notion seems based on ideas found in the Ṛigveda, although we have not, as far as I am aware, documentary evidence that it was recognized before the period of the Brāhmaṇas, but this in itself carries us back to a time prior to 600 B.C. . . . In the Brāhmaṇas the truth that is so potent is the truth of exactitude in the sacrifice, a ritual or ceremonial accuracy.*

As an illustration of the importance of this 'Act of Truth', Brown (p. 7) quotes A.B. Keith:

> "The sense of the importance of exactitude in the rite is seen in the famous ritual of confession which is performed at the Varuṇapraghāsas, when the priest, the Pratiprasthātṛ, asks the wife of the sacrificer [the question] with whom she consorts, other than her husband. It is essential that [if she is guilty of being unfaithful] she should confess since else it will go badly with her kinsfolk, an interesting assertion of the solidarity of the kin. The speaking out of the sin diminishes it, but not, it appears, by anything else than that it brings exactitude again into the order of things. . . ."**

Brown goes on to say: "This rite . . . illustrates the notion that the mere truth is able to render the sacrifice effective even though it be a truth that reveals a sin."

The Buddha, in his meditation, seems to have transformed this 'Act of Truth' (considered magical by the ancients) into a psycho-therapeutic ritual (free from any hint of magic) to combat the all too human tendencies to fail to follow the many precepts that monastics have chosen to adhere to. Since no other religion in the Mediterranean world had any similar ritual, the origin of Christianity's practice of 'confession and absolution' is thus clearly traceable back to Buddhism.

As we have noted, in Buddhism, it is a ritual practiced *only* by Buddhist monastics. In the Buddhist mission fields of the Western kingdoms around the Mediterranean, where Buddhism had gone underground, so to speak, hiding its Indian origin by masquerading in the form of Jewish organizations, we presume that these apparently Jewish organizations may *not* have followed any elaborate *Prātimōkṣa* ritual. In the first century A.D., reports by Philo and Josephus on the Essenes/Jessæans (the Therapeutæ and Qumranites), there is hardly a trace of any ritual of 'confession and absolution'. However, during the period of successive Jewish revolts of 66-135 A.D., the ex-monastics must have scattered to various groups with less obvious Jewish profiles such as 'voluntary associations' or private homes, carrying over some of their monastic traditions. Thus, some of these proto-Christian groups may have preserved truncated forms of the *Prātimōkṣa* ritual, which then were eventually passed down to their "descendants", the earliest Christians – truncated forms which have been preserved most clearly, today, in Roman Catholicism.

The ***Paraklêtos*** of John's Gospel is an allegorical personification of the *Prātimōkṣa* ritual – a "Substitute Teacher". The ***Paraklêtos***, thus, is not a divine being, but rather a transmogrification of the rules which the Buddha lay down for attaining Parinirvāṇa / Kingdom of Heaven. If one does not understand this allegory in John's Gospel, one will not understand this relationship between Buddhism and Christianity. The monastic life, in its own way, achieves the creation of a 'Heaven on Earth'. And in this heaven on earth, there is also no marrying nor being given in marriage. Or to be more specific, there is to be no involvement in sexuality – in thought or deed.

The first century A.D. saw the rise of Mahāyāna Buddhism, with a greatly increased influence of laypersons, and with less emphasis on the *prajñā* ('wisdom') of the monks and with more emphasis on the 'faith' of laypersons. During the Jewish revolts, before the canonical gospels were written, the balance of power was shifting from monastic organizations of Buddhist heritage to secularized organizations, such as 'voluntary associations' or home organizations of lay-members. With the writing of the works of the New Testament, especially *Acts*, the Epistles, and *Revelation*, there is a reflection of this shift from monasticism (with its *prajñā*) to a context of secular clerical sacramentalism (with its emphasis on 'faith').

---

*W.N. Brown, *The Indian and Christian Miracles of Walking on the Water* (Chicago: The Open Court Publishing Company, 1928), p. 6.

**Arthur Berriedale Keith, *The Religion and Philosophy of the Veda and the Upanishads*, vol. 32 (Cambridge, MA: Harvard University Press, 1925), p. 471.

• • • • • • • • • •

Aniconicism

The topic of 'Aniconicism' is deeper and more pervasive than my brief discussion of it (on p. 24) might indicate. Aniconicism is related to the invention of the Brāhmī script and its use of an "inherent '*a*' ". Virtually all of the Indic scripts have evolved over the centuries from Aśōkan Brāhmī. Prof. Gift Siromoney and I first published a paper, "The Invention of the Brāhmī Script", in the *Madras Christian College Magazine*, XLVI (1977). In the following year, our short paper was reprinted in the *Souvenir of the Fourth Annual Congress of the Epigraphical Society of India* (1978), pp. 31-33. And in 1992, it was again printed in *Indological Essays: Commemorative Volume II for Gift Siromoney*, which was edited by me for the Department of Statistics, Madras Christian College. Archive.org has made this book (and our paper) available freely as a PDF download on the internet: < http://archive.org/details/IndologicalEssays2 >.

The Brāhmī script was used for writing all of the Indo-European languages of India – and for all the Dravidian languages. The earliest form of the Brāhmī script is often referred to as 'Aśōkan Brāhmī', as it seems to have sprung forth as if from the head of Brahmā on monumental pillars and rock edicts of this king.

It has not been clear to palæographers how this marvelous script arose, the "mother" of all the scripts of the many languages of India, which have evolved over 2,250 years into the great variety of scripts we see today. In this brief note, however, I suggest that we have evidence that the invention of the Brāhmī script actually took place in Alexandria, Egypt. Before accusing me of Alexandria-mania, let me explain. The Tocharian language, spoken by an ethnic group well separated from India, geographically and culturally, used a version of the Brāhmī script in their writing. And, further, I note that the Meroitic script, which was an alpha-syllabic script said to have been originally derived from Egyptian hieroglyphs, and which was used in the Meroë Kingdom of Sudan, also has the "inherent '*a*' ", like all the languages in India and in South East Asia.

If Indians had invented the Brāhmī script in India, I doubt that the Tocharians, in such an out-of-the-way geographic location would have adopted Brāhmī. And how would we explain the appearance, in the 2nd century **BCE**, of that sophisticated element of Brāhmī, the "inherent '*a*' " in the script of an ethnic group in the Sudan? But if the Indians invented the Brāhmī script in Alexandria's great Library/Musæum, interacting with Western scholars, the immense prestige of those Egyptian institutions could more reasonably account for the world-wide distribution of the Brāhmī script and the appearance of the "inherent '*a*' " in the Meroitic Kingdom of Sudan – a kingdom which modeled itself very closely on that of the Egyptian pharaohs.

We know that scholars in the Library/Musæum of Alexandria went into great depth with the study of the grammar of various languages. It is reasonable that such studies were paralleled by the study of scripts. In fact, it would be a necessary discipline, because the Great Library was collecting written works from all over the world.

During Aśōka's reign, the Brāhmī script was used in most of the Indian sub-continent. A second script, Kharōṣṭī, was used in what is now Afghanistan, Pakistan, and North India. Kharōṣṭī, which also has the "inherent '*a*' ", is generally considered to have been patterned on the Aramaic script. As with Brāhmī, I would suggest that Kharōṣṭī was also developed by Indian scholars *in Alexandria*.

In the Dravidian Tamil language, there is an interesting characterization of consonants and vowels. The consonants are considered the physical elements forming the bodies of words, and the vowels are the vivifying elements of the consonants. Consonants, without vowels, can only form a dead body, a corpse – there will be no life in them. But connect a vowel or vowels to the consonants, and they will come alive and form pronounceable words or elements of a word. Vowels unattached to any consonants, on the other hand, can and do express words.

To get around the negative 'corpse' tag for consonants, the concept of an "inherent '*a*' " was devised so that all the consonants were thought of as possessing an "inherent '*a*' ", unless marked with another vowel or deliberately deprived of its "inherent '*a*' ".

The unmarked consonants, therefore, are understood as possessing an "inherent '*a*' " in them, and are pronounced, accordingly, with the sound of the short '*a*'. The sound of the short '*a*' can be viewed as the mystical source of all life (and the beginning of the sacred sound, '*Ōṁ*'), and treated as so sacred, holy, that it is not to be represented by any physical mark. Thus, the development of the "inherent '*a*' " device. And, as the short '*a*' is the most common vowel encountered in Indian languages, there is great economy, in writing, in not having to make a mark for it.

From this perspective, the Hebrew script of the Torah, which has no vowel letters or marks at all, can also be viewed as an example of aniconicism. All vowels are inherent! They are all sacred vivifiers. The breath of life. The context of the consonant patterns brings to mind the unwritten vowels. For the monomaniac inerrantists, I have a question: Could the writers of the Hebrew Bible have intended multiple implied readings in given words – a type of multiple entendre, intentionally allowing for a given Hebrew consonant cluster to convey multiple implied meaning?

Egyptians practiced the ritual of placing bread and wine before an image/idol of the deity. This is idolatry. The shewbread and wine ritual in the Jerusalem Temple was a hangover from a similar Jewish idolatrous background. But in the Second Temple era, there was no physical image of **YḤVḤ** in this idolatrous context. This is aniconicism.

The Rock Edict below is written in Aśōkan Brāhmī, with its use of the inherent '*a*'. Please also note Aśōka's mention of specific Buddhist scriptures and the clear presence of both Buddhist monks and nuns, the forerunners of those ascetic celibate men and women of the Therapeutæ, and, later, of Christian ascetic celibate men and women.

IV.20. ***The Calcutta-Bairāt Rock Inscription of Aśōka****, where he recommends the study of the Buddhist texts, namely, Vinayasamukasa, Aliyavaṁśas, Anāgatabhayas, Muni-gāthās, Mōnēya-suta, Upatisapasina and the Sermon to Rāhula as essential for the monks as well as the laymen. Stone, 3rd century B.C.*

This inscription proves beyond doubt Aśōka's personal allegiance to the religion of Buddha.†

[*The Way of the Buddha*, pp. 308-309]

'Piyadasi' [Aśōka], King of Magadha, saluting the Sangha and wishing them good health and happiness, speaks thus: "You know, reverend sirs, how great my faith in the Buddha, the Dhamma and Sangha is. Whatever, reverend sirs, has been spoken by Lord Buddha, all that is well-spoken."

These Dhamma texts – Extracts from *The Discipline*, *The Noble Way of Life*, *The Fears to Come*, *The Poem on the Silent Sage*, *The Discourse on the Pure Life*, *Upatisa's Questions*, and *The Advice to Rāhula* which was spoken by the Buddha concerning false speech – these Dhamma texts, reverend sirs, I desire that all the monks and nuns may constantly listen to and remember. Likewise the laymen and laywomen.

– Minor Rock Edict Nb. 3 (trans. S. Dhammika)

---

†Thanissaro Bhikkhu has provided a full English translation of these seven extracts from Buddhist works referred to by King Aśōka, together with an enlightening commentary, all freely available on the internet [second (revised) electronic edition, 1996]:

http://halfsmile.org/buddhadust/www.accesstoinsight.org/lib/modern/thanissaro/asoka.html

The title of Thanissaro Bhikkhu's paper is: *That the True Dhamma Might Last a Long Time: Readings Selected by King Aśoka.*

Crypto-Buddhism's 'Smoking Gun'

Christian Lindtner, quoted in Lockwood, *Buddhism's Relation to Christianity*, p. 278:

> Mahā-Parinirvāṇa-Sūtra 9: In the village of Nādikā a large number of brothers and sisters have passed away. What will become of them? It is explicitly said that "more than 500 brothers have passed away". This sentence is available in the Sanskrit (9:15) and in the Pāli (Waldschmidt, p. 166). The Pāli has been translated into English, e.g. by Trevor Ling: "More than five hundred devout men of Nādikā who have died" (*The Buddha's Philosophy of Man*, London 1981, p. 159). This accounts for the "more than five hundred brothers . . . of whom some have died", in *1 Cor. 15:6*, a statement that has always caused the greatest embarrassment to theologians. The more than 500 brothers are never mentioned in any other ancient Christian sources – with one exception, a Coptic source that says that the more than 500 were Indian priests (see R. Garbe, *Indien und das Christentum*, Süderbrarup 2004 [reprint of 1914 edition], p. 292). There is, as we have just seen, some truth in this. There was an Indian source for the 500.

Garbe, *Indien und das Christentum*, p. 292:

> Zu S. 60, Z. 11. Die echt buddhistische Rundzahl 500 hat schon einen alten koptischen Erklärer des Neuen Testaments, möglicherweise schon im vierten Jahrhundert, dazu bestimmt, den Vers I. Cor. 15, 6 zu indianisieren. Die dort erwähnten mehr als 500 Brüder, denen der auferstandene Christus erschienen sein soll, werden nämlich von diesem Ausleger für Brahmanen erklärt! S. Oskar von Lemm, *Der Alexanderroman bei den Kopten* (St. Petersburg 1903), 119-120:
>
> „Es ist in neuerer Zeit mehrfach der Versuch gemacht worden die Buddhalegende mit den evangelischen Berichten in Beziehung zu bringen; ein ähnlicher Versuch liegt uns nun bereits aus weit älterer Zeit vor – wenn der Verfasser wirklich Schenûte ist – also schon aus dem vierten Jahrhundert.
>
> . . .
>
> „Da in diesem Texte von den Brahmanen das gesagt wird, was sonst von den Buddhisten berichtet wird, so scheinen hier die einen mit den anderen verwechselt worden zu sein."

Translation

Garbe, *Indien und das Christentum*, p. 292:

> Re page 60, line 11. The genuinely Buddhist round number 500 already prompted an early Coptic commentator on the New Testament, possibly as far back as the fourth century, to Indianize the verse *1 Cor. 15:6*. That commentator describes the more than 500 brothers mentioned there to whom the risen Christ is said to have appeared as Brahmins! See Oskar von Lemm, *Der Alexanderroman bei den Kopten* (St. Petersburg 1903), 119-120:
>
> "Repeated attempts have been made in recent times to link the Buddha legend with Gospel stories; a similar [known] attempt dates back to much earlier times – if its author is indeed Schenûte – namely to the fourth century.
>
> . . .
>
> "Since that text says about the Brahmins what is otherwise said about Buddhists, it seems that here the former were mistaken for the latter."

* * * * * * * * *

Here rests the 'Smoking Gun' of crypto-Buddhism!
Delivered to us by two outstanding German scholars, Lemm and Garbe.

English translations (of parts) of Lemm's facing meta-page, 119:

The following appears to be the meaning of the text: Matthew is here compared with the Brahmin Dandamis; he is said to have abolished any variation in daily meals, and to have led the people not in the manner of the Olympian (i.e. Greek) peoples but rather following the example of the Brahmin Dandamis, meaning that, just as Dandamis was a model for the Brahmins with his undemanding nature, so was Matthew as leader of the monks.

And, finally, I found the Brahmins mentioned again in a passage of the *Cod. Borg.* CCXLVI (Zoëga 600), that may be of interest regarding the history of the spreading of the Buddha legend. Here a verse of the *First Epistle to the Corinthians* is explained curiously. The author, presumably Schenûte, writes:

[six lines of Coptic text, followed by 5 lines of German translation:]

As I said initially, many who do not interpret Scripture correctly are [mistaken], as I and those who agree with me have heard a great man say thus: The Apostle speaks of those who are known as Brahmins when he says: The Lord appeared to more than 500 brothers at once, many of whom are (alive) to this day.

The passage is in *1 Cor. 15:6* and reads:

Epeita ōphthē epanō pentakosiois adelphois ephapax ex hōn hoi pleiones menousin heōs arti tines de ekoimēthēsan.

'Then he appeared to over five hundred of our brothers at once, most of whom are still alive.'

In this passage, here, those to whom Christ appeared after his resurrection, are expressly called Brahmins. There have been several attempts in recent times to link the Buddha legend with Gospel stories; we now can refer to a similar, much older attempt – if the

gehenden, sondern ist wohl die Überschrift des darauf folgenden Abschnittes der Handschrift. Die Form ⲧⲉⲛⲇⲓⲁ, resp. ⲧⲉⲛⲧⲓⲁ für «Indien» ist uns schon aus der Geschichte des «Gesios und Isidoros» bekannt[205]).

Der Sinn dieses Textes dürfte etwa folgender sein. Matthäus wird hier verglichen mit dem Brahmanen Dandamis; es wird von ihm gesagt, dass er die Abwechselung in den Speisen abgeschafft habe und das Volk geleitet habe nicht nach Art der olympischen (d. i. griechischen) Völkerschaften, sondern vielmehr nach dem Muster des Brahmanen Dandamis d. h. also, wie Dandamis den Brahmanen ein Vorbild war in der Genügsamkeit, so wurde es auch Matthäus als Führer der Mönche.

Schliesslich fand ich die Brahmanen noch an einer Stelle des Cod. Borg. CCXLVI (Zoëga 600) erwähnt, die vielleicht für die Geschichte der Verbreitung der Buddha-Legende nicht ohne Interesse sein dürfte. Hier wird ein Vers des 1. Corintherbriefes auf eigenthümliche Weise erklärt. Der Verfasser, vermuthlich Schenûte, sagt dort: ⲕⲁⲧⲁ ⲑⲉ ϭⲉ ⲉⲛⲧⲁⲓϣⲣⲡ̄ⲛ̄[sic]ϫⲟⲟⲥ ⲟⲩⲛ ϩⲁϩ ⲉⲩⲃⲱⲗ ⲛ̄ⲛⲉⲅⲣⲁⲫⲏ ϩⲛ ⲟⲩⲥⲟⲟⲩⲧⲛ ⲁⲛ ⲛⲑⲉ ⲛⲧⲁⲓⲥⲱⲧⲙ ⲁⲛⲟⲕ ⲙⲛ ⲛⲉⲧⲛ̄ⲙⲙⲁⲉⲓ ⲉⲩⲛⲟϭ ⲛ̄ⲣⲱⲙⲉ ⲉϥϫⲱ ⲙ̄ⲙⲟⲥ. ϫⲉ ⲉⲣⲉ ⲡⲁⲡⲟⲥⲧⲟⲗⲟⲥ ϣⲁϫⲉ ⲉⲛⲉⲧⲟⲩⲙⲟⲩⲧⲉ ⲉⲣⲟⲟⲩ ϫⲉ ⲛ̄ⲃ̄ⲣⲉ[sic]ⲭⲙⲁⲛⲟⲥ. ϩⲙ ⲡⲧⲣⲉϥϫⲟⲟⲥ. ϫⲉ ⲁ ⲡϫⲟⲉⲓⲥ ⲟⲩⲱⲛϩ ⲉⲃⲟⲗ ⲛϩⲟⲩⲟ ⲉϯⲟⲩ ⲛϣⲉ ⲛⲥⲟⲛ ⲛⲟⲩⲥⲟⲡ ⲛⲟⲩⲱⲧ, ⲛⲁⲓ ⲉⲣⲉ ⲡⲉⲩϩⲟⲩⲟ ϣⲟⲟⲡ ϣⲁ ⲧⲉⲛⲟⲩ. «Wie ich zuerst gesagt habe, sind viele, welche die Schriften nicht richtig erklären, wie ich mit denen, die mit mir sind, einen grossen Mann also habe sagen hören: Der Apostel redet von denen, welche man Brahmanen nennt, indem er spricht: Der Herr erschien mehr als fünfhundert Brüdern auf einmal von denen viele bis jetzt (am Leben) sind».

Die Stelle findet sich 1 Cor. 15,6 und lautet: ⲙⲛ̄ⲛ̄ⲥⲱⲥ ⲁϥⲟⲩⲱⲛϩ ⲉⲃⲟⲗ ⲛϩⲟⲩⲟ ⲉϯⲟⲩ ⲛϣⲉ ⲛⲥⲟⲛ ⲛⲟⲩⲥⲟⲡ ⲛⲟⲩⲱⲧ. ⲛⲁⲓ ⲉⲣⲉ ⲡⲉⲩϩⲟⲩⲟ ϣⲟⲟⲡ ϣⲁ ⲧⲉⲛⲟⲩ ϩⲟⲓⲛⲉ ⲇⲉ ⲙ̄ⲙⲟⲟⲩ ⲁⲩⲛ̄ⲕⲟⲧⲕ. ἔπειτα ὤφθη ἐπάνω πεντακοσίοις ἀδελφοῖς ἐφάπαξ, ἐξ ὧν οἱ πλείονες μένουσιν ἕως ἄρτι, τινὲς δὲ καὶ ἐκοιμήθησαν.

Es werden hier also diejenigen, denen Christus nach seiner Auferstehung erschienen sein soll, ausdrücklich als Brahmanen bezeichnet. Es ist in neuerer Zeit mehrfach der Versuch gemacht worden die Buddhalegende mit den evangelischen Berichten in Beziehung zu bringen[206]); ein ähnlicher Versuch liegt uns nun bereits aus weit älterer Zeit vor — wenn

205) Ä. Z. XXI (1883), 146. Vergl. Kl. kopt. Studien I—IX, pag. 407/5.

206) Rudolf Seydel, Das Evangelium von Jesu in seinen Verhältnissen zu Buddha-Sage und Buddha-Lehre mit fortlaufender Rücksicht auf andere Religionskreise untersucht. Leipzig, 1882. — G. Marquardt, Der Verrat des Judas Ischariot — eine Sage. München (1900).

der Verfasser wirklich Schenûte ist — also schon aus dem vierten Jahrhundert. Es ist zu bedauern, dass uns der Name des Mannes, der den Ausspruch über die fünfhundert Brüder gethan haben soll, nicht mitgetheilt wird. Man vergl. aber zu unserem Texte R. Seydel l. l. pag. 285. «Paulus (1 Kor. 15,6) spricht von einer Erscheinung des Auferstandenen «*vor 500 Brüdern*». Gerade so viel beträgt nach dem Mahâparinibbâna-Sutta die Anzahl der versammelten «Brüder», an welche Buddha seine letzten Worte richtet, und in deren Gegenwart er stirbt. Darauf kommt der Jünger Kassapa mit ebenfalls «500 Brüdern» an, mit welchen er unterwegs war, als ihn die Todesbotschaft traf. Auch das erste Concil, welches *unmittelbar nach Buddhas Tode* zu Radschagriha zusammentrat, bestand aus 500 Bekennern. Oft ist es dieselbe Zahl, vor der Buddha predigt». Vergl. Marquardt, l. l. pag. 31 f.

Da in diesem Texte von den Brahmanen das gesagt wird, was sonst von den Buddhisten berichtet wird, so scheinen hier die einen mit den anderen verwechselt worden zu sein.

V. 11. — ϩⲛ ⲛⲁⲙⲏⲣⲓ «in den Homeriten»] ϩⲛ ⲛⲁⲙⲏⲣⲓ steht hier für ϩⲛ ⲧⲉⲭⲱⲣⲁ ⲛⲛⲁⲙⲏⲣⲓ «im Lande der Homeriten». Vergl. oben pag. 38 zu Fr. 2'18.

V. 12. — . . . . . ⲛⲃⲓⲟⲥ ⲛⲛⲉⲧⲉⲙⲙⲁⲁⲩ . . . . . «die Leben[sweise] jener».

V. 13. — . . . . . ⲓⲟⲟⲩ ⲛ̀ϩⲉϥⲥⲱ ⲙ . . . . . .] Bouriant theilt hier ab . . . . . ⲓⲟⲟⲩ ⲛ̀ϩⲉϥⲥⲱⲙ . . . . . , doch glaube ich, dass ϩⲉϥⲥⲱ für ϩⲉⲃⲥⲱ steht, wie in der folgenden Zeile und wir können vielleicht ergänzen . . . . . [ⲁϥϯ ϩ]ⲓⲟⲟⲩ ⲛ̀ϩⲉϥⲥⲱ ⲙ . . . . . . «[er legte] ihnen Kleider von . . . . . . an» oder [ⲁⲩϯ ϩ]ⲓⲟⲟⲩ ⲛ̀ϩⲉϥⲥⲱ ⲙ . . . . . . «[sie legten] sich Kleider von . . . . . . an».

V. 14. — . . . . . . ⲁⲁⲩ ⲛϩⲉⲃⲥⲱ . . . .] Hier ergänze ich: [ⲙⲛ ⲗ]ⲁⲁⲩ ⲛϩⲉⲃⲥⲱ [ⲧⲟ ϩⲓⲟⲟⲩ] «kein Kleid war ihnen angelegt» d. h. «sie hatten kein Kleid an». — Vergl. dazu Pseudo-Call. III, 9. ἐν γυμνότητι διαζῶντες. — In dem Cod. Copt. Paris. 43 f. 51 r. wird ein Land genannt: ⲡⲕⲁϩ ⲛ̄ⲃⲁϣⲁϩⲏⲩ ارض العريان «Terra nudorum»[207]). Hier werden vielleicht auch die Gymnosophisten gemeint sein.

Etwas ganz Analoges zu den Gymnosophisten findet sich mehrfach in koptischen Quellen, wo von nackten Anachoreten in der Wüste oder auf einer öden Insel die Rede ist. Vergl. besonders eine Geschichte aus dem Leben Makarius' des Grossen, die uns an verschiedenen Stellen überliefert ist:

---

207) Baciai in Ä. Z. XXIV (1886), pag. 89.

English translation (of part) of Lemm's facing meta-page, 120:

author is indeed Schenûte – namely one made in the fourth century. It is regrettable that we are not given the name of the man who is supposed to have made the statement about the five-hundred brothers. But compare our text with R. Seydel 1.1 page 285. "Paul (*1 Cor. 15:6*) speaks of an appearance of the risen [Christ] 'to 500 brothers'. According to the *Mahāparinibbāna-Sutta*, that is exactly the number of the assembled 'brothers' to whom the Buddha addresses his final words and in whose presence he dies. Then arrives the disciple Kassapa with also '500 brothers' with whom he was traveling when the news of the death reached him. The First Council, too, which assembled at [Rājagṛiha] immediately following the Buddha's death, consisted of 500 faithful. Often the Buddha preaches to the same number." Comp. Marquardt, 1. 1., page 31 f.

Chelidonura varians	
Scientific classification	
Kingdom:	Animalia
Phylum:	Mollusca
Class:	Gastropoda
(unranked):	clade Heterobranchia clade Euthyneura clade Euopisthobranchia clade Cephalaspidea
Superfamily:	Philinoidea
Family:	Aglajidae
Genus:	*Chelidonura*
Species:	***C. varians***
Binomial name	
Chelidonura varians Eliot, 1903	

Sir Charles was a marine biologist, in addition to being a diplomat, multi-linguist, and one who wrote with authority about India and Buddhism.

Illustration with information courtesy of Wikipedia.

THIRD APPENDIX

Charles Norton Edgecumbe Eliot, *Hinduism and Buddhism: An Historical Sketch*, Vol. 3 (London: Routledge & Kegan, Ltd., 1921), pp. 429-450:

CHAPTER LVI

INDIAN INFLUENCE IN THE WESTERN WORLD

The influence of Indian religion on Christianity is part of the wider question of its influence on the west generally. It is clear that from 200 B.C. until 300 A.D. oriental religion played a considerable part in the countries round the Mediterranean. The worship of the Magna Mater was known in Rome by 200 B.C. and that of Isis and Serapis in the time of Sulla (d. 78 B.C.). In the early centuries of the Christian era the cultus of Mithra prevailed not only in Rome but in most parts of Europe where there were Roman legions, even in Britain. These religions may be appropriately labelled with the vague word oriental, for they are not so much the special creeds of Egypt and Persia transplanted into Roman soil as fragments, combinations and adaptations of the most various eastern beliefs. They differed from the forms of worship indigenous to Greece and Italy in being personal, not national: they were often emotional and professed to reveal the nature and destinies of the soul. If we ask whether there are any definitely Indian elements in all this orientalism, the answer must be that there is no clear case of direct borrowing, nothing Indian analogous to the migrations of Isis and Mithra. If Indian thought had any influence on the Mediterranean it was not immediate, but through Persia, Babylonia and Egypt. But it is possible that the doctrine of metempsychosis and the ideal of the ascetic life are echoes of India. Though the former is found in an incomplete shape among savages in many parts of the world, there is no indication that it was indigenous in Egypt, Syria, Babylonia, Asia Minor, Greece or Italy. It crops up now and again as a tenet held by philosophers or communities of cosmopolitan tastes such as the Orphic Societies, but usually in circumstances which suggest a foreign origin. It is said, however, to have formed part of the doctrines taught by the Druids in Gaul. Similarly though occasional fasts and other mortifications may have been usual in the worship of various deities and though the rigorous Spartan discipline was a sort of military asceticism, still the idea that the religious life consists in suppressing the passions, which plays

429

such a large part in Christian monasticism, can be traced not to any Jewish or European institution but to Egypt. Although monasticism spread quickly thence to Syria, it is admitted that the first Christian hermits and monasteries were Egyptian and there is some evidence for the existence there of pagan hermits.[1] Egypt was a most religious country, but it does not appear that asceticism, celibacy or meditation formed part of its older religious life, and their appearance in Hellenistic times may be due to a wave of Asiatic influence starting originally from India.

Looking westwards from India and considering what were the circumstances favouring the diffusion of Indian ideas, we must note first that Hindus have not only been in all ages preoccupied by religious questions but have also had a larger portion of the missionary spirit than is generally supposed. It is true that in wide tracts and long periods this spirit has been suppressed by Brahmanic exclusiveness, but phenomena like the spread of Buddhism and the establishment of Hinduism in Indo-China and Java speak for themselves. The spiritual tide flowed eastwards rather than westwards; still it is probable that its movement was felt, though on a smaller scale, in the accessible parts of the west. By land, our record tells us mainly of what came into India from Persia and Bactria, but something must have gone out. By water we know that at least after about 700 B.C. there was communication with the Persian Gulf, Arabia and probably the Red Sea. Semitic alphabets were borrowed: in the Jātakas we hear of merchants going to Baveru or Babylon: Solomon's commercial ventures brought him Indian products. But the strongest testimony to the dissemination of religious ideas is found in Asoka's celebrated edict (probably 256 B.C.) in which he claims to have spread the Dhamma as far as the dominions of Antiochus "and beyond that Antiochus to where dwell the four kings named Ptolemy, Antigonus, Magas and Alexander." The kings mentioned are identified as the rulers of Syria, Egypt, Macedonia, Cyrene and Epirus. Asoka compares his missionary triumphs to the military conquests of other monarchs. It may be that the comparison is only too just and that like them he claimed to have extended his law to regions where his name was unknown.

---

[1]See Scott Moncrieff, *Paganism and Christianity in Egypt*, p. 199. Petrie, *Personal Religion in Egypt*, p. 62. But for a contrary view see Preuschen, *Monchium und Serapiskult*, 1903.

No record of the arrival of Buddhist missions in any Hellenistic kingdom has reached us and the language of the edict, if examined critically, is not precise. On the other hand, however vague it may be, it testified to two things. Firstly, Egypt, Syria and other Hellenistic states were realities to the Indians of this period, distant but not fabulous regions. Secondly, the king desired to spread the knowledge of the law in these countries and this desire was shared, or inspired, by the monks whom he patronized. It is therefore probable that, though the difficulties of travelling were great and the linguistic difficulties of preaching an Indian religion even greater, missionaries set out for the west and reached if not Macedonia and Epirus, at least Babylon and Alexandria. We may imagine that they would frequent the temples and company of the priests and not show much talent for public preaching. If no record of them remains, it is not more wonderful than the corresponding silence in the east about Greek visitors to India.

It is only after the Christian era that we find Apollonius and Plotinus looking towards India as the home of wisdom. In earlier periods the definite instances of connection with India are few. Indian figures found at Memphis perhaps indicate the existence there of an Indian colony,[1] and a Ptolemaic grave-stone has been discovered bearing the signs of the wheel and trident.[2] The infant deity Horus is represented in Indian attitudes and as sitting on a lotus. Some fragments of the Kanarese language have been found on a papyrus, but it appears not to be earlier than the second century A.D.[3] In 21 A.D., Augustus while at Athens received an embassy from India which came *via* Antioch.

It was accompanied by a person described as Zarmanochegas, an Indian from Bargosa who astonished the Athenians by publicly burning himself alive.[4] We also hear of the movement of an Indian tribe from the Panjab to Parthia and then

---

[1]Flinders Petrie, *Man*, 1908, p. 129.

[2]*J.R.A.S.* 1898, p. 875.

[3]Hultzsch, *Hermas*, XXXIX. p. 307, and *J.R.A.S.* 1904, p. 399.

[4]Nicolaus Damascenus, quoted by Strabo, XV. 73. See also Dion Cassius, IX. 58, who calls the Indian Zarmaros. Zarmanochegas perhaps contains the two words *Śramana* and *Ācārya*.

to Armenia (149-127 B.C.),[1] and of an Indian colony at Alexandria in the time of Trajan. Doubtless there were other tribal movements and other mercantile colonies which have left no record, but they were all on a small scale and there was no general outpouring of India westwards.

The early relations of India were with Babylon rather than with Egypt, but if Indian ideas reached Babylon they may easily have spread further. Communication between Egypt and Babylon existed from an early period and the tablets of Tel-el-Amarna testify to the antiquity and intimacy of this intercourse. At a later date Necho invaded Babylonia but was repulsed. The Jews returned from the Babylonian captivity (538 B.C.) with their religious horizon enlarged and modified. They were chiefly affected by Zoroastrian ideas but they may have become acquainted with any views and practices then known in Babylon, and not necessarily with those identified with the state worship, for the exiles may have been let to associate with other strangers. After about 535 B.C. the Persian empire extended from the valley of the Indus to the valley of the Nile and from Macedonia to Babylon. We hear that in the army which Xerxes led against Greece there were Indian soldiers, which is interesting as showing how the Persians transported subject races from one end of their empire to the other. After the career of Alexander, Hellenistic kingdoms took the place of this empire and, apart from inroads on the north-west frontier of India, maintained friendly relations with her. Seleucus Nicator sent Megasthenes as envoy about 300 B.C. and Ptolemy Philadelphus (285-247 B.C.) a representative named Dionysius. Bindusāra, the father of Asoka, exchanged missions with Antiochus, and according to a well-known anecdote,[2] expressed a wish to buy a professor [sophist]. But Antiochus replied that Greek professors were not for sale.

Egyptologists consider that metempsychosis is not part of the earlier strata of Egyptian religion but appears first about 500 B.C., and Flinders Petrie refers to this period the originals of the earliest Hermetic literature. But other authorities regard these works as being both in substance and language considerably

---

[1]See *J.R.A.S.* 1907, p 968.

[2]See Vincent Smith, *Early History of India*, edition III. p. 147. The original source of the anecdote is Hegesandros in Athenæus, 14. 652.

posterior to the Christian era and as presenting a jumble of Christianity, Neoplatonism and Egyptian ideas.

I have neither space nor competence to discuss the date of the Hermetic writings, but it is of importance for the question which we are considering. They contain addresses to the deity like "I am Thou and Thou art I". . . . If such words could be used in Egypt several centuries before Christ, the probability of Indian influence seems to me strong, for they would not grow naturally out of Egyptian or Hellenistic religion. Five hundred years later they would be less remarkable. Whatever may be the date of the Hermetic literature, it is certain that the Book of Wisdom and the writings of Philo are pre-Christian and show a mixture of ideas drawn from many sources, Jewish, Neoplatonic and Neopythagorean. If these hospitable systems made the acquaintance of Indian philosophy, we may be sure that they gave it an unprejudiced and even friendly hearing. In the centuries just before the Christian era Egypt was a centre of growth for personal and private religious ideas,[1] hardly possessing sufficient organization to form what we call a religion, yet still, inasmuch as they aspired to teach individual souls right conduct as well as true knowledge, implicitly containing the same scheme of teaching as the Buddhist and Christian Churches. But it is characteristic of all this movement that it never attempted to form a national or universal religion and remained in all its manifestation individual and personal, connected neither with the secular government nor with any national cultus. Among these religious ideas were monotheism mingled with pantheism to the extent of saying that God is all and all is one: the idea of the Logos or Divine Wisdom, which ultimately assumes that the Word is an emanation or Son of God; asceticism, or at least the desire to free the soul from the bondage of the senses; metempsychosis and the doctrine or conversion of the new birth of the soul, which fits in well with metempsychosis, though it frequently exists apart from it. I doubt if there is sufficient reason for attributing the doctrine of the Logos[2] to India, but it is possible that asceticism and the belief in metempsychosis received their first impulse thence. They [asceticism and metempsychosis] appear late and, like the phraseology of the

---

[1]See Flinders Petrie, *Personal Religion in Egypt before Christianity*, 1909.

[2]As I have pointed out elsewhere there is little real analogy between the ideas of *Logos* and *Śabda*.

Hermetic books, they do not grow naturally out of antecedent ideas and practices in Egypt and Palestine. The life followed by such communities as the Therapeutæ and Essenes is just such as might have been evolved by seekers after truth who were trying to put into practice in another country the religious ideals of India. There are differences: for instance these communities laboured with their hands and observed the seventh day, but their main ideas, retirement from the world and suppression of the passions, are those of Indian monks and foreign to Egyptian and Jewish thought.

The character of Pythagoras's teaching and its relation to Egypt have been much discussed and the name of the master was clearly extended by later (and perhaps also by early) disciples to doctrines which he never held. But it seems indisputable that there were widely spread both in Greece and Italy societies called Pythagorean or Orphic which inculcated a common rule of life and believed in metempsychosis. The rule of life did not as a rule amount to asceticism in the Indian sense, which was most uncongenial to Hellenic ideas, but it comprised great self-restraint. The belief in metempsychosis finds remarkably clear expression: we hear in the Orphic fragments of the circle of birth and of escape from it, language strikingly parallel to many Indian utterances and strikingly unlike the usual turns of Greek speech and thought. Thus the soul is addressed as "Hail thou who has suffered the suffering" and is made to declare "I have flown out of the sorrowful weary wheel."[1] I see no reason for discrediting the story that Pythagoras visited Egypt.[2] He is said to have been a Samian and during his life (c. 500 B.C.) Samos had a special connection with Egypt, for Polycrates was the ally of Amasis and assisted him with troops. The date, if somewhat early, is not far removed from the time when metempsychosis became part of Egyptian religion. The general opinion of antiquity connected the Orphic doctrines with Thrace but

---

[1]... From the tablet found at Compagno. Cf. Proclus in Plat. *Tim.* v. 330,... See J.E. Harrison, *Proleg. to the study of Greek Religion*, 1908, esp. XI. and appendix.

[2]Burnet, *Early Greek Philosophy*, p. 94, says that it first occurs in the Busiris of Isocrates and does not believe that the account in Herodotus implies that Pythagoras visited Egypt..

so little is known of the Thracians and their origin that this connection does not carry us much further. They appear, however, to have had relations with Asia Minor and that region must have been in touch with India.[1] But Orphism was also connected with Crete, and Cretan civilization had oriental affinities.[2]

The point of greatest interest naturally is to determine what were the religious influences among which Christ grew up. Whatever they may have been, his originality is not called in question. Mohammed was an enquirer: in estimating his work we have often to ask what he had heard about Christianity and Judaism and how far he had understood it correctly. But neither the Buddha nor Christ were enquirers in this sense: they accepted the best thought of their time and country: with a genius which transcends comparison and eludes definition they gave it an expression which has become immortal. Neither the substance nor the form of the teaching can reasonably be regarded as identical, for the Buddha did not treat of God or the divine government of the world, whereas Christ's chief thesis is that God loves the world and that therefore man should love God and his fellow men. But though their basic principles differ, the two doctrines agree in maintaining that happiness is obtainable not by pleasure or success or philosophy or rites but by an unselfish life, culminating in the state called Nirvana or the kingdom of heaven. "The kingdom of heaven is within you."

In the Gospels Christ teaches neither asceticism nor metempsychosis. The absence of the former is remarkable: he eats flesh and allows himself to be anointed: he drinks wine, prescribes its use in religion and is credited with producing it miraculously when human cellars run short. But he [Jesus] praises poverty and the poor: the Sermon on the Mount and the instructions of the Seventy can be put in practice only by those who, like the members of a religious community, have severed all worldly ties and though the extirpation of desire is not in the Gospels

---

[1]Whatever may have been the true character and history of the enigmatic people of Mitanni it appears certain that they adored deities with Indian names about 1400 B.C. But they may have been Iranians, and it may be doubted if the Aryan Indians of this date believed in metempsychosis.

[2]J.E. Harrison, *l.c.* pp. 450 and 564, seems to think that Orphism migrated from Crete to Thrace.

held up as an end, the detachment, the freedom from care, lust and enmity prescribed by the law of the Buddha find their nearest counterpart in the lives of the Essenes and Therapeutæ. Though we have no record of Christ being brought into contact with these communities (for John the Baptist appears to have been a solitary and erratic preacher) it is probable that their ideals were known to him and influenced his own. Their rule of life may have been a faint reflex of Indian monasticism. But the debt to India must not be exaggerated: much of the oriental element in the Essenes, such as their frequent purifications and their prayers uttered towards the sun, may be due to Persian influence. They seem to have believed in the pre-existence of the soul and to have held that it was imprisoned in the body, but this hardly amounts to metempsychosis, and metempsychosis cannot be found in the New Testament.[1] The old Jewish outlook, preserved by the Sadducees, appears not to have included a belief in any life after death, and the supplements to this materialistic view admitted by the Pharisees hardly amounted to the doctrine of the natural immortality of the soul but rather to a belief that the just would somehow acquire new bodies and live again. Thus people were ready to accept John the Baptist as being Elias in a new form. Perhaps these rather fragmentary ideas of the Jews are traceable to Egyptian and ultimately to Indian teaching about transmigration. That belief is said to crop up occasionally in rabbinical writings but was given no place in orthodox Christianity.[2]

With regard to the teaching of Christ then, the conclusion must be that it owes no direct debt to Indian, Egyptian, Persian or other oriental sources. But inasmuch as he was in sympathy with the more spiritual elements of Judaism, largely borrowed during the Babylonian captivity, and with the unworldly and self-denying lives of the Essenes, the tone of his teaching is nearer to these newer

---

[1]The question of the Disciples in John ix.2, Who did sin, this man or his parents, that he was born blind?, must, if taken strictly, imply some form of pre-existence. But it is a popular question, not a theological statement, and I doubt if severely logical deductions from it are warranted.

[2]The pre-existence of the soul seems to be implied in the Book of Wisdom viii. 20. The remarkable expression in the Epistle of James iii. 6 . . . suggests a comparison with the Orphic expressions quoted above and Saṁsāra, but it is difficult to believe it can mean more than "the course of nature."

and imported doctrines than to the old law of Israel.[1]

Some striking parallels have been pointed out between the Gospels and Indian texts of such undoubted antiquity that if imitation is admitted, the Evangelists must have been the imitators. Before considering these instances, I invite the reader's attention to two parallel passages from Shakespeare and the Indian poet Bhartṛihari [fl. c. 5th century CE]. The latter is thus translated by Monier Williams:[2]

Now for a little while a child, and now
An amorous youth; then for a season turned
Into the wealthy householder: then stripped
Of all his riches, with decrepit limbs
And wrinkled frame man creeps towards the end
Of life's erratic course and like an actor
Passes behind Death's curtain out of view.

The resemblance of this to the well-known lines in *As You Like It*, "All the world's a stage," etc., is obvious, and it is a real resemblance, although the point emphasized by Bhartṛihari is that man leaves the world like an actor who at the end of the piece slips behind the curtain, which formed the background of an Indian stage. But, great as is the resemblance, I imagine that no one would maintain that it has any other origin than that a fairly obvious thought occurred to two writers in different times and countries and suggested similar expressions.

Now many parallels between the Buddhist and Christian scriptures – the majority as it seems to me of those collected by Edmunds and Anesaki Masaharu – belong to this class.[3] One of the most striking is the passage in the Vinaya

---

[1]As in their legends, so in their doctrines, the uncanonical writings are more oriental than the canonical and contain more pantheistic and ascetic sayings. *E.g.* "Where there is one alone, I am with him. Raise the stone and thou shalt find me: cleave the wood and I am there" (*Oxyrhynchus Logia*). "I am thou and thou art I and wheresoever thou art I am [there] also: and in all things I am distributed and wheresoever thou wilt thou gatherest me and in gathering me thou gatherest thyself" (Gospel of Eve in Epiph. *Haer*. XXVI.3). "When the Lord was asked, when should his kingdom come, he said: When two shall be one and the without as the within and the male with the female, neither male nor female" (*Logia*).

[2]*Hinduism*, p. 549. The original is to be found in Bhartṛihari's *Vairogyaśatakam*, 112.

[3]*The Buddhist and Christian Gospels*, 4th ed. 1909.

relating how the Buddha himself cared for a sick monk who was neglected by his colleagues and said to these latter, "Whosoever would wait upon me let him wait on the sick."[1] Here the resemblance to Matthew xxv. 40 and 45 is remarkable, but I do not imagine that the writer of the Gospel had ever heard or read of the Buddha's words. The sentiment which prompted them, if none too common, is at least widespread and is the same that made Confucius show respect and courtesy to the blind. The setting of the saying in the Vinaya and in the Gospel is quite different: the common point is that one whom all are anxious to honour sees that those around him show no consideration to the sick and unhappy and reproves them in the words of the text, words which admit of many interpretations, the simplest perhaps being "I bid you care for the sick: you neglect me if you neglect those whom I bid you to cherish."

But many passages in Buddhist and Christian writings have been compared where there is no real parallel but only some word or detail which catches the attention and receives an importance which it does not possess. An instance of this is the so "called parable of the prodigal son in the Lotus Sūtra, Chapter iv, which has often been compared with Luke xv. 11 ff. But neither in moral nor in plot are the two parables really similar. The Lotus maintains that there are many varieties of doctrine of which the less profound are not necessarily wrong, and it attempts to illustrate this by not very convincing stories of how a father may withhold the whole truth from his children for their good. In one story a father and son are separated for fifty years and *both* move about: the father becomes very rich, the son poor. The son in his wanderings comes upon his father's palace and recognizes no one. The father, now a very old man, knows his son, but instead of welcoming him at once as his heir puts him through a gradual discipline and explains the real position only on his deathbed. These incidents have nothing in common with the parable related in the Gospel except that a son is lost and found, an event which occurs in a hundred oriental tales. What is much more remarkable, though hardly a case of borrowing, is that in both versions the chief personage, that is Buddha or God, is likened to a father as he also is in the parable of the carriages.[2]

---

[1]Mahavagga, VIII. 26.

[2]*Lotus*, chap. V.

One of the Jain scriptures called Uttarādyayana[1] contains the following remarkable passage, "Three merchants set out on their travels each with his capital; one of them gained much, the second returned with his capital and the third merchant came home after having lost his capital. The parable is taken from common life; learn to apply it to the Law. The capital is human life, the gain is heaven," etc. It is impossible to fix the date of this passage: the Jain Canon in which it occurs was edited in 454 A.D. but the component parts of it are much older. It clearly gives a rough sketch of the idea which is elaborated in the parable of the talents. Need we suppose that there has been borrowing on either side? Only in a very restricted sense, I think, if at all. The parable is taken from common life, as the Indian text truly says. It occurred to some teacher, perhaps to many teachers independently, that the spiritual life may be represented as a matter of profit and loss and illustrated by the conduct of those who employ their money profitably or not. The idea is natural and probably far older than the Gospels, but the parable of the talents is an original and detailed treatment of a metaphor which may have been known to the theological schools of both India and Palestine. The parable of the sower bears the same relation to the much older Buddhist comparison of instruction to agriculture[2] in which different classes of hearers correspond to different classes of fields.

I feel considerable hesitation about two other parallels. What relation does the story of the girl who gives two copper coins to the Sangha bear to the parable of the widow's mite? It occurs in Aśvaghoṣa's *Sūtrālaṅkāra*, but though he was a learned poet, it is very unlikely that he had seen the Gospels. Although his poem ends like a fairy tale, for the poor girl marries the king's son as the reward of her piety, yet there is an extraordinary resemblance in the moral and the detail of the *two* mites. Can the origin be some proverb which was current in many countries and worked up differently?

The other parallel is between Christ's meeting with the woman of Samaria and a story in the Divyāvadāna[3] telling how Ānanda asked an outcaste maiden for water. Here the Indian work, which is probably not earlier than the third century

---

[1]VII. 15-21 in *S.B.E.*, XLV. p. 29

[2]Sam. Nik. XLII. VII.

[3]Ed. Cowell, p. 611.

A.D., might well be the borrower. Yet the incident is thoroughly Indian. The resemblance is not in the conversation but in the fact that both in India and Palestine water given by the impure is held to defile and that in both countries spiritual teachers rise above such rules. Perhaps Europeans, to whom such notions of defilement are unknown, exaggerate the similarity of the narratives, because the similarity of customs on which it depends seem remarkable.

There are, however, some incidents in the Gospels which bear so great a likeness to earlier stories found in the Piṭakas that the two narratives can hardly be wholly independent. These are (a) the testimony of Asita and Simeon to the future careers of the infant Buddha and Christ: (b) the temptation of Buddha and Christ: (c) their transfiguration: (d) the miracle of walking on the water and its dependence on faith: (e) the miracle of feeding a multitude with a little bread. The first three parallels relate to events directly concerning the life of a superhuman teacher, Buddha or Christ. In saying that the two narratives can hardly be independent, I do not mean that one is necessarily unhistorical or that the writers of the Gospels had read the Piṭakas. That a great man should have a mental crisis in his early life and feel that the powers of evil are trying to divert him from his high destiny is eminently likely. But in the East superhuman teachers were many and there grew up a tradition fluctuating indeed but still not entirely without consistency, as to what they may be expected to do. Angelic voices at their birth and earthquakes at their death are coincidences in embellishment on which no stress can be laid, but when we find that Zoroaster, the Buddha and Christ were all tempted by the Evil One and all at the same period of their careers, it is impossible to avoid the suspicion that some of their biographers were influenced by the idea that such an incident was to be expected at that point, unless indeed we regard these so-called temptations as mental crises natural in the development of a religious genius. Similarly it is most remarkable that all accounts of the transfiguration of the Buddha and of Christ agree not only in describing the shining body but in adding a reference to impending death. The resemblance between the stories of Asita and Simeon seems to me less striking but I think that they owe their place in both biographies to the tradition that the superman is recognized and saluted by an aged Saint soon after birth.

The two stories about miracles are of less importance in substance but the curious coincidences in detail suggest that they are pieces of folklore which circulated in Asia and Eastern Europe. The Buddhist versions occur in the introductions to Jātakas 190 and 78, which are of uncertain date, though they may be very ancient.[1] The idea that saints can walk on the water is found in the Majjhima-nikāya,[2] but the Jātaka adds the following particulars. A disciple desirous of seeing the Buddha begins to walk across a river in an ecstasy of faith. In the middle his ecstasy fails and he feels himself sinking but by an effort of will he regains his former confidence and meets the Buddha safely on the further bank. In Jātaka 90 the Buddha miraculously feeds 600 disciples with a single cake and it is expressly mentioned that, after all had been satisfied, the remnants were so numerous that they had to be collected and disposed of.

Still all the parallels cited amount to little more than this, that there was a vague and fluid tradition about the superman's life of which fragments have received a consecration in literature. The Canonical Gospels show great caution in drawing on this fund of tradition, but a number of Buddhist legends make their appearance in the Apocryphal Gospels and are so obviously Indian in character that it can hardly be maintained that they were invented in Palestine or Egypt and spread thence eastwards. Trees bend down before the young Christ and dragons (*nāgas*) adore him: when he goes to school to learn the alphabet he convicts his teacher of ignorance and the good man faints.[3] When he enters a temple in Egypt the images prostrate themselves before him just as they do before the young Gotama in the temple of Kapilavastu.[4] Mary is luminous before the birth of Christ which takes place without pain or impurity.[5] But the parallel which is most curious, because the incident related is unusual in both Indian and European literature, is

---

[1]See Rhys Davids, *Buddhist India*, p. 206, and Winternitz, *Ges. Ind. Lit*. II. 91.

[2]Maj. Nik. VI.

[3]Gospel of Thomas: longer version, chaps. VI. XIV. See also the Arabic and Syriac Gospels of the Infancy, cf. Lalita-Vistara, chap. X.

[4]Pseudo-Matthew, chap. XXII.-XXIV. and Lal. Vist. chap. VIII.

[5]Pseudo-Matthew, XIII. Cf. Dig. Nik. 14 and Maj. Nik. 123. Neumann's notes on the latter give many curious medieval parallels.

the detailed narrative in the Gospel of James, and also in the *Lalita-vistara* relating how all activity of mankind and nature was suddenly interrupted at the moment of the nativity.[1] Winds, stars and rivers stayed their motion and labourers stood still in the attitude in which each was surprised. The same Gospel of James also relates that Mary when six months old took seven steps, which must surely be an echo of the legend which attributes the same feat to the infant Buddha.

Several learned authors have discussed the debt of medieval Christian legend to India. The most remarkable instance of this is the canonization by both the Eastern and the Western Church of St. Joasaph or Josaphat. It seems to be established that this name is merely a corruption of Bodhisat and that the story in its Christian form goes back to the religious romance called Barlaam and Joasaph which appears to date from the seventh century.[2] It contains the history of an Indian prince who was converted by the preaching of Barlaam and became a hermit, and it introduces some of the well-known stories of Gotama's early life, such as the attempt to hide from him the existence of sickness and old age, and his meetings with a cripple and an old man. The legends of St. Placidus (or Hubert) and St. Christopher have also been identified with the Nigrodha and Sutasoma Jātakas.[3] The identification is not to my mind conclusive nor, if it is admitted, of much importance. For who doubts that Indian fables reappear in Aesop or Kalilah and Dimnah? Little is added to this fact if they also appear in legends which may have some connection with the Church but which most Christians feel no obligation to believe.

But the occurrence of Indian legends in the Apocryphal Gospels is more important for it shows that, though in the early centuries of Christianity the Church was shy of this oriental exuberance, yet the materials were at hand for those who chose to use them. Many wonders attending the superman's birth were deliberately rejected but some were accepted and oriental practices, such as asceticism, appear with a suddenness that makes the suspicion of foreign influence legitimate.

---

[1]See Gospel of James, XVIII. and Lal. Vist. VII. *ad init.*

[2]See Rhys Davids, *Buddhist Birth stories*, 1880, introduction; and Joseph Jacobs, *Barlaam and Josaphat*, 1896.

[3]Nos. 12 and 537.

Not only was monasticism adopted by Christianity but many practices common to Indian and to Christian worship obtained the approval of the Church at about the same time. Some of these, such as incense and the tonsure, may have been legacies from the Jewish and Egyptian priesthoods. Many coincidences also are due to the fact that both Buddhism and Christianity, while abolishing animal sacrifices, were ready to sanction old religious customs: both countenanced the performance before an image or altar of a ritual including incense, flowers, lights and singing. This recognition of old and widespread rites goes far to explain the extraordinary similarity of Buddhist services in Tibet and Japan (both of which derived their ritual ultimately from India) to Roman Catholic ceremonial. Yet when all allowance is made for similar causes and coincidences, it is hard to believe that a collection of such practices as clerical celibacy, confession, the veneration of relics, the use of the rosary and bells can have originated independently in both religions. The difficulty no doubt is to point out any occasion in the third and fourth centuries A.D. when oriental Christians other than casual travellers had an opportunity of becoming acquainted with Buddhist institutions. But the number of resemblances remains remarkable and some of them – such as clerical celibacy, relics, and confession – are old institutions in Buddhism but appear to have no parallels in Jewish, Syrian, or Egyptian antiquity. Up to a certain point, it is a sound principle not to admit that resemblances prove borrowing, unless it can be shown that there was contact between two nations, but it is also certain that all record of such contact may disappear. For instance, it is indisputable that Hindu civilization was introduced into Camboja, but there is hardly any evidence as to how or when Hindu colonists arrived there, and none whatever as to how or when they left India.

It is in Christian or quasi-Christian heresies – that is, the sects which were rejected by the majority – that Indian influence is plainest. This is natural, for if there is one thing obvious in the history of religion it is that Indian speculation and the Indian view of life were not congenial to the people of Europe and western Asia. But some spirits, from the time of Pythagoras onwards, had a greater affinity for oriental ways of thinking, and such sympathy was specially common among the Gnostics. Gnosticism consisted in the combination of Christianity with the already mixed religion which prevailed in Alexandria, Antioch and other centres, and which was an uncertain and varying compound of Judaism, Hellenistic thought and the ideas of oriental countries such as Egypt, Persia and Babylonia. Its fundamental idea, the knowledge of God or Gnosis, is clearly similar to the Jñānakānda of the Hindus,[1] but the emphasis laid on dualism and redemption is not Indian and the resemblances suggest little more than that hints may have been taken and worked up independently. Thus the idea of the Demiurgus is related to the idea of Īśvara in so far as both imply a distinction not generally recognized in Europe between the creator of the world and the Highest Deity, but the Gnostic developments of the Demiurgus idea are independent. Similarly, though the Aeons or emanations of the Gnostics have to some extent a parallel in the beings produced by Brahmā, Prajāpati or Vāsudeva, yet these latter are not characteristic of Hinduism and still less of Buddhism, for the celestial Buddhas and Bodhisattvas of the Mahāyāna are justly suspected of being additions due to Persian influence.

Bardesanes, one of the latest Gnostic teachers (155-233), wrote a book on Indian religion, quoted by Porphyry. This is important for it shows that he turned towards India for truth, but though his teaching included the pre-existence of the soul and some doctrine of Karma. It was not specially impregnated with Indian ideas. This, however, may be said without exaggeration of Carpocrates and Basilides who both taught at Alexandria about 120-130 A.D. Unfortunately we know the views of these interesting men only from the accounts of their opponents. Carpocrates[2] is said to have claimed the power of coercing by magic the spirits who rule the world and to have taught metempsychosis in the form that the soul is imprisoned in the body again and again until it has performed all possible actions, good and evil. Therefore the only way to escape reincarnation (which is the object of religion) and to rise to a superior sphere of peace is to perform as much action as possible, good and evil, for the distinction between the two depends on intention, not on the nature of deeds. It is only through faith and love that a man can obtain blessedness. Much of the above sounds like a caricature, but it may be a

---

[1]As is also the idea that [*gnosis*] implies a special ascetic mode of life, the [*bios gnostikos*].

[2]Irenæus, I. XXV.

misrepresentation of something analogous to the Indian doctrine that the acts of a Yogi are neither black nor white and that a Yogi in order to get rid of his Karma creates and animates many bodies to work it off for him.

In Basilides we find the doctrines not only of reincarnation, which seems to have been common to Gnostic schools,[1] but of Karma, of the suffering inherent in existence and perhaps the composite nature of the soul. He is said to have taught that the martyrs suffered for their sins, that is to say that souls came into the world tainted with the guilt of evil deeds done in another existence. This guilt must be expiated by common-place misfortune or, for the nobler sort, by martyrdom. He considered the world process to consist in sorting out confused things and the gradual establishment of order. This is to some extent true of the soul as well; it is not an entity but a compound (compare the Buddhist doctrine of the Skandhas) and the passions are appendages. He called God [*ouk on theos*] which seems an attempt to express the same idea as Brahman devoid of all qualities and attributes (*nirguṇa*). It is significant that the system of Basilides died out.[2]

A more important sect of decidedly oriental affinities was Manichæism, or rather it was a truly oriental religion which succeeded in penetrating to Europe and there took on considerably more Christianity than it had possessed in its original form. Mani himself (215-276) is said to have been a native of Ecbatana but visited Afghanistan, Bactria and India, and his followers carried his faith across Asia to China, while in the west it was the parent inspiration of the Bogomils and Albigenses. The nature and sources of his creed have been the subject of considerable discussion but new light is now pouring in from the Manichæan manuscripts discovered in Central Asia, some of which have already been published. These show that about the seventh century and probably considerably earlier the Manichæism of those regions had much in common with Buddhism.

[1]It appears in the Pistia Sophia which perhaps represents the school of Valentinus. Basilides taught that "unto the third and fourth generations" refers to transmigration (see Clem. Al. fragm. sect. 28 Op., ed Klotz, IV. 14), and Paul's saying "I was alive without the law once" (Rom. vii. 9), to former life as an animal (Orig. in Eph. and Rom. v. Op. iv. 549).

[2]For Gnosticism, see "Buddhist Gnosticism", J. Kennedy in *J.R.A.S.* 1902, and Mead, *Fragments of a Faith Forgotten.*

A Manichæan treatise discovered at Tun-huang[1] has the form of a Buddhist Sūtra: it speaks of Mani as the Tathāgata, it mentions Buddhas of Transformation (*Hua-fo*) and the Bodhisattva Ti-tsang. Even more important is the confessional formula called Khuastuanift[2] found in the same locality. It is clearly similar to the Pātimokkha and besides using much Buddhist terminology it reckons killing or injuring animals as a serious sin. It is true that many of these resemblances may be due to association with Buddhism and not to the original teaching of Mani, which was strongly dualistic and contained many Zoroastrian and Babylonian ideas. But it was eclectic and held up an ascetic ideal of celibacy, poverty and fasting unknown to Persia and Babylon. To take life was counted a sin and the adepts formed an order apart who lived on the food given to them by the laity. The more western accounts of the Manichæans testify to these features as strongly as do the records from Central Asia and China. Cyril of Jerusalem in his polemic against them[3] charges them with believing in retributive metempsychosis, he who kills an animal being changed into that animal after death. The Persian king Hormizd is said to have accused Mani of bidding people destroy the world, that is, to retire from social life and not have children. Alberuni[4] states definitely that Mani wrote a book called Shāburkān in which he said that God sent different messengers to mankind in different ages, Buddha to India, Zarādusht to Persia and Jesus to the west. According to Cyril the Manichæan scriptures were written by one Scythianus and revised by his disciple Terebinthus who changed his name to Boddas. This may be a jumble, but it is hard to stifle the suspicion that it contains some allusion to the Buddha, Śākya-muni and the Bo [Bodhi] tree.

I think therefore that primitive Manichæism, though it contained less Buddhism than did its later and eastern forms, still owed to India its asceticism, its order of celibate adepts and its regard for animal life. When it spread to Africa and Europe it became more Christian, just as it became more Buddhist in China,

---

[1]Chavannes et Pelliot, "Un traité Manichéen retrouvé en Chine," *J.A.* 1911, I, and 1913, II.

[2]Le Coq in *J.R.A.S.* 1911, p. 277.

[3]Chatechetic Lectures, VI, 20 ff. The whole polemic is curious and worth reading.

[4]Alberuni, *Chronology of ancient nations*, trans. Sachan, p. 190.

but it is exceedingly curious to see how this Asiatic religion, like the widely different religion of Mohammed, was even in its latest phrases the subject of bitter hatred and persistent misrepresentation.

Finally, do the Neoplatonists, Neopythagoreans and other pagan philosophers of the early centuries after Christ owe any debt to India? Many of them were consciously endeavouring to arrest the progress of Christianity by transforming philosophy into a non-Christian religion. They gladly welcomed every proof that the higher life was not to be found exclusively or most perfectly in Christianity. Hence bias, if not accurate knowledge, led them to respect all forms of eastern mysticism. Apollonius is said to have travelled in India:[1] in the hope of so doing Plotinus accompanied the unfortunate expedition of Gordian but turned back when it failed. We may surmise that for Plotinus the Indian origin of an idea would have been a point in its favour, although his writings show no special hostility to Christianity.[2] So far as I can judge, his system presents those features which might be expected to come from sympathy with the Indian temperament, aided perhaps not by reading but by conversation with thoughtful orientals at Alexandria and elsewhere. The direct parallels are not striking. Plato himself had entertained the idea of metempsychosis and much that seems oriental in Plotinus may be not a new importation but the elaboration of Plato's view in a form congenial to the age.[3] Affirmations that God is [*to on*] and [*to en*] are not so much borrowings from the Vedānta philosophy as a re-statement of Hellenic ideas in a mystic and quietist spirit, which may owe something to India. But Plotinus seems to me nearer to India than were the Gnostics and Manichæans, because his teaching is not dualistic to the same extent. He finds the world unsatisfying not because it is the creation of the Evil One, but because it is transitory, imperfect and unreal.

---

[1]The account in Philostratus (books II. and III.) reads like a romance and hardly proves that Apollonius went to India, but still there is no reason why he should not have done so.

[2]He wrote, however, against certain Gnostics.

[3]Similarly Sallustius (*c.* 360 A.D.), whose object was to revive Hellenism, includes metempsychosis in his creed and thinks it can be proved. See translation in Murray, *Four Stages of Greek Religion*, p. 213.

His system has been called dynamic pantheism and this description applies also to much Indian theology which regards God in himself as devoid of all qualities and yet the source of the forces which move the universe. He held that there are four stages of being: primæval being, the ideal world, the soul and phenomena. This, if not exactly parallel to anything in Indian philosophy, is similar in idea to the evolutionary theories of the Sānkhya and the phases of conditioned spirit taught by many Vishnuite sects.

For Plotinus neither moral good nor evil is ultimate: the highest principle, like Brahman, transcends both and is beyond good [*uperagathon*]. The highest morality is a morality of inaction and detachment: fasting and abstinence from pleasure are good and so is meditation, but happiness comes in the form of ecstasy and union with God. In human life such union cannot be permanent, though while the ecstasy lasts it affords a resting place on the weary journey, but after death it can be permanent: the divine within us can then return to the universal divine. In these ideas there is the real spirit of India.

CHAPTER LVII

PERSIAN INFLUENCE IN INDIA

Our geographical and political phraseology about India and Persia obscures the fact that in many periods the frontier between the two countries was uncertain or not drawn as now. North-western India and eastern Persia must not be regarded as water-tight or even merely leaky compartments. Even now there are more Zoroastrians in India than in Persia and the Persian sect of Shiite Mohammedans is powerful and conspicuous there. In former times it is probable that there was often not more difference between Indian and Iranian religion than between different Indian sects.

Yet the religious temperaments of India and Iran are not the same. Zoroastrianism has little sympathy for pantheism or asceticism: it does not teach metempsychosis or the sinfulness of taking life. Images are not used in worship,[1] God and his angels being thought of pure and shining spirits. The foundation of the system is an uncompromising dualism of good and evil, purity and impurity, light and darkness. Good and evil are different in origin and duality will be abolished only by the ultimate and complete victory of the good. In the next world the distinction between heaven and hell is equally sharp but hell is not eternal.[2]

The pantheon and even the ritual of the early Iranians resembled those of the Veda and we can only suppose that the two peoples once lived and worshipped together. Subsequently came the reform of Zoroaster which substituted theism and dualism for this nature worship. For about two centuries, from 530 B.C. onwards, Gandhara and other parts of north-western India were a Persian province. Between the time of Zoroaster (whatever that may be) and this period we cannot say what were the relations of Indian and Iranian religions, but after the seventh

---

[1]They are forbidden by strict theology, but in practice there are exceptions, for instance, the winged figure believed to represent Ahura Mazda, found on Achæmenian reliefs.

[2]Though the principles of Zoroastrianism sound excellent to Europeans, I cannot discover that ancient Persia was socially or politically superior to India.

century [B.C.] they must have flourished in the same region. Aristobulus,[1] speaking of Taxila in the time of Alexander the Great, describes a marriage market and how the dead were devoured by vultures. These are Babylonian and Persian customs, and doubtless were accompanied by many others less striking to a foreign tourist. Some hold that the Zoroastrian scriptures allude to disputes with Buddhists.[2]

Experts on the whole agree that the most ancient Indian architecture which has been preserved – that of the Maurya dynasty – has no known antecedents in India, but both in structure (especially the pillars) and in decoration is reminiscent of Persepolis, just as Asoka's habit of lecturing his subjects in stone sermons and the very turns of his phrases recall the inscriptions of Darius.[3] And though the king's [Asoka's] creed is in some respects – such as his tenderness for animal life – thoroughly Indian, yet this cannot be said of his style and choice of themes as a whole. His marked avoidance of theology and philosophy, his insistence on ethical principles such as truth, and his frank argument that men should do good in order that they may fare happily in the next world, suggest that he may have become familiar with the simple and practical Zoroastrian outlook,[4] perhaps when he was viceroy of Taxila in his youth. But still he shows no trace of theism or dualism: morality is his one concern, but it means for him doing good rather than suppressing evil.

---

[1]See Strabo, XV. 62. So, too, the Piṭakas seem to regard cemeteries as places where ordinary corpses are thrown away rather than buried or burnt. In Dīg. Nik. III. the Buddha says that the ancient Śākyas married their sisters. Such marriages are said to have been permitted in Persia.

[2]"He who returns victorious from discussions with Gautama the heretic," Farvadin Yasht in *S.B.E.* XXIII. p. 184. The reference of this passage to Buddhism has been much disputed and I am quite incompetent to express any opinion about it. But who is Gautama if not the Buddha? It is true that there were many other Gautamas of moderate eminence in India, but would any of them have been known in Persia?

[3]The inscriptions near the tomb of Darius at Nakshi-Rustam appear to be hortatory like those of Asoka. See William Jackson, Persia, p. 398 and references. The use of the Kharoshtī script and of the word *dipi* has also been noted as indicating connection with Persia.

[4]Perhaps the marked absence of figures representing the Buddha in the oldest Indian sculptures, which seems to imply that the holiest things must not be represented, is due to Persian sentiment.

End of the "Eliot" Appendix

FOURTH APPENDIX

Three Articles from *The Catholic Encyclopedia* Touching on Consecrated Celibate Women

Widow*

I. Canonical prescriptions concerning widows in the Old Testament refer mainly to the question of remarriage. If a man died without children, his widow was obliged to marry her deceased husband's brother, and if the latter refused to take her to wife he was put to shame before the people (*Deuteronomy 25:5-10*). The high-priest was forbidden to marry a widow (*Leviticus 21:14*), but other members of the priesthood were at liberty to take to wife the widow of another priest, but not the widow of a layman (*Ezekiel 44:22*). Outside of these prescriptions, there is no law in the Old Testament restricting a widow's remarriage. The support of widows was commended to the charity of the Israelites, and they were to have the gleanings of the cornfields, olive trees, and vineyards (*Deuteronomy 24:19-22*). In the third year of tithes (or the great tithe) widows were to have their share of the offering (*Deuteronomy 26:12*), and at the three principal solemnities of the year they were to be invited to feast with the nearest house-holder (*Deuteronomy 16:11*). In the times of the Maccabees money was deposited and provisions were kept in the Temple at Jerusalem for the subsistence of widows (*2 Maccabees 3:10*), and the spoils of battle were also shared with them (2 *Maccabees 8:28*). For their protection, there was a prohibition against taking their garments in pawn (*Deuteronomy 24:17*). In the Book of Job the taking away of a widow's ox for a pledge is considered a wicked action (*xxiv, 3*), from which commentators generally gather that the law of Deuteronomy was later extended to all a widow's possessions. Besides legal prescriptions for the protection of widows, the Old Testament contains many general precepts commending them to the reverence and benevolence of the chosen people and bitter denunciations of their oppressors and defrauders. The lot of the widow in Old Testament times was generally a hard one, and Christ refers to the widow's mite as an offering from the poorest of the poor (*Mark 12:44*). He also strongly denounces the Pharisees: "because you devour the houses of widows" (*Matthew 23:14*). Under the Old Dispensation some widows devoted themselves to a life of special religious observance, as is recorded of Anna the Prophetess, "who departed not from the temple by fastings and prayers serving night and day" (*Luke 2, 37*).

II. In primitive Christian times the support of widows was made a special duty by the Apostles, who collected alms for them and gave care of them to the deacons (*Acts 6:1*). This support of needy widows has always been considered a particular charge of the ministers of the Christian Church and many decrees of popes and councils make mention of it as specially incumbent on bishops, parish priests, and holders of benefices. In Apostolic times widows were employed in certain capacities in the ministry of the Church, directing that one to be chosen must be "of no less than threescore years of age, who hath been the wife of one husband. Having testimony for her good works" [*1 Timothy 5:9*]**, and some see in this reference to the order of deaconess, while others do not. Shortly after, however, the office of deaconess was referred to as "widowhood" (St. Ignatius, *Smyrnæans* 8.1). As to the remarriage of widows in the Christian Church, though St. Paul declares that widowhood is preferable to the married state (*1 Corinthians 7:8*), yet he does not forbid remarriage (*1 Corinthians 7:39*). Second nuptials are valid by ecclesiastical law if the first marriage bond has been really dissolved and if there is no canonical impediment, as is the case for clerics in major orders in the Oriental rites. In the mind of the Church, however, second nuptials are less honourable than a first marriage (Council of Ancyra, canon 19; Council of Laodicea, canon 1), and [for widows] the state of widowhood is more commendable as a more perfect good [than remarriage] (*Conc. Trid., sess.* xxiv, de matr., can. 10).

---

*William Fanning, "Widow," *The Catholic Encyclopedia*, Vol. 15 (New York: Robert Appleton Company, 1912). Ecclesiastical approbation: *Nihil Obstat,* October 1, 1912, Remy Lafort, S.T.D., Censor; *Imprimatur*: John Cardinal Farley, Archbishop of New York.

**Throughout this appendix, the square bracketed clarifications and the bolding emphases are ML's.

Double Monasteries*

Religious houses comprising communities of both men and women, dwelling in contiguous establishments, united under the rule of one superior, and using one church in common for their liturgical offices. The reason for such an arrangement was that the spiritual needs of the nuns might be attended to by the priests of the male community, who were associated with them more closely than would have been possible in the case of entirely separate and independent monasteries. The system came into existence almost contemporaneously with monasticism itself, and like it had its origin in the East. Communities of women gathered around religious founders in Egypt and elsewhere, and from the life of St. Pachomius [ca. 292–348] we learn many details as to the nuns under his rule and their relation to the male communities founded by him. Double monasteries, of which those of St. Basil [ca. 329-379 A.D.] and his sister, Macrina, may be cited as examples, were apparently numerous throughout the East during the early centuries of monasticism. It cannot be stated with any certainty when the system found its way into the West, but it seems probable that its introduction into Gaul may be roughly ascribed to the influence of Cassian, who did so much towards reconciling Eastern monasticism with Western ideas. St. Caesarius of Arles, St. Aurelian, his successor, and St. Radegundis, of Poitiers, founded double monasteries in the sixth century, and later on the system was propagated widely by St. Columbanus and his followers. Remiremont, Jouarre, Brie, Chelles, Andelys, and Soissons were other well-known examples of the seventh and eighth centuries. From Gaul the idea spread to Belgium and Germany, and also to Spain, where it is said to have been introduced by St. Fructuosus in the middle of the seventh century. According to Yepes there were in Spain altogether over two hundred double monasteries.

Ireland presents only one known example – Kildare – but probably there were others besides, of which all traces have since been lost. In England most of the early foundations were double; this has been wrongly attributed by some writers to the fact that many of the Anglo-Saxon nuns were educated in Gaul, where the system was then in vogue, but it seems more correct to ascribe it to the religious influence of the missionaries from Iona, since the first double monastery in England was that of St. Hilda [614-680 A.D.] at Whitby, established under the guidance of St. Aidan [d. 31 Aug. 651] and there is no evidence to show that either St. Aidan or St. Hilda was acquainted with the double organization in use elsewhere. Whitby was founded in the seventh century and in a short time England became covered with similar dual establishments, of which Coldingham, Ely, Sheppey, Minster, Wimborne, and Barking are prominent examples. In Italy, the only other country besides those already mentioned where double monasteries are known to have existed, they were not numerous, but St. Gregory speaks of them as being found in Sardinia (*Ep.* xi), and St. Bede mentions one at Rome (*Hist. Eccl.*, IV, i). The Danish invasions of the ninth and tenth centuries destroyed the double monasteries of England, and, when they were restored, it was for one sex only, instead of for a dual community. The system seems to have died out also in other countries at about the same time, and it was not revived until the end of the eleventh century when Robert of Arbrissel inaugurated his reform at Fontevrault and gave the idea a fresh lease of life. It is not surprising to find that such a system was sometimes abused, and hence it was always an object of solicitude and strict legislation at the hands of ecclesiastical authority. Many synodal and conciliar decrees recognized its dangers, and ordered the strictest surveillance of all communications passing between monks and nuns. Too close proximity of buildings was frequently forbidden, and every precaution was taken to prevent any occasion of scandal. Very probably it was this scant favour shown by the Church towards it that caused the gradual decline of the system about the tenth century.

In many double monasteries the supreme rule was in the hands of the abbess, and monks as well as nuns were subject to her authority. This was especially the case in England, e.g. in St. Hilda's at Whitby and St. Etheldreda's at Ely, though elsewhere, but more rarely, it was the abbot who ruled both men and women, and sometimes, more rarely still, each community had its own superior independent of the other. The justification for the anomalous position of a woman acting as the superior of a community of men is usually held to originate from Christ's words from the Cross, "Woman, behold thy son; Son, behold thy mother"; and it is still further urged that maternity is a form of authority derived from nature, whilst that which is paternal is merely legal. But, whatever may be its origin, the supreme rule of an abbess over both men and women was deliberately revived, and sanctioned by the Church, in two of the three medieval orders that consisted of double monasteries. At Fontevrault (founded 1099) and with the Bridgettines (1346), the abbess was the superior of monks as well as nuns, though with the Gilbertines (1146) it was the prior who ruled over both. In the earlier double monasteries both monks and nuns observed the same rule mutatis mutandis; this example was followed by Fontevrault and the Bridgettines, the rule of the former being Benedictine, while the latter observed the rule of St. Bridget. But with the Gilbertines, whilst the rule of the nuns was substantially Benedictine, the monks adopted that of the Augustinian Canons. Little is known as to the buildings of the earlier double monasteries except that the church usually stood between the two conventual establishments, so as to be accessible from both. From excavations made on the site of Watton Priory, a Gilbertine house in Yorkshire, it appears that the separation of nuns from canons [monks!] was effected by means of a substantial wall, several feet high, which traversed the church lengthways, and it is probable that some similar arrangement was adopted in other double monasteries. [Shades of the Therapeutæ's "wall"! See Meta-Appendix, p. 183 – ML]

---

*George Cyprian Alston, "Double Monasteries," *The Catholic Encyclopedia*. Vol. 10 (New York: Robert Appleton Company, 1911). Ecclesiastical approbation: *Nihil Obstat* (October 1, 1911), Remy Lafort, S.T.D., Censor; *Imprimatur*: John Cardinal Farley, Archbishop of New York.

Deaconesses*

We cannot be sure that any formal recognition of deaconesses as an institution of consecrated women aiding the clergy is to be found in the New Testament. There is indeed the mention of Phebe (*Romans 16:1*), who is called *diakonos*, but this may simply mean, as the Vulgate renders it, that she was "in the ministry [i.e. service] of the Church", without implying any official status. Again, it is not improbable that the **"widows"** who are spoken of at large in *1 Timothy 5:3-10*, may really have been **deaconesses**, but here again we have nothing conclusive. That some such functionaries were appointed at an early date seems probable from Pliny's letter to Trajan concerning the Christians of Bithynia (*Ep.* X, 97, A.D. 112) There he speaks of obtaining information by torture from two *ancillae quae ministrae dicebantur*, where a technical use of words seems to be implied. In any case there can be no question that before the middle of the fourth century women were permitted to exercise certain definite functions in the Church and were known by the special name of *diakonoi* or *diakonissai*.

History and consecration

[• 451 A.D. (4) Council of Chalcedon: Its Canon #15 (**1**) declared the following: *No woman under 40 years of age is to be ordained a deacon, and then only after close scrutiny*. – ML]

Most Catholic scholars incline to the view that it is not always possible to draw a clear distinction in the early Church between deaconesses and widows (*cherai*). The *Didascalia*, *Apostolic Constitutions* and kindred documents undoubtedly recognize them as separate classes and they prefer the deaconess to the widow in the duty of assisting the clergy. Indeed, the *Apostolic Constitutions* (III, 6) enjoin the widows to be obedient to the deaconesses. It is probable also, as Funk maintains, that in the earlier period it was only a widow who could become a deaconess, but undoubtedly the strict limits of age, sixty years [*1 Timothy 5:9*], which were at first prescribed for widows, were relaxed, at least at certain periods and in certain localities, in the case of those to be appointed to be deaconesses; for example, the Council of Trullo in 692 fixed the age at forty. Tertullian [c. 160 – c. 225 A.D.] speaks with reprobation of a girl of twenty *in viduatu ab episcopo collocatam*, by which he seems to mean ordained as a deaconess. There can again be no question that the deaconesses in the fourth and fifth centuries had a distinct ecclesiastical standing, though there are traces of much variety of custom. According to the newly discovered "Testament of Our Lord: (c. 400 [A.D.]), widows had a place in the sanctuary during the celebration of the liturgy, they stood at the anaphora behind the presbyters, they communicated [took communion] after the deacons, and before the readers and subdeacons, and strange to say they had a charge of, or superintendence over the deaconesses. Further it is certain that a ritual was in use for the ordination of deaconesses by the laying on of hands which was closely modeled on the ritual for the ordination of a deacon. For example, the *Apostolic Constitutions* say:

> Concerning a deaconess, I, Bartholomew enjoin O Bishop, thou shalt lay thy hands upon her with all the Presbytery and the Deacons and the Deaconesses and thou shalt say: Eternal God, the Father of Our Lord Jesus Christ, the creator of man and woman, that didst fill with the Spirit Mary and Deborah, and Anna and Huldah, that didst not disdain that thine only begotten Son should be born of a woman; Thou that in the tabernacle of witness and in the temple didst appoint women guardians of thy holy gates: Do thou now look on this thy handmaid, who is appointed unto the office of a Deaconess and grant unto her the Holy Spirit, and cleanse her from all pollution of the flesh and of the spirit, that she may worthily accomplish the work committed unto her, to thy glory and the praise of thy Christ.

Comparing this form with that given in the same work with that for the ordination of deacons we may notice that the reference to the outpouring of Holy Ghost in the latter case is much more strongly worded: "fill him with the spirit and with power as thou didst fill Stephen the martyr and follower of the sufferings of thy Christ". Moreover, in the case of the deacon, prayer is made that he "may be counted worthy of a higher standing", a clause which not improbably has reference to the possibility of advance to a higher ecclesiastical dignity as priest or bishop, no such praise being used in the case of the deaconess.

---

*Herbert Thurston, "Deaconesses," *The Catholic Encyclopedia*, Vol. 4 (New York: Robert Appleton Company, 1908). Ecclesiastical approbation: *Nihil Obstat,* Remy Lafort, Censor; *Imprimatur*: John M. Farley, Archbishop of New York.

The subject of the precise status of the deaconess is confessedly obscure and confused, but two or three points at any rate seem worth insisting on. In the first place there were no doubt influences at work at one time or another which tended to exaggerate the position of these women-helpers [deaconesses]. This tendency has found expression in certain documents which have come down to us and of which it is difficult to gauge the value. Still there is no more reason to attach importance to these pretensions than there is to regard seriously the spasmodic attempts of certain deacons to exceed their powers and to claim, for example, authority to consecrate. Both in the one and the other case the voice of the Church made itself heard in conciliar decrees and the abuse in the end was repressed without difficulty. Such restrictive measures seem to be found in the rather obscure 11th canon of Laodicea [c. 363–364 A.D.] and in the more explicit 19th canon of the [Second] Council of Nicaea [787 A.D.] which last distinctly lays down that deaconesses are to be accounted as lay persons and that they receive no ordination properly so called (Hefele-LeClercq, *Conciles*, I, 618). In the West there seems always to have been considerable reluctance to accept the deaconesses, at any rate under that name, as a recognized institution of the Church. The Council of Nismes in 394 reproved in general the assumption of the levitical [priestly] ministry by women, and other decrees, notably that of Orange in 411 (can. 26) forbid the ordaining of deaconesses altogether. It follows from what has been said that the Church as a whole repudiated the idea that women could in any proper sense be recipients of the Sacrament of Order. None the less in the East, and among the Syrians and Nestorians much more than among the Greeks (Hefele-LeClercq, *Conciles*, II, 448), the ecclesiastical status of deaconesses was greatly exaggerated.

Another **source of confusion** has always been introduced by those who have interpreted the word *diaconissae*, on the analogy of *presbyterae* and *presbytides*, *episcopae* and *episcopissae*, as the wives of deacons who, living apart from their husbands, acquired *ipso facto* an ecclesiastical character. No doubt such matrons who generously accepted this separation from their husbands were treated with special distinction and were supported by the Church, but if they became deaconesses, as in some cases they did, they had, like other women to fulfill certain conditions and to receive a special consecration. With regard to the duration of the order of deaconesses we note that when adult baptism became uncommon, this institution, which seems primarily to have been devised for the needs of [instruction for] women catechumens, gradually waned and in the end died out altogether. **In the time of Justinian (d. 565) the deaconesses still held a position of importance. At the church of St. Sophia in Constantinople the staff consisted of sixty priests, one hundred deacons, forty deaconesses, and ninety subdeacons; but Balsamon, Patriarch of Antioch about A.D. 1070 states that deaconesses in any proper sense had ceased to exist in the Church though the title was borne by certain nuns ([Deaconess Cecilia] Robinson, *Ministry of Deaconesses* [1898], p. 93), while Matthew Blastares declared of the tenth century that the civil legislation concerning deaconesses, which ranked them rather among the clergy than the laity had then been abandoned or forgotten (Migne, *P.G.*, CXIX, 1272).** In the West in spite of the hostile decrees of several councils of Gaul in the fifth and sixth centuries, we still find mention of deaconesses considerably after that date, though it is difficult to say whether the title was more than an honorific name attributed to consecrated virgins and widows. Thus we read in Fortunatus that St. Radegund was "ordained deaconess" by St. Medard (about A.D. 540 – Migne, *P.L.*, LXXXVIII, 502). So also the ninth Ordo Romanus mentions, as forming part of the papal procession, the "*famine diaconissae et presbyterissae quae eodem die benedicantur*" and *diaconissae* are mentioned in the procession of Leo III in the ninth century (Duchesne, *Lib. Pont.*, II, 6). Further the Anglo-Saxon Leofric missal in the eleventh century still retained a prayer *ad diaconissam faciendam* which appears in the form *Exaudi Domine*, common to both deacons and deaconesses. The only surviving relic of the **ordination of deaconesses** in the **West** seems to be the delivery by the bishop of a stole and maniple to Carthusian nuns in the ceremony of their profession.

Functions of deaconesses

There can be no doubt that in their first institution the deaconesses were intended to discharge those same charitable offices, connected with the temporal well being of their poorer fellow Christians, which were performed for the men by the deacons. But in one particular, viz., the instruction and baptism of catechumens, their duties involved service of a more spiritual kind. The universal prevalence of baptism by immersion and the anointing of the whole body which preceded it, rendered it a matter

it a matter of propriety that in this ceremony the functions of the deacons should be discharged by women. The *Didascalia Apostolorum* (III, 12; see Funk, *Didascalia*, etc., I, 208) explicitly directs that the deaconesses are to perform this function. It is probable that this was the starting point for the intervention of women in many other ritual observances even in the sanctuary. The *Apostolic Constitutions* expressly attribute to them the duty of guarding the doors and maintaining order amongst those of their own sex in the church, and they also (II, c. 26) assign to them the office of acting as intermediaries between the clergy and the women of the congregation; but on the other hand, it is laid down (*Const. Apost.*, VIII, 27) that "the deaconess gives no blessing, she fulfills no function of priest or deacon", and there can be no doubt that the extravagances permitted in some places, especially in the churches of Syria and Asia, were in contravention of the canons generally accepted. We hear of them presiding over assemblies of women, reading the Epistle and Gospel, distributing the Blessed Eucharist to nuns, lighting the candles, burning incense in the thuribles, adorning the sanctuary, and anointing the sick (see Hefele-LeClercq, II, 448). All these things must be regarded as abuses which ecclesiastical legislation was not long in repressing.

Deaconesses in Protestant communions

Outside the Catholic Church the name of deaconesses has been adopted for a modern revival which has had great vogue in Germany and to some extent in the United States. It was begun in 1833 by the Lutheran pastor Fliedner at Kaiserswerth near Düsseldorf. His first inspiration is said to have been derived from the Quakeress Elizabeth Fry, and through the celebrated Miss Florence Nightingale, who organized a staff of nurses in the Crimean War and who had previously been trained at Kaiserswerth, the revival at a later date attracted a good deal of attention in England. The main work of deaconesses is the tending of the sick and poor, instruction and district visiting, but with more subordination to parish needs than is usually compatible with the life of an Anglican sisterhood. In the United States more particularly, community life is usually not insisted upon, but a good deal of attention is given to training and intellectual development. Both in the Anglican Church, and in the Protestant Episcopal Church, and Methodist Episcopal Church of America, deaconesses are "admitted" in solemn form by the bishop with benediction and the laying on of hands. In Germany the movement has taken such hold that the Kaiserswerth organization alone claims to number over 16,000 sisters, but it is curious that relative to the population the institution is more popular in Catholic districts, where probably the familiar spectacle of Catholic nuns has accustomed the people to the idea of a community life for women.

* * * * * * * * *

Meta-Appendix

In the Watton Priory, a double-monastery in Yorkshire (see bottom, page 180), there was a "substantial wall, several feet high, which traversed the church lengthways" and which thus effected a partial separation of the nuns from the monks during their joint church services. Compare this wall with the "partition" wall in the sanctuary of the Therapeutæ, which similarly separated the women monastics from the men, as described by Philo:

> [O]n the seventh day they get together for a general assembly and seat themselves in order according to their age [seniority as to the date of their joining the community – another Buddhist touch! – ML] with the proper dignity. . . . Then the eldest who is also best versed in their doctrines comes forward, and composed both in expression and in voice, holds forth with reasoned arguments and wisdom. . . .
>
> This common sanctuary in which they meet every seventh day is a double enclosure, one part set off for the men, the other for the women. For women too customarily form part of the audience possessed by the same fervor and sense of purpose. The partition between the two chambers is built up to three or four cubits [roughly breast high] above the floor in the form of a breastwork, while the space above up to the roof is left open. This serves two purposes: that the modesty proper to women's nature be maintained and that the women seated within ear-shot with nothing to obstruct the voice of the speaker may obtain easy apprehension.*

**Philo of Alexandria: The Contemplative Life, The Giants, and Selections*, translation by David Winston (Mahwah, NJ: Paulist Press, 1981), p. 47.

Buddhist-Christian Parallels discussed in *Buddhism's Relation to Christianity*

1. a) The Bōdhisattva (Buddha-to-be), from Heaven, takes birth on Earth,'virginally' conceived – born to a royal family (***BRC*, pp. 16-17**).

   b) Jesus in Heaven takes birth on Earth, 'virginally' conceived, of royal lineage (***John 1:1-2***).

2. a) Angels (*devas*) announce to King Śuddhōdana the impending ('virginal') birth of the Bōdhisattva to his wife (***BRC*, p. 22**).

   b) Angel announces to Joseph the impending virginal birth of Jesus to his wife (***Matt 1:20-21***).

3. a) Queen Māyā gives birth to the Bōdhisattva in the Lumbinī Grove on the journey to *her* ancestral home (***BRC*, p. 24**).

   b) Mary gave birth to Jesus on the journey to Bethlehem, Joseph's ancestral home (***Luke 2:5-6***).

4. a) The elderly sage, Asita, in the royal palace, holds and praises the baby Bōdhisattva (***BRC*, pp. 30-31**).

   b) At the Jerusalem Temple, the elderly Simeon holds and praises the baby Jesus (***Luke 2:25-32***).

5. a) Royal genealogy given for the Bōdhisattva (***BRC*, p. 29**).

   b) Royal genealogies given for Jesus (***Matt 1:1-17 & Luke 3:23-38***).

6. a) The 29 year old Bōdhisattva leaves home for homeless wandering and is initiated by the ascetic Kālāma (***BRC*, pp. 252-253**).

   b) The 29 year old Jesus is baptized and thus initiated by the ascetic John the Baptist (***Mark 1:9***).

7. a) The Bōdhisattva is tempted by the devil, Māra, in the forest wilderness (***BRC*, pp. 36-37**).

   b) Jesus is tempted in the wilderness by the devil (***Luke 4:1-13***).

8. a) The Bōdhisattva fasts in the wilderness and is waited on by angels (*devas*) (***BRC*, p. 39**).

   b) Jesus fasts in the wilderness and is waited on by angels (***Mark 1:12-13***).

9. a) The Buddha walks on water (***BRC*, p. 40**).

   b) Jesus walks on water (***Matt 14:25-27***).

10. a) The Buddha's disciple, Śāriputra, walks on water (***BRC*, p. 41**).

    b) Jesus's disciple, Simon Peter, walks on water (***Matt 14:28-31***).

11. a) The courtesan Āmrapālī (the Indian alter ego of Mary Magdalene) with her women companions *were the first* to salute the deceased body of the Buddha; she held the Buddha's feet and her tears wet them (***BRC*, pp. 43-46**).

    b) Mary Magdalene held Jesus's feet (when he was alive!) and her tears wet them – and later, after his crucifixion, she and her women companions *were the first* to see the resurrected Jesus (***Matt 28:9***).

12. a) The Buddha's body, wrapped in 500 layers of cotton cloth, was entombed in a casket filled with oil (***BRC*, p. 43**).

    b) Joseph of Arimathea and Nicodemus wrapped Jesus's body with about 100 pounds (!) of spices, in strips of linen cloth, and laid it in a new, unused rock-cut tomb // casket/womb (***John 19:39-42***).

13. a) The Buddha's body was cremated, the smoke rising heavenward (***BRC*, p. 47**).

    b) Jesus was resurrected and ascended into heaven (***Mark 16:19; Luke 24:51***).

14. a) The relics of the Buddha were peacefully divided among eight contesting clans, after their soldiers had faced off to force the issue (***BRC*, p. 48**).

    b) Jesus's clothes were divided (***Psalm 22:18***) peacefully among soldiers (***Luke 23:34; John 19:23***) [Metaphorically, the body is the "clothing" of one's soul. – ML].

15. a) In the third century, BCE, the Indian king, Aśōka, sent Buddhist missionary monks to western countries around the Mediterranean as Conquistadors for 'Righteousness' (The Dharma) – a dramatic contrast to *military* conquest – it was the world's first 'Salvation Army' (***BRC*, pp. 50-51**).

   b) Christianity has its own distinct version of this 'Salvation Army'.

16. a) In his 10th Rock Edict inscription, engraved in the 3rd century, BCE, the Buddhist king, Aśōka, states (in verse six) that 'it is more difficult for the rich than the poor to attain the happiness of heaven (in the "Other World")'! (***BRC*, p. 56**).

   b) Jesus declares that it is easier for a camel to pass through the eye of a needle than for a rich man to enter the kingdom of God (***Mark 10:25***).

17. a) King Aśōka's 9th Rock Edict records his recommending and spreading abroad the Buddhist Dharma (the "Living Water" of the Buddha): Aśōka declares (in verse xvii of this edict) that by the practice of Dharma (Righteousness), one can attain "***endless*** merit . . . in the Next World" (***BRC*, p. 60**).

   b) Jesus: "the water that I shall give . . . will be an inner spring always welling up for ***eternal*** life" (***John 4:14***). [emphasis added – ML]

18. a) The story of the early life of Prince Siddhārtha (the Buddha-to-be = the Bōdhisattva) was transmuted into the most widespread legend of Christian sainthood during medieval times, in which the young Indian prince – now called 'Josaphat' (from 'Bōdhisattva') – is converted to Christianity by the ascetic sage, Barlaam! (***BRC*, pp. 61-64**)

   b) **Note:** It was really the crypto-Buddhist Christians, probably in Alexandria, Egypt, who deliberately reversed the true direction of conversion in this story, thus hiding the fact that Christianity actually springs from Buddhism! (***BRC*, pp. 61-64**)

PARALLEL PARABLES

19. a) The Buddhist Parable of the Prodigal Son (***BRC*, pp. 66-68**).

   b) The Christian Parable of the Prodigal Son (***Luke 15:11-32***).

20. a) Passages from the Buddhist *Lotus Sūtra*, in which it is pointed out that different people attain Nirvāṇa after different number of rebirths (different lengths of time) (***BRC*, pp. 71-72**).

   b) Jesus illustrates this idea by metaphor in the Parable of the Laborers in the Vineyard (***Matt 20:1-16***).

21. a) The Buddhist meta-Parable of the Outcaste Woman at the Well (***BRC*, pp. 74-77**).

   b) The Christian meta-Parable of the Samaritan Woman at the Well (***John 4:7-30***).

22. a) Buddhist passages which are prototypical – and therefore parallels – of the Christian Parable of the Good Samaritan (***BRC*, pp. 78-79**).

   b) Jesus's Parable of the Good Samaritan (***Luke 10:29-37***).

PARALLEL SAYINGS

23. a) The Buddha said: 'Phagguno, if any one . . . were to give thee a blow with hand, clod, staff or sword, thou should renounce all common feelings . . . and train thyself in the thought: "I will not let evil speech escape, but continue kind and compassionate, with a loving heart instead of a hateful one"' (***BRC*, p. 80**).

   b) Jesus said: 'Do not set yourself against the man who wrongs you. If someone slaps you on the right cheek, turn and offer him your left' (***Matt 5:39***).

The Buddha and Jesus were both asked, "Are you the Promised One?"

24. a) Pōkkharasati said, 'Gautama is staying in the dense jungle. It is reported that this Blessed Lord is a fully enlightened Buddha. Now go and find out whether the report is correct or not.' (***BRC*, p. 82**).

   b) The story of what [Jesus] had done ran through all parts of Judæa. . . . John [the Baptist] too was informed of all this by his disciples. Summoning two of their number he sent them to the Lord with this message 'Are you the one who is to come, or are we to expect some other?' (***Luke 7:16-19***).

Both the Buddha and Jesus were born from Spirit:

25. a) [The Buddha said:] 'There are these two gifts, the carnal and the spiritual. Of these two gifts the spiritual is preëminent. He who has made the spiritual offering – such a one, the best of mankind, is honored by all beings as one who has gone beyond' (***BRC*, p. 82**).

    b) Jesus answered, 'In truth I tell you, no one can enter the kingdom of God without being born from water and spirit. Flesh can can give birth only to flesh.' (***John 3:5-7***).

Both the Buddha and Jesus consorted with sinners:

26. a) The Bōdhisattva, to demonstrate the evils of desire, 'even entered brothels – to establish drunkards in correct mindfulness, he entered the taverns' (***BRC*, p. 82**).

    b) 'When Jesus was at table in the house, many bad characters – tax-gatherers and others – were seated with him and the disciples' (***Matt 9:10-13***).

Both promoted freedom from worldly attachments:

27. a) 'Then the Lord [Buddha] addressed the monks, saying: "I am free from all snares. And you, monks, are free from all [worldly] snares"' (***BRC*, p. 82**).

    b) [Jesus] said to them, 'When I sent you out barefoot without purse or pack, were you ever short of anything?' 'No', they answered (***Luke 22:35***).

Both had similar ideas about what defiled a person:

28. a) The Buddha held that 'stealing, deceiving, adultery; this is defilement. Not the eating of meat' (***BRC*, p. 83**).

    b) Jesus: ['N]othing that goes into a man from outside can defile him; no, it is the things that come out of him that defile a man . . . evil thoughts, acts of fornication, of theft, murder, and adultery. . .' (***Mark 7:15, 21***).

Both stressed compassion for the poor and sick:

29. a) [The Buddha said to his monks:] 'If you do not tend one another, then who is there to tend you? Whoever would tend me, he should tend the sick' (***BRC*, p. 83**).

    b) [Jesus said to his disciples:] "I tell you this: anything you did for one of my brothers here, however humble, you did for me" (***Matt 25:40***).

Both laid down similar commandments:

30. a) [The Buddha said:] 'Abstain from killing and from taking what is not given. Abstain from unchastity and from speaking falsely. Do not accept gold and silver' (***BRC*, p. 83**).

    b) [Jesus said:] 'You know the commandments: "Do not murder; do not commit adultery; do not steal; do not give false evidence; do not defraud; honour your father and mother"' (***Mark 10:19***).

Both preached freedom from worldly corruption:

31. a) [The Buddha said:] 'Just as, brethren, a dark blue lotus or a white lotus, born in [muddy] water, rises . . . to the surface and stands unspotted by the water, even so, . . . the Buddha, having come to full growth in the world, passing beyond the world, abides unspotted by the world' (***BRC*, p. 83**).

    b) [Jesus prayed:] 'I have delivered thy word to them, and the world hates them because they are strangers in the world, as I am' (***John 17:14-16***).

Both are credited with similar miracles:

32. a) 'As soon as the Bōdhisattva was born, the sick were cured; the hungry and thirsty were no longer oppressed by hunger and thirst. Those maddened by drink lost their obsession. The mad recovered their senses, the blind regained their sight, and the deaf could once more hear.' (***BRC*, p. 83**).

    b) Then [Jesus] gave them his answer: 'Go', he said, 'and tell John what you have seen and heard: how the blind recover their sight, the lame walk, the lepers are made clean, the deaf hear, the dead are raised to life, the poor are hearing the good news . . .' (***Luke 7:22-23***).

Both spoke of mega-miracles possible by those with great faith or concentration:

33. a) [The Buddha:] 'A monk who is skilled in concentration can cut the Himālyas in two' (***BRC*, p. 84**).

b) [Jesus said:] 'Your faith is too small. I tell you this: if you have faith no bigger even than a mustard-seed, you will say to the mountain, "Move from here to there!", and it will move' (***Matt 17:20***).

Both criticized opposing religious leaders as the blind leading the blind:

34. a) [The Buddha:] 'When these Brahmins teach a path that they do not know or see, saying, "This is the only straight path," this cannot possibly be right. Just as a file of blind men go on, clinging to each other, and the first one sees nothing, the middle one sees nothing, and the last one sees nothing – so it is with the talk of these Brahmins' (***BRC*, p. 84**).

b) [Jesus told] them a parable: 'Can one blind man be a guide to another? Will they not both fall into the ditch?' (***Luke 6:39***).

Both are portrayed as though establishing a line of succession after their departure:

35. a) [The Buddha said:] 'When it said of anyone: "He is the son of the Blessed One [the Buddha], born of his breast, an heir in the dharma, not an heir in material things," it is of my follower Sāriputta that this should be said' (***BRC*, p. 84**).

b) Then Jesus said: 'Simon son of Jonah, you are favoured indeed! You did not learn that from mortal man; it was revealed to you by my heavenly Father. And I say this to you: You are Peter, the Rock; and on this rock I will build my church' (***Matt 16:17-18***).

Both advocated the forsaking of family ties in order to become their followers:

36. a) [The Buddha said:] 'Just as the great rivers, on reaching the great ocean, lose their former names and identities and are reckoned simply as the great ocean, so do my followers lose their former names and clans and become sons of the Buddha's clan' (***BRC*, p. 84**).

b) And looking round at those who were sitting in the circle about him [Jesus] said, 'here are my mother and my brothers. Whoever does the will of God is my brother, my sister, my mother' (***Mark 3:34-35***).

Both live on in their 'Word' ('Logos'/'Dharma'):

37. a) And the Lord [Buddha] said: 'It may be that you will think: "The Teacher's instruction has ceased, now we will have no teacher." It should not be seen like this, for what I have taught and explained to you will, at my passing, be your teacher' (***BRC*, p. 84**).

b) [Jesus said:] 'But when your Advocate [Paraklêtos / Pratimōkṣas ('Substitute Teacher': the Four Noble Truths)] has come, whom I will send you from the Father – the Spirit of truth that issues from the Father – he will bear witness to me' (***John 15:26***).

Both warn of the Karmic 'Wages of Sin':

38. a) [The Buddha said: 'S]ome man is of an angry and irritable character; when criticized even a little, he is offended, becomes angry, hostile, and resentful, and displays anger, hate, and . . . after death, he reappears in a state of deprivation, in an unhappy destination, in perdition, or even in hell' (***BRC*, p. 85**).

b) [Jesus:] 'I tell you this: Anyone who nurses anger against his brother must be brought to judgement. If he abuses his brother he must answer for it to the court; if he sneers at him he will have to answer for it in the fires of hell' (***Matt 5:22***).

And both warn of future degeneration setting in because of misguiding leaders and false prophets:

39. a) [The Buddha:] 'Monks who are untrained will give guidance to others, and they will not be able to lead them in the way of higher virtue. And those in turn who have not been trained will give guidance to others and will not be able to lead them' (***BRC*, p. 85**).

b) [Jesus:] 'Many false prophets will arise, and will mislead many: and as lawlessness spreads, men's love for one another will grow cold' (***Matt 24:11-12***).

40. a) **MISSIONARIES**: The Buddha, in the 5th century BCE, sent his monks to spread his teaching throughout India; and Aśōka, 3rd century BCE, sent missionary monks abroad in all directions (***BRC*, pp. 88-89**).
    b) Christian missionary activity begins only in the early Common Era (***BRC*, p. 89**).

41. a) **MONASTICISM**: The Buddha had established, in the early fifth century BCE, a form of monasticism which prefigures the monasticism of the Qumranites (second century BCE to 68 CE) and the Therapeutæ community living near Alexandria, Egypt, described in detail by Philo in the mid-first century CE (***BRC*, p. 90**).
    b) The earliest recorded evidence of Christian monasticism comes from Egypt: the communities of Saints Antony and Pachomius in the 3rd and 4th centuries CE (***BRC*, p. 188**).

42. a) **NUNS' SUBJECTION TO MONKS**: In Buddhism, the most senior nun, according to their literature, was subordinate to the most junior monk (***BRC*, pp. 91-94**).
    b) This Buddhist bias has been carried over into Christian monasticism (***BRC*, p. 94**).

43. a) **LINEAGES OF MASTERS**: Dharma lineages ("family trees" of Buddhist traditions) begin with the Buddha, extending upward through a line of Buddhist Masters to the present (***BRC*, pp. 96-99**).
    b) Various Christian churches or sects trace their authority from 'Jesus' and one or another of the 'original Apostles' in "Lineages of Patriarchs" (***BRC*, pp. 96-98**).

44. a) **BŌDHISATTVAS ("SAINTS")** are beings which are widely venerated in Buddhism. They are considered intermediate between ordinary folk and the Buddha, whom Mahāyānists, from the first century BCE, had raised to the superhuman, abstract status of a god (***BRC*, p. 101**).
    b) Christian saints have provided a similar function, especially in Roman Catholicism.

45. a) The **VENERATION OF RELICS** of the Buddha and Bōdhisattvas was present from the very beginning (***BRC*, pp. 103-106**).
    b) Centuries later, a similar veneration of relics of saints is seen in Catholicism (***BRC*, pp. 106-109**).

46. a) "**CONFESSION AND ABSOLUTION**", for Buddhism, was a *psychological* strategy realized by the Buddha (fifth century BCE) during his meditation and introduced by him into the communal fortnightly ceremonial recitation of the Buddhist rules of moral discipline, the *Prātimōkṣa*. No supernatural power or authority was involved! (***BRC*, pp. 111-114**)
    b) Christian 'Confession and Absolution' claims divine authority (***BRC*, pp. 114-115**).

47. a) The first 4 **BUDDHIST COUNCILS** were convened in order to prevent divisions in practice and doctrine (***BRC*, pp. 116-117**).
    b) The first 7 Ecumenical Christian Councils were convened for similar reasons (***BRC*, pp. 118-119**).

48. a) Buddhism invented mechanical **PRINTING OF SCRIPTURES**, 2nd to 11th cent., CE (***BRC*, pp. 120-121**).
    b) Christianity (Gutenberg) followed, in the 15th century.

49. a) The **ALMS-ROUND** was adopted by Buddhism in the sixth cent., BCE (***BRC*, pp. 122 &126-129**).
    b) From its early days, Christianity followed this Buddhist practice (***BRC*, pp. 122-125**).

* * * * * * * * *

END